A UNITED NATION

Croatians are proud of their country – and they have every right to be, though geography and history have made it a land of at least two parts

However much emphasis Croatians put on a single identity, the country's odd wishbone shape has created a nation of two flavours in which history and geography have both played a part. One half of the country stretches inland across Central Croatia to the capital, Zagreb, and here the Germanic correctness of the Habsburgs is evident. The other, lapped by the blue Adriatic from Istria down through hundreds of islands and the Dalmatian coast, is exuberantly Latin.

Though its identity goes back to the Illyrians, it was the Hrvati Slavs, arriving in the 6th century, who created an independent Croatian kingdom. Subdued by Venetians and Austro-Hungarians, and harried by the Ottomans, the nation was subsumed into 20th-century Yugoslavia. But all this while, the people continued to believe in a cohesive Croatian (Hrvati in Croatian) identity that faces west, towards Catholic Rome and not east towards the Orthodox Byzantium of the Serbs or the Islam of the Ottoman Turks.

The 1991–5 Homeland War has left scars: Vukovar in the far east of the country was the first European city to have been razed to the ground since World War II. The other hotspot was Knin behind the Dalmatian coast. Both had large Serbian populations driven out by Croats and replaced by refugee Croatians from Serbia and Bosnia. Some Serbs have since returned, too, but around 90 percent of the country's population is now officially Croatian.

The first tourists on the coast were the Viennese aristocracy who adored the Opatija Riviera. In Communist times, Croatia was the richest

of Yugoslavia's six provinces, much of its money derived from visitors attracted to the clean Adriatic water and beautiful beaches, and it still is today, with destinations such as Hvar now rivalling the best of the Mediterranean's rivieras. The country's physical diversity means that there is a variety of holidays to enjoy, from the lovely wooded farmlands of Slavonia to the winelands of Istria and the sparkling resorts on the coast. ❑

PRECEDING PAGES: Plitivice National Park; Rovinj waterfront; cathedral built into Diocletian's Palace in Split. **LEFT:** Croatia's potential for tourism is huge. **ABOVE LEFT:** Zagreb woman. **LEFT:** cathedral gardens, Split. **RIGHT:** an Istrian vineyard.

LAND AND PEOPLE

Different empires and different landscapes have
created two distinct kinds of Croatian – one
central European, the other Latin

Croatia amounts to around 146,000 sq km (56,500 sq miles), about the size of England and Wales, or the state of Iowa, and though not large, it often seems less like a single country than a league of nations and small city-states. This partly reflects its odd, boomerang shape: one arm flung eastwards along the verdant Pannonian plain, cupping the soft underbelly of Hungary, the other stretching south over the dry mountains that run like a spinal cord along the Adriatic Sea.

One part was ruled for centuries by the Habsburg Austro-Hungarians and the other was governed for a similar length of time by Venice. No wonder that continental and maritime Croatia have evolved into such different societies – one more reserved, polite and distinctly Germanic, the other all Mediterranean flair and bravado.

Central European Slavonia

Croatia's borders today lie along five countries, clockwise from the north: Slovenia (455km/285

> *Never make the error of telling Croatians they are "Balkan" unless you have time to rebut a lecture on the past thousand years of Croatian history; they are Central European and determined to remain so.*

miles), Hungary (329km/204 miles), Serbia and Montenegro (241km/150 miles), Bosnia Herzegovina (932km/580 miles) and Montenegro

LEFT: Motovun, one of Croatia's hilltop towns.
RIGHT: weighing up the options in Dolac Market, Zagreb.

(25km/16 miles). Central Europe's great Pannonian Plain, once a sea, comes down from Hungary into central and eastern Croatia, and into Serbia. Taking its name from the Roman province of Pannonia, the Croatian part of this plain largely accords with the ancient region of Slavonia (not to be confused with Slovenia, the country to the north, though both roughly mean a region settled by Slavs). This is mostly flat land of forests and farms, and their bounty can be seen in the big markets at Bjelovar, as well as in the daily Dolac market in Zagreb. The islands in this ancient sea are now hills, such as those in Papuk Nature Park where the volcanic pillars of Rupnica became the first geological monument in the country to have a protected status. Other former islands are Psunj, Slavonia's highest peak at 986 metres (3,235ft), and the 152-metre (500ft) hill at Požega, which provided the fortress on the River Sava between Vukovar and Zagreb.

The Sava is Slavonia's drain in the south, the Drava in the north, both running east to reach the Danube at, respectively, Vukovar and just beyond the Slavonian regional capital of Osijek. The Danube, Europe's great water highway, forms Croatia's eastern border, creating a flood plain by its confluence with the Drava that is described as "Europe's last remaining wetlands".

drove out all the Serbs. Almost overnight, a Serb population of 150,000 or so fled to Bosnia or Serbia, leaving many towns and villages entirely empty. Vukovar, bombed to rubble in the punishing Serb siege of autumn 1991 *(see page 53)* has about a third of the population it had before the war. Serbs returned in 1998, and they live in uneasy proximity with Croats, outnumbered now by around two to one. The Serb population overall in Croatia is down now from around 12 percent before the war to around 4 percent of the total.

The greatest problem facing the Krajina is its poor economy. Bio-diesel fuels are starting

The southern part of Slavonia is part of the Vojna Krajina, a military buffer zone that stretched from the Adriatic all along the border and into modern Bosnia Herzegovina, and east into Serbia. The Ottomans, who had reached the gates of Vienna 300km (190 miles) north of Croatia, occupied much of Slavonia for around 150 years. As they retreated, the Hungarians carved out this military border to shield their empire from Turkish invasions, populating it with conscript volunteers. Heavily settled over several centuries by Orthodox Serbs, the character of Karijna changed drastically in 1991 when Serb separatists drove out all the local Croats, and equally drastically again in July 1995, when the Croatian army

to produce around 200,000 tonnes a year, but these are not a big employer, and although the government has tried to restart the tourism industry, especially in the popular Plitvice Lakes National Park (a Unesco World Heritage Site) between Zagreb and Zadar on the coast, there are few job prospects. The global recession has not helped. With a small, elderly population, it is difficult to see this ruggedly beautiful region ever realising its massive tourist potential.

Fair and flaxen haired

By contrast, the Zagorje in western central Croatia has a healthy economy that comes from a rolling landscape of green hills, elegant castles and popular spas, which bring weekenders from

Zagreb. Stretching north of the capital to the most northerly city, Varaždin, this is a favourite place of escape, not much explored by foreign visitors. Further stretches of quiet countryside lie west of Zagreb in the sparsely populated Žumberak mountain range, where conditions are ideal for growing vines, especially around the Samabor hills.

Almost 90 percent of Zagreb's 1.2 million inhabitants are identified as Croats. But the flaxen hair and fair complexions of so many Slavonians reflect centuries of intermarriage between Croats, Germans, Hungarians and a dozen other nationalities settled in the region

architecture of Zagreb's National Theatre and the other grand civic buildings of the capital as well as in nearby cities such as Osijek and Baroque Varaždin. But it is not just the buildings. Much of Zagreb looks and feels like a slice of Old Vienna that has been airlifted south, from the *wiener schnitzels* and *strudels* served in the restaurants to the formidable old ladies dressed in pork-pie hats walking tiny fluffy dogs through the parks in the morning. That other pillar of Viennese life – coffee and cream cake consumed over the daily newspaper in the hushed, high-ceilinged precincts of the city café – remains sacrosanct to many Zagrebians.

by the Empress Maria Theresa in the 18th century, including Czechs, Slovaks, Ruthenes and Ukrainians. Many of these settler communities maintain a distinct identity, which distinguishes the places where they have settled: the Czechs around Daruvar and Pakrac in western Slavonia; the Hungarians in the Baranja region, north of Osijek; and the Slovaks in Ilok, on the border with Serbia.

The stamp of Habsburg rule and the cultural influence of Vienna hangs heavily over this part of the world in the monumental neoclassical

LEFT: Zagreb women in traditional clothing. **ABOVE LEFT:** central Croatian farmer at work. **ABOVE RIGHT:** colourful dwelling in the Kumrovec old quarter.

THERMAL SPAS

In the wooded interior of Croatia, water bubbles up from underground at high temperatures in a number of spa centres that have been enjoyed since Roman times. In the very north of the country there are traces of a Roman settlement by the baths at Varaždinske Toplice in the woods above Varždin, where sulphurous waters come out of the ground at near body temperature – 37°C (98.6°F). There are a number of spa retreats between here and Zagreb, in the Zagorje. In the countryside north of Istria, Istaske Toplice has large indoor and outdoor pools. Many of the modern spas date from the late 19th century, when railways and better roads brought rich Viennese in search of cures.

Mediterranean Dalmatia

A few hours away by car in Dalmatia and you might as well have crossed a continent. In fact what you will have crossed is the Dinaric Alps, which run for 645km (400 miles) along the Adriatic coast, sheltering it from cold easterly winds and hemming much of it tightly against the sea. Corroded by water, these rocks are Swiss cheeses of caves, canyons and grottoes. They produces the dramatic gorges of rivers such as the Neretva, while other rivers spring up from their depths, fully formed, their sediment-free waters sparklingly clear. The great falls at Plitvice Lakes, one of the country's top

since the times of the ancient Greeks that it has become a Unesco World Heritage Site.

The Adriatic, a spur of the Mediterranean, is an omnipresent influence on life in Dalmatia. It has shaped the inhabitants' dreams and poems, inspired their art and architecture and informs their religion.

It has also fed them. Seafood is an important part of Dalmatian life. Forget *schnitzels*, fruit-filled *strudels* and the other Austrian winter-warmers that are so beloved further north. This is the land of garlic and fish, sold fresh from the quaysides at the crack of dawn every morning. Visitors may fall for tourist menus offering

attractions, are a shining example of how this rock can work its wonders. In Central Dalmatia is Vilebit, the largest mountain range in the country, whose white walls rise from the sea between Sinj and Knin, and whose escarpments are a challenge to climbers.

Reluctant to give up the land, these limestone crags tumble deeply into the sea, only to emerge again shortly afterwards in a series of islands that make this coast so appealing. Here the contrast between the old world and the new are nowhere more striking than on the island of Hvar, where the main town attracts the mega-yacht brigade and the likes of Kevin Spacey and Gwyneth Paltrow, while the island's Stari Grad Plain has a cultural landscape so little changed

SUBTROPICAL ISLAND

The most southerly part of Croatia is Palagruža, an island 1.4km (nearly 1 mile) long and 300 metres/yds wide with a climate that is subtropical. At its 90-metre (295ft) summit is a lighthouse, which offers accommodation in one of the most remote spots in Europe. The island is a nature reserve and there are two pebble beaches with safe, shallow waters. The island and its surrounding islets lie midway between the Gargano peninsula in Italy and Lastovo, the island to the south of Korčula, from where boats bring visitors on a 2½-hour journey. Palagruža was an important stop between the two shores in Mesolithic times, and a resident archaeological dig is tracing its past.

> At 1,392 metres (4,570ft) deep, Lukina jama in the northern Velebit massif is the deepest cave in Croatia. Discovered in 1992, it was named after Ozren Lukic, a keen caver and volunteer who had been shot by a sniper the previous year.

pork chops and pizza; the locals will be eating their favourite dish of squid risotto, washed down with some of the Mediterranean's most delicious – though least known – wines, the best of which are produced on the islands and on the Pelješac peninsula.

Dark and noisy

Here the black hair and flashing eyes of the local people reveal centuries of intermingling with Italians and, before them, Greeks. This is a no-holds-barred Mediterranean society that has little time for what the Dalmatians see as Zagreb's stiffness and "hauteur". Brash and noisy, the Dalmatians take their manners, their fashion sense – and their ideas of what constitutes an acceptable noise level in a restaurant – from neighbouring Italy. Immaculately pressed white shirts and dark glasses are *de rigueur* for

---

LEFT: raising a glass of Dalmatian wine on the island of Vis. **ABOVE:** captain of one of the many Adriatic island excursion boats.

the suave, not to say arrogant, young men swaggering through the narrow streets of Split on the evening *corso*, or revving up their motorbikes on the sea front.

Though the Homeland War happened a generation ago there are still a few unhealed scars left on the coast, which was shelled from the sea and an easy target for Bosnian Serbs looking down from mountain tops above. Serbs formed more than three quarters of the population of Knin, a former Croatian capital, and a main transport hub between Zagreb and the coast. In 1991 they seized control of the city, declaring the region the Republic of Serbian Krajina. Croatia's Operation Storm drove them out, and leaders on both sides were charged with war crimes. Croat refugees from Bosnia were encouraged to re-settle the town, and today they make up most of the population. Knin has a rather fly-blown look and the refugees eke out an existence in the company of equally impoverished Serb returnees.

Italianate Istria

Istria, the pendulous, tear-shaped peninsula is yet another country. Geographically it covers slightly more than the Croatian territory, spilling north into Slovenia, with which it has a border dispute that has threatened its attempted EU membership. It also touches Italy just below Trieste, making this the land entry point to the country for Italians. Ceded to Italy after World War I and returned to Yugoslavia after World War II, Istria had first an influx, then an exodus of Italians. A number still remain, and Grožnjan is the only town in the country where non-Croatians (Italians, representing 51 percent of the population) outnumber Croatians.

Istria's undulating landscape, vineyards, the hilltop towns and the soaring campaniles on the village churches evoke frequent and understandable comparisons with Tuscany. Istrians, however, consider themselves first and foremost Istrian. Street signs written in Italian in the main town of Pula reflect their relaxed patriotism and easy-going relationship with their big next-door neighbour – a sentiment that worries and angers more orthodox Croat nationalists living further east. Strong pro-autonomy movements, the Istrian Democratic Party and the Istrian Social Democratic Forum, reflect most people's determination not to be pushed around by Zagreb.   ❏

DECISIVE DATES

EARLIEST TIMES

2500 BC
The statue of the Vučedol dove confirms neolithic settlements in the region.

4th century BC
Greeks established on the coast, living side by side with native Illyrians.

1st century BC
Roman colony of Illiricum established, divided into Dalmatia (southern) and Pannonia (northern) provinces.

AD 300
Roman Emperor Diocletian builds palace at Spalatum (Split).

365
Collapse of Roman Empire. Eastern (Orthodox) church established in Constantinople (Byzantium).

7th century
Slav invasions. Croats settle in Dalmatia and Pannonia.

c.910
Tomislav crowned king of Croatia.

FOREIGN RULE

1089
Invasion by Hungary.

1094
Bishopric of Zagreb founded.

1102
Croatian autonomy under Hungary with its own *ban* (governor, or viceroy) and *sabor* (parliament).

1126
The destruction of Biograd by Venice.

1202
The sack of Zadar by Fourth Crusaders.

1238
Mongol invasion destroys Zagreb cathedral.

1320–30
Seizure of Split, Trogir and Pula by Venice.

1389
Serbs defeated by Ottoman Turks at battle of Kosovo

1493
Croat nobles slaughtered by Ottomans at the Battle of Krbava Fields.

1526
Most of Croatia falls to the Ottoman Turks.

HABSBURG EMPIRE

1527
Croatian crown goes to Habsburg Archduke Ferdinand of Austria.

1566
Siege of Siget. *Ban* Nikola Subic Zrinski's heroic defence of the city against Ottoman advance.

1593
Ottomans repulsed at Battle of Sisak, south of Zagreb, and the tide turns.

1630
Serb Orthodox settlers in Krajina offered freedoms in exchange for a life of military service.

1671
Execution of heads of Zrinski and Frankopan families for conspiring against the Habsburg crown.

1797
Dalmatia comes under French rule as the Illyrian Provinces.

1815
The Congress of Vienna: Dalmatia incorporated into Austrian Empire following the defeat of Napoleon.

NATIONAL REVIVAL
1848
Josip Jelačić made *ban* of Croatia and leads Croats against Hungarians.

1861
Party of Rights founded by Ante Starcević who opposes the idea of South Slav, or "Jugoslav", union proposed by his rival, Bishop Strossmayer.

1867
Austrian Empire divided into Austria-Hungary. Croatia becomes part of Hungary, Dalmatia remains under Austria.

1883–1903
Rule of Charles Khuen-Hédervàry as *ban* of Croatia, who advances Hungary's interests.

1905–6
Croatian-Serbian coalition wins elections in Dalmatia and Croatia.

20TH CENTURY
1914
Assassination of Archduke Ferdinand in Sarajevo (Bosnia Herzegovina) brings Croats into World War I on the side of Austria-Hungary.

PRECEDING PAGES: Murad I is killed in the Battle of Kosovo. FAR LEFT TOP: the Battle of Kosovo. FAR LEFT: Emperor Diocletian. LEFT CENTRE : Archduke Ferdinand. TOP RIGHT: from a 1944 Partisan poster *Everyone into the Battle for the Freedom of Croatia*. RIGHT: Tudjman's grave.

1918
The kingdom of Serbs, Croats and Slovenes proclaimed in Belgrade by Serbian Prince Aleksandar.

1934
Assassination of King Aleksandar.

1939
Croatian autonomy within Yugoslavia.

1941–5
World War II: German invasion. Ustaše proclaim Independent State of Croatia, Nezavisna Drzava Hrvatska (NDH).

1945
Partisans enter Zagreb. The Nezavisna Drzava Hrvatska army massacred. Croatia becomes federal republic in Yugoslavia under the Partisan leader Tito.

1990
Multi-party elections in Croatia and Slovenia end Communist rule. Franjo Tudjman and his Croatian Democratic Union (HDZ) win power.

1990
Serb revolt in Knin, northern Dalmatia, backed by Milošević and Yugoslav Army.

1991–5
Homeland War: Croatia proclaims its independence. Dubrovnik shelled. Vukovar destroyed. The conflict ended with Operation Storm (known in Croatian as Oluja) in the summer of 1995.

21ST CENTURY
2001
Major war crimes trials commence in The Hague in the Netherlands.

2003
New parliamentary elections held and reformed HDZ party wins under leadership of Ivo Sanader, who becomes prime minister. Croatia applies for EU membership.

2008
Croatia joins Nato. A Croatian general is the first to be jailed for war crimes by a court inside Croatia.

2009
Jadranka Kosor becomes first woman prime minister.

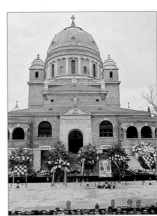

EARLY DAYS

The Slavic Hrvati, one of the tribes that arrived in the Balkans when the Roman Empire fell, formed the first Croatian state

R ecent visitors to Croatia may have noticed posters and pictures of a squat stone bird and wonder what it is. This ancient drinking vessel is the Vucedol Golubica, the Vucedol dove. Discovered in 1938, its iconic role as a symbol of the nation was given added poignancy during the siege of Vukovar *(see page 141)* in 1991–2. Dating from at least 2,500 BC, it came to represent a nation's ancient heritage under threat.

The dove is one of many finds to suggest that a rich Neolithic culture flourished in what is now the Eastern Slavonia region of Croatia. Other artwork from the same period has been found on the coast of Dalmatia (*Dalmacija* in Croatian), where neolithic settlers gave way first to Phoenicians and, by the 4th century BC, to Greeks. The Greeks left many traces of their presence on the coast. Their settlements can be plotted in place names that come from Greek words, such as the island of Hvar, from *pharos*, meaning lighthouse, while vineyards on the nearby island of Korčula dating from classical times produce famous wines called Grk, which simply means "Greek".

Roman Dalmatia and Pannonia

By the 3rd century BC Greek cultural and economic dominance over the Adriatic was giving way to the superior force of Rome. Expanding steadily into what they called Illyricum, Roman armies gradually subdued the Illyrians of the interior, incorporating the region into the empire by around 59 BC. Illyrians not absorbed into Roman society pushed deep into

the mountains, and the inhabitants of modern Albania may well be their descendants.

Most of modern Croatia and Bosnia became part of the Roman province of Dalmatia, while the north became part of the province of Pannonia. Greek settlements on the islands of Hvar and Korčula evolved into Latin towns and the Romans developed new cities on the mainland. Many Croatian coastal towns date their continual settlement from the Roman era, including Zadar (*Jader* in Latin), Trogir (*Tragurium*) and Dubrovnik (near *Epidaurum*, modern Cavtat).

Roman Dalmatia's most famous son was the Emperor Diocletian, who retired to his home town of Salona (now Solin, a suburb of Split)

LEFT: depiction of a Croat, dating from the 18th century. **RIGHT:** the Emperor Diocletian hailed from Salona (now a suburb of Split).

around AD 300 and built a vast home for himself a few miles away at Spalatum, overlooking the harbour. Ironically, the octagonal mausoleum of this dedicated persecutor of Christians eventually became Split's cathedral. The thick walls, soaring arches and massive supporting

> Around 3,000 Christians are thought to have died under Diocletian's purges. The last pagan Roman Emperor, Diocletian was succeeded by Constantine, who converted to Christianity and founded Constantinople.

cessive invasions, security in Dalmatia collapsed. Christian Visigoths, Germanic Vandals, Central Asian Avars and other tribes raced through, looting and sacking the wealthy towns en route.

In 396, St Jerome, the great biblical scholar who was born in Strido, wrote movingly from Istria of the general distress he had witnessed in this time of trouble. "Bishops have been captured, priests killed, horses tied to Christ's altars and martyrs' relics cast around," he declared. "Everywhere there is sorrow, horror and the image of death."

The fact that by the 5th century Pula's magnificent arena was functioning as a menial cat-

columns of the immense compound where Diocletian spent his retirement survive to this day, framing Split's old city like an exoskeleton.

The old city of Split is, perhaps, Rome's most impressive legacy in Croatia. But it has a great rival in the north, in the forum at Pula, in Istria. Constructed from about 20 BC to AD 70, Pula's amphitheatre – three tiers high with 72 arches – is considered second only to the Colosseum in Rome in terms of size and preservation. It is still used today as a theatre and film venue.

After the division of the Roman Empire in AD 395 into an eastern half governed from Constantinople (Byzantium) and a western half ruled from Rome, Dalmatia was awarded to the west. But as Rome buckled under the weight of suc-

tle market shows how far the region's economy and culture had declined. Some of the more exposed Roman settlements in Dalmatia shrank into insignificance.

Others, like Salona, disappeared altogether and people were forced to move elsewhere. In the early 7th century, in search of security, refugees from ravaged Salona began pouring into the ruins of the walled palace at Spalatum, transforming Diocletian's palace into a town. Further south, the inhabitants of Epidaurum fled their old home to build a new city a few miles away in a marshier, less accessible position. In so doing they laid the foundations of what would later become the great merchant city of Ragusa, or Dubrovnik.

Slavic Hrvati (Croats) arrive

While the Latin, or Latinised, inhabitants of the Dalmatian coast struggled to adapt to their deteriorating circumstances, momentous demographic changes were taking place in the interior. Emigrating from their homeland in modern Ukraine and Belarus, Slavs had begun to surge into the Balkan pensinsula. These migrants may have come, at least initially, at the invitation of the Byzantine emperors, who saw the Slavs as a potential bulwark on the empire's depopulated frontier against invading barbarians.

Regardless of whether this was fact or legend, from the 7th century onwards the shattered Latin faith of their Latin neighbours – though their mass evangelisation may have owed more to the Frankish army of Charlemagne, which conquered the area in the 9th century. The earliest surviving examples of *starohrvatski* (Old Croatian) architecture, such as the 9th-century Holy Cross Cathedral in Nin, suggest that the Croats were much more interested in imitating Latin civilisation than attacking it.

From a mass of small principalities, a single Croatian polity began to merge in the 8th and 9th centuries. By the 820s, a ruler called Vladislav was styling himself Duke of the Croatians and Dalmatians. Thirty years later,

settlements of the Dalmatian coast found themselves living in proximity to the Slavic Croats. Their name, Hrvati, may point to distant Iranian antecedents, for Greek writers of around 200 BC described the Horvatos as an Iranian tribe. But they were undoubtedly a Slavic society by the time they settled Dalmatia and Pannonia.

The immigrants seem to have acted as a stabilising force, as there is no record of armed conflict between the surviving Latins on the coast and the Croats in the neighbouring interior. In fact the Croats seemed to have assimilated easily, rapidly taking on board the Christian

LEFT: a 19th-century drawing of Pula.
ABOVE: Pula's Roman amphitheatre today.

ISLAND ESCAPES

The islands around the Adriatic provided protection for the Latinised communities when the Slavic invasions began. In Italy, they formed the first settlements on the lagoons at Venice. Dubrovnik was founded at the same time, as an island retreat, with the Slavs settling on the coast just a few meters away. Nin, one of the major early centres of Croatia, occupied an island that covered just half a square kilometre. But some islands had long been occupied: seafaring Liberians who traded with Phoenoicians and Greeks, had a stronghold on three rocky outcrops that became the city of Zadar. Illyrian Rovinj was also an island settlement, which remained unconnected to the mainland until 1763.

a successor, Trpimir, invited the Benedictine order to Croatian lands, a significant step in strengthening ties between the Croats and western Christendom.

The first king of Croatia

The early Croatian state reached its apogee under Tomislav, who, according to legend, was crowned first King of Croatia in 925. The legend may be apocryphal, as there is no contemporary surviving evidence that this ceremony ever took place. What is certain is that Croatia's rise to power had attracted international attention. In his contemporary handbook, Porphyrogenitus

describes Croatia as a substantial power. The early Croatian state did not maintain its independence, however. The more advanced states of Hungary to the north and Venice to the west both cast acquisitive glances over the strategically important Dalmatian coastline. Of the two, Venice was the more dangerous and by the beginning of the 11th century the doges ominously had assumed the title of dukes of Dalmatia.

Gregory of Nin

A significant weakness of the infant Croatian state had been its failure to promote an autonomous church, which could act as a pillar of the state. Gregory (Grgur) of Nin, a Slav bishop, had championed the use of an indig-

enous Croatian alphabet, known as Glagolitic (*see page 193*), as well as the performance of Mass in the vernacular. As a result there was an attempt to make Nin, just north of Zadar, the ecclesiastical centre of the kingdom. But the Latin clergy in other coastal towns in Dalmatia fiercely resisted the idea. After appeals to Rome, the papacy sided with the established Latins against the Croat newcomers, elevating Split, instead of Nin, to the rank of archbishopric in 925. In spite of this setback, the Croat kingdom enjoyed an Indian summer from 1058 to 1074 under Kresimir IV, who moved the capital from Knin, in the Dalmatian interior, to Biograd on the coast. He also founded a new Slav city on the coast south of Biograd to rival the older Latin foundations. This was Šibenik. Kresimir's death without an heir left the kingdom rudderless and divided. Power fell into the hands of Zvonimir, the *ban* (governor) of the northern, Pannonian, region.

The Hungarians move in

On Zvonimir's death in 1089, Croatia's northern neighbour seized the opportunity to invade. Claiming the crown as the brother of Zvonimir's surviving queen, Jelena, King László of Hungary moved an army south, seizing much of Croatia's northern plains and founding a bishopric in 1094 at Zagreb, which was then an insignificant settlement. His brother, Koloman (in Hungarian Kálmán, King of Croatia 1095–1116) continued the campaign to subdue the Croats but decided to buy off the resistance of the Croat nobles rather than wage a protracted war of conquest.

The fruit of Koloman's deliberations was the *Pacta Conventa* of 1102, under which Hungary pledged to respect the ancient rights of the Croatian kingdom. Koloman's coronation in Biograd was a victory of sorts for the Croat noble class. The ceremony confirmed that the Croat kingdom would retain a separate identity under the Hungarian crown. The Croats would have their own *ban* to govern them in the king's name and would keep their own *sabor* (parliament). Nevertheless the Croats were no longer masters of their own destiny. They would not rule themselves again for another eight centuries. ❏

LEFT: the Glagolitic alphabet commemorated in the village of Hum in Central Istria.
RIGHT: bronze of Grgur of Nin (1927) in Split, by the famous Croatian sculptor Ivan Meštrović.

THE MIDDLE AGES

The Croatian crown passed from the Hungarians
to the Habsburgs, but the biggest upset was
the Ottomans, enemies of Venice and the Pope

The union of the Croatian and Hungarian crowns under Koloman did not bring the Croats security against Venice, or any other invaders. After Koloman's death in 1116, Venice attacked Šibenik, Zadar and Biograd, practically demolishing the old coronation town in 1126. The most infamous assault occurred in 1202, when thousands of soldiers who had arrived in Venice for the Fourth Crusade were given supplies in return for the prize of Zadar. The city surrendered after a punishing bombardment. Ignoring the crosses hanging from its walls as a sign of submission, the crusaders simply massacred many of the city's inhabitants. The slaughter and looting of churches so outraged Pope Innocent III that he excommunicated the Venetians for their infamy.

The sack of Zadar was only the beginning of Venetian expansion in the Adriatic. In the 1320s and 1330s the Italian city-state took control of Split, Trogir, Šibenik and Pula. In 1409 King Ladislas of Naples, claimant to the Hungarian

The word "argosy" to describe a fleet of mercantile ships is derived from the word Ragusa, the old name for the seafaring city of Dubrovnik.

crown, sold his rights over Zadar and the rest of Dalmatia to Venice for 100,000 ducats. In little more than 10 years Venice had obtained control

LEFT: *The Capture of Cattaro* (modern-day Kotor in Dalmatia) by the Venetians under Vittorio Pisani in 1378, from a painting by Andrea Micheli (1539–1614). **RIGHT:** Mongolian warriors in a Persian miniature.

of most of Dalmatia, which it retained until the French revolutionary army terminated Venice's own independence in 1797.

The Mongol invasion

The Hungarian crown had been equally ineffective in resisting an invasion of Mongols from the east, who tore through Hungary and Croatia in 1238 with devastating effect, demolishing Zagreb cathedral, which had been completed just 21 years earlier. King Bela IV of Hungary-Croatia was chased as far down as the Dalmatian city of Trogir, which risked sharing Zagreb's fate when it refused to hand him over. Mysteriously, however, the Mongol army abruptly retreated east and Trogir was spared.

One consequence of these debilitating invasions was a decline in royal power and the growth of semi-independent feudal lordships. Two families that would long exercise quasi-royal authority over much of Croatia were the Frankopans and the Subics, later known as the Zrinskis. The base of the former was the island of Krk, while the Subic fastness was located at Bribir, near Knin. The other consequence of colonisation was that Croatia's axis shifted north from Dalmatia to the plains of Pannonia, now known as Slavonia (*Slavonija* in Croatian). As Dalmatia declined under Venetian rule and its cities lost their lustre,

The Muslim Ottomans

In the 14th century a new threat from the east appeared in the shape of the Ottoman Turks. This danger was to prove far more durable than that posed by the Mongol hordes. The Battle of Kosovo in 1389, though an indecisive military encounter, marked the beginning of the end of neighbouring Serbia as an independent state. By temporarily reoccupying much of Bosnia, which had collapsed by 1463, King Matthias Corvinus (1458–90) of Hungary-Croatia energetically repelled the Ottoman advance, but the process of Muslim conquest was only slowed, not reversed. At a decisive

Zagreb began its slow rise to pre-eminence. In spite of the severity of the Mongol assault, the cathedral was rapidly rebuilt in the new Gothic style and in 1242 Zagreb was awarded the status of a royal free city by King Bela IV.

Medieval Zagreb was soon large and prosperous enough to afford the luxury of vigorous territorial battles, pitting the clerical lords of the Kaptol area, surrounding the cathedral, against the lay masters of the town, known as Gradec. The bone of contention usually concerned control over the mills in the stream dividing the two areas. The street that bears the name Krvavi Most, or Bloody Bridge, recalls the spot where one of these furious encounters took place in 1295.

battle at the Krbava Fields in the Lika region of western Croatia in 1493 the Turks routed a Croatian force and cut down the flower of its nobility.

At the turn of the 16th century, armies of Ottoman Turks had penetrated the Dalmatian coast and were rapidly overrunning everything in their path, except for those coastal cities held by Venice and the prosperous city-state of Dubrovnik, which offered the Ottoman Sultan nominal allegiance in 1526 in exchange for retaining effective independence.

By then the Turkish advance was only a few kilometres south of Zagreb. The ecclesiastical authorities had already frantically supervised the erection of defensive towers and high city walls in expectation of a siege, completing them by 1520. This gave the cathedral the appearance of a fortress, which it retained until the walls were finally torn down in the 19th century.

The piecemeal occupation of Croatia by the Ottomans was relentless but it encountered fierce resistance. From Rome, an anxious papal court watched the country's steady collapse with a mixture of alarm for the security of Italy and admiration for the Croats' valour in defence of their land. When the military genius Suleyman the Magnificent became Sultan in 1520, Hungary-Croatia suffered a further

the Lutheran revolt against the Church, which threatened to plunge the whole of Europe into civil war. Preoccupied with the religious chasm that was opening up within his own domains, Charles V left the Croats to their own fate.

Hungary-Croatia's end came five years after the fall of Belgrade. In August 1526 at the Battle of Mohacs in southern Hungary, the Ottomans annihilated a joint Hungarian-Croat army, killing King Ludovik II and opening the way to the Hungarian capital of Buda. Most of Hungary fell quickly to the Ottomans. In December a remaining portion in the northwest of the country accepted the Habsburg claim to the

series of defeats and more land was overrun by the Turkish invaders.

Croatian nobles desperately canvassed outside powers for support. Bishop Simun Kozicic of Modrus went to Rome to plead Croatia's cause before the Catholic bishops, who were attending the Fifth Lateran Council in 1513. Nobles such as the 82-year-old Bernardin Frankopan attended the Diet of Nuremberg, summoned by the Habsburg Holy Roman Emperor Charles V, in 1522. But the timing of their appeals was unfortunate. The papacy and the Holy Roman Empire were both weakened and distracted by

> *Suleyman, victor at Mohacs, was the Ottomans' greatest ruler, who doubled the size of the empire during his reign (1520–66). Dubbed "The Magnificent", he preferred the title of "Lawgiver".*

Hungarian crown. Croatia promptly followed suit. On New Years Day 1527, the Diet of Cetin offered the Habsburg Archduke Ferdinand of Austria the Croatian crown.

The long era of Hungarian domination was thus over and the baton was passed to the Austrians. Few might have predicted that they would keep hold of it for almost 400 years.

LEFT AND ABOVE: Turkish forces under the command of Suleyman the Magnificent.

Ottoman rule

The Ottoman conquest had vast, overwhelmingly negative consequences for the Croats. Serbs, Greeks, Bosnians and Albanians all resented subjugation to a Muslim emperor but, deep inside the Ottoman domains, they were able to reap some material benefits from the imposition of a stable government. The Ottomans built roads and bridges through their lands and erected fine administrative local capitals. In addition, the Orthodox Christian Serb and Greek churches revived to a degree, taking advantage of the Ottoman Empire's tolerance of the Orthodox faith. Many Albanians and Bosnians, meanwhile, converted to Islam, uniting their fates with that of the Ottoman Empire.

The Croats on the other hand were condemned to endure all the disadvantages of life on a shifting and unstable frontier. Their Roman Catholic religion was anathema to the Turks, who viewed the pope as one of their most dangerous political foes. The result was the virtual depopulation of many areas of Croatia and radical ethnic and religious changes in others. In the half-empty lands of Slavonia new communities of Muslim Turks and Slav converts settled the deserted towns of Osijek and Ilok. Bihac, in western Croatia, also underwent a complete change after the Otto-

RAGUSA.

THE CROATIAN RENAISSANCE

Many Renaissance writers and poets in Dubrovnik and Venetian Dalmatia explored ideas of racial solidarity among the Slavs, while others used the new medium of printing to write the first works in Croatian as opposed to Latin, marking the liberation of Croatian culture from purely religious themes. A landmark was the publication of *Judita* (Judith), the first epic poem in Croatian, by the Split poet Marko Marulić. It was written in 1501 and published in Venice in 1521. Marulić's poem enjoyed huge popularity. Its story of a widow struggling to retain her faith, dignity and independence in circumstances of extreme adversity was an obvious allegory of the plight of Croatia as a whole.

The Golden Age of Croatian literature was typified in the work of Ivan Gundulić (1589–1638), a poet from Dubrovnik, who celebrated the combined strengths of the Slavic nations in a famous epic, *Osman*.

Another highly significant figure in this Croatian Renaissance period was the Benedictine abbot Mavro Orbini, from the island of Mljet. His book *Il Regno degli Slavi* (The Kingdom of the Slavs), published in Italy in 1601, provided the first comprehensive account of all the Slavic nations. This flowering of Slavic consciousness among the Croat intelligentsia, whose sons were often sent to be educated in Italian universities, stimulated the production of many books and plays.

mans captured and sacked the city in 1592, and repopulated it almost entirely with Muslims. While towns were restocked with Muslim settlers, the empty countryside was repopulated with migrating herdsmen and shepherds. Most were ethnic Vlachs who belonged to the Serbian Orthodox Church.

Intellectual flowering

The Turkish occupation did have a few positive side effects for the Croats, however. There was an influx of thousands of Catholic refugees from Bosnia and Croatia to the city-state of Dubrovnik (then known as Ragusa) and to the

Venetian-ruled towns in Dalmatia. Many were highly educated professionals and they quickened the pace of intellectual life, stimulating a new interest in the place that Croats held in the wider family of Slav nations.

The late 15th and early 16th centuries also saw the publication of numerous books in the Glagolitic script that Grgur of Nin had championed many centuries earlier. But the decision of poets such as Marko Marulić to use Latin instead of Cyrillic letters (still used today in Serbia) was prescient. The dice were loaded against

ABOVE: Ragusa, the name given to the independent republic of Dubrovnik, thrived as an entrepôt between the 15th and 18th centuries, even rivalling Venice.

a permanent revival of Glagolitic. The Renaissance anchored Croatian culture more firmly than ever within a Western European orbit, where the use of the Latin alphabet was universal. Glagolitic would survive but it became increasingly marginalised, finally fading from the picture in the 19th century.

Subordinate to Venice

While Croatian culture flourished in 16th-century Venetian Dalmatia – and benefited from Venice's role as a European centre for the book trade – the Croats were always conscious of their subordinate place in the hierarchy of the Italian city-state. Moreover, colonial rule brought few economic benefits to the Adriatic towns and cities, which were exploited as staging posts and military garrisons. Venice imported raw materials from Dalmatia – mainly wine, cheese, salt and animal skins – but strongly discouraged manufacturing. Under this unfavourable economic regime many Adriatic cities took on an increasingly petrified appearance. In Trogir new building work virtually ceased after Venice took over in the 15th century. The great age of the Adriatic cities appeared to be over.

The Republic of Dubrovnik

The shining exception to this overall picture of economic decline in the Adriatic was the republic of Dubrovnik, then known as Ragusa. Never a particularly large city, with a population of only a few thousand, it had retained its liberty, pride and wealth through its merchant fleet, which plied the shipping lanes from the Levant in the east to Flanders in the north. The city functioned as a great entrepôt for the Ottoman-ruled territories in the Balkans, where Dubrovnik's enterprising merchants established many commercial interests.

Though a republic, Dubrovnik was no democracy. As in Venice, power resided in the hands of a noble elite who controlled the Grand Council. But as a wealthy, beautiful, Slav and Catholic city, Dubrovnik provided a beacon for many Croatian writers and intellectuals at a time when all their other hopes appeared to be dashed.

Dubrovnik's golden age came to an abrupt end in 1667, when a massive earthquake levelled most of the city and killed half the population. Until then, the Croats serenaded the city as their "Croatian Athens". ❏

THE HABSBURGS

Austrian measures to repel the Ottoman threat had important consequences for Croatia: it sowed the seeds for future conflict

The first decades of Habsburg rule in Croatia began ominously. Further Turkish incursions led to the loss of more territory, so that by the end of the 16th century all that was left was a small patch of land surrounding Zagreb. This was the dismal inheritance that the Croatian Sabor mournfully referred to as the *Reliquiae Reliquiarum*, the "Remains of the Remains" of the once great Kingdom of Croatia.

But in the second half of the century the tide began to turn. A seminal event was the Siege of Siget (Szigetvar in Hungarian) in southern Hungary in 1566, where for a month a Croat force under *Ban* Nikola Subic-Zrinsky held up a vastly superior army under Suleyman the Magnificent. Although the Ottomans eventually overwhelmed the town, the *ban*'s exploits made him a hero among Croats and thrilled all Christian Europe, while the Ottomans' image of invincibility was dented by the death of the great Sultan himself at the siege. Then, in 1593, a powerful Turkish assault on the last Croatian stronghold south of Zagreb was repulsed in the landmark Battle of Sisak. Although the Turks would menace Croatia – and indeed Vienna – for another century, there was a sense that the Turkish Empire had reached a high-water mark.

The Vojna Krajina

The Austrians, meanwhile, strengthened their defences in Croatia. In a development of great significance for the nation's political future, they established a string of garrisons along the Croatian border with Turkey, removing the surrounding territory from the jurisdiction of the *sabor* and placing it under the direct control of the Austrian military. The Vojna Krajina, or military border was designed to act as a break-

water against further Ottoman incursions. Most importantly, the Austrians turned the entire population of the Krajina into a permanent standing army, obliged to spend their active lives in the emperor's direct service and beyond the jurisdiction of the *sabor*. Owing to the depopulation of the frontier zone, the Habsburgs also encouraged Orthodox Christian Vlachs and Serbs to migrate into Krajina, permanently altering Croatia's ethnic and religious composition.

The Croat nobles in the *sabor* resented their loss of control over such a large portion of Croatia's remaining territory and the immigration of so many non-Catholics. They also resented the immigrants' status as free peasants exempt from feudal control. The *sabor* called for its own jurisdiction to be restored over the new inhabitants of the Krajina who infinitely preferred their status as armed warriors serving the emperor to that of menial serfs serving the Croat nobility. Ignoring the *sabor*'s demands, Ferdinand II confirmed the incomers' civil and religious freedoms in the *Statuta Valachorum* (Statute of Vlachs) of 1630, and granted them the powers to elect their own judges and local chiefs.

Anger over the shape of the Vojna Krajina and a growing sense of disillusion over the Habsburgs' failure to roll back the tide of Ottoman conquest formed the background to a series of anti-Austrian plots by the Croatian

arrested. On 30 April 1671 they were executed and their lands were broken up.

The longed-for end to Ottoman rule over Croatia followed remarkably soon, though it was the Turks, not the Austrians, who initiated the chain of events leading up to it. Their fatal tactical error was the siege of Vienna in 1683, which finally roused the Austrians to a decisive counterblow. After the siege was broken, Habsburg armies ploughed deep into the Balkans, reaching Kosovo in southern Serbia in 1689. Ten years later the Peace of Srijemski Karlovski left Turkey with most of its Balkan empire intact but Hungary and Slavonia

nobles. Their frustration peaked when Austria defeated the Turks at Szeged in 1664 only to concede yet more territory. The conspiracy was headed by Croatia's two leading families, the Frankopans and Zrinskis, who hawked the Croatian crown around France and Poland. In desperation, they even offered it to the Sultan in exchange for the reconstitution of all or most of the old Croatian kingdom. Not surprisingly, there were no takers and when news of the plot was leaked, the heads of both families were

The destruction of the Frankopans and Zrinskis opened the way for a new German, or Germanised, aristocracy whose loyalties lay with the Habsburgs but who had none of their pretensions to national leadership.

were re-united under the Habsburg sceptre.

To the annoyance of the *sabor*, most of liberated Slavonia was added to the Vojna Krajina, over which they had no control. However, thousands of Croats were able to settle the virgin lands, along with Orthodox Serbs, Germans, Hungarians and others, turning Slavonia into an ethnic mosaic.

LEFT: the double-headed eagle – symbol of the Austro-Hungarian Empire – in Rijeka, Croatia.
ABOVE: the Relief of Vienna in September 1683 marked a turning point in the battle against the Turks.

Prosperous peace

The century that followed proved to be a golden age for the new aristocracy and the middle classes. The towns of Croatia-Slavonia took on an appearance that many retain to this day, their skylines dominated by onion-domed Baroque churches and some impressive civic buildings. The Baroque chateaux that pepper the landscape, such as the massive and imposing Eltz castle in Vukovar, and the Odeschalchi chateau in Ilok, show the prosperity of the new noble families who had been rewarded for their services to the dynasty with large estates.

The Kingdom of Illyria

The years of peace and plenty – for the rich – came to end after the French Revolution in 1789, though it was not so much the handful of Jacobins in Croatia who disturbed the old order as the French occupation of Venice in 1797. Overnight, the centuries-old Venetian Empire collapsed and Dalmatia was incorporated into a new Napoleonic creation, the Kingdom of Illyria, including Dubrovnik, which was overrun in 1806.

This French client state was not popular. Dalmatia's impoverished Catholic peasants believed in their priests, who told them that the French were atheistic devils come to rob them of their religion. They boycotted the schools and academies that the French set up in suppressed Catholic convents and monasteries. They did not appreciate the new talk of being "citizens" and they could not read the new progressive newspapers such as the *Kraljski Dalmatin* (The King's Dalmatian), which the French encouraged. They knew only that they were being heavily taxed.

The Illyrian experiment folded with the defeat of Napoleon and Dalmatia's incorporation into the Habsburg Empire in 1815. But there could be no outright return to the moribund political order that had prevailed before the 1790s. Though the Dalmatian peasants remained sceptical of French notions of progress, an urban minority had drunk deeply from the well of French thought and they became a restless element in the ultra-conservative Austria of Prince Metternich. Austria's failure to revive Dalmatia's economy and its firm refusal to

THE LANGUAGE OF A NATION

The 19th-century national revival was centred on the issue of language. At this time a multitude of tongues was spoken throughout Croatia-Slavonia and Dalmatia. While the aristocracy and the urban elite spoke German or Hungarian in Croatia, their counterparts in Dalmatia used Italian. Several mutually incomprehensible Slav dialects were in competition among the peasants. In the 1920s and 1930s, a group of young intellectuals instigated the "Illyrium Movement" with the aim of standardising the language.

Inspired by the example of neighbouring Serbia, where a talented lexicographer, Vuk Karadzic, undertook the wholesale reform of the Serbian language and alphabet

with royal support, Lujevit Gaj attempted a similar reform in Croatia. Gaj himself spoke Kajkavian, the dialect of Zagreb, and though this had a strong literary tradition, he turned instead to the *stokavski* dialect of Dubrovnik, the national standard. It was also a language that was understood by Serbs, Bosnians and Montenegrans.

The movement was popular but, more importantly, it received the discreet support of the authorities in Vienna, who were increasingly wary of Hungary's pretensions. As a result, Gaj's allies had no problems with the government when they published the first newspapers, *Novine Horvatske* (Croatian News) and a literary supplement, *Danica* (Morning Star) in their standardised Croatian.

allow Dalmatia's union inside the empire with Croatia-Slavonia fed a sense of national frustration. This was heightened as an increasingly assertive Hungary began to flex its muscles and promote its ancient claims to Croatia as part of the Hungarian crown.

> Karl Marx and other revolutionary figures never forgave Jelačić and the "dying nationalities" for wanting to "restore the status quo of AD 800". Jelačić's statue in Zagreb was removed in 1947, but restored in 1990.

dynasty, Josip Jelačić, a popular army officer from the Vojna Krajina, was installed as *ban* of Croatia amid unprecedented popular rejoicing. A wave of changes followed, including the abolition of feudalism, the reform of the *sabor*, the unification of Croatia and Slavonia and the adoption of Croatian as the exclusive language of government and education.

But Croatia's moment of freedom did not outlive the crushing of the Hungarian uprising in 1849. Once Kossuth was safely defeated, with Russian aid, Vienna no longer felt it needed to indulge Jelačić and the Croats, and the Austrians had no intention of permitting Croatia and

Nationalist revival

Hungarian pressure only stimulated a national revival among the Croats. The new national party in Croatia had its chance in 1848, the "Year of Revolutions", when bourgeois radicals toppled the French monarchy, drove the Pope from Rome and threw most of Europe's ruling houses on the defensive. In Hungary a nationalist uprising under the radical parliamentarian Lajos Kossuth threatened the Habsburg Empire with destruction. It also gave the Croat reformers their opportunity. Pledging loyalty to the

LEFT: Napoleon Bonaparte. The Venetian Empire collapsed with French occupation of Venice in 1797.
ABOVE: Josip Jelačić enters Zagreb as *ban*.

Dalmatia to unite into a powerful bloc. Most of the reforms in Croatia were undone and a new emphasis on Germanisation prevailed. In 1859 Jelačić died a broken man.

The ideas of the *narodnjaki*, or nationals, as the patriotic party was called, did not perish, even though their powerlessness encouraged constant factional splits. In the last quarter of the 19th century two broad strands developed in Croatian political thought. The Party of Rights under Ante Starcević (1823–96) rallied those who wanted Croatia to develop its national programme alone. Those hankering for a wider Slavic union embracing Croats, Serbs and others leaned to the National Party led by Juraj Strossmayer (1815–1905), the Catholic Bishop of Đakovo. The difference between the two groups was exacerbated by intense personal rivalry between these two doughty old bachelors. Though their party ideologies were often blurred, they undoubtedly represented diverging answers to a perennial question: could a nation as small and weak as the Croats survive as a self-contained entity, or did it need to subsume its identity into a larger Slavic association? The question would dog Croatia right up to independence in the 1990s.

The empire's division into Austria-Hungary in 1867 increased popular pressure on all political factions in Croatia to form a common front. After a crushing military defeat at the hands

Hungarian interests, manipulating the *sabor* and playing on the mistrust between the Catholic Croats and the large Serb Orthodox minority to divide and rule. Though outwardly successful in his aims, Khuen-Hedervary unintention-

> *The Hungarians are a proud, egotistical and in the highest degree tyrannical race and my poor nation is persecuted, oppressed and ill-treated.*
> Strossmayer to William Gladstone

of Prussia, Austria devised a "dual monarchy", effectively splitting the empire between Vienna and Budapest. But Hungary gained its freedom from Vienna at the expense of the Croats, Serbs, Romanians and other nationalities, who found themselves under the thumb of a highly nationalistic government in Budapest. The Hungarians tried to head off Croatian unrest with a special agreement, the Nagodba. This granted Croatia a measure of self-government within an autonomous Hungary. In practice, the Nagodba was subverted because effective power resided not with the *sabor* but with the *ban* appointed by the Hungarian government.

The *ban* from 1883 to 1903, Charles Khuen-Hedervary, was a particularly devoted servant of

ally closed the gap between the parties and nationalities in Croatia, who increasingly saw through his motives. The result was the formation of an historic coalition, uniting most Croat and ethnic Serb parties under a programme of national equality, and the union of Dalmatia and Croatia. In 1905–6 this Croatian-Serbian coalition swept the board in elections to both the Dalmatian and Croatian assemblies. These coalition victories alarmed the authorities in Vienna and Budapest. In Croatia-Slavonia, Hungary's puppet *bans* repeatedly dissolved the *sabor* and called for new elections in the hope of different results. In 1908 the authorities put 52 ethnic Serb politicians on trial for treason, sentencing 31 of them to jail.

Emigration and World War I

Economic depression fuelled the sullen mood in Croatia and Dalmatia. While cities such as Zagreb expanded and were beautified in this period, modest industrialisation failed to absorb the landless poor who began emigrating to the New World. Between 1900 and 1913 about half a million Croats left for North America.

The outbreak of World War I in 1914, precipitated by the assassination at Sarajevo in Bosnia Herzegovina of the heir to the Austrian throne, the Archduke Ferdinand and his wife Sophia, by Yugoslav nationalists, was a dramatic distraction. Tens of thousands of Croats dutifully answered

that the victorious Entente powers might bargain away their land. In the secret 1915 Pact of London, Britain and France had been ready to offer Istria and Dalmatia to Italy as a bribe for abandoning the Triple Alliance and entering the war on their side. Fear of Italian designs on the Adriatic were a powerful incentive for Croats to throw in their lot with neighbouring Serbia.

A Yugoslav state

At the Serbian headquarters in exile on Corfu in 1917 a Yugoslav Committee, comprising Croatian politicians, intellectuals and artists, set out to negotiate terms for a new south-Slav, or

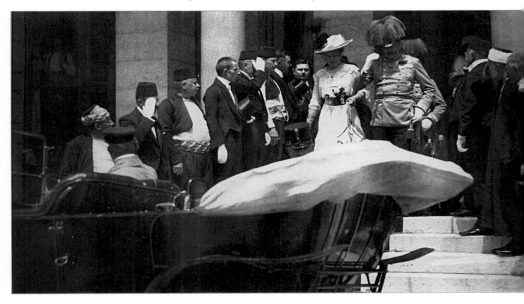

the call up to the imperial army. Among them was a young Croat called Josip Broz, known later as "Tito" when he became the Communist ruler of the new state of Yugoslavia. The empire was too weak to withstand a protracted war, however, and the death of the Emperor Franz Josef in 1916 effectively marked the end of the long Habsburg era. The new emperor, Charles, struggled on until Austria's defeat set the nationalities on paths to independence. The Croats' greatest worry was

yugoslav, state with the Serbian prime minister, Nikola Pasić. The Croats were encouraged by the entry of the United States into the war that year. President Woodrow Wilson stated his support for the principle of national self-determination.

In October the empire's southern front collapsed and Austria-Hungary sued for an armistice. A National Council of Croats, Serbs and Slovenes was set up in Zagreb as a provisional government for the empire's southern Slavs. The Croatian *sabor* declared independence and on 1 December a delegation in Belgrade presented the agreed terms for unification to Prince Aleksandar, the heir to the Serbian throne. Aleksandar I Karadordević then proclaimed the new state, the Kingdom of Serbs, Croats and Slovenes. ❏

FAR LEFT: Strossmayer, proponent of pan-Slavism. LEFT: Emperor Franz Joseph; his death in 1916 signalled the end the Habsburgs. ABOVE: Archduke Ferdinand before his assassination in Sarajevo, the event that triggered World War I.

THE MODERN AGE

Whether to seek independence alone, or in
alliance with other small states, was a
question hotly debated for a century

The Croats soon regretted the haste with which they had negotiated the terms of union with Serbia. The Vidovdan (St Vitus Day) Constitution of June 1921 abolished Croatia as a separate entity and established a centralised state in Belgrade under Serbia's Karajdordjević royal family. The Treaty of Rapallo with Italy the previous year was another disappointment, as it ceded Zadar, Istria and the islands of Lošinj, Cres and Lastovo to Italy. The city of Rijeka (Fiume in Italian) was made a League of Nations trusteeship but subsequently also fell into Italian hands.

Croatian resentment of the post-war political and territorial settlement was articulated through the Croatian Republican Peasants Party (HRSS) led by Stjepan Radić. The idol of the rural masses, Radić waged an unsuccessful, non-violent struggle for Croatian autonomy, his popularity increased by regular spells in jail. His assassination in 1928 in the Belgrade parliament by a Serbian nationalist deputy from Montenegro, Punisa Racić, threatened the country with civil war and gave King Aleksandar an opportunity to suspend parliamentary government and proclaim a royal dictatorship the following year.

Direct rule by the monarch failed to heal any of the bitter divisions and the renaming of the Kingdom of Serbs, Croats and Slovenes as Yugoslavia was interpreted by the people merely as a cosmetic gesture.

LEFT: "Long live the elections for a constituent assembly, the expression of statehood and sovereignty of the people of Croatia" – Communist party poster dating from 1946. **RIGHT:** Aleksandar I, Prince of Serbia and King of Yugoslavia (1921–34).

The Fascistic Ustaše

Ethnic and political polarisation led to the creation of a right-wing authoritarian movement in Croatia modelled on Benito Mussolini's Fascists in Italy. The Ustaše (from *ustanak* meaning uprising), led by a lawyer, Ante Pavelić, rejected the Peasants Party's parliamentary politics, its programme of non-violent agitation and its willingness to accept autonomy rather than complete independence. Based mainly in Italy, the Ustaše was sponsored by Mussolini as a useful tool with which to destabilise his neighbour and keep the question of sovereignty over Dalmatia alive.

The assassination of King Aleksandar in Marseilles in France in 1934, in which the Ustaše were implicated, opened the way for a new political settlement in Yugoslavia. The dead king's cousin, Prince Paul, became regent during the new King Peter's minority. With Hitler now in power in Berlin, and Mussolini in Rome, the regent resolved to prevent Europe's expansionist dictators from playing on Yugoslavia's divisions. For this, he engineered an historic compromise between the Serbs and Croats. The terms of the 1939 national *Sporazum*, or agreement, established a Croatian Banovina with considerable autonomy. The deal was a triumph for Vlatko Maček, Radić's successor as head of the Peasants Party, but it did not have long to prove itself.

claimed in Zagreb on 10 April. The credibility of the new regime was boosted by a public blessing from Croatia's Catholic leader, the Archbishop of Zagreb, Alojzije Stepinac.

The popularity the new regime gained by proclaiming independence dwindled when the Ustaše's Italian patrons imposed a humiliating territorial settlement. In the Rome Agreement of 18 May 1941, Italy added the port of Susak, near Rijeka, the islands of Krk, Rab and Pag and the north Dalmatian coast from Zadar to Split to its Dalmatian domains. A much wider area was designated Italy's "sphere of influence", in which the Italian military were paramount.

World War II

The outbreak of World War II in September 1939 made it certain that Yugoslavia would be drawn into the conflagration, especially after Mussolini's abortive invasion of Greece in 1940. Succumbing to overwhelming German pressure, Yugoslavia signed the Tripartite Pact with Germany, Italy and Japan in the following March, triggering a British-inspired military coup in April. This led to a German invasion and hopes raised by the *Sporazum* were destroyed.

While the Germans occupied Serbia, setting up a puppet government under General Nedić, their Italian allies sponsored an Ustaše takeover of Croatia. The Independent State of Croatia, Nezavisna Drzava Hrvatska (NDH) was pro-

The loss of most of Croatia's historic heartland guaranteed the resolute hostility of most Dalmations to the new regime.

As compensation, the NDH was granted Bosnia-Hercegovina, with a result that 2 million of the enlarged state's 6.3 million population were Orthodox Serbs. Serb hostility to the new order was guaranteed by Ustaše mass killings and deportations of Serbs and Jews and the establishment of concentration camps for the regime's political and racial enemies, most notoriously at Jasenovac, south of Zagreb.

By the summer of 1941 the NDH faced a full-scale revolt by Serb royalist "Chetniks" under Draza Mihajlović. The NDH's problems were augmented after anti-Fascist Croats and Serbs rallied to a left-wing uprising proclaimed by the Yugoslav Communist Party leader, Josip Broz "Tito", in June 1941. Tito's Partisans were initially a less important force than the Chetniks but in 1944, after a British secret agent, Fitzroy Maclean, parachuted into Yugoslavia and praised the Partisans' fighting abilities to the wartime leader, Winston Churchill, the allies switched support from Mihajlović to Tito.

At a series of stage-managed conferences at Bihac in 1942 and at Jajce in 1943 the Anti-Fascist

in Argentina in 1957. His army was less lucky. Fleeing to Austria to escape Partisan retribution, thousands of soldiers accompanied by their families were turned back at the border by British occupation forces. Partisans executed almost all of them at the village of Bleiburg.

Tito in power

With the Partisans now in control of Yugoslavia, the pretence at a coalition government was abandoned and a strict Communist regime imposed. Non-Communists were rapidly eased out of the government and their parties suppressed. A single-list "election" in November 1945 gave Tito's

Council for the National Liberation of Yugoslavia (AVNOJ) presented its programme for a new settlement, based on Yugoslavia's division into six federal republics, Serbia, Croatia, Slovenia, Bosnia Herzegovina, Macedonia and Montenegro.

The Allied invasion of Normandy and Russia's advance westwards in 1944 heralded Germany's defeat and with it the fall of Pavelić's NDH and other satellite regimes. In November 1944 Tito entered Belgrade and on 8 May 1945, the day Germany surrendered, the Partisans entered Zagreb. Pavelić escaped and would die

LEFT: Ante Pavelić, leader of the Ustaše and later the NDH, in Zagreb in 1941.
ABOVE: a clandestine Partisan meeting, 1944.

Popular Front the predictable 95 percent of votes it sought. With the politicians jailed, silenced or exiled, the regime turned to the Catholic Church, arresting Archbishop Stepinac in 1946 for collaboration. Incriminated by his public support for the NDH in 1941, he was imprisoned, then placed under house arrest, dying in 1960.

Purges were not restricted to non-Communists. In 1948 the former wartime leader of the Croatian Communists, Andrija Hebrang, was arrested and never seen again. A nationalist as well as a Communist, his popularity in Croatia made him a potentially dangerous rival to Tito. The break with Stalin in 1948 and Yugoslavia's expulsion from the Cominform (Communist Information Bureau) brought no let-up in the repressive regime, or in the ubiquitous activities of the secret police, the OZNa, later known as the UDBa. However, the government's resistance to Soviet pressure was popular. In Croatia, the return of Italian-occupied Dalmatia, Istria and Rijeka also boosted the Communists' standing and gave them a more patriotic profile than Communists enjoyed elsewhere in Eastern Europe.

In the early 1960s a political thaw set in. A vigorous debate on the virtues of economic decentralisation was permitted, and mass tourism was encouraged in Dalmatia, signalling a more general opening-up to the West. Within Croatia, the death of Archbishop Stepinac –

and the impressive funeral the authorities permitted – eased the path towards a less fraught relationship between Church and State.

The Croatian Spring

At the same time a new generation of Communist leaders emerged that was less timorous than its elders about pressing for greater autonomy and liberalisation. Led by Mika Tripalo and Savka Dabčević-Kučar, their movement would soon become known as the Croatian Spring, or as the "masspok", from *masovni pokret*, meaning mass movement.

At first Tito tolerated the reformists, especially

TITO THE BOSSY BOSS

Born in 1892 in a small stone house in Kumrovec *(see page 119)* to a Croatian father and Slovenian mother, Josip Broz became a sergeant major in World War I. He was captured fighting the Russians and while in prison learned to speak their language. He met his wife, Pelagija Beloussova, in Siberia and fought with the Red Guards in the Russian Civil War.

On his return Broz became active in the Yugoslav Communist Party and was frequently imprisoned and, having to work clandestinely, he adopted the name Tito to conceal his identity.

Tito is Croatian for Titus, but his wartime advocate Fitzroy Maclean maintains that he earned the name for

ordering people about, pointing first at them and then at what was to be done, saying: "you" *(ti)* "that" *(to)*.

As post-war leader of the country, his ability to hold the disparate elements of the Balkans together while refusing to ally the country with either the Soviet Union or the West, made Tito one of the most remarkable figures in the history of the region.

On his death in 1980 thousands of Croats lined the railway line to watch his famous Blue Train carry the presidential coffin back from the clinic in Ljubljana, where he had died, to Belgrade.

Even now Tito is remembered by many members of the older generation with affection.

when they offered him crucial backing against the Soviets during the invasion of Czechoslovakia in August 1968, which he condemned. In the same year Savka Dabčević-Kučar became the head of the Croatian League of Communists and when, two years later, she fought off a challenge by party hardliners, she unleashed a wave of public rallies that made her a national heroine – a highly dangerous position in a Communist society.

The number of enemies of the Croatian Spring began multiplying to include many of Croatia's ethnic Serbs, who feared a revival of Croat nationalism, long-time Croatian Communist stalwarts, the Serb-dominated Yugoslav People's Army and the hardline leaders of neighbouring Bosnia-Hercegovina. Abroad, the Soviet Union denounced events in Croatia and on a visit to Yugoslavia in September 1971, Soviet leader Leonid Brezhnev virtually ordered Tito to remove anti-Communist elements.

The crunch came in November when radical students engulfed Croat university campuses with strikes, enraging Tito who was then on a visit to the United States. On his return, he summoned the Croat leadership to the old hunting lodge of the Serbian royal family at Karadjordjevo on 1 December and ordered them to resign. A widespread purge of the universities, newspapers, radio and television and the League of Communists followed. Thousands lost their jobs and hundreds served jail terms.

After Tito

Tito's last decade was marked by ideological stagnation and a marked rise in living standards that took the edge off discontent. Most Yugoslavs turned away from politics towards the pursuit of the good life, their new prosperity underpinned by seemingly limitless Western credits. The ideological straitjacket was made more comfortable by greatly increased access to foreign holidays and consumer items that the inhabitants of other Communist countries could only dream about. But by the time of Tito's death in 1980, the artificial boom of the 1970s, purchased on the strength of foreign loans, had saddled the country with a US$20 billion debt.

Foreign media predictions that Yugoslavia would collapse without his guiding hand were at first unfounded. The official slogan, *Nakon*

Tita bit ce Tito (After Tito there will be Tito), testified to the political elite's determination to maintain his legacy.

His final political settlement, the 1974 constitution, left the Yugoslav presidency to a rotating collective, representing all the republics. Within a few years, however, this inheritance began to unravel as a severe economic crisis hit home. As high inflation and wage cuts hit the workers and shortages of goods hit the shops, an acrimonious argument erupted between the republics on how to restore Yugoslavia's finances, pitting the four poorer republics against the two richest – Croatia and neighbouring Slovenia.

These two demanded radical solutions, including greater autonomy for the republics, cuts in the massive army budget and an end to subsidies for failing enterprises.

In Slovenia a new liberal Communist leadership under Milan Kučan took power in 1986 and began reaching out to non-Communists, ecological groups and other sympathetic parties, horrifying the guardians of Communist orthodoxy in Belgrade and the Yugoslav Army. They began to accuse the Slovene Communists of treason.

Milošević's bid for a Greater Serbia

In Serbia, affairs moved in a different direction. There, growing anger over the ethnic turmoil in

LEFT: Tito as a Partisan in 1942.
RIGHT: Tito the statesman.

the province of Kosovo propelled an authoritarian Communist, Slobodan Milošević, to assume the party leadership in 1986. The Kosovo crisis had been years in unfolding. It was poor, overcrowded and overwhelmingly Albanian, but the Serbs insisted that it was the medieval cradle of their state and had to remain inside Serbia. They bitterly resented the local Albanian-led government that had been given some autonomy under the 1974 constitution.

Serb frustration over their loss of control created a groundswell of opinion in favour of Milošević's "big stick" tactics. The new Serbian leader encouraged massive tumultu-

ous rallies throughout Serbia, where Kosovo's Albanian leaders and other "enemies" of the Serbs were lambasted as traitors. With the support of the Yugoslav Army's mostly Serb leaders, Milošević scrapped Kosovo's autonomy in 1989 and crushed Albanian demonstrations. Celebrating his victory, he was the star of a rally in Kosovo of about a million of his supporters, held to mark the 600th anniversary of the Battle of Kosovo in June.

A growing fear outside Serbia that Milošević aimed at achieving a dictatorship over the whole of Yugoslavia on the back of Serbian populism propelled the Slovene Communists to unveil their own trump card. In January 1990 they walked out of the last Yugoslav Commu-

nist summit, ditched their Communist labels, re-branded themselves as Social Democrats and announced that multi-party elections would be held in Slovenia in April. Croatia followed suit, announcing its own multiparty poll at the same time. Yugoslavia was set for a showdown.

A new Croatian party

The Slovene and Croatian Communist leaders both planned to benefit at the polls from posing as champions of Western-style democracy against Serbian authoritarianism. But while Kučan coasted into office as Slovenia's first elected president, his Croatian counterpart, Ivica Račan, stumbled. The suppression of the Croatian Spring had left a legacy of bitterness in Croatia that Račan's winning manner could not overcome, and many Croats twinned Communist ascendancy, however it was reformed, with Serbian domination.

Victory swung instead to an elderly outsider, Franjo Tudjman, and his Croatian Democratic Union, Hrvatska Demokratska Zajednica (HDZ). Born in 1922 into a Peasants Party family, Tudjman had joined the Partisans in World War II, rising to the rank of general in 1961. In the Croatian Spring he was active within the Matica Hrvatska publishing house, receiving a two-year jail sentence for nationalism in 1972 (reduced to nine months) and another three-year term in 1981.

In spite of his Communist, Partisan background, Tudjman boldly reached out to the traditionally right-wing Croat diaspora in the US, Canada, Australia and Argentina for money, ensuring his campaign was well financed. Campaigning almost exclusively on a nationalist platform, the HDZ trounced the opposition.

The Homeland War

Tudjman's triumph was short-lived. After using Serbian agitation to swallow up Kosovo, Milošević, bidding for a Greater Serbia, set his sights on Croatia, where 600,000 ethnic Serbs, a majority in large parts of the old Vojna Krajina (the Austrian military frontier lands that were to be a buffer against the Ottomans), proved amenable to his rhetoric about the HDZ being the new Ustaše, bent on completing the genocide of 1941. The town of Knin in the Dalmatian interior became the centre of militant Serb opposition to HDZ rule and the presence of a large Yugoslav Army base ensured the rebels could act with impunity.

By the summer of 1990 a full-scale Serb revolt had erupted in the Krajina, aided by supplies of weapons delivered by the army. With Serbian encouragement, the rebels, led by a former dentist, Milan Babić, and a former policeman, Milan Martić, proclaimed the Autonomous Province of Serbian Krajina in August, declaring independence from Croatia shortly after.

While Babić's men rolled unimpeded through the Krajina in 1990, Serb militants opened new fronts in the spring of 1991 in Eastern Slavonia, on the border with Serbia round Vukovar, and in Western Slavonia, round the town of Pakrac. Their advances almost cut Croatia into three segments and the government lost control of about 30 percent of its territory.

In spite of American and international opposition, Slovenia and Croatia decided further discussions with Milošević were useless and that it was time to go for independence. Both states proclaimed their sovereignty on 25 June 1991. The two new countries' circumstances could not have been more different. After a brief skirmish with the Slovenes, the Yugoslav Army evacuated Slovenia with hardly a murmur.

Croatia, on the other hand, found itself gearing up for a long hot summer of desperate fighting against a coalition of local Serbs, the Yugoslav Army and paramilitary formations from Serbia proper. While many towns suffered severe bombardment, the most savage fighting enveloped Vukovar, which for both sides became a symbol of victory (see page 141). By the time of the surrender of Vukovar on 17 November it had been reduced to rubble and thousands were dead. Its capture was followed by a brutal war crime – the massacre of almost 300 Croat patients in Vukovar hospital. Their bodies were buried in a mass grave on a nearby sheep farm.

However, from October 1991 international attention focused more on the siege of Dubrovnik by the Yugoslav navy and Montenegrin troops, who trapped the 50,000 inhabitants behind the medieval city walls and shelled this priceless Unesco landmark.

That autumn, the Serbs' blatant aggression awoke sympathy in Germany and Aus-

tria, which had large Croat communities. Germany's Foreign Minister, Hans-Dietrich Genscher, emerged as a trenchant critic of the West's hands-off policy and of the arms embargo that hurt the lightly-armed Croats much more than Serbia and the Yugoslav Army. Fearful of a split in EU ranks, both Britain and France dropped their opposition and agreed to Europe's joint recognition of Slovenia and Croatia in December 1991.

The Vance Plan

Serbia's desire to wind down the war, partly to concentrate on Bosnia Herzegovina, which

The phrase "ethnic cleansing", synonymous with the war in Yugoslavia, was first used by the Croatian Supreme Council in July 1991 to describe Serbian actions against Croatians.

also now demanded independence, prompted Milošević to throw his weight behind a ceasefire signed on 3 January 1992 and a UN-brokered peace plan for Croatia. Drawn up by former US Secretary of State, Cyrus Vance, the Vance Plan involved the withdrawal of the Yugoslav Army from Croatia and the deployment of UN peacekeepers in UN Protected Areas, known as UNPAs. Controversially, in Croatia, the plan did

LEFT: Tudjman posing with Croatian national basketball players during a triumphal visit to Serb capital, Knin, in August 2006. RIGHT: Siege of Dubrovnik.

not address the question of Krajina's sovereignty, or the return of refugees. Nor were the local Serbs disarmed. Dissatisfaction with a deal that left the Serbs in possession of their territorial gains destabilised the agreement, ensuring Croatia's first years of independence were dominated by demands for the recovery of the Krajina.

Pact with Milošević

While public attention in Croatia focused on the Krajina, Tudjman pursued a disastrous adventure in Bosnia Herzegovina, effectively endorsing Milošević's partition policy on the understanding that Croatia would receive a chunk in the

which was confident it could take on the Krajina Serbs. In a test strike in April 1995, named Operation Flash (*Bljesak* in Croatian) the Croats overran the smallest UNPA, in western Slavonia, within hours. In retaliation, Krajina forces shelled Zagreb.

Milošević's impassive reaction to Operation Flash indicated a loss of interest in the Krajina. The *casus belli* for another strike came in July, when the Bosnian Serb army attacked and overran the UN-proclaimed "safe areas" of Srebrenica and Zepa in eastern Bosnia, murdering some 7,000 Muslims. With US encouragement, Bosnia and Croatia signed a mutual

southwest, where many Bosnian Croats lived. Condemned in the West, Croatia's military intrigues in Bosnia lost it the sympathy it had briefly attracted over Vukovar and Dubrovnik. The policy was unpopular at home, too, where the idea of a tacit alliance with Milošević against the Bosnian Muslims revolted public opinion. Ordered by the US to disengage from a messy war in Bosnia in spring 1994, or face global sanctions, Tudjman's prestige hit an all-time low and the media clamoured for his removal.

The end of the Bosnian conflict, however, concentrated minds on the Krajina. By the spring of 1995 Tudjman's defence minister Gojko Šušak had transformed the ragged army of 1991 into a well-armed fighting force,

defence pact in Split in July, and on 4 August Tudjman sent 200,000 soldiers into the Krajina on Operation Storm (*Oluja* in Croatian). The Croats routed the Serb forces within 24 hours, triggering an epic exodus of at least 150,000 Serbs, fleeing towards Serb-held Bosnia and Serbia. The recovery of the Krajina was severely marred by the killing of several hundred Serb civilians who had remained behind, many of them elderly, and resulted in several army officers being pursued for war crimes.

With the fall of the Krajina, the recovery of the rest of occupied territory was only a matter of time and Milošević quickly backed a plan to return the last slice of Serb-held land around Vukovar to Croatia, in eastern Slavonia.

Peace with some prosperity

The war had savage economic consequences and, tired of nationalist slogans, people became restive about the rampant corruption that allowed a clique of HDZ officials to asset-strip state enterprises under the guise of "privatisation". Although vast crowds attended

The ruins of Vukovar and their surroundings were returned to Croatia in December 1995, within three years of the signing of the UN-mediated Basic Agreement at Erdut.

Crimes Tribunal for former Yugoslavia, mend fences with Bosnia Herzegovina and facilitate the return of Serb refugees. The coalition was buffeted by large popular protests against the extradition of Croatian officers to face war crimes charges, and Croatia's application to join the EU in 2004 was held up until General Ante Gotovina was tracked down and indicted for crimes against humanity. Milošević was already on trial for genocide, but he died in 2006 amid the proceedings. But the authorities have also shown that they are capable of meting out justice at home: in May 2009 former General Branimir Glavas became the first Croatian politician

Tudjman's funeral on 13 December 1999, the people wanted change. The subsequent elections restored the former League of Communists leader, Ivica Račan, to the helm as prime minister of a centre-left coalition. The vote for the presidency went to Stipe Mesić, a former Tudjman ally who had turned against him over his Bosnia policy.

The new government showed its determination to improve Croatia's profile by pledging to cooperate fully with the International War

to stand trial for crimes against Serbs. A court in Zagreb found him guilty of torturing and murdering 12 Serbs in 1991 and sentenced him to 10 years in prison. Unfortunately the general then fled the country.

The economy has shown slow but steady growth since the Homeland War ended, though problems remain for Stipe Mesić, elected for a second term in 2005. Croatia still relies heavily on tourism, a weakness exposed in the global downturn of 2008–9. But fiscal and structural reforms that have been carried out since being accepted as a candidate for the European Union in 2004 have helped keep the country on a steady course for full membership, scheduled for 2010. ❏

LEFT: elected President of Croatia three times, Tudjman's fortunes were in decline by the time he fell ill with cancer in the 1990s. **RIGHT:** the scars of war are still evident along this now-peaceful Vukovar road.

RELIGION AND SOCIETY

Catholicism is at the heart of Croatian identity, which
is bolstered through folk traditions. But it doesn't
mean everyone goes to church

According to Freud, the smaller the real difference between peoples, the larger it is bound to loom in their imaginations. This point is made by the writer/broadcaster Michael Ignatieff, son of a Canadian ambassador to Yugoslavia, in *Blood and Belonging*. The book describes his journeys to Croatia during the Homeland War, and to other world hotspots, to discover what binds nations and gives people their identity, and how they crave recognition of that identity.

When the social and political experiment that was Yugoslavia fell apart, its constituent populations sought to show their identities in large part through their faiths. For Croatians to profess their Roman Catholicism was as much about telling the world that they looked to the West for their identity as it was to say that they turned their back on Eastern Orthodox Christianity, in other words the Serbs, not to mention those who believed in Islam. This difference, to Croatians, is very important indeed.

Statistically around 90 percent of the country

The Orthodox rite involves complex iconography, and the Icon Museum next to the Serbian Orthodox Church in Dubrovnik is a place to see it.

is Roman Catholic, and statistically around 90 percent of the population is Croatian. To many Croatians, it amounts to the same thing.

That does not mean most people go to church

PRECEDING PAGES: Tintoretto altarpiece, St Mark's Cathedral, Korčula. **LEFT:** Croatians are devout Roman Catholics. **RIGHT:** Byzantine frescoes inside the Basilica of Euphrasius in Poreč.

regularly, or that everyone likes the clergy. Church attendance in urban areas is low and Croatia has an old left-wing, anti-clerical tradition, which has no time for organised religion. However, there is a strong Marian cult, and professions as well as towns and villages have patron saints. The popularity of annual pilgrimages and saints' festivals is a reminder of the powerful grip that the Roman Catholic Church still exercises over the Croat imagination, in spite of years of atheistic indoctrination under the Communists. Weddings in church have also become more common, though the union has first to be sanctioned by a civil ceremony.

There are eight active Benedictine convents

for nuns in the country, mostly on the islands, and one monastery for monks on the island of Pasman near Šibenek. Nuns work in schools and hospitals and they are a common sight in the streets. Most people still grant the Church a leading position in society as the historic guardian of the nation's identity, a role cemented in the Communist era and increased to a still greater degree in the 1990s, when war with Serbia at times assumed the aspect of a religious as well as a national struggle.

The Church strongly supported the country's bid for independence and drummed up support for Croatia's diplomatic recognition

Religious differences

The Balkan peninsula has long been a great soup of peoples and faiths. Ottomans, who occupied much of it for more than 500 years, practised some religious tolerance, with the local governing councils (*millets*) being made up of leaders of each religious community. But until the 19th century Catholicism would have no other god but its own, a god who responded only to a Latin liturgy. Diocletian, in his palace at Split, had been the last Roman Emperor to persecute Christians, which he did with a vengeance. His successor, Constantine, converted to Christianity and founded Constantinople

in the Vatican. In return the government of Franjo Tudjman restored religious education in schools – though attendance is not compulsory – and returned much of the Church property that the Communists had seized since 1945. But in his bid to unite the nation Tudjman failed to condemn the wartime Fascist Ustaše – against whom he had fought.

The beatification in 1998 of Alojzije Stepinac, Croatia's wartime Archbishop of Zagreb, was a significant and controversial political event. Pope John Paul II's act delighted Catholics and nationalists as much as it angered the greatly diminished Serb and Jewish communities, many of whom have always seen Stepinac as an apologist for the wartime Fascist regime of Ante Pavelić.

and the Byzantine empire where, at the fall of Rome, the Eastern Church grew under the Orthodox rite that was fundamentally Greek. In Croatia Glagolitic rites were sanctioned by the pope, and the Latin, Western Church continued its missions from Aquileia down the Adriatic coast, where the outposts of Venice and Ragusa (Dubrovnik) kept the pope's torch burning.

The Cyrillic alphabet, invented in the 9th century by saints Cyril and Methodius to write down the speech of the Slavs, created a third language in the Christian church: Old Church Slavonic, which came to be used in the Serbian, Bulgarian and Russian Orthodox churches.

The Serbo-Croat language that evolved in the Balkans after the fall of the Ottomans became the official language of Yugoslavia, but in the break up of the state, it was rejected by Croatia at the first opportunity. A written language with familiar Western, Latin letters, replaced the Cyrillic alphabet that was seen as an instrument of repression. And though today the language may sound pretty similar to Serbian – or to Russian or any other Slavic language – such a suggestion should never be made to a Croatian.

During the Balkans conflict ecclesiastical buildings were seen as targets on all sides, especially when religious leaders gave support to the fighting forces. In Croatia during the Homeland War dozens of Serbian Orthodox churches and

much of Yugoslavia. It still practises the Byzantine rite and has about 6,000 adherents.

Mosques in Ottoman-occupied Slavonia were all torn down by the Catholic Austrians at the start of the 20th century. Now there are around 50,000 Muslim Bosnians in the country, about 1.3 percent of the population, and they have two mosques and 11 *masjids* (small mosques). The first of the modern mosques was built in Zagreb at the end of the Communist era, in 1987. There are currently plans for several more on the coast.

The churches of Croatia to be seen today are therefore almost exclusively Roman Catholic, and there are some very beautiful buildings

some monasteries, along with their treasures and graveyards, and around 5,000 icons were destroyed, damaged or looted, and the *eparchies* (dioceses) of Karlovac, Slavonia and Dalmatia were abandoned. After 1995 priests and bishops returned and the buildings have been largely restored, but congregations are diminished.

Old Church Slavonic, with Cyrillic script, used in the Serbian Orthodox Church is also adopted in the Croatian Greek Catholic Church established in the Eparchy of Križevci in central Croatia, whose parish once extended through

LEFT: boys will be boys on the island of Hvar.
ABOVE: elderly males lead a more sedentary lifestyle – frequently in cafés.

CUSTOMS AND MANNERS

On the whole, Croatians are formal, punctual, respectful and neatly dressed. They shake hands, speak their minds and put store by family and age. Except for close friends and family, they address each other formerly, as Gospodin (Mr), Gospodja (Mrs) and Gospodice (Miss). Friends get an embrace or a kiss on each cheek. Invited to a house, guests will take flowers, but not chrysanthemums, which are reserved for funerals and, according to custom, there should be an odd number of stems. Guests should eat with enthusiasm and try to agree to second helpings if pressed. All this is a generalisation, of course: the rules of a more reserved interior and a rather Latin coast still apply.

among them – the Basilica of Euphrasius in Poreč and the Cathedral of St James in Šibenik are world-class treasures. Many have once again become places of prayer, but some remain museums or social spaces for concerts and other events. But any local church is appreciated by its congregation, especially during festivals, when it is obvious just how much they are a focus of daily life.

Equality of opportunity

Religious tolerance and ethnic reconciliation have been among the demands for joining the European Union, though these may have been achieved, to a greater or lesser extent, anyway. Equality of gender rights was never an issue under Communism, when women were used to salaried work and to taking high office in the League of Communists. Savka Dabčević-Kučar, a Dalmatian, famously led the ill-fated Croatian Spring reform movement in the late 1960s. Milka Planinc, a far less popular figure, was another Croatian woman in the driving seat as Yugoslav premier in the early 1980s. And in July 2009 the Croatian Democrat Union (HDZ) leader Jadranka Kosor, a former journalist, became prime minister when Ivo Sanader stepped down. In the previous presidential

FABRICS OF THE NATION

The wonderful traditional costumes of Croatia, in which women can wear up to three bodices and seven underskirts, are a chance to show off the skills of weavers, embroiderers, lacemakers, leatherworkers, silver- and goldsmiths, seamstresses and jewellers.

Silk has a long tradition in the country, which is why there are so many white mulberry trees, as the silk moth feeds on their leaves. There was a time when Croatian women would keep a cacoon between their breasts to ensure their skills would be perpetuated. Today the cravat or tie, Croatia's main fashion gift to the world, remains a good outlet for silk products.

Dubrovnik's silver- and goldsmiths were once famous, and you can still find filigree buttons for sale in the town. But perhaps the most emblematic of the country's costume crafts are the wide-hatted lacemakers in the town of Pag, on the island of the same name. You can see women today at their doorsteps creating intricate patterns with their special sewing needles.

The embroiderer's art may seem arcane, but in Croatia it has been brought to the brink of artistic achievement by Ivan Rabuzan who designed the drop curtain for the Takarazukla Theatre in Tokyo. Measuring 1.4 by 24 metres (4ft 6in x 79ft), it depicts a naïve landscape of cherry trees, sunny hills and fluffy clouds. It took 24 weavers three months to make.

elections, she was defeated in the run-off by the incumbent head of state, Stipe Mesić. She speaks fluent English and has published two volumes of poetry and two books on the Homeland War. Taking over at a time of economic uncertainty and following the blocking of accession talks with the EU by Slovenia because of the border dispute, Kosor promised to lead the government with "a strong female hand".

Today, even in more conservative country districts, women are far from submissive. Indeed, many believe Croatia is really a matriarchy, a state of affairs summed up in the old Dalmatian proverb: *Zena drzi tri kantuna od kuce* – A woman holds three corners of the house. In 2005 the women of Lozisca on the island of Brac won all seven seats on the local council after proclaiming they were sick of seeing the village men doing nothing for the community.

The Croats' selective approach to religion is also reflected in their attitude towards contraception. Long before the Communists began methodically to undermine religious teaching, the Catholic clergy was bemoaning the refusal of its flocks to take any notice of Rome's prohibition of birth control. The evidence for this was a rapid decline in the size of the average family from the early 20th century. It is a trend that continues to worry demographers, as constantly shrinking families fail to compensate for the death rate, resulting in an overall decline in population. There are predictions that many rural areas will be depopulated if the trend is not reversed in the next quarter-century.

As in the rest of the West, woman are also getting married later, and while many of the old religious taboos, such as no sex before marriage, seem to have crumbled away in urban areas, others remain pretty much in place. There is still pressure on women to get married and little respect for single women, childless women (unless they are nuns) or single mothers. Divorce is hardly unknown but it is not common.

Economic reality means that many people live at home until they are married. In rural areas, where couples tend to marry at a younger age, traditional weddings can still last several days and visitors may well get caught up in them. The family remains the centre of every-day life, and relatives stay close, offering the first port of call for any help and support. Children are expected to look after their parents and the elderly are more likely to move in with their families rather than to be put in a home.

Same-sex relationships are recognised in law, and though homosexuality is still frowned upon by many, Gay Pride is now a regular feature in Zagreb every June, with more than 500 participants, and each year more and more gay tourists, many of them Americans, are discovering the freedoms of the coast. The HIV rate is extremely low, affecting less than 0.1 percent of the Croatian population.

Fashion fiends

While the demographers cite low wages and the small size of socially owned flats as some of the causes of the current baby shortage, another factor is the national obsession with fashion. Croatians are fanatical followers of every latest trend, and there isn't much that the average female city dweller won't do to maintain a wasp waistline, fill her wardrobe with designer-label clothes and dedicate every minute after work to the trendy bars and cafés that fill to bursting each long, hot summer night in Zagreb, Split and elsewhere. None of these activities is compatible with becoming the mother of a large brood, and even young mothers pushing prams can look as if they have just come off the catwalk.

LEFT: votive candles at Stone Gate Chapel, Zagreb.
RIGHT: selling olive branches on Palm Sunday, Split.

Most foreign visitors wonder how the inhabitants of a country with such low average wages can afford to go out so often and dress up so glamorously. Are they secretly rich? No they aren't. The answer is that most Croats (and Serbs for that matter) would rather starve than wear last year's gear. And far more than in most Western countries, Croatian parents and grandparents unthinkingly sacrifice their own creature comforts for their children. There is another trick to the Croats' uncanny ability to go out a lot on next to nothing – much of the time all they need to do is walk up and down, and unlike in Britain or the US, where waiters usually drive out diners as soon as they have finished their meals, Croats cling undisturbed to their seats in their favourite cafés for hours. If need be they will nurse a single coffee and ice cream all night to indulge the nation's favourite pastime – people-watching.

Sport: the other religion

Catholicism is not the Croats' only religion. The other is sport, and it's one that dovetails neatly with the national obsession with politics and regional pride. The only crowds large enough to rival political protest rallies and church pilgrimages are those watching Zagreb's Dinamo football team slug it out against Hajduk of Split. In 2009 a group of 19 Benedictine nuns from a convent in Zadar bought around 3,600 euros' worth of shares in Hajduk Split, making them one of the club's top 20 shareholders. Most nuns in the convent know little of football, but they promised to pray for their newly adopted team.

At a time when Croatia was isolated, and even reviled during the war in Bosnia, world-class footballers such as Davor Šuker and Zvonimir Boban – the two pillars of Croatia's World Cup bid in 1998 that took Croatia to the semi-finals – put the country on the world map in a positive way. Croatia marched all the way to third place in the World Cup that year, taking the scalps of Germany and Holland on the way and giving the hosts and eventual winners, France, a real run for their money in the semi-final This was the "Golden Generation" of Croatian football, but the team remains world class. It knocked England out of the 2008 World Cup qualifiers by beating

SPORTING HEROES

Croatia's most famous sporting icon is the tennis player Goran Ivanišević, who surprised everyone in 2001 by becoming the first "wild card" entry ever to win the Wimbledon singles championship. On his return to his native Split more than 100,000 fans lined the waterfront and in typically Goran style he stripped off to his underwear to salute his slightly bemused followers.

Following on Ivanišević's heels was Mario Ancic, who made his debut at Wimbledon on the centre court as a teenager, beating Switzerland's Roger Federer. He led the Croatian team that won the 2005 Davis Cup.

Meanwhile in Zagreb and northern Dalmatia, basketball competes with football for attention. Zadar and Šibenik both have excellent teams and have supplied players who have been successful in the National Basketball Association leagues in the United States. The Croatian Basketball Federation was founded in 1948.

Perhaps Croatia's most surprising sporting success of all time came in 2002 at the Salt Lake City Winter Olympics in America when Croatian skier Janica Kostelić not only won Croatia's first-ever Olympic medal, but also its second, third and fourth in a haul that included an impressive three golds. In swimming Duje Draganja, an Olympic silver medallist, became the fastest man in the water in 2009 when he finished the 50-metre freestyle in just 20.81 seconds.

them twice, making a hero out of Ivan Klasnic – though they suffered retribution when England removed them from the qualifiers for 2010.

Croats know that football supremos and tennis stars like Goran Ivanišević have done far more for their country's image abroad than any number of diplomats, writers or singers. These

Croatian parents often go without to keep their children supplied with the latest prestige goods and clothes, and enough pocket money to show off in bars and clubs.

from central government. Innovation, an ability to think for oneself outside safe bureaucracies and known rules from the past, can take a generation to learn. But there is a new generation, one that knew neither Communism nor civil war. Young Croats are well educated – literacy is over 98 percent – and the majority of them speak English and German. They tend to be optimistic and determined to succeed in a world that remains alien to many of their parents. They are computer-literate and internet-smart. Travelling overseas in search of money and experience is increasingly common, but so is coming back to set up small businesses in Croatia. They are not

days, Croatia's sports stars tend to get poached by wealthy clubs outside the country, but they still wield a lot of political influence back home. When Suker and Boban signed a protest letter in 2001 against the decision to surrender two war crimes suspects to the Hague tribunal, the government trembled.

Profit and loss

The early days of cavalier capitalism are over, the warlords have returned to their restaurant businesses or their farms, and the country has settled into capitalism's maw, with a strong role still

afraid of work, and may often have more than one job to try to make ends meet. Germany and the US have the highest emigrant populations, with around half million in each.

In the aftermath of independence, some Croats worried that their distinctive traditions were crumbling under the impact of relentless exposure to Western mass media. Regional dialects, proverbs and traditional songs seemed to be fading and the country's wonderful regional costumes were sometimes put on only for the benefit of tourists or for "Vinkovacki Jeseni" – the annual autumn folklore festival held in Vinkovci. But the reality of capitalism has set in, with the realisation that it is not a cure for all ills, that money does not turn up the moment

LEFT: choir boys outside the cathedral in Split.
ABOVE: national football shirts for sale in a Zagreb shop.

that free markets are introduced and five-star tourist hotels built. There were aspects of life under Tito's Communism that many still recall with nostalgia. Though towns remain by and large clean and orderly, much of the simple country life has gone.

As the quest for identity continues, traditions today are not just clung to, but are enriched. New festivals are introduced, old crafts are resuscitated, and customs have re-emerged as popular as ever.

The pull of the West and the almost universal desire, especially prevalent among the young, to imitate everything American, from accents

Organised crime, on the other hand, is a symptom of newly independent states. It began with the break up of Yugoslavia when arms embargoes against the country led to criminal activity that would finance arms buying, and it continues through a murky underworld of drugs, prostitution, extortion and corruption.

According to journalist Goran Flauder, "Where Italy is a state with a mafia, Croatia is a mafia with a state." Flauder has suffered a number of physical attacks as a result of his investigative articles, including stories about the assassination by car bomb in Zagreb of Ivo Pukanic, editor of the *Nacional* newspaper, and its marketing chief Niko

to dress sense, has created a more homogenised society. But swings in one direction are invariably followed by reactions in another. That is the one lesson in Croatian history. And as the country's favourite poet, Gustav Matos, once reassuringly put it: *Dok je srca bit ce Kroacije* – While people have hearts (or rather, courage) there will always be Croatia.

Organised crime

Western ills as well as benefits have also infiltrated daily life. Violent crime – virtually unknown a generation ago – is creeping into cities. Even so, it remains comparatively low, and, beyond the usual safety precautions, visitors have little to concern themselves with.

Franjic in 2008. Two weeks earlier 26-year-old Ivana Hodak, the daughter of a prominent lawyer, was shot in the back of the head in Zagreb. These events led to the British Foreign Office issuing warnings to visitors about the threat from organised crime, and to the EU raising doubts about Croatia's fitness as a potential member. This is a threat the government must have viewed seriously. It took a while for Croatia to be recognised by the UN. Next to that, membership of the EU is the highest accolade a fledgling European nation can aspire to: it will be a big step towards confirming a national identity. ❑

ABOVE: to see and be seen in Brač, dark glasses are essential.

Naked Passions

Encouraged by the government and approved by romping royals, naturism on Croatia's bays and beaches has a long and healthy tradition.

Naturism and Croatia go back a long way and the country could even claim to be the spiritual home of modern European naturism, with devotees flinging off their clothes on its Adriatic beaches as early as the start of the 20th century. But it was in 1936, when Edward VIII stripped down to his crown jewels on the Kvarner Gulf island of Rab, that naturism really took off. The British monarch requested permission from the local authorities, which allowed him to bathe naked in Kandarola Bay (now dubbed "English Beach"). It was not recorded whether Mrs Simpson chose to join him, but the musical *The Naked King* is based on Edward's notorious visit to Rab.

With the advent of mass tourism and jet airline travel in the 1960s naturist resorts, beaches and camps sprang up all along the Croatian coastline as more than 100,000 naturists flocked to the coast every summer. Today, encouraged by government and the tourism boards, the numbers are probably not far short of this. But it's hard to draw a line between dedicated, paid-up naturists, and holidaymakers who briefly slip away from the textile world.

Croatians, however, are thought to make up only about 5 percent of naturists on the country's beaches. Some put this down to the effects of the Catholic Church, which preaches a more private attitude to their bodies. That said, compared with other Catholic countries, Croatia is fairly liberal when it comes to nudity. Even outside naturist areas it is common for local women to go topless.

More than 20 official naturist centres take various forms, and can be beaches, campsites, apartments, bungalows and hotels with plenty of sporting facilities and places to eat and drink. Istria has a string of naturist resorts around Umag, Poreč, Vsar and Rovinj. The Alpe-Adria Encounter is a well-established sports gathering of national naturist associations with a standard diet of sporting contests, dinners and dances.

Casanova is said to have swum naked on both his visits to the islet Koversada, a fact that encouraged it to hold the 1972 World Naturist Congress. Vrsar, on the shore opposite, now has an annual Casanova festival of erotica.

Further south in the Kvarner Gulf, where the first official naturist centre was set up on Rab in 1934, naturism is still popular, with resorts also located on the islands of Cres, Mali Lošinj, Krk and Pag. The Northern Dalmatian cities of Zadar and Šibenik also have nearby naturist resorts, while the Dalmatian islands of Brač, Hvar and Korčula have all-nude beaches and resorts. Even Dubrovnik has its own naturist centre.

Areas without official naturist resorts will often

reserve a section of beach for naturists. Look out for the FKK signs (an abbreviation taken from the German for Free Body Culture), indicating where nude sunbathing is allowed – usually away from family areas. These don't have the same facilities as the naturist resorts, but there is no entrance charge and you can just stop off if you are passing by. Some boat trips also revolve around naturist beaches – again look out for the FKK sign.

Today's naturists are a cosmopolitan bunch, coming mostly from Hungary, Germany and Austria, as well as Italy, the Netherlands and the Czech Republic. For more information on naturist holidays, for feedback from previous visitors, and for details of nudist sailing holidays, look up www.cronatur.com. ❑

RIGHT: look for signs saying FKK if you want to find a nudist beach.

FESTIVALS

When it comes to celebrating, Croatians like to dress up – in the kind of costumes their forefathers wore

Traditional costumes, folk music and dance have been extraordinarily enduring in Croatia, not only surviving the vicissitudes of the 20th century, but seeming to grow in genuine popularity. Many towns have a day on which to dress up in costumes that show exactly where the participants come from – fur and thick capes in the interior, beautiful embroidery in Slavonia and high lace hats on the island of Pag. Rich and colourful, the costumes are given added sparkle with jewellery and gold thread. Costumed groups come together at the annual International Folklore Festival in Zagreb in July, started in 1965, which attracts folk performers not just from Croatia and the Balkans, but from all over the world, while the Zlatna Sopela (The Golden Flute) festival in Poreč in late June brings people from around the Mediterranean. People don't need much excuse to dress up to celebrate their past – you can meet Diocletian, Marco Polo and Prince Banimir, while in June Opatija remembers the days when it was a favourite watering hole of the Austrian aristocracy, and people dress up in courtly style. The main pre-Lent carnival is in Rijeka, with many masked figures, and there is a big summer carnival in Pag.

One of the most famous folk dances is the Moreška, a ritualised sword dance representing the triumph of Christians over Turks, which takes place in Korčula Town on the feast of St Theodor on July 27. It recounts the tale of two kings, who battled for the affection of a maiden.

ABOVE: dressed for the 10-day autumn festival in Vinovci, Slavonia, a region renowned for sumptuous costumes.

LEFT: the *tambura*, a five-string instrument, forms part of any band.

ABOVE: the Lindo Folk Ensemble have a permanent venue in Dubrovnik, where the perform dances from various parts of the country.

LEFT: the "Triestino" accordion is a popular instrument in Istria ar an annual festival take place in Roc.

DUBROVNIK'S LIBERTAS

The hoisting of the Libertas, the flag of Ragusa, heralds the start of the renowned Libertas Festival on 10 July each year in Dubrovnik. Held since 1949, it attracts top artists, but there are no mass concerts in huge arenas; all performances are staged among 70 mostly open-air venues in the historic buildings of the old town. Perhaps the most dramatic setting is Lovrijenac Fort, the stone bastion on the edge of the old town, with the Adriatic lapping at its base. Daniel Day Lewis is just one of several Hamlets to have stalked its ramparts. The Dubrovnik Symphony Orchestra and the Lindo Folk Dance Group are perennials.

Street performers fill the old town during the seven-week event and for much of the day cafés are full of festival-goers soaking up the carnival atmosphere. For further information visit the Libertas website: www. dubrovnik-festival.hr; or tel: 020 326100, fax: 020 326116.

: Christians and
s do battle in the
eška dance on the
d of Korčula. This
lised sword dance
s from the 15th
tury.

HT: embroidery and
at the International
Festival in Zagreb.

OW: Klapa singers, a
tion on the coast:
nnual competition
almation singers is
at Omiš.

TOP: the walls of Dubrovnik provide a dramatic backdrop for the annual Libertas Festival, and its forts are ready-built venues.

ABOVE: the vibraphone of Boško Petrović, fusing jazz with traditional Croatian music, is a regular at the Libertas Festival.

BELOW: with the coats of arms of Croatia, Dubrovnik, Dalmatia, Istria and Slavonia, the national flag is waved at every festival.

THE CULTURAL SCENE

Tradition is central to all the arts, particularly music, in which Croatians excel. Luckily, there are many wonderful venues where you can see them perform

Seasons in Croatia can be measured by their festivals of music, art, film, dance and drama, which fill the diaries of both professional and amateur performers. These make the best use of some of the country's most beautiful buildings, from the dramatic castles and gilded theatres of Zagreb and Slavonia to the pretty churches of Istria and Dalmatia. What better place to attend a film festival than in the Roman Amphitheatre at Pula, or to listen to a classical concert than in St Donat's in Zadar, or the Rector's Palace in the city of Dubrovnik?

Mad about music

Of all the arts, however, music is the one that seems to course most easily through Croatian blood. In many towns and villages you may be walking down a street when the sounds of choirs in rehearsal, of instruments being blown, struck and plucked, drift out from behind closed doors. You may hear, too, the unique Croatian *ganga*, an exciting singing style in which a soloist is accompanied by a wailing chorus; or come across a group of boisterous a cappella *klapa* singers, particularly in the coastal regions.

In Varaždin in the north of Croatia, music seeps onto every pavement, from a School of Music, its 15 churches, its Baroque evenings, and from a 10-day international music festival, Špancirfest, held every August. If you are visiting, you might also drop in at the workshop of Vladimir Proskurnjak, "the Stradivarius of Varaždin", a master craftsman of violins and other stringed instruments, to see how they are made and hear how they sound.

Violins, violas, cellos, guitars – Croatians have

a great ability to make strings sing. The Zagreb Soloists is a world-class chamber orchestra of more than a dozen string instrumentalists. Founded in 1954 and made up mostly of graduates from the capital's Music Academy, they play without a conductor and are great exponents of Croatian composers.

The guitar is also a popular instrument on which to play classical music in Croatia. You can hear it played by such talents as Zoran Dukić, one of the most prominent players today.

Croatian stars

The international reputation is growing of a number of young stars such as Robert Belinic, who in 1991, at the age of eight, starred in

Tale of Croatia, the first film made in the newly independent nation. Piano soloists are highly accomplished, too. Martina Filjak, who debuted with the Zagreb Soloists at the age of 12, is a name to watch.

Many towns have orchestras and choirs, some with reputations outside their own parish. Zvjezdice (Little Stars) is an all-girl choir from Zagreb that has gained accolades around the world, winning twice at the Llangollen Eisteddfod. One of the oldest amateur choirs is the Kolo singing society in Šibenik, which has been performing for more than a century, though its numbers are down on the 900 or so

song. Over the centuries the many distinctive regions of the country developed their own folk songs, and most villages and towns produced colourful performers whose repertoires would include tragic stories of their history and lost love, as well as songs for local weddings and festivities.

Their repertoire developed alongside traditional instruments. Perhaps the best known is the *tamburitza*, which has either three or five strings and offers a sound much like a mandolin. It was brought to eastern Croatia in the 14th century by the Ottomans and was at first confined to the Slavonia region. Today

before the Homeland War. Šibenik, incidentally, has a beautiful 19th-century theatre, and any chance to watch a performance here is something to cherish – perhaps for an event at the annual International Children's Festival of Performing Arts.

Folk music

Folk songs are at the root of all Croatian music. They were developed under the first kings in the 11th century and in the church music of the same period, involving Glagolitic

LEFT: Croatia's classical guitarist, Zoran Dukić.
ABOVE: a Croatian folk dancing troupe performing in Dubrovnik.

PROMINENT COMPOSERS

In the sphere of classical music Croatia lays claim to the composer Franz Joseph Haydn, who was born in a Croatian enclave of Austria in 1732. Of those composers born within the present borders of Croatia two of the earliest were Andrija Motovunskjanin, who hailed from inland Istria in the 15th century, and his contemporary Franjo Bosanac. During the Renaissance Julite Skjavetic was both a composer and the conductor at Šibenik's acoustically impressive cathedral. Further south Luka Sorkocević rose to prominence in Dubrovnik in the 18th century. His two sisters followed in the musical tradition by becoming the first female composers in the country.

it has become the most recognised Croatian folk instrument, used by groups all over the country, and it is the central instrument in the national Kolo folk dance. Also common in the coastal areas and islands of Dalmatia and the Kvarner Gulf are two variations of the bagpipe: the *gajde* and the *dude*.

Fine art

As in music, local traditions inform the most distinctive of Croatian art, Naïve painting *(see pages 142–3)*. Under Austro-Hungarian rule, painters followed mainstream Western movements, as can be seen in the modern galleries of the

Museum of Arts and Crafts in Zagreb, where the pastoral and romantic paintings of artists such as Nicola Maöić and Vlaho Bukovac (1855–1922) followed the fashion for painting en plein air. Communism required more revolutionary art, and a significant practitioner was Edo Murtić (1921–2005), whose work, which can also be

> Resorts in Istria, the Kvarner Gulf and Dalmatia all hold huge one-off outdoor dance parties in summer, usually lasting all night and attracting big name DJs.

CROATIAN POP

Ivo Robic (1923–2000) was a Croatian prodigy and pop singer who had a German hit in Europe and the USA with the song *Morgen*. He studied piano, clarinet, flute, sax and double bass at the Zagreb Music Conservatoire and was a guest star on many US TV shows, including The Ed Sullivan Show. His hit sold more than a million copies, hence his nickname "Mr Morgen".

Other notable Croatian stars include pop singer Tereza Kesovija, the well-known singer and actress Dunja Rajter, and Radojka Šverko – one of the country's greatest female singers, known for her beautiful interpretations of Croatian songs.

seen at the museum, progressed fluently from figurative to abstract Expressionism.

The Contemporary Art Museum in Zagreb, with a permanent collection of works dating from the early 20th century, brings the story up to date. The film and video collection was started here back in the 1960s, shortly after the wartime thriller *Don't Turn Around, My Son* made Dubrovnik-born director Branko Baur, the leading figure in the fledgling Yugoslav film industry.

There are some excellent artists working today throughout Croatia, particularly on the coast where the Mediterranean light infuses their work with a great vibrancy. Paintings, prints and drawings can make lasting souvenirs. You might visit the inspirational artist communities in the hilltop villages of Grožnjan and Motovun in Istria, join the tourists browsing Rovinj's gallery-lined Grisia street, centre of an arts festival on a Sunday in August, or seek out the works of sunny artists like Dubrovnik's Josip Pino Trostmann.

Ivan Meštrović *(see page 224)* is the country's best-known sculptor, and was considered by some as the finest since the Renaissance. In a different league but rather more fun is Nikola Bašić, who has been brightening up the seafront in Zadar. His *Sea Organ* is an award winning sonic sculpture set in marble steps on the

many translated for the first time. Published in 2005, the book has given its name to a continuing part of the annual Festival of Alternative Literature (FAK) run by the playwright and novelist Borivoj Radaković, which brings together leading British and Croatian writers. As the critic Tibor Fischer says in the introduction to the book: "*Croatian Nights* was born out of a shared fondness for hard drinking and a contempt for regular employment."

Drinking is one way of forgetting. The Rijeka-born journalist Slavenka Drakulić, wrote about the abuse of women during the Homeland War in the fictionalised *As If I Am Not There* and

Riva seafront and powered by wind and waves that pass through its tubes and cavities. Nearby is Bašić's *Greetings to the Sun*, a 22-metre (72ft) circle containing 300 glass plates covering photovoltaic cells that produce a glittering light show as the sun goes down.

Literature

Contemporary Croatian literature is celebrated in *Croatian Nights*, a collection of contemporary short fiction by the most exciting and innovative writers from Britain and Croatia,

chronicled the trials of war criminals in The Hague in *They Would Never Hurt a Fly*. Her other non-fiction works, *How We Survived Communism and Even Laughed* and *Café Europa: Life after Communism*, are brilliant insights into daily life in the country's recent history.

But Croatia's towering literary figure remains Ivo Andrić (1892–1975). The son of Croatian parents, he was born in Bosnia, and his stunning classic, *The Bridge over the Drina*, published in 1947, is still in print. This is an extraordinarily vivid account of life under successive rulers in the Balkans and it is no surprise that in 1961 he was made a Nobel Laureate. The author's life's work is archived in the city of Zagreb. ❑

LEFT: Vlaho Bukovac depicted his wife and daughter in *During Reading (c.*1905). **ABOVE:** the pretty hilltop village of Rovinj has a thriving arts scene.

FOOD AND DRINK

Whether you enjoy fresh oysters and lobster or
rich schnitzels and strudels, you will find
plenty of diverse dishes on the menu

In a country with such a complex history it
comes as no surprise to learn that Croatia's
cuisine is a smörgåsbord of influences. The
dishes of central and eastern Croatia have
more in common with rich, hearty Hungarian
cooking, while Istria and Dalmatia favour
Italian-influenced seafood and pasta dishes.
Turkish influences also feature, particularly in
the east.

Common to all areas is the abundance of fresh
produce. Much of Croatia's food production is
still small scale involving family-run farms and
businesses, and though locally sourced produce
may be played up in tourist areas, in many
respects it is simply following tradition.

Coastal cuisine

When it comes to the differences between the
regional cuisines the major fault line is between
inland and coastal cooking. While inland areas
focus on hearty meat dishes, broths and stews,

The bountiful Dolac central market in Zagreb
is the daily meeting place of both housewives
and culinary stars. "It is here," they say, "that
we start cooking."

as soon as the Adriatic Sea is within striking
distance seafood dominates the menus and restaurant tables move outside.

Croatia's seafood is among the best in
Europe, as this is one of the cleanest corners of
the Mediterranean. Fish and shellfish, cooked

simply in olive oil and fresh herbs, dominate
the menus of the smallest and simplest restaurants; comprise the dish of the day in cheap
and cheerful tourist restaurants; and come in
all manner of delicious guises in the top end
establishments, such as Valsabbion in Pula
(with tasting menu and gourmet lab), Šumica
in Split and Villa Kaliopa on the island of Vis.
In Southern Dalmatia the small town of Ston
is a place of pilgrimage for gastronomes, who
come just for the quality of its seafood.

Coastal menus tend to be similar to menus
across the Adriatic in Italy, though prices are
considerably lower. Menus follow a familiar
pattern with a first course of seafood risotto

LEFT: first course with the herb-flavoured aperitif
Biska. **RIGHT:** a typical *konoba* (rustic inn) on Hvar.

(*rizot*), *škampi na buzaru* (shrimps cooked in their own juice), octopus and spring onion salad or spaghetti, followed by a main course of freshly grilled fish (*riba na žaru*) or grilled squid (*ligne*). Variations on the risotto include *crni rizot*, a black risotto cooked in cuttlefish ink, and *skampi rizot*, made with shrimps' tails.

> One of the tastiest ways of eating fish is to cook it on a rostilj (barbecue) and then serve it with blitva sa krumpirom (beetroot and potato smothered in olive oil and garlic).

In all cases, garlic and olive oil are used liberally. For a real feast, order a fish platter featuring the best of the local catch and available on almost every menu.

Commonly caught fish include John Dory, sardines, sole, hake, mackerel and sea bream. Oysters, crab, mussels and prawns are also abundant. A close relation of French *bouillabaisse* is the old peasant dish *brodetto* (also known as *brodet*), a fish stew served traditionally in Dalmatia. It consists of chunks of various types of fish that have been cooked slowly with parsley, garlic, bay leaves and tomato – all mopped up with polenta (*pura*).

ISTRIA'S TRUFFLES

To connoisseurs truffles are the ultimate gastronomic extravagance; to nervous first-timers they usually smell disgusting and taste overpowering. Whether you like them or not there is no doubt that the white truffles found in inland Istria are considered as delectable as anything Italy or France have to offer. A whopping 1.3kg (nearly 3lb) white truffle was found in the Motovun woods in 1999, fetching $212,000.

Istrian truffles (*tartufi* in Croatian) were reputedly enjoyed by the Romans, who valued them as an effective aphrodisiac. However, they didn't really make much impact until after World War I, when, it is said, a sharp-nosed Italian soldier who had noticed the geographical

similarities between Istria and his native land, went back in search of truffles.

Today the Istrian truffle harvest (from September to October) is a growing industry. Many of the truffles, which are unearthed by specially trained dogs in the inland forests, are harvested illegally, but a large-scale operator, cea (www.zigantetartufi.com), runs slick shops in Livade, Pula, Buje and Buzet, selling all manner of truffle products, such as truffle oil and pasta sauce, slices of truffle and sheep's cheese infused with white truffle. The truffles, white or black, look nothing special, just hard lumps no bigger than a tennis ball, but their smell and taste is unmistakable.

Inland influences

Inland Dalmatia, the Kvarner Gulf and Istria have tasty meat dishes, though most of these originate away from the Adriatic. Don't miss the wonderful *pršut*, smoked Dalmatian ham, which is often served as a starter with cheese (ideally from the island of Pag) or melon. At its best this salty full-flavoured ham is more than a match for Italian *prosciutto* and Spanish *jamon serrano*.

Roe from trout found in the rivers and lakes of the Lika region around Plitvice is sought after by gourmets, and soups from freshwater fish and crabs here are a speciality.

In central Croatia spit-roasted lamb and the schnitzel that appears on menus all across the Croatian interior. In many ways the capital has the best of both worlds, with all the hearty meat dishes of the interior as well as good quality fish, and a wide variety of international and ethnic restaurants.

Perhaps the most distinctive regional cuisine originates from Slavonia in Eastern Croatia. Here fish makes a come back with carp and pike, caught in the Drava and Danube rivers, meeting the influence of Hungary with delicious results, such as *fiš paprikaš*, a spicy fish stew. Slavonia is also home to the excellent *kulen* spicy sausage, flavoured with red peppers, garlic and salt. Not

pig can be seen slowly turning outside many restaurants. Head north into the Zagorje and the calories mount as Austrian and Hungarian influences begin to take over, with creamy, richly flavoured sauces featuring strongly. Spicy *gulas* is a mainstay of many menus.

Other specialities include *mlinci*, a rich pastry cooked with turkey, duck or goose, which is particularly popular in Varaždin.

Zagreb has its own signature meat dish, *Zagrebački schnitzel*, veal stuffed with ham and cheese and cooked in breadcrumbs, similar to

> In Dalmatia and Istria you're bound to hear of peka or čirepnja. *This is a traditional method of cooking meat and vegetables beneath a metal dome buried in glowing embers.*

dissimilar to Spanish *chorizo*, it is perfect for picnics but also often incorporated into red meat and poultry stews. Slavonia is also a good place to sample more unusual meat dishes such as wild boar and various types of game.

Cheese and dessert

Croatia has some renowned cheeses. The Kvarner Gulf island of Pag is famous for *paški sir*, a

LEFT: fishermen mending nets in Rovinj harbour, Istria.
ABOVE: the layered-pastry dish, *štrukli,* is comfort food from the Zagorje region.

sheep's cheese. The saltwater-blasted extremities of the island, on which the sheep graze, help produce a cheese with a unique flavour that visitors often grow to love. It goes well with *pršut*, olives or tomatoes, but is great just with bread.

Ice cream *(sladoled)* is especially good in Istria where the Italian influence and expertise are at

> Most beers are lager beers. One notable dark beer is the Zagreb-produced Tomislav, a hearty, yeasty brew that tempts the palate of many a visiting real ale drinker.

their strongest. Much of the ice cream that you will find along the coast more than matches Italian *gelati*. *Rožata*, similar to crème caramel, is also popular, as are *štrudle* filled with *jabuka* (apple), *trešnja* (cherry) or *sir* (cream cheese) and *palačinke* (pancakes), laden with creamy toppings that get more elaborate the further you head towards Austria and Hungary.

Equally calorific is *baklava*, filo pastry smothered in honey and nuts, introduced to the Balkans by the Turks.

Fast food

Pizza is found everywhere. Usually this has a thin crust and some of the wood oven pizzas are every bit as good as you will find in Naples, though in Slavonia they tend to bulk up the base and overdo the toppings. Pizzas are very affordable and enjoyed as much by locals as visitors.

A number of international fast-food chains have moved into the big cities and towns, but take-away burgers and fries are nowhere near as popular as they are in Germany or the UK. The indigenous fast food products include meat kebabs and snacks of Turkish origin common to all the countries in the region, such as *burek* (cheese baked in filo pastry) and *štrukli*, a speciality of Zagorje, parcels of fresh pasta filled with curd cheese served with toasted or fried breadcrumbs.

If you can manage to pronounce *ćevapčići* correctly you will be served with mixed kebabs, including spicy sausages.

Wine, beer and spirits

Croatia produces good wines *(see opposite)* and excellent beers *(pivo)*. Perhaps the best of all Croatian beers is Karlovačko, a 5.2 percent lager beer with a full flavour and a pleasant aftertaste, perfect for a hot summer's day on the coast and equally at home in a cosy Zagreb beer hall *(pivnica)* in winter. Its main rival is Ožujsko, a Zagreb-produced lager that is again very drinkable, though some connoisseurs complain of a slightly chemical aftertaste. In Istria, Favorit is a rather insipid beer hardly ever drunk by the locals, but Slavonia has its own enjoyable Osiječko.

The Croats are also a big nation of spirit drinkers, whether it be an aperitif or a fiery *grappa* to finish off a meal. In many restaurants a shot of Croatian grappa is offered with the compliments of the house, but beware, as it is a long way from the smooth variety that you find in Italy. The most popular spirit is Slivovitz, a rather abrasive plum brandy, but others include Maraschino, a cherry liqueur produced in Zadar, and Biska, a herb-flavoured aperitif from inland Istria.

A very good dessert wine, normally produced along the Dalmatian coastline and islands, is Prošek, which is the perfect accompaniment to the very sweet desserts.

To end a meal, coffee is the preferred beverage, usually drunk very strong in tiny cups. Turkish coffee and cappuccino are sometimes available, along with herbal teas. ❑

LEFT: one of Croatia's many top-notch beers.

Wine Country

Croatian wines aren't something you often find at home – but they have been impressing visitors since the times of the ancient Greeks.

The ideal conditions for viniculture in this region were recognised by the Greeks and Romans, who produced their wine often in the same places, and with similar types of grapes, as today's vineyards. Athenian writers in the 4th century BC sang the praises of white wines from the Dalmatian island of Vis, and rudimentary Greek and Roman wine-making equipment and goblets have been found during archaeological digs.

Today there is a healthy industry producing 50 million bottles a year in 300 geographically identifiable regions, in Slavonia, Istria and in central and southern Dalmatia. Two-thirds of the wine produced is white, with reds mainly coming from the coast. Champagne-method wines are also produced, and make a popular aperitif.

Large commercial concerns make high quality wines with international reputations, but there are also many small-scale producers, often at a village or family level. Croats like to drive out to the countryside at weekends and fill up containers with fresh, inexpensive wine – in Zagreb people head for the Samobor hills.

Most of Croatia's wine is produced near or along the coast. In the north over 70 percent of Istria's production is white wine, with Muscatel and Malvazija the ones to look out for, while Teran is a reliable red. Check the local tourist office for details of wine roads and cellar open days. Further south in Dalmatia, Šibenik produces Plavina and Babić wines, as well as an acceptable rosé. Neighbouring Primošten makes its own excellent Babić.

The Pelješac peninsula, north of Dubrovnik, is rightly famous for its seafood, but it is also home to the Dingač, perhaps Croatia's finest wine, as well as its most expensive. High in alcohol content, this ruby-red wine holds its own against many French and New World competitors, although the export market is still very much at an embryonic stage. Pelješac is also home to the cheaper red Plavac, which can still be a quality tipple in the hands of the local producers.

RIGHT: a Dalmatian vineyard.

Tours of the Pelješac wine makers, often just small farmers, are offered to visitors to Dubrovnic, usually with a stop for a meal at Ston along the way. The Konavle wine district south of Cavtat, which produces the Dubrovnik Malvasia blanc, can also be visited.

Tucked on the end of the Pelješac peninsula is the island of Korčula, renowned for its Kaštelet, Pošip and the especially good Grk, all varieties of white.

Vis, the island mentioned by the Athenians, today has myriad small vineyards specialising in Viški Plavac and Vugava. On the Dalmatian island of Brač there is another version of Plavac, while Hvar has its Zlatan Plavac and Faros wines. Perhaps the best of all the island wines is Vrbnička

Žlahtina. From the rich slopes around the town of Vrbnik, in the north of the Kvarner Gulf island of Krk, this straw-yellow wine is superb, the perfect accompaniment to fish dishes.

Slavonia in eastern Croatia has some excellent wines, which, like the local food, are highly distinctive. Look out for the best of them all, the very consistent Graševina and Kutjevo Chardonnay, both of which go well with the local fish dishes. The famous cellars at Ilok on the Danube can be visited. Slavonia also produces the oak to make wine barrels used in both Croatia and Italy.

Many Croatians choose to dilute their wine with a little plain water (*a bevanda*) or add a touch of sparkling mineral water (*a gemišt*), and Vrbnička Žlahtina works well with both of these. ❑

THE GREAT OUTDOORS

Whether you want to cycle, climb, hike or dive,
Croatia offers many exhilarating ways of
enjoying the elements

Croatia has a wide variety of flora and fauna, and much of the most interesting and wildly beautiful parts of the country have been well preserved. Conservation is taken seriously, for Croatians tend to have a great respect for outdoor living. The country's first national park at Paklenica was provisionally set up in the 1920s and there are now eight official national parks dotted around the mainland and islands, as well as many smaller nature reserves and conservation areas.

Five of the eight national parks are on the mainland, with Paklenica, Risnjak and Northern Velebit, Croatia's newest national park (set up in 1999), all covering harsh mountainous terrain. Velebit, beside the Kvarner Gulf, is a protected Unesco World Biosphere Reserve, the first such area in Croatia.

Krka National Park in northern Dalmatia is a wetland area, while further north in central Croatia Plitvice Lakes National Park comprises forested wetlands.

The Kornati Islands are perfect for canoeing – crystal-clear waters, numerous islands, consistently low winds and a real sense of getting away from it all.

The three island national parks are: Brijuni Islands in Istria, once Tito's private retreat; the Kornati Islands, a stark but beautiful archipelago in Northern Dalmatia; and lush Mljet in Southern Dalmatia.

LEFT: rock climbing in Paklenica National Park.
RIGHT: Eurasian brown bears at play.

From bears to vultures

A number of rare species can be found on the Croatian mainland and islands. In Plitvice Lakes and Risnjak national parks, for example, there are brown bears, while Risnjak, Plitvice and Velebit are now home to lynx, which only recently returned to Croatia from across the border in the Slovenian mountains. Griffon vultures are thriving in their own sanctuary on the island of Cres, while further south, on Mljet, rare monk seals, which were once prevalent throughout the Mediterranean, are often spotted, and have been sighted in several other places in recent years. Both the Krka and Plitvice national parks also support the threatened European otter.

Outdoor activities

Life in Croatia is lived outdoors, and there are always activities close at hand. The lakes, rivers and coast offer every kind of water-borne opportunity, from sailing, windsurfing, canoeing and scuba diving to fishing and rafting. The landscape is ever ready to take on rock climbers, hikers, cyclists and skiers, and practitioners of extreme sports. There are a number of "adventure racing" events, combining various activities in different degrees of difficulty, organised around the country each year.

Croatia's rugged terrain makes it a popular destination for rock climbing. Among the best

Hiking, cycling and skiing

Those looking for a gentler mountain experience will find many opportunities for hiking. Both Paklenica and Risnjak national parks have well-marked hiking trails and mountain huts. Further south the Biokovo mountain range offers a multitude of hiking trails, many of which are accessible from the resorts along the Makarska Riviera. North of Zagreb are the Samobor Hills, where Tito first laced up his hiking boots; they remain a pleasing bucolic escape in the warmer months. The Gorski Kotar range between Karlovac and the Kvarner Gulf also has a network of trails and hiking

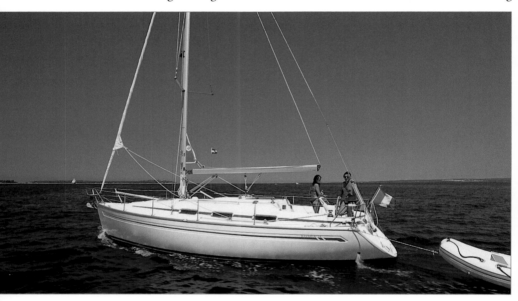

venues are the sheer limestone walls of the Paklenica National Park at the southern fringe of the Kvarner Gulf. At the entrance to the main gorge a steep rock wall is used for practising, training and for showing first-timers the ropes. Some adventurous free climbers also use these walls, and they also come together every July or August at the Vanka Regule (Without Rules) extreme sports festival in Sutivan on the island of Brač (*see page 229*).

Further north, Risnjak National Park is a quieter alternative to Paklenica with fewer facilities, but equally stunning scenery and challenging climbing. Beware of the winter weather in both parks, as the fierce bura winds and heavy snow make conditions treacherous.

Despite the country's limited ski slopes, Croatian Janica Kostelić, now retired, is the only woman to win four gold medals in alpine skiing – at the 2002 and 2006 Winter Olympics.

opportunities, and overlooking the Kvarner Gulf is the Učka range, with trails that are easily accessible from the Opatija Riviera resorts. As yet facilities remain basic and the country is not set up for walks of more than one or two days, but that is likely to change as hiking becomes more developed.

Cycling also has great potential. The Adriatic Highway would make a wonderfully scenic route from Rijeka to Dalmatia and on towards Dubrovnik, though its traffic is a considerable concern. More suitable are the quieter islands, where bikes are an excellent way of getting around. A lazy bike ride around the lakes of Mljet's two national parks is a great way to spend a day.

There are several MTB mountain bike routes, particularly in the Velebit area, and on the islands of Kvarner and Rab.

Croatia is not a significant ski destination. Skiers and snowboarders who happen to be in the country when conditions are right may want to venture on to the slopes But there is

little appeal in planning a whole skiing holiday in Croatia. Zagreb's Mt Medvednica has a number of runs, as does Mt Bjelolasica in the Gorski Kotar region. There is also a modest ski slope at Snježik in the Risjnak National Park.

Horse riding

Riding is a great way to appreciate the countryside and there are equestrian clubs throughout the country, notably in the Cetina Valley, Velebit, Istria and on the plains around the rivers Sava, Drava and Danube. Croatia has a long equestrian tradition, developing a number of local breeds – the Tulipan in Slavonia, the Istrijanic in Istria, and the Posavina, descendants of Mongol horses. Even if you don't want to ride, you might like to visit the Lipizzaner stud farm in Dakovo, Croatia's leading breeding farm and one of Europe's oldest, first mentioned in 1506.

Water sports

Whitewater rafting is possible in Croatia's southern uplands and also in the mountains of Dalmatia. The Kupa River, near the city of Karlovac, offers some of the best rafting in Central Croatia. Down towards the Adriatic, in the Gorski Kotar of central Croatia, it is possible to arrange a rafting trip on the Dobra river. From the Dalmatian towns and resorts it is easy to get to the Cetina river, where there are regular whitewater rafting trips through spring and summer.

Croatia is not a big windsurfing destination, but there are a couple of worthwhile locations. The most renowned is at Bol on the island of Brač, a scenic spot close to Zlatni Rat beach in a channel that separates Brač from the neighbouring island of Hvar. Another recommended area lies further south around Orebić on the Pelješac peninsula, itself an attractive resort surrounded by a string of decent beaches, all within sight of the island of Korčula. Equipment is available for hire in the main resort; in summer there is a windsurfing school at Bol.

Keen canoeists will be at home in Croatia, especially if they prefer coastal kayaking to shooting river rapids. There are numerous

SAVE THE DOLPHINS

One of Croatia's most successful conservation initiatives is the Adriatic Dolphin Project, set up around the Kvarner Gulf islands of Cres and Lošinj in 1987 and reaffirmed with the establishment in 2006 of the Losinj Dolphin Reserve. Today there are around 100 bottlenose dolphins in the area. The project takes on volunteers – see www.blue-world.org for details. Weather permitting, the time is spent out at sea recording, dating and tracking the creatures, and direct contact is common. Meanwhile the country's commitment to conservation was reinforced with an Animal Protection Act introduced in 2007, which prevented a proposed dolphinarium from operating in Vodnjan.

LEFT: sailing around the protected Brijuni Islands in one of the country's three island national parks.
ABOVE: setting off on a gentle hike.

opportunities for coastal kayaking all around Istria, the Kvarner Gulf and in Dalmatia, but the Kornati Islands provide an idyllic setting. It is also possible to canoe the Dobra and Kupa rivers in central Croatia.

Sailing

With more than 1,185 offshore islands, Croatia is an ideal sailing destination. Throw in the favourable winds, the 48 marinas that are dotted up and down the coast and the often idyllic weather from May right through to September and it is no surprise that Croatia is a top sailing destination and a serious rival to Greece.

The 48 marinas range from the resort of Umag in northern Istria right down south to the marina at Cavtat on the edge of the Montenegrin border. The facilities of each marina do vary, but they all provide a safe place to moor for the night, the chance of a shower and somewhere to relax with a bite to eat and drink. Adriatic Croatian International (ACI) is the biggest operator, managing 21 of the marinas. Some of the larger marinas are almost resorts in themselves with all the trappings that go with it, while others such as Trogir and Rab bring you right alongside the heart of the old town.

Places that do not have dedicated marinas usually have harbours where, for a small fee,

you can tie up a boat for the night. Any vessels over 3 metres (10ft) are required to register on arrival so make sure you find someone from whom you can buy the necessary ticket if you want to avoid a frustrating brush with Croatian bureaucracy.

Beginners only

The main choice when organising a trip is whether to go "bareboat" and just hire the boat or hire a skipper as well. For bareboat you will need at least one member of the party to be a qualified skipper who can use a VHF radio and you will also have to be prepared to do a lot of the leg work. If you choose the skippered option the cost goes up and you can take one fewer person in your party, but the toughest parts of sailing, such as navigation, will be taken out of your hands (you will still have to help with tasks such as unfurling sails, wrenching them up and keeping the boat clean).

For those who have not sailed before the Kornati Islands are a perfect first time destination. A number of companies run "learn to sail" holidays in the calm and protected waters of the Kornatis, with the chance to gain a "competent crew" certificate, which basically means you have shown you can be useful around the yacht and know the basics.

Seasoned sailors

More experienced sailors might consider either heading further north and trying out the resort-strewn Istrian coastline, or perhaps even better the indented and island-studded Dalmatian coast where local winds, such as the *bura*, *maestral* and *yugo*, can make life more interesting, as can sudden summer thunderstorms. The Dalmatian coastline is laden with historical towns and the islands are increasingly geared towards yachts arriving for lunch or evening stopovers.

The length of the Croatian coastline means there is a lot of ground to cover between the key attractions, so a good option is to arrange a one-way sail. A popular route is to head south from the central Dalmatian marinas at either Trogir or Split, via the islands of Hvar or Korčula, before making for southern Dalmatia and the city of Dubrovnik, which offers one of the most dramatic sea arrivals in Europe. ❑

LEFT: rafting on the Kupa River.

Diving

With visibility up to 40 metres (130ft), pleasant temperatures, sheer drops and caves, the waters of the Adriatic are a diver's delight.

C roatia is a major European dive destination and scuba enthusiasts flock from all over the continent to explore the warm, crystal-clear waters of the Croatian Adriatic, with its many shipwrecks and good dive facilities.

Organised scuba diving in the country began in World War I when the first scuba course was offered on the Dalmatian island of Vis. Now it is a major sport, popular with locals and foreign visitors. There are official dive centres all the way from Umag in northern Istria, right down to the resort town of Cavtat in the extreme south, near the border with Montenegro. Some of the most popular are at Rovinj and Poreč in Istria, Mali Lošinj and Baška in the Kvarner Gulf and Sali (Dugi Otok), Murter, Vodice, Bol, Makarska and Trogir in Dalmatia.

Vis remains the top place to head for, with dive centres in both Vis Town and Komiza. As Vis was on the main trade routes during Roman and Venetian times, routes that were also busy during World War II and are still active today, there are more than half a dozen diveable wrecks within easy reach of the island. They include the *Brioni*, an Austrian cargo ship, the *Teti*, an Italian merchant vessel, the *Vassilios*, a Greek commercial ship, as well as the remains of a World War II bomber and a sprinkling of Roman relics. Water clarity is good and the temperature balmy in summer, making for enjoyable diving conditions.

Just off Vis is the small island of Biševo, usually reached from the southern Vis town of Komiza. In summer Biševo's "Blue Grotto" offers a spectacular visual phenomenon as light bathes the cave in an eerie blue sheen. Experienced scuba divers get to appreciate it much more than the dry tourists on the bobbing boats in the bay. They can delve down the main channel into the central chamber of the cave itself before coming out through a second route.

Other top dive sites include the Kornati Islands, Mezanj Island near Dugi Otok, Rovinj and, to the south, the shipwreck of the *Tottono*, which sank off the Dalmatian coast near the city of Dubrovnik after being struck by a mine during World War II. The myriad dive operators know where all the best sites are and they offer a variety of day dives and night dives, as well as three-, five- and seven-night adventures, either on board or based at the centres themselves.

Scuba diving is strictly regulated and no one is allowed to dive without first obtaining a diving certificate. These cost 100 kuna, are valid for one year from the date of issue and allow qualified divers to dive in any permitted area, provided they pay any necessary fees that may apply, for exam-

ple in areas of national parks where diving is allowed. The certificate allows divers to descend to a depth of 40 metres (130ft).

Some divers complain about the need for the certificate, but the Croatian Diving Association stresses that the funds raised are used to ensure the preservation of the dive sites for future generations. The certificate is only available to those with proof that they have already passed an internationally recognised dive course such as SSI, CMAS or PADI. These courses are run by many different dive centres.

Safety is taken seriously in Croatia and there are decompression chambers at Pula and Split, which are ready around the clock to deal with any divers suffering difficulties. ❑

RIGHT: young scuba diver.

ARCHITECTURE

Many of Croatia's finest buildings tell the story of the country's past

The history of Croatia is displayed in its architecture. Starting with the Roman grandeur of Pula's amphitheatre and Split's Diocletian Palace, it leads on to early Christian buildings such as the pre-Romanesque church of St Donatus in Zadar. Byzantium brought the mosaic glister of the Euphrasian Basilica in Poreč, and the Renaissance, courtesy of the Venetians, helped produce the Cathedral of St James in Šibenik, the palaces of Dubrovnik and many fortresses and castles, as well as the sturdy walls of the one-time capital, Varaždin. The Franciscan and Dominican monastic orders brought in Gothic, which shaped Zagreb's cathedral, and with the Jesuits came Baroque, a popular style that invaded domestic architecture, created glittering Habsburg ballrooms and gave the pilgrimage churches of Vinagora and Belec the aesthetics of a candy store.

Zagreb saw the flowering of 19th-century Croatian aspirations in the palaces of Opaticka Street. Most brilliant is No. 10, reconstructed by Izidor Krsnjavi in 1895, and decorated with painting and sculptures that turned its Golden Hall into a gallery of Croatian art.

Just as important is the country's home-grown architecture, from *kažuni* Neolithic stone huts to wooden buildings. The timber homes and farmsteads of central Croatia are particularly appealing. The Turopolje region east of Zagreb has fine wooden mansions called *kurija* and handsome wooden chapels, beautifully carved, such as the the Chapel of St Barbara in Velika Mlaka, which dates from 1642.

ABOVE: Tkalčićeva Street in Zagreb shows the rich Baroque influence of the Habsburgs. **BELOW:** the Euphrasian Basilica in Poreč is one of the finest Byzantine buildings in Europe.

ABOVE LEFT: St Donat, Zadar, built in the 9th century with stones from the old Roman Forum.

LEFT: *Fisherman with Serpent*, by Simeon Roksandic (1874–1943) in Jezuitski Square, Zagreb.

THE VENETIAN LEGACY

Venice did not own or conquer all of the Croatian coast, but through trade and agreements, treaties and example, it has left its mark from Rovinj to Dubrovnik. Sometimes this is evident in stone carvings of the Lion of St Mark, symbol of the Most Serene Republic, but most often it is through the buildings, which seem to belong more to the Italian peninsula than to Croatia.

Many towns and villages on the coast started life as offshore islands, a strip of sea acting as a moat to protect them from landward invaders – just as Venice itself had done. As trade among the communities prospered in the 11th century, an abundance of stone allowed a flowering of buildings and the start of some urban planning. By the 14th century, much of Venice was being built with Pietra d'Istria, quarried in the village of Kirmenjak near Porej. By the 15th century Venice had all of Dalmatia, except the south, under its control and builders and sculptors worked and travelled freely between Croatia and Italy. It was known that the dazzling, durable Pietra d'Istria limestone actually increased in strength when exposed to the atmosphere and could be easily carved into attractive tracery, balustrades and decorative crenellations. And so mini-Venices were built up and down the coast.

Above: the Lion of St Mark, in Korčula: the Republic stamped its symbol along the coast.

Left: angel on Zagreb Cathedral by the Viennese sculptor Anton Dominic Fernkorn (1813–78).

VE: part of the old town walls of the former
:al, Varaždin **Left:** cloister of the
:iscan monastery in Dubrovnik.

PLACES

A detailed guide to the entire country, with principal sites clearly cross-referenced by number to the maps

Though only about four times the size of Connecticut, scythe-shaped Croatia has the rich diversity of a country many times its size. Inland, lovely thick woods and limestone mountains drip with lakes and waterfalls; on the coast, myriad islands, from lush Hvar to the ethereal Kornatis, bask in warm, clear waters, capable of reviving even the most jaded traveller's spirits.

Zagreb, meanwhile, is in many ways a typical Central European capital, with more than a whiff of Vienna or Budapest in its coffee houses and ancient architecture. In the Samobar Hills north of the capital, vineyards, castles and 19th-century spa towns are ideal for exploring by car.

In two weeks or so it is possible to sample all these different aspects of Croatia, but you could just as easily spend that time pottering about in Istria (think Tuscany-on-sea) or spend a month or more island-hopping off Dalmatia. It is also worth trying to catch one of the country's many festivals, which illustrate how the Croatians are defining their national identity and distinguishing themselves from fellow Slavs.

But Croatia's varied natural beauty and lively traditions are not its only attractions. Over the centuries, invaders, traders and other migrants have left elegant imprints. Italian artists and architects were active in Dalmatia and Istria, and exquisite Gothic and Renaissance art and architecture are among the Adriatic coast's glories. Meanwhile, encounter the Austro-Hungarian Empire's splendour in the Baroque civic buildings of central and eastern Croatia – delightful, unexpected evidence of refinement in an agricultural and now sparsely populated region.

Croatia's EU entry will of course increase its mass-market appeal to international tourists but it would be better for anyone with an adventurous spirit to come and visit the unspoilt delights before the country risks suffering commercial sanitisation. ❏

PRECEDING PAGES: waterfall, Plitvice National Park; Hvar and islands; rooftops of Korčula. **LEFT:** Split viewed from its cathedral bell tower. **ABOVE LEFT:** Pazin Abyss and Castle. **TOP AND BOTTOM RIGHT:** cobbled lane and cathedral angel, Zagreb.

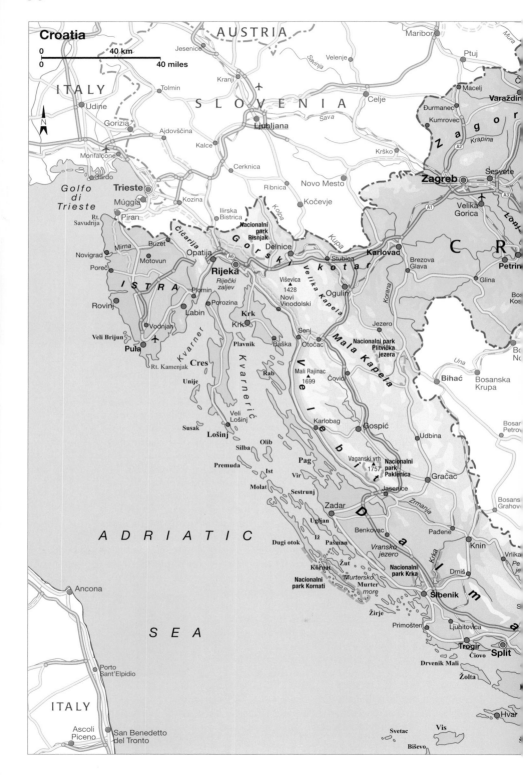

Croatia

0   40 km
0   40 miles

AUSTRIA

Maribor

Jesenice

Velenje   Ptuj

ITALY

Kranji

Macelj   **Varaždin**

Tolmin

Đurmanec

Kumrovec

Udine

SLOVENIA

Celje

Gorizia

Krapina

A2

Ajdovščina

Ljubljana

Zagreb

Kalce

Krško

Sesvete

Monfalcone

Cerknica

A3

Grado

Novo Mesto

Velika Gorica

Trieste

Kozina

Ribnica

Kočevje

Golfo di Trieste

Múggia

Ilirska Bistrica

Kolpa

Karlovac

CR

Piran

Rt. Savudrija

Nacionalni park Risnjak

Kupa

Brezova Glava

Petrin

Novigrad

Mirna

Buzet

Čičarija

Gorski kotar

Delnice

Stubica

ISTRA

Opatija

Rijeka

Velika Kapela

Glina

Bos Kos

Poreč

Motovun

Plomin

Rijeki zaljev

Viševica 1428

Ogulin

Rovinj

Labin

Porozina

Novi Vinodolski

Jezero

Veli Brijun

Vodnjan

Krk

Krk

Plavnik

Baška

Senj

Otočac

Nacionalni park Plitvička jezera

Bo No

Pula

Rt. Kamenjak

Kvarner

Cres

Kvarnerić

Rab

Mali Rajinac 1699

Čovici

Bihać

Bosanska Krupa

Unije

Karlobag

Gospić

Bosan Petrov

Susak

Veli Lošinj

Udbina

Lošinj

Silba

Olib

Pag

Vaganski vrh 1757

Nacionalni park Paklenica

Gračac

Premuda

Ist

Vir

Bosan Grahov

Molat

Sestrunj

Jasenice

Zrmanja

Zadar

Uglian

Benkovac

Pađene

Knin

Vrlika

ADRIATIC

Iž

Pašman

Vransko jezero

Krka

Drniš

Pe je

Dugi otok

Žut

Murterško more

Nacionalni park Krka

Ancona

Kornat

Nacionalni park Kornati

Murter

Šibenik

SEA

Žirje

Primošten

Ljubitovica

Porto Sant'Elpidio

Trogir

Čiovo

Split

Drvenik Mali

Žolta

ITALY

Ascoli Piceno

San Benedetto del Tronto

Svetac

Vis

Biševo

Hvar

ZAGREB

With its medieval Upper Town and elegant Lower Town, Zagreb is typical of many Central European cities. But its vibrancy is wholly its own, fuelled by one of Europe's youngest populations

A city of almost one million inhabitants, Zagreb (www.zagreb.hr) has come a long way since 1991, when Serbian rockets hit the suburbs and President Tudjman narrowly escaped assassination in a Yugoslav air-force raid as he sat in his presidential palace. Today bustling Zagreb has wholeheartedly embraced capitalism and modernisation and – partly thanks to low-cost carriers such as Wizz Air – become an increasingly popular city-break destination.

The city has a scenic location, spread out on a plain with the Sava River sealing off the older parts of the city from the post-World War II suburbs and the hulk of Mt Medvednica, often visible to the north. The city's old sections in Gradec and Kaptol in the Gornji grad (Upper Town) are reminiscent of Prague or Riga, while in the Donji grad (Lower Town), a grid-like 19th-century central business district, neon lights and designer shops have moved in alongside the elegant Austro-Hungarian buildings.

Zagreb was never designed to be a capital and at times, especially in July and August when many of its residents head to the coast, it can feel more like a provincial Austrian city than a European capital. At its best, though, on a warm spring or autumn evening when the cafés are full to bursting point, it is an invigorating place to be. The young Croatians in its clubs and bars are every bit as style-conscious as their counterparts in London or Milan. Expanding in parallel with Zagreb's nightlife scene and café culture are its hotel and restaurant industries. These have seen huge improvements since independence, with the result that the city is firmly established as both a popular offbeat city break for other Europeans and as a business destination. Its success as a business centre is partly due to its central location and good transport links: Austria, Hungary, Slovenia, Italy and Bosnia are all within easy driving distance.

Main attractions
THE CATHEDRAL
DOLAC MARKET
ALTAR OF THE HOMELAND
ARTS AND CRAFTS MUSEUM
MIMARA MUSEUM
LOTRŠĆAK TOWER
ST MARK'S CHURCH
ZAGREB CITY MUSEUM

LEFT: golden guardian angel, Zagreb Cathedral.
BELOW: Zagreb's Dolac Market.

One of 200 sculptures in Mimara Museum dating from antiquity to the 20th century.

Organising your visit

If time is short, one can cover Zagreb's sights in a day by spending the morning in the Donji grad and the afternoon in the Gornji grad, but this only scratches the surface of the city, as places such as the Mimara Museum and the Meštrović Atelier can take a whole day in themselves. On the outskirts are several attractive natural attractions such as Lake Jarun, Maksimir Park and Mt Medvednica, as well as Mirogoj, one of Europe's most beautiful cemeteries.

It is also worth exploring the city's cultural life. Increasingly Zagreb is attracting musicians and thespians from around the world and there are good venues for theatre, opera and classical music. The huge Maksimir Stadium hosts big pop and rock acts as well as Dinamo Zagreb and the Croatian national football team. On a more traditional note, there is the Zagreb International Folklore Festival in July, celebrating Croatia's rich folk-culture tradition and welcoming folk groups from all over Europe.

Lower Town and Kaptol

A good place to start a tour of the Donji grad is outside the main **railway station ❶** (Glavni kolodvor), which neatly divides the most interesting parts of the city (Donji Grad and Gornji grad) to the north from the modern post-World War II suburbs to the south. From the station Zagreb's central parks are visible as well as the spires of the cathedral in the distance.

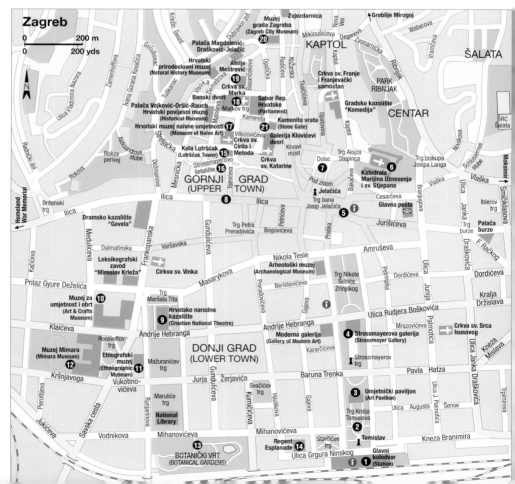

Designed by the Hungarian architect Ferenc Pfaff, the station opened in 1892 when Zagreb became the main gateway to Vienna and Budapest. Its pastel-yellow neoclassical facade retains something of its original splendour and there is an old steam train on display just to the east of the passenger platforms.

Just across the tram lines in front of the station the chunky statue of King Tomislav I welcomes new arrivals from his horse, with an outstretched sword raised in one hand. Tomislav was the first king of Croatia (925–8) and Frangeš Mihanović's depiction of the monarch has become a popular central meeting place for the locals as well as one of the most recognisable symbols of the city.

Stretching north of the equestrian statue is the elegant **Trg Tomislava ❷**, the first of a string of parks extending north towards the city's main square and its oldest quarters. In summer Trg Tomislava is alive with students reclining on the benches, backpackers trying to catch some sleep between train rides, and roller-bladers gliding around the fringes. At the northern end is the yellow Art Nouveau **Art Pavilion ❸** Umjetnički paviljon; Mon–Fri 11am–7pm, Sat 10am–1pm; charge), which holds regular temporary exhibitions and has a good restaurant. In front of the pavilion look out for the statue of the Croatian Renaissance painter Andrija Medulić by the sculptor Ivan Meštrović (see page 224).

The next park is dedicated to Bishop Josip Juraj Strossmayer (1815–1905), proponent of pan-Slavism, which contains **Strossmayer's Old Masters Gallery ❹** (Strossmayerova galerija starih majstora; tel: 01-481 3344; www.mdc.hr/strossmayer; Tue–Sun 10am–1pm, Tue also 5–7pm, closed public holidays; charge), founded by the Slavonian prelate in 1884. Today it houses a collection of work by Italian masters such as Tintoretto and Veronese, dating from the 14th to 19th centuries, as well as paintings by Dutch masters, includ-

ing Brueghel, and the less well-known Croatian painters Andrija Medulić and Federiko Benković.

Also here is the Baška Tablet, from the Kvarner Gulf island of Krk (see page 191), which is the oldest example of Croatian Glagolitic script in existence. It dates from around 1100. Look out for the statue of Strossmayer by Ivan Meštrović, himself a campaigner for pan-Slavism, outside the gallery.

Walk north for another five minutes through the green belt of parks, past the fountains and sculptures, to Zagreb's heart, **Trg bana Josipa Jelačića ❺**, which rapidly dispels many preconceived notions of what a former Communist city might look like. Funky new trams zip across a square packed with Armani-suited professionals chatting into mobiles, bright-shirted students and camera-toting tourists. Presiding over the scene are the elegant facades of some of Zagreb's most impressive Austro-Hungarian-era buildings.

At the centre of the square, and a popular meeting place, is the equestrian statue of Count Josip Jelačić of Bužim, the work of Viennese sculptor

TIP

If you spend more than a day in the capital, the Zagreb Card is a good investment. Valid for three days, it offers 50 percent off admission to many galleries and museums, free public transport and discounts at many theatres, restaurants and nightclubs.

BELOW: relaxing in a central Zagreb café.

One of the four angles surrounding Fernkorn's Madonna outside Zagreb's cathedral.

RIGHT: the Arcades, Mirogoj Cemetery.

Anton Dominik Ritter von Fernkorn (1813–78). When the Communists took power after World War II they removed Jelačića's statue, deeming it to symbolise the drive for an independent Croatia, but they never finished the job of disposing of the statue and instead it ended up in storage. During the early 1990s and the backlash against Communism, it magically reappeared to reclaim its place in the heart of Zagreb's main square.

The cathedral

From the square take a detour from the Donji Grad, up the small Kaptol hill to the **Cathedral of the Assumption of the Blessed Virgin Mary and St Stephen** ❻ (Katedrala Marijina Uznesenja i sv. Stjepana; Mon–Sat 10am–5pm, Sun and public holidays 1–5pm), where another work by Fernkorn stands outside. This startling gold Madonna is surrounded by four equally striking angels. Despite the scaffolding that seems set to hang around the voluminous spires for many years to come this elegant building is one of the most attractive in the city. An earlier Roman-

esque church existed on the site, and the first cathedral dates back to the time of the first Croatian kings in the 10th century. Today's incarnation has its origins in the 13th century, but there have been countless modifications and revamps over the centuries, the most significant following a catastrophic earthquake in 1880. Outside the cathedral look out for the walls built to protect it from Ottoman attacks.

Inside, the high central nave appears stark and bare, but there is plenty to see. The most controversial part of the cathedral is the tomb of Archbishop Alojzije Stepinac, a man convicted under Tito of high treason and war crimes for colluding with the Nazi puppet regime established in Croatia during World War II, although later exonerated and beatified by Pope John Paul II. Whatever the politics, Ivan Meštrović's relief of Christ with the bishop is striking. Look out also for a series of 13th-century frescoes that have survived the cathedral's numerous traumas. The treasury above the sacristy is home to Baroque banners and tapestries, as well as church plate.

Mirogoj Cemetery

There is no question that the smartest place to be buried in Zagreb is in the Mirogoj Cemetery (Groblje Mirogoj; www.gradskagroblja.hr) – one local joke suggests that most of its tombs are better than many homes in the city. Built in 1876, it occupies the site of the summer mansion of Ljudevit Gaj, the leader of the Illyrian Movement. After his death the local authorities bought the land and commissioned the naturalised Croatian architect Hermann Bollé to design the cemetery, which is divided up according to religion. The entrance is suitably grand, with high ivy-clad walls, neoclassical colonnades, cupolas and a large central dome. Inside lie many of Croatia's artistic, military and political luminaries, including President Franjo Tudjman, laid to rest here on 15 December 1999. His grave is not as elaborate as his character suggested it might be, but like many of the tombs it receives plenty of fresh flowers and candles.

Some of the tombs are works of art in their own right. In particular, look out for Ivan Meštrović's bust of painter Vladimir Becić (1886–1954) and work by fellow Dalmatian sculptor Ivan Rendić (1849–1932). The cemetery is also home to a collection of sculptures, giving it the feel of a huge open-air art gallery. Getting to Mirogoj is easy. Take the No. 106 bus from outside the cathedral on Kaptol (journey time 15–20 minutes). Entrance to the cemetery is free.

Dolac Market ❼, just a short walk down the hill from the cathedral, offers a glimpse of Zagreb life that is a world away from both the calm and order of the cathedral and the slick modernity of Trg bana Josipa Jelačića. Every morning this raffish square becomes a bustling produce market selling fruit and vegetables fresh from the countryside. There are a number of basic restaurants and cafés above the market – one open all hours – where you can have breakfast and survey the activity.

Memorials and museums

Stretching away to the west from Trg bana Josipa Jelačića is **Ilica** ❽, at 6km (4 miles) the longest street in Zagreb, and probably the oldest, as it dates back to Roman times. Ilica is the haunt of Zagreb's nouveau riche, who come here to buy designer-name fashion and to see and be seen. On a more sombre note much further along Ilica (take tram Nos 6 or 11) is the **Altar of the Homeland** (Oltar domovine), with the names of the Croatian dead inscribed across the bricks.

A 10-minute walk west of Vincek, at 18 Ilica (*see margin tip*), and south down Francopanska is the **Croatian National Theatre** ❾ (Hrvatsko narodno kazalište; www.hnk.hr) dating from 1894. Just outside the theatre look out for an early sculpture by Ivan Meštrović dating from 1905. *The Well of Life*, a small fountain enclosed by a sprawl of bronze figures, lies just below street level. On the same square is fellow sculptor Fernkorn's vivid depiction of *George Slaying the Dragon*.

Just across Runjaninova is the **Arts and Crafts Museum** ❿ (Muzej za umjetnost i obrt; Sun 10am–2pm, Tue–Sat 10am–7pm, Thur until 10pm, closed public holidays; charge), designed by Croatia's leading architect, Herman Bollé (1845–1926), who also designed the grandiose Mirogoj Cemetery (*see page 102*). The exhibits include a wide range of ceramics and furniture as well as textiles. The top floor houses clocks, silverware and glass, while the second displays domestic ceramics and furniture and the ground floor religious art, porcelain and more furniture.

EAT

At 18 Ilica, Vincek sells arguably the city's finest ice cream, in myriad flavours, along with excellent cakes and pastries. The queues are slow but well worth it.

BELOW: the neoclassical National Theatre.

Visit the Hotel Regent Esplanade to see its sumptuous Art Deco foyer and have a drink in its tempting pavement café.

BELOW: the Mimara Museum, devoted to fine art and archaeology.

A block further south is the **Ethnographic Museum** ⑪ (Etnografski muzej; tel. 01-455 8544; www.emz.hr; Tue–Thur 10am–6pm, Fri–Sun 10am–1pm; charge, free on Thur), mainly devoted to costume. The ground floor displays indigenous clothing, with everything from traditional peasant attire through to military uniforms, while the lower level has an eclectic range of exhibits brought to the city by adventurous Croatians from all corners of the globe. Other artefacts include weapons and musical instruments as well as fine examples of the intricate lace produced on the Kvarner Gulf island of Pag for centuries.

Behind the Ethnographic Museum is the **Mimara Museum** ⑫ (Muzej Mimara; Tue–Sat 10am–5pm, Sun 10am–2pm; charge), founded on the 4,000-strong collection of a mysterious Dalmatian collector called Ante Topić Mimara, who died in 1987. It was never clear how Mimara had made his fortune and the collection has been the subject of much controversy. Taken at face value it is one of Europe's great art galleries with an exciting range of European masters but the art world has cast doubts on the authenticity of some of the paintings. On show are works attributed to Raphael, Caravaggio, Rembrandt, Rubens, Van Dyck, Velásquez, Gainsborough, Turner, Delacroix, Renoir, Manet and Degas.

The museum, which is a work of art in itself, also has an extensive archaeological collection, again amassed by Mimara. It includes classical pieces from antiquity as well as the famous Vučedol Dove. The China collection contains 300 pieces of indigenous art. There is also a rich collection of sculpture, including works by Rodin, della Robbia and Verocchio.

Restful interlude

Walk south towards the railway line and just before you get there head back east along Mihanovićeva to one of the city's most charming and relaxed oases, the **Botanical Garden** ⑬ (Botanički vrt; www.botanic.hr; May–Sept Mon–Tue 9am–2.30pm, Wed–Sun 9am–7pm, Apr and Oct Mon–Tue 9am–2.30pm, Wed–Sun 9am–6pm;

free). Though modest in comparison with the world's great botanical gardens, Zagreb's version still makes a pleasant diversion on a warm day. The gardens were opened in 1890, their design influenced by gardens in France and Britain. The network of paths, ponds and greenhouses includes some 10,000 plant species.

From the Botanical Garden it is only a five-minute stroll further east to the railway station where this tour began, but first it is worth popping into the **Hotel Regent Esplanade** ⓮, occupying a prime position across from the railway station and fronted by a large fountain. Built in 1925 to cater for the discerning needs of the passengers of the Orient Express, it is Croatia's classiest hotel. The Art Deco foyer is dazzling, with funky clocks showing the time in various world cities and huge leather armchairs. If you are hungry you can have lunch or dinner here, or just relax with a coffee in its pavement café. At night you can return to the casino to mingle with Zagreb's movers and shakers – as well as some shady-looking characters.

Upper Town

The Upper Town, or Gornji grad, is home to Gradec, the oldest part of the city. It still retains much of its medieval shape, though many parts of the original defensive walls have been dismantled or destroyed over the centuries. The fun way of getting to the Gradec is to take the old **funicular**, built in 1888. It rumbles up the hill from just off Ilica, revealing views of the Donji Grad and its blend of 19th-century and modern architecture as it goes. At 55 seconds, it is probably the world's shortest funicular ride. Initially steam powered the funicular, until electrification during World War II, and it originally had first- and second-class carriages. If you are feeling energetic, you can walk up the stairs beside the tracks.

Across from the funicular terminus in Gradec is **Lotršćak Tower** ⓯ (Kula Lotršćak; Tue–Sun 11am–7pm), a sturdy construction topped by an orange-tiled roof and an observation deck offering sweeping views of the city. The lower floors of the towers have a souvenir shop and a modest and regularly changing array of modern art,

It is a steep climb to the Upper Town (Gornji grad) – you may want to take the funicular.

BELOW: the Botanical Gardens.

The short and sweet Zagreb funicular was built in 1890 and is under 100 metres (328ft) long.

BELOW: view over Gradec, the oldest part of Zagreb, with the chequered roof of St Mark's clearly visible.

some of which is for sale. Be alert as it approaches midday, when a single cannon round goes off. This was originally meant to scare off the Ottoman threat; today it serves only to sort the tourists from the locals.

Walk east of the museum to enjoy the views from **Strossmayer Parade** 16 (Strossmayerovo šetalište), built in the 19th century when the town walls were removed. You can see the Donji Grad falling away below, the cathedral to the left and Novi Grad (New Town) spreading over the far bank of the Sava River to the south. This tree-lined boulevard has benches and old-fashioned gas lamps, as well as a silver-finished bronze figure of Modernist literary hero Antun Gustav Matoš (1873–1914) reclining on a bench, the work of Ivan Kožarić (www.ivankozaric.net), born in 1921.

Continue north from the terminus of the funicular and you will soon come to the **Croatian Museum of Naïve Art** 17 (Hrvatski muzej naivne umjetnosti; www.hmnu.org; Tue–Fri 10am–6pm, Sat–Sun 10am–1pm, closed public holidays; charge), housed in an old palace. The naïve tradition in Croatia originated amongst untutored painters in the rural areas and was developed by Krsto Hegedušić. He scoured the Croatian interior looking for local artists, which he found in abundance, and the results are on show in the gallery's six rooms. Some of the key names to look out for are Ivan Generalić, Franjo Mraz and Ivan Lacković, with the most startling work a portrait of Sophia Loren – something of a departure from the traditional depictions of rural life.

Zagreb's most distinctive church, restored to glory after a 25-year project is **St Mark's** 18 (Crkva sv. Marka) which looks like something out of a Brothers Grimm fairytale with its chequered red, white and blue roof tiles incorporating the Croatian coat of arms in its design. The roof's colourful pattern was added at the end of the 19th century, but the church dates back to the 13th century. The interior, perhaps more arresting than that of Zagreb's cathedral, includes one of Ivan Meštrović's best works, a haunting depiction of the Crucifixion with

the figure of Christ stretched out in the sculptor's typical style.

After a day or two in Zagreb you may feel that you have had your fill of this Split-born artist, but the **Meštrović Atelier** ⑲ (Atelje Meštrović; tel: 01-485 1123/4; www.mestrovic.hr; Tue–Fri 10am–6pm, Sat–Sun 10am–2pm, closed public holidays; charge) is worth visiting. The 17th-century house where he lived from 1924 to 1942 contains sketches and plans for some of his most significant projects, such as the Crucifixion in nearby St Mark's Church and the statue of Grgur of Nin, outside Diocletian's Palace in Split. The museum helps to fill in the blanks about Meštrović and provides a useful context for the statues, sculptures and reliefs that dot the city.

Further north on Opatička is the **Zagreb City Museum** ⑳ (Muzej grada Zagreba; tel: 01-485 1361/2; www.mgz. hr; Sun 10am–2pm, Tue, Wed and Fri 10am–6pm, Thur 10am–10pm, Sat 11am–7pm; charge, free guided tour Sat and Sun 11am). As the name suggests, it tells the story of the city from medieval times to the present, using well con-structed arrangements and information in English as well as Croatian. The scale models of Zagreb show how the city has metamorphosed over the centuries. The most interesting section covers Zagreb during the 1990s' war.

From Gradec a good route back down towards Trg bana Josipa Jelačića is Tkalčićeva, an old cobbled lane that hugs the old walls. Today it's lined with cafés, where the young, trendy and rich congregate on summer evenings. Running parallel to Tkalčićeva is Radićeva, which also ends at Trg bana Josipa Jelačića, with interesting shops and a few more cafés on the way and passing close to the 13th-century **Stone Gate** ㉑ (Kamenita vrata), the only one of four city gates still standing. It contains a small chapel, built to commemorate a fire of 1731 that razed the wooden buildings huddled about the gate but left a picture of the Virgin Mary unscathed. The chapel is a place of pilgrimage.

City escapes

The largest park in Zagreb is **Maksimir**, a short ride east from the Donji Grad on

Zagreb has produced two Nobel Prize winners, both chemists. Lavoslav Ružička was honoured in 1939 and Vladimir Prelog in 1957. The latter was also a first-class athlete who managed to combine his research with winning the World Pentathlon Championship in 1923.

BELOW: attending church on All Saints' Day.

Day of the Dead

Roman Catholics worldwide celebrate All Saints' Day (1 Nov) and All Souls' Day (2 Nov), also known in Croatian as Dan Mrtvih (the Day of the Dead) or Dan Spomina na Mrtve (Remembrance Day). The first is an occasion to revere all the myriad martyrs and saints one might not have got around to remembering the rest of the year, while the second is a chance to remember and pray for the souls of lesser mortals who may need a little helping hand from the living to ease their path heavenwards. Croatians mark All Saints' Day by attending church and lighting candles over the graves of loved ones. If you can get any transport there, it is a marvellous time to visit Mirogoj Cemetery – where practically the whole population of Zagreb decamps in late after-noon – to experience the eerie glow of the thousands of candles after dark.

TIP

For an easy escape from the heat and dust of Zagreb head down to the banks of the Sava River immediately south of the centre. Take a tram to the foot of Miramarska and descend to the river bank from there.

tram No. 11 or 12 from Trg bana Josipa Jelačića. Covering 316 hectares (781 acres), the park owes its appearance to a makeover in 1843 that was modelled on the English garden concept. It has artificial lakes, meadows, oak forests, a zoo, a café (mobbed on summer weekends) and a large somewhat dilapidated stadium founded in 1912. It hosts the home matches of both Dinamo Zagreb and the Croatian national football team but plans are afoot to build a more suitable replacement.

To the southwest of the Donji Grad, accessible by tram from Trg bana Josipa Jelačića (tram No. 17), is **Lake Jarun** (Jezero Jarun), Zagreb's "artificial sea", another popular destination in summer. The park spreads around a rowing lake and there is a small shingle beach as well as several cafés. On summer evenings it is a favourite haunt for teenagers, who head here from the city centre at around 10pm, bringing their own drinks with them.

Bear Mountain

To the north of the city the bulk of **Mt Medvednica**, meaning "Bear Moun-

tain", beckons, its cooling breezes a godsend on a scorching summer's day. It offers a range of hiking trails and – if you are feeling particularly energetic – you can ascend to the peak of Sljeme at a height of 1,035 metres (3,396ft) though a cable car will take you most of the way. In winter, when condition are right, a modest ski run operates with equipment available for hire.

It is possible to walk west from the Sljeme peak to **Medvedgrad** (Bear Town), a fortress on the forested slopes (allow three hours each way). Built *c.* 1250 to ward off Tartar attacks it fell into a dilapidated state before a reincarnation as the Altar of the Homeland (Oltar domovine). An eternal flame burns in the interior and the site has become a controversial symbol of the rapid nation-building that has taken place in Croatia, with solemn state ceremonies and re-enactments of medieval battles held in a fortress that can claim no deep historical significance and was just a ruin until the 1990s. It also houses a museum and a fine restaurant with north Croatian specialities.

BELOW: springtime break on Trg Tomislavov.

Café Culture

These days, Zagreb's café culture is stronger than ever, with young citizens often preferring to spend their evenings with espressos rather than getting drunk on beer.

C offee and café culture have been part of the fabric of social life in Zagreb ever since the days of the Austro-Hungarian occupation, when the best Viennese brews were all the rage. These days, during warmer months, all Zagreb seems to be reclining in a pavement café, as tables sprout up everywhere. Even during cooler months, at the first glimpse of sunshine locals will be out looking for a table in the sun.

A café is a *kavana* and a *kafić* is more like a café-bar, though both sell coffee and alcohol and often a variety of pastries and ice cream, and both close around midnight. *Kafići* tend to be popular with a youngsters. A *slastičarnice* is a patisserie, where there is no alcohol, but a full range of coffees backed up by a wider range of snacks, ice creams and cakes than either *kavane* or *kafići* offer.

The range of coffees available in the Croatian capital is almost as confusing as the different venues for drinking it in. If you ask for a simple coffee *(kava)* you can usually expect a heart-pumping espresso, and many *kavane* open well before rush hour to allow bleary-eyed citizens their pre-work caffeine shot. *Kava s mlijekom* is an espresso slightly diluted with a dash of milk, closely related to the *macchiato* that Dalmatians enjoy. *Bijela kava* is quite simply "white coffee", similar to a latte, while most cafés also serve up an at least acceptable cappuccino *(kapučino)*. *Kava sa šlagom* is a highly calorific coffee loaded with a dollop of full-fat cream.

City centre café society

The city centre is the best place to experience the vibrant café culture. One of the liveliest streets, Tkalčićeva, winds down the Gornji grad's eastern edge. The street has over a dozen cafés, many open late into the night in summer, some not getting going until after 10pm. Some of the street's best coffee is at Argentina (No. 9) and Café Bar Bonn (No. 22), while Cica (No. 8) has probably

RIGHT: coffee and newspapers in a café on Radićeva.

Zagreb's most comprehensive range of artisan *rakija* (fruit brandy).

If you want to fit in with the local cognoscenti on Tkalčićeva, don your trendiest clothes and begin with a quick espresso in one café, making sure everyone notices you as you go in, and then cruise up and down the cobbles a couple of times, before deigning to favour another lucky café with your presence.

This time, just order an extravagant coffee creation and spin it out for an hour or so. Repeat until the cafés close, when you can move off with fellow poseurs to one of the city's chic nightclubs.

The Dubrovnik café

Trg bana Josipa Jelačića has a couple of notable long-established cafés that tend to be busiest during the day. Belonging to the eponymous hotel, the best is the classy Dubrovnik, a meeting place for politicians, journalists and business people. Its coffee is excellent, served in Viennese style with a glass of water, and its sumptuous cakes and ice cream are divine. It is one of the oldest and most popular places in Zagreb and a meeting place for politicians, journalists and business people. There is an outdoor terrace for drinks and snacks.

Another fruitful district is Trg Petar Preradovića and Bogovićeva, where myriad cafés rub shoulders with shops and bars.   ❑

CENTRAL CROATIA

Tourists mostly overlook it, yet this region has scenery every bit as spectacular as the coast's. Its outstanding attraction is the Plitvice Lakes region

Zagreb

Foreign visitors largely neglect this large frontier region encircling Zagreb, bordered by Hungary to the north, Bosnia to the east, the Kvarner Gulf to the south and Slovenia to the west, often ignoring it apart from the Plitvice Lakes National Park, on Unesco's World Heritage list.

Yet the Plitvice Lakes are by no means Central Croatia's only scenic attraction. Head north and west of Zagreb and the scenery is every bit as spectacular in its own way as the coastline, with rugged heavily forested hills forming a natural border with the surrounding countries. These natural fortifications have put the region in the very fault-line of political and religious Europe for centuries, when Christian Europe stared over the brink of the Ottoman Empire to the south. Both the Croats and the Serbs lay claim to this region, which spelt trouble in the Homeland War of the 1990s when fighting rippled through the eastern sections of Central Croatia. The conflict began around the Plitvice Lakes when the rebel Serbs overran the national park.

Today the Plitvice Lakes are back on the tourism map, and the northern city of Varaždin is on the "tentative list" for World Heritage status from Unesco. Other attractions north of Zagreb include a string of castles that used to form the old defensive line and a number of spa towns, built to cater to the 19th-century fashion for spas among Austro-Hungarians. Head fur-

ther south and the Samobor Hills are a popular weekend retreat for the citizens of Zagreb. They offer gently rolling hills, a rustic way of life, clean air and high-quality wines, produced on a pleasingly local scale.

South of Zagreb is Karlovac, once a bulwark against the Ottomans and more recently where the Croats made a desperate stand against the rebel Serbs and the Yugoslav army. Had the city fallen the Serbs could have rolled up the motorway all the way to Zagreb. The scars of war are evident in Karlovac and the neighbouring village of Turanj, where an outdoor Homeland

Main attractions
VARAŽDIN
TRAKOŠĆAN CASTLE
KRAPINA
VELIKI TABOR AND KUMROVEC
KRAPINSKE TOPLICE
SAMOBOR
KARLOVAC
PLITVICE LAKES
OGULIN
MT BJELOLASICA

PRECEDING PAGES: rural scene near Kumrovec. **LEFT:** typical landscape in the Žumberak region. **BELOW:** locals in Varaždin.

Central Croatia

War museum is one of few of its kind in the country.

On the southern reaches of Central Croatia before the Kvarner Gulf travellers can choose between heading straight for the Plitvice Lakes or using the old road over the mountains to the port city of Rijeka. Either route has plenty to recommend it.

North of Zagreb and the Zagorje

The E71, a fast road, soon to become part of the A1 motorway, runs north from Zagreb towards the Hungarian border, providing easy access to the **Zagorje**, a picturesque mountain region replete with trim villages, hilltop castles and spa retreats. Long a favourite getaway for Zagreb's inhabitants, this bucolic oasis receives few tourists and traffic is relatively light even at the peak of high season.

The city of **Varaždin ❶** is an excellent base for exploring the Zagorje, though it is possible to access the region by taking a number of day trips from Zagreb using public transport or, more conveniently, with a hired car. Varaždin itself has enough to see to justify a few days' stay; Unesco is even considering including its historic Baroque core, popularly known as the Karlovac star (Karlovačka zvijezda), for inclusion on the list of World Heritage Sites.

The best place to start a tour of the city is at its original raison d'être, the **Stari Grad Dubovac Fortress** (Stari grad Dubovac; Tue–Fri 10am–5pm, Sat–Sun 10am–1pm; charge), a stark white 16th-century creation, whose graffiti-stained walls cannot disguise the beauty of a meticulous restoration programme during the 1980s. Scramble up the old grass mounds to get a real feel for its history, on the frontier between Christian Europe and the Ottoman Empire. When the Turkish threat finally receded Stari Grad fell under the control of the wealthy Erdödy family, who gave it a more elaborate appearance in keeping with its new domestic purpose.

The fortress was converted into a branch of the city museum in the 1920s. This is well presented with clear displays, helpful explanations in

TIP

You may be able to catch a football match at Varaždin's modern football stadium, where the local team Varteks inspires civic pride. The Croatian national team also occasionally plays here.

BELOW: the Stari Grad Fortress.

Border Dispute with Slovenia

One of the main obstacles to Croatian entry to the European Union has been a complicated dispute with an existing member, Slovenia, over the maritime border in a body of water known in Croatian as the Savudrija Bay (Piranski zaljev) and in Slovenian as the Gulf of Piran (Piranski zaliv). In this case, international law on maritime borders is confused and a succession of arbiters from the UN to Nato have failed to resolve the dispute. The issue was never of relevance when both states were part of Yugoslavia but since independence the two countries have had a prickly relationship and Slovenia, which joined the union in 2007, has had an excellent opportunity to press its case against its poorer neighbour, as border disputes with existing members pose a bar to entry.

EAT

A culinary speciality of Varaždin, usually served with coffee, is the Varaždin roll *(Varaždinski Klipi)*, a type of breadstick made of flour, salt, milk, caraway, sugar, egg and fresh yeast. The town square is a good place to try it.

English and friendly English-speaking staff. The exhibits, spread over several rooms, include rifles, pistols, axes and swords from the old frontier days. Look out in particular for the hallway lined with bullet-studded 19th-century wooden hunting targets that were given to the winners of local hunting competitions as trophies. In one wing is the simple St Lovro Chapel (Kapelica sv. Lovre), with its novel mobile altar and wide slits for firing cannons, which enabled a quick turnaround from chapel to artillery position. In the basement, accessed on the way to the exit, there are often temporary exhibitions showcasing the work of local artists.

From the fortress head through the only gate that remains from the original city walls and you will come to the small Trg Stančića, which has a hard-to-resist café and Varaždin's **Old and Contemporary Masters' Gallery** (Galerija starih i novih majstora; Tue– Fri 10am–2pm, Sat–Sun 10am–1pm; charge). The gallery is housed in a grand old 17th-century palace and features the modern work of local artists as well as a number of Dutch, French and German paintings.

Baroque architecture

Proceed down Kranjčevića to **Franjevački trg**, in parts an impressive boulevard lined with the expertly restored homes of Varaždin's wealthy merchants and in others a shabby thoroughfare scarred by rundown facades, indicating just how much work has still to be done to restore Varaždin's Baroque splendour. The city's richest merchants and nobles used to build their ostentatious homes and palaces on Franjevački trg and their coats of arms and various symbols adorn many of the buildings.

Also on Franjevački trg is the hulk of the Franciscan church of **St John the Baptist** (Crkva sv. Ivana Krstitelja), inside which are some interesting 18th-century frescoes. Just outside the church look out for a copy of Ivan Meštrović's *Bishop Grgur of Nin*, a much smaller version of the original statue that presides over the northern entrance to Diocletian's Palace in Split. The polished and gleaming toe is evi-

BELOW: flowers for sale in a market in Varaždin.

lence of local faith in the efficacy of the statue as a good luck charm.

Head east along Franjevački trg and you will come to the expanse of **Trg kralja Tomislav** and its brace of pavement cafés. Lording it over the square is the town hall (Gradska vijećnica), dating from 1533, though today's incarnation is largely a Gothic reconstruction. During civic events the local guard, the Purgari, don their immaculate blue uniforms and parade proudly past the town hall. Local pageantry also takes over on Saturdays with an elaborate changing of the guard ceremony. On the same square look out for the **Jacomini House** (Kuća Jacomini), an old confectionery shop whose interior is adorned with stucco decorations bearing the initials of its original owner.

A short stroll southeast is Varaždin's **cathedral** (katedrala), whose opening times are erratic, though you can always peer into the interior through the windows of the main door. This portal bears the coat of arms of the Drašković family, local nobles who were influential in the region for centuries. Inside, the highlight is the extravagant multi-coloured altarpiece with its panoply of saints, angels and cherubs.

The most bizarre museum in Varaždin is without doubt the **Entomological Museum** (Entomološki odjel; closed for restoration), housed in the Herzer Palace. More than 10,000 insects, painstakingly mounted and displayed by Franjo Koscec, make up the collection. Koscec was a local high school teacher who dedicated much of his life to his unusual hobby, opening the museum in 1954 and bequeathing it to the city in 1959. His daughter, Ruzica Koscec, herself a biology professor, took up the reins from 1962 until 1980 and further expanded the collection.

Varaždin is also a good place to try the cuisine of the Zagorje, especially as dining out here is shockingly cheap by Croatian standards. The city's bakers have a formidable reputation. Culinary specialities include a stodgy but very popular snack called *strukli*, a cottage-cheese pastry. Also often on the menu are turkey with *mlinci* (a form of pasta) and buckwheat porridge. Those with a sweet tooth may want to try the traditional sugary cake

TIP

In September Varaždin, itself a celebration of Baroque architecture, hosts the Varaždin Baroque Evenings (Varaždinske barokne večeri; www.vbv.hr), a 10-day celebration of chamber music in suitably period venues.

BELOW: the impeccable ramparts of Trakošćan.

Trakošćan castle rising picturesquely above its lake.

BELOW: inside the church of St Mary of Bistrica.

zlevka. And as well as the local wines there is the tasty local Knaput beer.

Castles in the air

The Zagorje is renowned for its gloriously Baroque castles, which line this mountainous region, some just crumbling old ruins and others spruced up as tourist attractions. Arguably the most impressive castle and less than an hour's drive west of Varaždin is **Trakošćan Castle ②** (Dvorac Trakošćan; daily 9am–6pm, until 4pm in winter; charge), parts of which date from the 13th century. The castle is associated with the ubiquitous Draškovic dynasty, who lorded over Trakošćan from the 16th century right through to the early part of the 20th. Today's incarnation owes much to a late 19th-century reworking, which nearly bankrupted the family. Some point out that their rather outlandish tastes mean that some of the embellishments have more in common with Disney than defence, but that does not deter the citizens of Zagreb and Varaždin, who make secular pilgrimages here in droves on summer weekends.

Once most visitors have delved inside the castle they head straight back to their cars and return home, but it is worth exploring the castle grounds too. The narrow tree-shrouded lake offers an opportunity to escape the crowds, good views of the castle and also, if you are lucky, encounters with the resident deer. The only noise to break the bucolic calm are the annoying pedalos that thump around the lake – great for kids, but an aural intrusion for others.

A short drive further east from Trakošćan Castle is the town of **Krapina ③**. It is home to one of the most important palaeolithic sites in the world, **Hušnjakovo**, on a hill on the edge of the town. The bones of dozens of Neanderthals and various animals, as well as a scattering of artefacts such as scrapers and stone axes, possibly dating from 30,000 BC, were found here in the late 19th century. Krapina's Museum of Evolution (Muzeji hrvatskog zagorja; closed for restoration; www.mhz.hr) displays archaeological finds from local digs, but the real prize, "Krapina Man", the bones of some 20 Neanderthals, are now in the Croatian Natural History

Museum in Zagreb. Today a motley collection of artists' impressions of what "Krapina Man" and the animals may have looked like is all that remains of the find on Hušnjakovo.

Krapina itself is an appealing town in one of the prettiest parts of the Croatian Zagorje. The old core of the town is a little ramshackle, with nothing much to do apart from try one of the cafés or restaurants. A short walk away from the centre is the Franciscan monastery (Franjevački samostan) and the attached church of St Catherine. Look out for the coat of arms above the entrance, the symbol of the Keglevic family who paid for its construction in the 17th century. Also outside the town, in and around the Krapina and Sutla rivers, are opportunities for hunting and fishing, which one can organise from the town. Krapina also proffers a livelier cultural scene than most of the other settlements in the Zagorje, with regular classical concerts and exhibitions.

After Krapina those on a day trip may want to head back south on the motorway to Zagreb, possibly making a relaxing stop off at the spa town of Krapinske Toplice on the way *(see page 120)* or to the pilgrimage church of **St Mary of Bistrica ❹**, (Crkva Marije Bistricvke) southeast of Krapina, whose Black Madonna, dating from the late 15th century, draws hundreds of thousands of pilgrims each year. The statue was discovered in 1684, immured in the church wall, where it had been hidden from the Ottomans some 34 years previously. Apparently, a miraculous beam of light had indicated its presence. The current church, designed by Hermann Bollé, architect of Zagreb's cathedral and Mirogoj Cemetery, is a good place to see Croatian piety in action – in particular the many women who come to petition the Madonna. Regular buses run direct from Zagreb.

Towards Slovenia

It is well worth exploring the area bordering Slovenia, a contested border for the European Union. One of the most dramatic features of this region is **Veliki Tabor ❺** (closed for renovation until 2011; www.veliki-tabor.hr), a ruggedly impressive fortress presiding over the surrounding countryside. The original fortifications on the site date back to the 12th century, though today's version is mainly the result of a 15th-century renovation. The sturdy construction and orange slate roof may not be as magical as Trakošćan but the castle feels more "real" and there are fewer visitors.

Further west and a little south, close to the border with Slovenia, is the unassuming village of **Kumrovec ❻** (direct bus and rail connections with Zagreb). It would have remained as sleepy and unheralded as any other village in this hilly region were it not for its most famous son, Josef Broz Tito, who was born to a local peasant family in 1892 when the region was part of the Austro-Hungarian Empire. The house where the future Yugoslav president was born is said to have been the first brick building in the village. In 1947 it was revamped by the Zagreb Museum of Arts and Crafts and in

Tito depicted in his prime in Kumrovec, the birthplace of the great leader.

BELOW: Veliki Tabor.

Grapes from the Samobor Hills.

1948 a statue of Tito by the Croatian sculptor Antun Augustinčić (1900–79) was erected. Those travelling to Kumrovec just to visit the house may be a little disappointed as there is little to see bar one of his old uniforms and some mementoes.

More interesting is the **Staro Selo Ethnographic Museum** (Muzej staro selo; daily Apr–Sept 9am–7pm, Oct–Mar 9am–4pm; charge), formerly the Marshal Tito Memorial Museum, which was set up in the old quarter of Kumrovec in 1953. This open-air attraction has over 40 19th- and early 20th-century buildings that shed light on the way of life in Tito's day. On show are dwellings, a blacksmith's, a toy shop, a pottery, a gingerbread-maker's and a vintner's, as well as a school, displays on local wedding traditions and musical instruments. There are even a few rooms for those looking to stay the night in Tito's old stamping ground, and a restaurant serving local dishes.

Spa country

BELOW: Samobor is renowned for its vineyards.

As well as the castles and pretty scenery, Zagorje has some wonderful spas.

Many came to the fore during the 18th and 19th centuries when spa bathing was all the rage for the moneyed classes of the Austro-Hungarian Empire. One of the best spa towns, conveniently located if you are on the way back to Zagreb, is **Krapinske Toplice** ❼ Some of the pools are currently being upgraded as part of a major modernisation project that is set to include new hotels, but four hot pools are still open to the public during the revamp. The temperature varies from lukewarm to extremely hot, with the cooler pools large enough to swim in. Protecting your modesty in the communal changing areas can be tricky, but the Krapinske Toplice spa offers a real taste of an activity that is so much a part of the culture of the Zagorje.

The most obvious way of getting back to Zagreb is by joining the Slovenia–Zagreb motorway, but there is an alternative. After Krapinske Toplice spa avoid the motorway junction and instead head south on the minor road that runs alongside the motorway for a while before rambling off through the countryside. This old main road is a lot

Wine Tasting

Croatia overflows with vineyards, with the most celebrated wines emanating from Dalmatia and Istria. All over the country, though, there are tiny pockets in which top-quality wine is produced in inauspicious surroundings. One of the best areas is the Samobor Hills, a short drive out of Zagreb to the southwest, where the quite sweet white wine is similar in some respects to German Riesling.

Many Zagreb citizens like to spend their weekends in the rolling hills, stocking up on wine. The hills are covered in vineyards, with a number of wine cellars open to the public (makeshift signs welcome visitors). In Croatian, wine cellar is *kleti*; so look out for signs pointing you towards the small-scale, often family-run, operations.

Public transport around the Samobor Hills is not very extensive or efficient; you need your own wheels to explore the area. If you want to stay the night there are a number of good value hotels dotted around the road from the town of Samobor towards Jastrebarsko (which eventually joins up with the motorway south to Karlovac).

The hearty local food is well worth trying and works well with the local wines. A scenic spot for lunch is the Restoran Ivančić in the village of Plešivica. Its pleasant terrace offers sweeping panoramic views out over the Samobor Hills.

uieter and much more enjoyable for
hose not in so much of a hurry, as it
akes a far more languorous approach
> the capital.

South of Zagreb and the Samobor Hills

Heading south of Zagreb the temptation is to join Croatia's busiest road,
the motorway to Karlovac, which is
fine if you are in a rush to get to the
coast. However, if you have your own
transport and want to take a more
interesting route, head southwest
out of Zagreb towards the vine-clad
Žumberak region and specifically the
Samobor Hills. Just 20km (12 miles)
from Zagreb, the town of **Samobor** ⑧
is a scenic little place huddled around
the sleepy Gradna River. It is known
for a number of Epicurean treats, such
as *samoborska kremšnita*, a delicious
warm vanilla custard cake, *bermet*, a
deep red aperitif that is something
of an acquired taste, and *samoborska
mustarda*, a fine mustard that has
been produced in the town for over
a century and which goes well with a
range of local meat dishes. The town

also has a lively pre-Lenten carnival,
with parades, traditional masks and a
firework display.

If you want to take your exploration
of Samobor beyond eating *kremšnita* in
one of the glut of cafés on Trg kralja
Tomislava, then you will find that
the town has an interesting history.
In the Middle Ages it was on a par
with emerging Zagreb and it came to
prominence in the 19th century when
composer Ferdo Livadić was part of
the movement to awaken Slavic consciousness amidst the confines of Austro-Hungarian domination. His story
unfolds in his old house, which Franz
Liszt once visited, on Trg kralja Tomislava, now the **Town Museum** (Tue–Fri
9am–3pm, Sat–Sun 9am–1pm; charge).
It also contains paintings of local
luminaries, as well as displays of crude
farming implements gathered from the
surrounding fertile farmland.

If you are keen to work off the effects
of the *kremšnita* further then you can
also head out on one of the hiking trails
around Samobor. Hiking is popular with
the citizens of Zagreb, who gather here
on summer weekends. Tito held one of

*Karlovac is home to
what many beer
lovers rate as
Croatia's number one
brew. Karlovačko is a
5.2 percent full-
flavoured lager with
a pleasant aftertaste
and few additives.
According to locals,
it will not give you a
hangover.*

BELOW: a café-bar
in Samobor.

Karlovac is typical of the region's fine Austro-Hungarian buildings. Many were damaged during the Homeland War and are now being restored.

BELOW: Holy Trinity Church in Karlovac.

his first clandestine Communist Party meetings near Samobor under the guise of the annual hiking festival. The easiest trail is just up from the town to its old medieval castle, but there are many different options, though for some of them you may want to drive further on to the village of Veliki Lipovec and set off from there.

Delving further south, the road cuts through picturesque scenery with rolling hills, tiny churches, villages of little more than a few houses and husband-and-wife farming teams ambling along on ancient tractors. The area is also covered in vineyards and is renowned for the excellent quality of its wine, something that few tourists really discover. The best times to visit are at weekends when the vineyards are open to visitors – the many cars from Zagreb will provide guidance on where to go.

The road through the Samobor Hills leads south and ultimately joins the motorway to **Karlovac ⑨**, a city often overlooked by tourists as they sweep past on their way to the Adriatic Sea. Karlovac is well worth a stop off, though, both for its Austro-

Hungarian heritage and for its pivotal role in the Homeland War. In Croatian terms Karlovac is something of a new arrival, built by the Austro-Hungarians in 1579 as a bulwark in the frontier defences against the Ottoman Empire. Though the historic centre had its moat drained and walls torn down in the 19th century, the moat is now part of a leafy greenbelt and the charm of the old town is still intact. Many of its buildings, though, were damaged during Serb shelling, which was at its peak between 1991 and 1992 but resumed in 1993 and did not stop until the Croatian Army ousted Serb forces from the city's outskirts in 1995.

The heart of Karlovac is Trg bana Jelačića, still not completely restored after bomb damage. Also patched up on the edge of the square is the Holy Trinity Church (opening times vary) whose sturdy exterior conceals an interior with good Baroque frescoes. Nearby, the **Town Museum** (Gradski muzej; Mon–Fri 7am–3pm, Sat–Sun 10am–noon; charge, free Wed) is housed in one of the city's oldest buildings, the 17th-century Baroque Franko-

an Palace. On display is a collection of traditional costumes from the region, as well as swords, guns and military paraphernalia. The most interesting exhibit is a scale model of the original fortifications that shows the virtually impregnable star-shaped design.

Just 5km (3 miles) south of the city is the battle-scarred village of **Turanj** ⑩, which was at the front line during the Homeland War and fell under Serbian occupation. An open-air museum (daily 24 hours) dedicated to the events of 1991–5 has a large collection of military hardware and other relics of the conflict. It is one of the few official places in the country where visitors can find out more about the war. Perhaps the most poignant exhibit is a tractor that was converted into an armoured vehicle by desperate local people as they tried to halt the advance of the Serb tanks. Across the road from the museum a simple marble memorial commemorates the local dead.

South to the Plitvice Lakes

From Turanj the drive south to the Plitvice Lakes ⑪ (Plitvička jezera),

one of Croatia's most popular tourist attractions, is a fairly uneventful one. You can break it, though, with a stop off at one of the restaurants that line the road side. These are good value and of an excellent standard, specialising in spit-roasted lamb and pork. Just keep a keen eye on the upcoming road and choose a place that suits – the most attractive look out over meadows or gurgling streams.

Call them emerald, call them turquoise, call them what you will, but the tumbling waters of Plitvice are undeniably a visual circus as they bubble and churn their way through a series of 16 densely forested lakes. Already protected as a national park, Plitvice Lakes earned a place on the Unesco World Heritage List in 1979, a fact that failed to deter rebel Serbian forces from trashing the park and looting its hotels between 1991 and 1995. Today Plitvice has recovered its tranquillity and it makes an excellent place to spend a day or, better still, several days. A variety of wildlife, including the occasional bear, shares the park with humans in relative harmony.

A scenic walkway brings visitors close to spectacular falls.

BELOW: rainbow formed in the spray of the Great Falls at Plitvice Lakes.

The lakes are linked by bridges and encircled by raised wooden footpaths.

BELOW: Veliki slap, Plitvice National Park's highest and most dramatic waterfall.

The best places to stay are the three park hotels (some rooms have views of the park and lakes), as negotiating the car parks and fighting for a space can be a problem for those travelling in from outside. There is also a campsite. Getting around the park is straightforward once you have paid the admission fee, which includes using the boats and tourist trains that aid getting around. There is a variety of trails, all linked by the trains and boats, and plenty of information assistants are on hand at the two entrances.

Try to visit the most popular parts of the lakes in the early morning or late evening when there are fewer people and the ever-changing light creates fabulous effects on the greeny-blue waters. To escape from fellow visitors, try heading for the more remote upper lakes to the south by taking the boat across **Lake Kozjak** Ⓐ (the park's largest lake) from Entrance 2 and following the path that skirts Lake Gradinsko. Just past the lake is a series of spectacular waterfalls. From here proceed on the trail south past the Labudovac Falls to Lake Proščansko.

The vast, tree-shrouded **Lake Proščansko** Ⓑ looks more like something that you would expect to find in the US or Scandinavia than in this corner of Europe. Be careful not to follow the rickety wooden walkway around the lake as this leads to a dead end requiring a dangerous jump on to the lake shore. Instead head for the train pick-up point and then keep on south past the waiting passengers. Alas there is no lakeside trail and so you have to make do with the road, but there are few other visitors up here and a little way along there is a disused wooden pier where you can relax and take in the view in peace.

From Lake Proščansko it is also possible to embark on a 7km (4-mile) trek up to one of the sources of the water that runs through the park – ask at the park information kiosks as the main maps do not mark this route.

With the lower lakes so overrun by tourists in high season it is tempting just to stay in the quieter southern half, but in doing so you would miss out on some of the most impressive scenery. Again, take a boat from the hotels near

Plitvice Lakes National Park

0   5 km

0   5 miles

ntrance 2 across Lake Kozjak, but this ime take the boat heading north to the ar end of the lake, where you can stop or a lunch of spit-roasted chicken before arrying on. There is a small beach here ut, as in the rest of the park, swimming s strictly prohibited. The path cuts way from the boat landing and down series of waterfalls and small lakes that re criss-crossed by paths and wooden valkways, the scene hemmed in by lime- tone cliffs on both flanks. The culmina- on is **Veliki slap** ●, the park's largest vaterfall, a spectacular drop that sprays nlookers with a gently cooling mist.

While one can negotiate the park on rushed day trip it is a much better lea to allow a couple of days. That way ou can plan on an early morning start nd beat the worst of the crowds and lso enjoy a relaxed evening spent on balcony overlooking the lake, watch- ng the sun set and complete calm escend over the park. The rerouting f the main highway between Zagreb nd Zadar (which used to cut right hrough the heart of Plitvice) was a wel- ome move. There are also long-term lans to discourage day-trippers, while providing more facilities and detailed information for people staying longer. Such measures should ease the current problems of overcrowding.

South towards Rijeka

Instead of heading from Karlovac for the Plitvice Lakes it is possible to take the old road across the mountains towards the Kvarner Gulf port city of Rijeka, although there is also a less sce- nic motorway. Be aware that the wind- ing old road can be tortuous and the tight bends and crawling trucks make overtaking dangerous and difficult, even without the icy conditions pre- vailing in winter. If in a hurry you can fly; otherwise go carefully, taking time to enjoy the scenery and visit the small towns and villages along the way.

The road and rail routes from Zagreb both run straight through the heart of the wild and relatively unspoilt **Gor- ski kotar**, the aptly named "wooded region", a rugged landscape of thickly wooded forests and deep river valleys that swirls around the Slovenian border from Karlovac right down to the very edge of the Kvarner Gulf. The region is

Aquatic life is plentiful in Plitvice National Park.

BELOW: the lakes are known for their deep turquoise colour.

With numerous tranquil pools amidst travertine waterfalls, the river Mzernica is ideal for rafting and swimming.

BELOW:
wild flowers bloom
from a crevice.

scattered with small road-side villages where you can savour the produce of the local countryside, with spit-roasted pork a ubiquitous speciality.

One of the highlights of the Gorski kotar is the area around the town of **Ogulin** ⑫, 55km (34 miles) south of Karlovac, on the main rail line and not far from the chief road artery south. The town clusters around a 16th-century castle that in the 1930s served as a prison for Tito. On the edge of the old town is Dula's Abyss, a steep fall in the River Dobra named after a local girl who hurled herself to her death here after a tragic love affair. When the Dobra joins the Mreznica River they combine to form two lakes offering opportunities for fishing, swimming and sailing. Parts of the River Dobra are used for whitewater rafting.

High spots

Ogulin is also a good base for tackling the peak of Klek, which rises 1,184 metres (3,885ft) above sea level in the Velika Kapela mountain range. It is hard to miss the distinctive presence of Klek, as it is visible for miles around.

Ascending the mountain is easy – yo can either tackle it the long way fro Ogulin (a 4-hour trek) or from th smaller village of Bijelsko, where the is a well-marked trail that takes aroun 2½ hours each way.

From Klek you can see a fami iar sight if you have been watchin Croatian TV, **Mt Bjelolasica**, whic always appears on TV weather report At 1,530 metres (5,022ft) above se level, the mountain is much high than Klek and it is a relatively straigh forward ascent, though long and tirin in summer. The Croatian governme is trying to push the Bjelolasica Olyn pic Centre as a ski resort, but althoug it may be one of the best ski resorts i Croatia it doesn't compare with an where in the Alps or even in neigh bouring Slovenia. The facilities a basic, but include overnight accon modation and a chair-lift, which on gets busy in the brief ski season th runs any time between December an February depending on condition The resort caters for beginners an intermediates, and there is a good fa run for more experienced skiers.

Flora and Fauna of the Plitvice Lakes

The Plitvice Lakes are home to a remarkably rich diversity of flora and fauna from brown bears to beech trees.

The harsh karst land that ripples across Central Croatia generally supports only sparse vegetation and forms a formidable natural barrier that cuts off the Northern Dalmatian coast. But right in the heart of this rugged terrain, in the midst of the mountains of Mala Kapela and Plješivica, is the lush wonderland of the Plitvice Lakes (Plitvička jezera), a Unesco World Heritage Site since 1979.

The lakes were formed through the process of travertine sedimentation as limestone deposits and moss and fungi reacted to build up the travertine beds and divert the water flow of the Bijela (white) and Crna (black) rivers. Instead of smoothly flowing rivers they become an 8km (5-mile) long network of dams, caves and waterfalls that tumble down in a series of 16 lakes and countless streams and brooks. The travertine process remains ongoing as the landscape evolves, making the area the focus of scientific research.

The size of the national park is roughly 300 sq km (115 sq miles), with 230 sq km (85 sq miles) of that area covered in thick forest and 220 hectares (540 acres) sunk under fresh water. The bulk of the forests are made up of beech, fir and spruce trees, but the unique microclimate also encourages the flourishing of more exotic species, such as hop hornbeam, white Italian maple, flowering oak and sycamore.

If anything the park's array of fauna is even more impressive. The highlights are the brown bears who thrive in and around the park. After losing their natural suspicion of humans in recent years, the bears have become bolder – not least because of irresponsible visitors ignoring regulations and leaving food for them – and even a little troublesome, and so the park authorities are keeping a close eye on them.

Packs of wild wolves, extinct in many of their natural habitats in Europe, also find sanctuary here. Other animals include otters, rabbits and foxes, lynx, wild cats, badgers and pine martens.

On recent estimates there are at least 126 bird species in Plitvice and of those at least 70 are thought to be nesting within the confines of the reserve, making it something of a paradise for ornithologists. Species include owls, cuckoos, thrushes, starlings, kingfishers, wild ducks, grouse, capercaillie and the rarely spotted black storks, as well as wild ospreys. A wide variety of butterfly species also thrives and makes for a spectacular sight in summer as they flit around the edges of the lake. Plitvice is also renowned for its large and particularly picturesque orchids.

Life also flourishes beneath the water in the form of a large population of trout as well as fire salamanders and various crustaceans, though keen fishermen will be frustrated as fishing, like hunting, is banned within the park's boundaries and the trout have grown fat and lazy as a result. Zoologists are at a loss to explain why the lakes have quite so many of them.

If you want to get a feel for the park's flora and fauna and how it evolves and adapts throughout the year, plan at least two trips to cover different seasons. The park is open year-round and there is no bad time to visit.

The Plitvice Lakes on a baking hot summer's day are altogether different on a bright spring morning when life is returning after the chill of the winter. In winter the park is caked in a sheet of snow and ice clogs up many of the waterways. ❏

RIGHT: a brown bear snoozing in the park.

EASTERN CROATIA

Eastern Croatia is not the rural backwater it first appears. Its towns and cities – most gloriously, Osijek – are rich in Baroque architecture, and it has significant natural resources, not least a huge untapped tourist potential

While the 1990s' war often feels like a distant bad dream in much of Croatia, many of the people of Eastern Croatia are still living with the all too real consequences of a conflict that did not see all of the region handed back by the Serbs until 1998. The region remains Croatia's poorest, with the highest unemployment rate and lowest GDP per head among other unenviable economic indicators, although job prospects for land mine disposal experts remain healthy. Many visitors choose to avoid this troubled part of the country and stick to the idyllic towns and balmy waters of the coast, but in doing so they miss an undiscovered part of Europe where tourists are very much a novelty. If you have any desire to learn more about the conflict and the way in which it has shaped the national consciousness, then a visit is highly recommended. Far from being considered ghoulish war tourists, such visitors can expect a hearty welcome from most locals. Aside from the legacies of war, which are all too evident in Osijek, Slavonski Brod and especially shattered Vukovar, Eastern Croatia also has two of Central Europe's finest cathedrals, a string of historic old towns and its own Slavonian cuisine.

There are also the natural attractions of the Kopački rit and the Lonjsko polje nature parks and the broad sweep of the Danube, which cuts through the region creating a natural border with Serbia. Much of Eastern Croatia, especially the segment east and northeast of Zagreb *(see page 132)*, is of little scenic interest compared with other destinations in the country, with large areas of flat land, punctuated by a few rolling hills, perfect for farming but of little real interest to tourists. Also, conditions on some of the minor roads are poor and routes are prone to flooding at all times of year. Most visitors therefore make a beeline east along the motorway from Zagreb straight to the Slavonia region, where most places of interest are located.

Main attractions
LONJSKO POLJE NATURE PARK
JASENOVAC MEMORIAL
    MUSEUM
SLAVONSKI BROD
ĐAKOVO
OSIJEK
VUKOVAR
OVČARA, ILOK AND HLEBINE

PRECEDING PAGES:
Gallery of Naïve Art,
Hlebine. **LEFT:**
cycling through
Bjelovar. **BELOW:** a
typical Podravina
region house.

Stork's nest in Lonjsko polje Park.

Today Eastern Croatia undoubtedly has its problems with high unemployment, the decline of traditional industries, uncleared minefields and the ethnic tensions between Croats who suffered through the war and Croatian Serbs who sat out the war in Serbia or assisted the attacking forces. But for visitors the only remaining danger is the threat of (well-marked) minefields that make the war more real than anywhere else in the country. It is wise not to express any strong opinions you have on the Balkans in this part of Croatia, though once the local people feel comfortable they are often more than happy to fill visitors in on the personal stories behind the TV news reports.

East of Zagreb

The Croatian word for motorway is *autocesta* and this is the nickname given to the once crucial artery connecting Zagreb with Eastern Croatia and on towards Serbia and Belgrade. It is a final ironic nail in the Yugoslav coffin that the road once called the "Motorway of Brotherhood and Unity" by Tito is now effectively the

road to nowhere with few users venturing across the new border with Serbia although it is open. There are, though, a handful of worthwhile diversions to break the journey to the Slavonia region, where most of the interesting parts of Eastern Croatia are.

Lonjsko polje Nature Park (www.pp-lonjsko-polje.hr) ❶, less than 100km (60 miles) along the motorway from Zagreb, is a worthwhile diversion. Hugging the banks of the River Sava with Bosnia to the south, this long, thin area of seasonal wetlands is not really set up for overnight visitors, and so is ideal for a few hours or even as a day trip from Zagreb. Visitors are advised to bring their own food and drink, to wear anti-mosquito spray, long trousers, shirts with long sleeves and a sunhat. The birdlife includes storks, which swoop in every summer, herons and the rarely encountered white-tailed eagle. With over 600 pairs of storks Lonjsko polje has the greatest concentration in Europe. On land, local semi-wild Posavlje horses, the spotted Turopolje pig, wild boar, deer, beaver and wild cats can also be seen. The pigs have

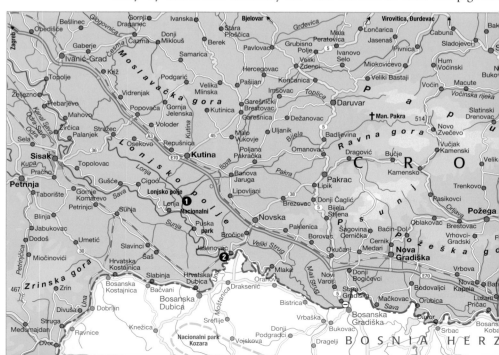

adapted to their watery environment by being excellent swimmers. **Sisak** is a useful base for exploring the area as it has places to stay and restaurants; the villages inside the reserve, such as Čigoć and Lonja, are not as well equipped for visitors. However, there is an information point in Čigoć (tel: 044 715115).

Jasenovac

It is possible to follow the old road from Sisak (22km/13 miles west of the *autocesta*) through the wetlands to **Jasenovac** ❷ (also just 10km/6 miles south of the *autocesta* itself). Visiting the town is not a trip that many Croatians recommend – indicative perhaps of the fact that Croatia still has to come to terms with what happened at Jasenovac and to accept some measure of national responsibility. Jasenovac was a Croatian Ustašeun concentration camp in World War II where anything from 70,000–1 million (depending on whose figures you believe) Serbs, Jews, Gypsies and political prisoners were executed by Croatians only too keen to follow and even exceed the Nazi blueprint. Even Hitler's representative in Zagreb, General Edmund

Glaise von Horstenau, was shocked at the conditions in the camps, describing them as "the epitome of horror" and admonishing the Ustaše in letters to his superiors. Today there is little left of the original camp, but the voluminous grass void tells its own story. At its heart is a huge metallic sculpture, a monument to all who perished in the camp.

The **Memorial Museum** (Javna ustanova Spomen-područje Jasenovac; www.jusp-jasenovac.hr; Tue–Fri 9am–5pm, Sat–Sun 10am–4pm; free) has three permanent exhibitions, including a list of individual victims. The village of Jasenovac saw war return in 1991 when the local Serbs, backed up by the Yugoslav Army, took the town, expelled Croatian residents and dynamited the Catholic churches. In a vicious circle of retaliation that was repeated throughout Croatia in 1995 the Croatian Army and Croatian irregulars sought their revenge by expelling Serbs and defacing the Orthodox churches.

Industrial belt

Continuing along the *autocesta*, you reach **Slavonski Brod** ❸, 180km (112

A sign warning of the danger of land mines, which are still a significant hazard in eastern Croatia.

TIP

Getting good value accommodation in Eastern Croatia can be a problem as the region is not really set up for tourism. The few hotels that do exist cater mainly for business people. Often the best bet is to ask at the local tourist office for details of residents who let out rooms in their homes.

miles) from Zagreb. Before the war few tourists ever breezed into this industrial city and the trickle stopped completely during the fighting as the city lies right on the River Sava, which forms a natural border with Bosnia. The local authorities are trying hard to rebuild the city centre and attract tourists.

The highlight is the Baroque 18th-century **Brod Fortress**, once a pivotal bulwark against the Ottoman Empire, with much of the original perimeter in the Vauban style still standing today. As late as the Homeland War it retained its original purpose, housing soldiers of the Yugoslav Army. An ongoing reconstruction is designed to breathe life back into what was once the focus of the town, with school buildings, local government offices and a rebuilt chapel taking shape inside the old walls and the former moat refilled with water for its new role as a town park. Progress so far has been impressive if slow, because of lack of funds, and it is a sign of the town's determination to shake off the effects of a conflict whose bullet holes still scar many public buildings, not to mention civilian apartment blocks.

Other things to see in Slavonsk Brod include the Ružić Gallery (Galer ija Ružić), opened in 1995 inside th largest building in the fortress with collection of modern Croatian art an sculpture, as well as the work of th late Croatian sculptor Branko Ružić who was born in the town and died i Zagreb. The House of the Brlić Fam ily (Kuća Brlićevih) is a neoclassica building, whose original occupant entertained many of Croatia's leadin luminaries of culture and politics. I is now a museum and art gallery. Th **Museum of the Sava Valley** (Muze brodskog posavlja; Mon–Fri 10am 1pm and 5–8pm, Sun 10am–1pm charge) spreads across two building and houses artefacts dug up from a over Slavonia. Exhibits include fos sils of an elephant, Bronze Age piece and leg armour dating back to Roma times. The Baroque 18th-century Fran ciscan Monastery is another Slavonsk Brod highlight.

Strossmayer's cathedral

Another 35km (22 miles) along th *autocesta* and then a 30km (18-mile drive north along a minor road is th town of **Đakovo ❹**, which would hav remained fairly anonymous were it no for one of Croatia's most colourful reli gious figures, Bishop Strossmayer. Th bishop's epic vision of a pan-Slavi nation at a time when the regio was firmly suppressed under Austro Hungarian rule is echoed in the volu minous sweep of the twin towers o the cathedral that he commissioned As you approach Đakovo the tower loom like huge space rockets awai ing lift-off; the interior is equally eye catching, with large, brightly coloure paintings of biblical scenes stretchin along the walls, the work of Alexan der and Ljudevit Seitz. The **cathedra** (daily 6am–noon, 3–8pm) was built i the 19th century in the Gothic style b Baron Frederick Schmidt. Look ou for the tomb that holds the remain of the controversial bishop and als in the road opposite, for the statue o

BELOW: Brod Fortress was built as a defence against the Ottoman forces.

trossmayer pointing proudly towards his architectural legacy, described by Pope John XXIII as "the most beautiful church between Venice and Istanbul".

If you want to take your interest in this turbulent priest further then head next door to the **Strossmayer Museum** (Muzej Jj Strossmayera; Tue–Fri 8am–8pm, Sat 8am–1.30pm) with its small collection of his scribblings and other artefacts that give a taste of his life. Continue down Kralja Tomislava, a pedestrianised thoroughfare that has a number of attractive outdoor cafés where you can have a coffee or savour the local Slavonian beer, Osiječko. At the end of the street is a squat church that was built into an old mosque. Continue in the same direction and you will come to a modern sculpture, *The Three Crosses*, erected in 1991. This gleaming tangle of steel provides an interesting visual counterpoint to the spires of the cathedral at the other end of town and commemorates all those who died in the Homeland War.

Slavonia's largest city

Half an hour farther north by road is Osijek ❺, Slavonia's largest settlement and an intriguing city that justifies a stay of a few days, especially if you are using it as a base for exploring the rest of the region. The history of the city dates back to the Romans who breezed through town in the first century, though barbarian attacks wiped out all traces of Roman Osijek. Osijek went on to serve as a fortress town for the Ausro-Hungarian Empire in its efforts to keep the Ottoman Empire at bay and here are many 18th-century reminders of that period as well as some handsome 19th-century buildings.

Although memories of war rarely fade quickly in this corner of Europe – Osijek endured a nine-month battering at the hands of the Serbs, which left around ,000 inhabitants dead and many buildings badly scarred – there are many signs that its once legendary cosmopolitan café life and joie de vivre are returning, especially in summer when the water-

front is once again crowded with people relaxing in its cafés and bars.

Upper, lower and old town

The city is split into three distinct areas that huddle on the banks of the fast moving Drava River: Gornji grad (Upper Town), the Tvrđa old town and Donji grad (Lower Town), the first two of which are of most interest to visitors. The centre of Osijek is still dominated by the **Cathedral of St Peter and St Paul** (Katedrala sv. Petra i Pavla), commissioned by Bishop Strossmayer, who was born here. This voluminous red-brick edifice, with its 90-metre (300ft) tall tower, was designed by German architect Franz Langenberg, but his original plans had to be modified after his sudden death in 1895 and the Viennese architect Richard Jordan took over the reins. The interior is graced with impressive stained-glass windows and brightly coloured paintings by Mirko Rački.

Walk further away from the Drava on the same street and you will soon come to the **Croatian National Theatre** (Hrvatsko narodno kazalište),

Croatia has a long tradition of breeding thoroughbred Lipizzaner horses, highly prized by professional equestrians. Founded in 1905, its largest stud farm is near the Slavonian town of Lipik. In 1991 many of the horses died after a napalm-bomb attack and the Serbs took the remaining ones to Serbia. The stud farm remained empty until 2007, when the Serbian government returned some of the stolen horses.

BELOW: phoning home in Đakovo.

Osijek's 18th- and 19th-century heyday is recalled by its fine buildings, though many are scarred by bullet holes from the Homeland War.

whose ground floor has been occupied, much to the chagrin of many locals, by a well-known international fast-food chain, but its facade has been impressively restored. A marvellous example of the Venetian-Moorish style, the theatre was built in 1866, and is one of only four national theatres in Croatia.

Head back past the cathedral to Trg Ante Starčevića and then walk east and you will come to Europska avenija, once one of Croatia's grandest boulevards and still a superb ensemble of Art Nouveau architecture. On both sides wealthy Austro-Hungarian and German families erected grand testaments to their fortunes, each with their own unique and often delightfully overblown decorative touches. Nos 12 and 22 are particularly fine. The thoroughfare was badly damaged during the Homeland War, but painstaking restoration work is bringing it back to its former glory. Financing this work remains a problem: larger investment interests such as banks are able to renovate but, as in much of central and eastern Europe, there is little state or private money to cover

the rest. The **Gallery of Fine Art** (Galerija likovnih umjetnosti; www gluo.hr; Tue, Wed and Fri, 10am–6pm Thur 10am–8pm, Sat–Sun 10am–1pm charge; free on Tue and Sun) at No 9 is one of the country's finest show cases of Croatian painting from the 18th century onwards.

Baroque fortress

A brace of Osijek's 17 parks envelope Europska as it heads east towards Tvrđa – look out for the plaque to the lef marking the spot where Croatian force dynamited a statue of a woman cradling a child that commemorated all victim of World War II, including both loca Croats and Serbs. As you walk through the park the Baroque fortress of **Tvrđa** rises up on the riverside. Built in stage in the first half of the 18th century, the fortress was intended to prevent the Ottomans from ever occupying the town again – the Turks having been forced out of Osijek as late as 1687.

After World War II the Yugoslav Army used Tvrđa as a base and it fell into disrepair before suffering furthe in 1991–2 when the same forces bom barded it with shells from outside the city. Money from the Croatian gov ernment has helped in the rebuilding process and the Catholic Church ha helped to address the severe beating meted out to Tvrđa's churches. Life i slowly returning to Tvrđa with Osijek University moving into many of the former barracks and old administration blocks. While most of Tvrđa's roofs and roads have been shored up there is stil a lot of work to be done, work which may accelerate if Osijek is successful in its current attempts to get Tvrđa place on the Unesco World Heritage List.

The centrepiece of Tvrđa is **Trg sveto Trojstva**, a grand square surrounded b impressive Austro-Hungarian militar buildings. At its heart is a plague co umn commissioned in 1729 by the wif of a local commander in thanks for th city being relieved of an outbreak o the disease. On the western flank o the square is the main guard building

with a clock tower, colonnaded exterior and a couple of small cannons. A sprinkling of cafés and bars now also occupy one end of the square, and at night the laughter and rowdy escapades of local students breathe life into the area.

Also in Tvrđa is **St Michael's Church (Crkva sv. Mihaila)**, with its signature twin towers, whose gleaming appearance inside and out is the result of an almost total reconstruction.

Back past the main square the church of Tvrđa's **Franciscan Monastery** (Franjevački samostan) has been impressively renovated and although it is rarely open to the public you can see the dimly-lit Baroque interior, with its impressive 15th-century statue of Mary and Judas, through the glass.

From the monastery head downhill towards the only one of the four original gates still left standing, with the only surviving Tvrđa defensive tower nearby. Leaving the gate brings you out on to the banks of the Drava River, in its final flourish before the mighty Danube swallows it up just downstream. Look across the water and there is the surreal apparition of the ambitiously named Copacabana – a modest stretch of riverside sand, backed up with swimming pools, a water slide and a restaurant. However, hardcore beach lovers may be better off looking a little bit farther along the coast.

Spa treat

The legacy of war, sparse tourist facilities and long distances on the motorway can make visiting Slavonia a gruelling experience, but there are two great places to recuperate near Osijek. You can either spend a day or two in the Kopački rit Nature Park, just 12km (8 miles) from Osijek *(see page 139)*; or in the spa of **Bizovač ❻**, 20km (12 miles) west of the city. From a depth of 2km (1¼ miles) below the earth's surface bubbling water gushes forth into four indoor and two outdoor pools. The waters are said to be of particular benefit for skin conditions and stress disorders. In addition there are swimming pools, whirlpools, a small water park with slides and tennis courts. It is easy to visit the spa on a day trip, but for more relaxation overnight accommodation is available on-site.

BELOW: inside Osijek's cathedral of St Peter and St Paul.

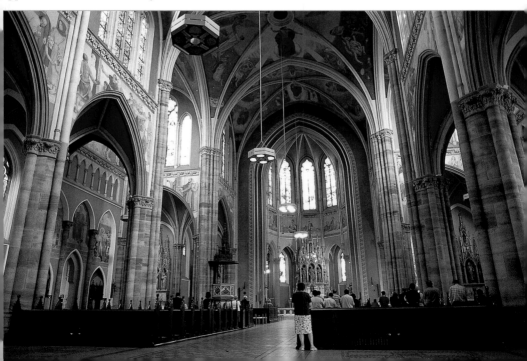

EAT

While in Eastern Croatia try *fiš paprikaš*, a delicious spicy fish stew native to Slavonia, that features river fish such as carp, catfish and pike.

Battle-scarred Vukovar

Today it takes around 30 minutes to drive south from Osijek to **Vukovar** ❼; during the war in the early 1990s the journey through the flat cornfields was suicidal. Vukovar is a name synonymous with Croatian suffering, a name that evokes a reaction in every Croat when it is mentioned. For three months in 1991 the lightly armed inhabitants of the Baroque town of Vukovar, which hugs a picturesque bend in the River Danube, were subject to the sort of savage and devastating siege not experienced in Europe since World War II *(see page 141)*.

Visiting is not an enjoyable experience as such, but by and large the locals are very keen on outsiders coming to learn more about their experiences and to bring in some much needed cash to help in the rebuilding work. Visiting the town is completely safe: all ordinance has been removed and all central areas de-mined, though walking around the surrounding cornfields is dangerous. Venturing into the embittered Serbian suburb of Borovo Selo is also inadvisable without local contacts.

Today Vukovar is trying to rebuild, but one of its main problems is that it is a geopolitical anomaly. Before the war the majority of its population was Croat, with a large Serbian minority. Today the balance has shifted, with only about a third of the original population left and roughly equal numbers of highly polarised Croats and Serbs, most living in segregated conditions, with separate schools and other institutions. The Serbs may have "won" the battle over Vukovar, but the UN passed the town back to Croatian control in 1998, and it appears that the central government is reluctant to channel vast funds into a now half Serbian town when so many other areas of the country still need attention. Also, many of the 20,000 Croat refugees who left in 1991 have shown little interest in returning to the economically depressed town, where jobs and accommodation are in short supply.

An essential first stop is the tourist office on the main street, which can give information on current rebuilding projects and, with a few days' notice, provide English-speaking guides (tel: 032 442889; www.turizamvukovar.hr).

A fallen city

Vukovar town centre is a sad shadow of its former self. Most of the buildings have new roofs and the roads have been resurfaced, but many beautiful Baroque buildings are skeletons, including Radnički dom (House of the Workers) where one of the first meetings of the Yugoslav Communist Party took place in 1920. The jumble of ruined buildings leads down to the river and a memorial where many Croats, who watched the plight of Vukovar unfold on their television screens, come to lay flowers. Do not enter abandoned buildings, which may still have landmines or be in danger of collapse, and take care to stick to footpaths on the edge of town.

Before the war Vukovar's most graceful 18th-century building was the Eltz Palace, built by a local noble family and reconstructed after the war. It contains a small **Town Museum** (Gradski

BELOW: a quiet street in Vukovar.

muzej; daily 7am–3pm; charge) containing a few prehistoric and Roman pieces, portraits of local nobles and luminaries from the 18th-century golden age of Vukovar. Much of the museum's collection was looted in the war and returned from Serbia in 2001 after painstaking diplomacy, while many of the paintings were donated by artists around Europe.

Uphill from the town centre is the **Franciscan Monastery** (Franjevački samostan). The Franciscans were hugely important in the history and culture of Vukovar and had seven monasteries here in the Middle Ages. The exterior has been impressively renovated, disguising the sad dereliction of the interior, although regular services once again take place here. Like many projects in Vukovar the original rush of funds to shore up buildings has dried up. One structure that may never be renovated is the voluminous water tower, visible from many parts of the town.

Another symbol of the war is the **Place of Memory** (Mjesto sjećanja; Županijska ulica 37; Mon–Fri 1–3pm) in the basement of the city hospital that kept going through heavy shelling, with exhibits poignantly recapturing life under the siege.

On a plain on the outskirts of Vukovar is the **war cemetery** (Memorijalno groblje žrtava iz Domovinskog rata), separated between the defenders of Vukovar and civilians, though the division between the two during the siege was blurred as many had little choice but to become involved. In the centre are hundreds of white crosses marking those whose bodies were never found.

Border land

Close to the border with Serbia, 7km (4 miles) from Vukovar, is **Ovčara** ❽, where one of the worst atrocities of the war took place. On capturing Vukovar, Serbian forces removed around 300 local hospital patients from under the noses of the International Red Cross. After being badly beaten, the prisoners were held for three days and then taken off and shot. A simple memorial now marks the spot where they were murdered. Some of the higher-ranking officers involved have been indicted by the Hague War Crimes

Slavonia's rich soil makes it the most important region for agriculture.

BELOW: Kopački rit Nature Park.

Kopački rit Nature Park

Kopački rit Nature Park is a must for ornithologists but also a wonderful day trip for less committed bird lovers. One of the largest inland wetlands in Europe, sprawling across 180 sq km (70 sq miles) at the confluence of the Danube and Drava rivers, it has over 260 species of bird, including white-tailed eagles, woodpeckers, kingfishers and black storks. The waters teem with over 40 fish species from pike and perch, through to carp and catfish. The park is also home to deer, pine martens, wild cats and wild boar.

During the war of the 1990s, the park was occupied by Serb forces and heavily mined. Most areas have now been cleared but it is essential to stick to trails designated as safe. The best way to discover the park is to take a guide. For further information, visit www.kopacki-rit.com.

Tribunal, but some Croat residents of Vukovar complain that the ordinary soldiers and irregulars involved were never brought to justice. There is no public transport to the memorial and the minor road there is difficult to follow, so it is advisable to get detailed instructions from the tourist office before setting out.

Frontier town

Heading 29km (18 miles) further east from Vukovar you reach **Ilok** , a small town – Croatia's easternmost – with a real frontier feel, overlooking the Danube and right on the Serbian border. Before the war this ethnically mixed town with large Slovak, Serb and Hungarian minorities was a prosperous agricultural centre renowned for the quality of its wine – Traminer, Burgundy and Grasevina. There are signs of a recovery in production; the grape harvest takes place at the end of September/beginning of October.

Architecturally the town is also interesting with Islamic styles blending into the traditional Pannonian buildings, a legacy of the days when Ilok was a tolerant multiethnic hub. It is encouraging to witness the residents of a town who have every reason to feel bitter and depressed, getting back on their feet and managing to kick-start their lives.

Northern area

From the Osijek region the only possibility is to turn around and travel back. For a change of scene you can return via the northern route rather than along the *autocesta*, initially flanking the Drava River and the Hungarian border and cutting south at **Đurđevac**, which has a medieval castle, to **Bjelovar** with its superb farmer's market (Mon–Sat) or the pleasant town of **Varaždin**, a good base for exploring the Zagorje *(see page 115)*. The agricultural flatlands of corn and sunflowers interrupted by tidy villages and towns have few sights and even fewer hotels, but the route gives an insight into rural and provincial life.

One such insight is to be found at **Hlebine**, near the administrative centre of Kroprivnica on the way to Varaždin. This typical Podravina village evolved into a centre for naïve art following the discovery of the work of the self-taught painter Ivan Generalić by the Paris-trained artist Krsto Hegedašic in the 1930s. Its **Hlebine Gallery of Naïve Art** (Galerija naivne umjetnosti Hlebine; Mon–Sat 10am–4pm; charge) contains the work of many naïve artists, including Generalić and his son Josip. Among the most notable paintings on display are Ivan Generalić's *The Tower (see picture, pages 128–9)*.

The Hlebine School, which evolved from a local art club, explores rural themes, using intense colours and metaphor. It was championed by the Croatian Peasant Party (HSS) and viewed as an authentic expression of Croatian culture free of Western influences.

Koprivnica also has a showcase of naïve art, the **Koprivnica Gallery** (Galerija Koprivnica; Mon–Fri 8am–2pm, Sat 10am–1pm), as well as a 17th-century Franciscan monastery and an 18th-century Orthodox church catering to the town's large Serbian minority. ❑

BELOW: native art in the village of Ernestinovo, near Osijek.

The Vukovar Siege

Since World War II, few places in Europe have been better witness to the worst aspects of nationalism and the futility of war than Vukovar.

I t is hard to comprehend the full horror of the Siege of Vukovar. For three months the might of the Yugoslav Army, with more than 40,000 troops and 600 tanks, was brought to bear on a Baroque town whose residents scraped by with no electricity or running water and precious little food. Almost every building was shattered, 2,000 citizens were killed and more than 4,000 wounded as the town was razed to a hollow shell of its former self.

The determination of Vukovar's residents to resist the attacks was replayed nightly on Croatian TV, but international media attention was concentrated on the less bloody siege further south in Dubrovnik. Inevitably the town fell. The stiff resistance of Vukovar, though, slowed up the Serbian advance, weakened Yugoslav Army morale and dispelled any notions that dragging Eastern Croatia into "Greater Serbia" was going to be easy.

Before the conflict, in the spring of 1991, Vukovar had more than 44,000 citizens, roughly 44 percent Croat and 37 percent Serb, with significant Bosnian, Hungarian, German and Slovak minorities. As tensions rose around the rest of the country attempts were made to mediate between local Croats and Serbs, but the Serb population clandestinely received arms from elements of the Yugoslav Army and the Serb-dominated suburb of Borovo Selo became a no-go area for Croats.

On 2 May 1991, a bus load of Croat policemen was ambushed and massacred in Borovo Selo. The Yugoslav Army became involved on the pretext that it was there to separate the skirmishing Croats and Serbs. However, the army joined forces with Serb irregulars and mounted a ferocious siege using mortars, howitzers, bomber jets and navy gunships, surrounding the Croats on all sides.

The defenders of Vukovar – mainly Croats but also some Serbs and other ethnic minorities – were armed with little more than hunting rifles or old World War II relics, if they had any weapons at all. The battle lines were drawn across the mined cornfields on the town's perimeter and while the defenders were able to confront the infantry and tank attacks they could do little about the shells raining in from afar. At the height of the siege up to 10,000 explosives a night pummelled Vukovar, driving the residents to their cellars. Both the Yugoslav Army and Serb irregulars thwarted repeated attempts by international organisations to relieve Vukovar and evacuate the wounded. For those not fit or rash enough to make the dangerous dash for freedom across the cornfields there was no escape.

By the start of November the dwindling number of defenders could offer less and less resistance. On 18 November the Serbs rolled into Vukovar. Men of fighting age were rounded up and there were summary executions. More than 2,000 people are still listed as missing.

The irony is that the Serbian victory was a hollow one. The town they inherited was virtually worthless and Serbia handed it back to Croatia in 1998 through the UN. As the international community began to comprehend the extent of the atrocities that had been committed there was a stiffening resolve to avoid "another Vukovar".

On the eastern approach road to Vukovar the biggest mass grave in Europe assembled since World War II – with 938 white crosses – is an eerie and oddly compelling aspect of a visit to the town. ❑

RIGHT: the memorial by the river in Vukovar.

NAÏVE ART

A speciality of Croatia, "peasant" painting on glass has never gone out of fashion

If anything is guaranteed to cheer you up, it is a visit to the The Croatian Naïve Art Museum in Zagreb. On the second floor of the 18th-century Raffay Palace, it opened with state finance in 1952, and was hailed as the first museum of naïve art in the world. Its collection of life-affirming works of art date from the 1930s and the Hlebine School (see opposite) to the present day.

The style is deeply rooted in central European peasant painting mixed with a touch of Breughel. These delightful scenes of rural life are rich in imagination and exquisitely executed. The earlier, pre-war paintings had a serious side, depicting social injustice. Later works became more abstract and dreamy, but retained their essential peasant soul, with fetes and weddings, harvests and winter landscapes, and animated scenes of village life.

Many are *sous verre*, painted in oils in reverse on glass, a tricky technique that emerged in central Europe and around the Ottoman empire in the late 19th century. It involves putting the final touches on the glass first and working up into the background. This technique gives the colours, viewed through the glass, a luminous quality.

The town of Hlebine, near the Hungarian border, birthplace of the great Ivan Generalić (1914–92) and fellow artists Franjo Mraz (1910–81) and Mirko Virius (1889–1943), also has a museum collection of its eponymous school associated with the town.

These paintings today can command high prices. In 2008, 100 works of Croatian reverse-glass naïve art were a highlight of the prestigious Art Basel in Miami, and prices were over $5,000. A few months earlier a Generalić sold at auction for just over $10,000.

ABOVE: this landscape Ivan Rabuzin (1921–2008) has the qual of a quilt.

BELOW: the artistic tradition continues around the country.

ABOVE RIGHT: *Farm in the Snow*, by Ivan Lacković (1932–2004) from Padrovina, one of many self-taught artists who found international acclaim.

THE HLEBINE SCHOOL

Krsto Hegedušić, the founder of Croatia's 20th-century naïve art movement, was born in 1901 into a family who came from the village of Hlebine on the misty Panovina plain near the Drava river. On entering the Arts and Crafts College in Zagreb at the age of 19, he began painting his home village from memory and a few years afterwards, on a scholarship to Paris, he became entranced by the work of Pieter Breughel. On his return to Croatia he organised an exhibition at the Zagreb Art Pavillion for a prolific 17-year-old artist from Hlebine – this was Ivan Generalić, the son of local peasants whose thatched, single storey, mud-rendered building looked out over a pond where geese and pigs roamed. A member of Zemlja ("soil"), group of Marxist artists, Hegedušić founded the Hlebine School in 1930. After the war he became a professor at the Zagreb Academy, illustrating books and designing theatre sets, while his protégé, Generalić, went on to become the finest exponent of Croatian naïve art.

Above: the Croatian Museum of Naive Art in Hlebine, centre of the 20th-century movement.

Right: wood carving in the naive art park at Ernestinovo, near Osijek, where a colony was founded in 1974 by Peter Smajić

ʌʙᴏᴠᴇ: this painting in the Croatian Naïve Art Museum is by Emerik ʃ who used matchsticks instead of paintbrushes.

THE ISTRIAN COAST

Though geared to package tourism, Istria's resorts have a distinctive Croatian-cum-Italian character, and in between the modern developments there are impressive archaeological sites

• Zagreb

he northern region of Istria is practically a country in itself, a sun-kissed peninsula given over to the demands of mass tourism for much of the year. Indeed, many locals often describe themselves as feeling more Istrian than Croatian, a sentiment that probably owes more to the amount of revenue generated by Istria's tourist industry for central government coffers in Zagreb than it does to any real desire for separatism.

With Istria capable of accommodating more than 200,000 visitors a night, it is by far Croatia's most developed and tourist-oriented enclave. The temptation to write it off as one big tourist resort, however, does not do justice to what is a visually dazzling corner of Croatia. The main tourist resorts – Rovinj and the granddaddy of them all, Poreč – are extensive, but they retain Croatian character and historical interest. Many of Istria's most interesting sights, such as the amphitheatre in Pula and the Basilica of Euphrasius in Poreč, date from Roman times. Smaller coastal resorts such as Umag and Novigrad also have much to offer.

The last two centuries have proven traumatic times for Istria with the peninsula's ownership passing from the Austro-Hungarian Empire to Napoleonic France and back again, before Italy wrested sovereignty in 1918. This was followed by a brief stint under Nazi Germany's grip, after which Istria was incorporated into Yugoslavia. It

finally became part of the independent Republic of Croatia in the early 1990s. Istria escaped direct involvement in the conflict of those years thanks to its westerly location. The region's future has never looked brighter as tourists return to the coastal resorts and more adventurous visitors head inland on *agroturizam* programmes.

Italian influences abound. The peninsula was part of Italy for 25 years between 1918 and 1943 and although there was a large exodus of ethnic Italians (around 200–350,000) when it

Main attractions
PULA
BRIJUNI ISLANDS
ROVINJ
POREČ
NOVIGRAD, UMAG AND
    SAVUDRIJA
RAŠA, LABIN AND RABAC

PRECEDING PAGES:
on the corniche, Vrsar.
LEFT AND BELOW:
views from the tower of St Martin's church, Vrsar.

A café in Pula, Istria's oldest town and largest port.

became part of Yugoslavia, thousands still live here. Most Istrians speak fluent Italian, Venetian-style architecture characterises the main towns, many signs are bilingual and Istrians frequently slip between Italian and Croatian in the same sentence. Pasta, truffles, balsamic vinegar and prosciutto are on the menus and the pizzas are often as good as in Italy.

Ancient and modern in Pula

As the only city in Istria, with a smattering of industry and the working port that goes with it, **Pula ❶** has gained something of an unwarranted reputation as the ugly sister to its more illustrious siblings further west. The sprawl of docks are an eyesore –

although Pulans are generally proud of them – and the traffic can be infuriating, but Pula is Istria's oldest town with a captivating Roman history a the town of Polensium, founded 4 BC. As the Romans built roads, villa and settlements all over Istria, Pula was garrisoned as the main hub.

Latin remained the principal language even after the division of the Roman Empire, when Pula slipped under Byzantine control.

Pula also served as the Austro-Hungarian Empire's main naval base and it is Istria's largest port today, a well as being home to the region' only international airport.

The Roman legacy surfaces all over Pula. World War II Allied bombing raids actually helped uncover more

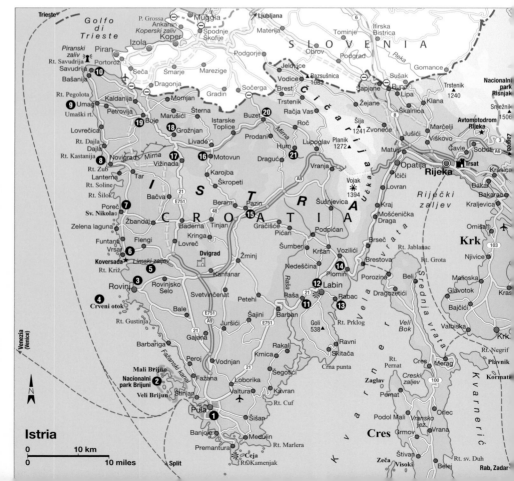

Istria

0   10 km

0   10 miles

f Pula's Roman heritage. The most impressive, and the most obvious point at which to begin a tour is the st-century **amphitheatre** (amfiteatar; aily, June–Sept 8am–9pm, Oct–May am–4.30pm; charge) set just back rom the waterfront on a street rather ptly called Gladijatorska. The amphi-heatre, also commonly known as the rena, is the world's sixth largest and he best for studying Roman building echniques; some 23,000 spectators ttended gladiatorial contests, naval attles and other amusements during s heyday. After wandering around the utside be sure to delve below ground nto the old holding cells where pris-ners were imprisoned whilst awaiting heir gruesome fate. The wild animals ere caged in the subterranean cellars.

The amphitheatre was built on a lope, partly to save money by reduc-ng the number of stones needed, and o has three floors on the side facing ne sea, two on the opposite side. Origi-ally it had about 20 entrances and it mployed a highly efficient network of nnels to ensure spectators got to and om their seats quickly.

The amphitheatre itself has survived various assaults over the past 2,000 years. Over the centuries whole lime-stone blocks, including much of the original seating, was removed to build local houses and in 1583, during Pula's stint as an outpost of the Venetian Republic, plans brewed to transport the whole structure across the Adriatic to Venice. The amphitheatre even suf-fered the ignominy of serving as a cat-tle market in the 5th century.

Today the gladiators and lions may be long gone, but the amphitheatre regularly hosts plays, festivals, classical concerts and, somewhat surreally, pop concerts by such artists as Sir Elton John and Sting. The annual Pula Film Festival at the end of July is also staged here. A highlight of a visit to Pula is catching any kind of performance amongst the ghosts of this mighty tes-tament to Istria's Roman heritage. It also houses a free exhibition of Roman amphorae salavaged from shipwrecks, and other equipment used for making and storing wine and olive oil.

A short walk south of the amphi-theatre, past Pula's main tourist infor-

When Mussolini ruled Istria he attempted to wipe out the indigenous culture. The Croatian language was banned in public and Croatian surnames were outlawed.

LEFT: Pula's Roman amphitheatre.

The Mummies of Vodnjan

There are few more eerie sights in all of Croatia than the "Mummies of Vodnjan". The desiccated bodies of three saints and the relics of others are preserved in St Blaise's Church in what is an otherwise unassuming town. St Blaise's itself is notable for being the largest par-ish church on the Istrian peninsula and also for having its highest cam-panile, which at 60 metres (200ft) tall matches the height of St Mark's in Venice. However, most visitors travel the 10km (6 miles) north of Pula to see the mummies, which are tucked behind a shroud of curtains to the rear of the main altar.

On display in a remarkably well-preserved state are the corpses of St Nikolosa Bursa, St Giovanni Olini and St Leon Bembo. The last of these, also known as St Leon Bembo the Blessed, is said to have turned his back on the intrigues of Venetian diplomacy to take up the austere life of a monk and cultivate his skills as a faith healer. Some Croatians still believe that the mummies possess magical powers, citing as evidence the uncannily preserved bodies.

Public buses from Pula to Rovinj and Poreč both stop off at Vodn-jan, dropping passengers off a short stroll from the church itself. The town is also notable for its large Italian-speaking community, who know it simply as Dignano.

TIP

In summer, concerts take place in the Sculpture Garden of the Archaeological Museum. Listening to classical music drifting through the statues on a warm evening is one of the best ways of experiencing the museum.

RIGHT: Pula's statue of James Joyce; the writer lived in the city for six months between 1903 and 1904.

mation centre, is the **Archaeological Museum of Istria** (Arheološki muzej Istre; May–Sept Mon–Sat 9am–8pm, Sun 10am–3pm, Dec–Apr Mon–Fri 9am–3pm; charge), which delivers less than it should in a city with such a rich ancient heritage, as many items are poorly displayed. Exhibits date from the Histrian era to the Slavs' arrival in the 7th century. The museum is, however, worth visiting for the sculpture garden alone.

Slightly further south is the **Triumphal Arch of Sergius** (Slavoluk obitelji Sergijevaca), dating from 27 BC, celebrating the powerful eponymous local family with a tribute etched into the stone. The arch was left looking rather forlorn when the original city walls were torn down in the 19th century. Continuing on through the arch and down Sergijevaca, you will come to the old **Roman forum**, once the hub of Polensium society, home to a medley of temples and public buildings where the minutiae of Roman life unfolded. Little of the original forum remains intact apart from the impressive **Temple of**

Augustus (Augustov hram; high season 9am–6pm; charge), built as a dedication to the eponymous emperor. The temple's construction took over a decade, with a grand facade of four Corinthian columns giving it a solid appearance. Inside are just some of the Roman artefacts, such as portraits and bronze pieces, unearthed from a city where myriad treasures still lie buried beneath the streets.

Back towards the east is the **Museum of Istrian History** (Povijesni muzej Istre; daily high season 8am–9pm, low season 9am–5pm; charge), inside a 17th-century Venetian fortress on the former site of the Roman Capitol (the hilltop site is a hot hike in summer).

Highlights include scale models of shipping vessels from various stages of Pula's maritime history, and displays relating to Italy's occupation of Istria during World War II, locally known as the "People's War of Liberation in Istria". The Romans chose the site well; it affords good views across the city and also of the seaward approaches to Pula.

Tito and Brijuni

Away from prying eyes of the vast majority of Yugoslav citizens, Tito ran the Brijuni islands as his private estate. In establishing Brijuni as his summer residence and luxury playground, he was in good company, as the remains of opulent villas built by Roman patricians attest. In the 19th century an Austrian magnate, Paul Kupelwieser bought the archipelago as an exotic retreat and built villas there for himself and his friends. After World War II the Brijuni Islands became part of Yugoslavia and in 1948 Tito made them his summer residence, renovating Kupelwieser's villas for himself and his guests. As the celebrity leader of the Non-Aligned Movement he hosted, with some extravagance, many world leaders such as Queen Elizabeth II, Emperor Haile Selassie, Indira Gandhi, Nasser and Nehru, as well as film stars including Sophia Loren, Elizabeth Taylor and Richard Burton. Tito's main palace was on the island of Vanga – currently off-limits to visitors without a special permit – while the larger island of Veli Brijun accommodated his guests. His Vanga palace also has historical importance as the place where Tito, Nasser and Nehru in 1956 formed the Non-Aligned Movement, a counterweight to the superpowers during the Cold War. It was common for state visitors to bring animals as presents and these formed the nucleus of today's Brijuni menagerie. Tito died in 1980 and the islands became a national park three years later.

The cathedral and south

Back down the hill, just before Pula's sprawling docks, is the **Cathedral of St Mary** (Katedrala sv. Marija; high season daily 10am–1pm and 4–8pm, low season Mass only), showing the city offers more than just its Roman heritage. Built on the site of a former Roman temple, the cathedral is home to a 3rd-century sarcophagus said to contain the remains of an 11th-century Hungarian king. The cathedral is a melange of architectural designs with the Renaissance facade the most memorable, though traces also remain of a 5th-century mosaic unearthed from beneath the cathedral's main body. Much of the 17th-century belfry recycles stone scavenged from the Roman amphitheatre.

South of the city centre is the green oasis of the **Verudela inlet**, where the city's busy marina is based. Austrian, British and German voices are an indication of the popularity of the yacht charters that use Pula as a base for exploring the spectacular coastlines and islands of Istria, the Kvarner Gulf and Dalmatia. The tree-lined bay makes for a pleasant stroll away from the city bustle.

Brijuni Islands

Set adrift in the Adriatic Sea just to the north of Pula are the **Brijuni Islands** ❷ (Brijunski otoci; www.brijuni.hr), once the private playground of yacht-loving Tito, who is said to have spent half his year on his favourite retreat. The 14 islands gained protected national park status in 1983 and public access to those without their own boats is only allowed on two of them, **Veli Brijun** and **Mali Brijun**, and even then visitors must either be staying at one of the hotels or villas on Veli Brijun or be part of an organised day tour.

Even before Tito brought the islands fame and entertained world leaders here, artists and writers such as James Joyce and Thomas Mann visited the islands. Franjo Tudjman also spent his summers as Croatian president here, though his successor since 2000, Stjepan Mesić, is reportedly less enthusiastic about spending time at this symbol of Communist decadence. Apart from the abundant wildlife other attractions include the ruins of a Byzantine castle, a small museum dedicated to Tito, with photographs of the celebrities he enter-

Istria is a favourite for family holidays. It was the only region in which tourism still functioned during the Homeland War and has long been a particular favourite of Italians.

BELOW: sailing to the Brijuni Islands.

tained during his long stint as Yugoslav leader, and the strange apparition that is the **Brijuni Safari Park**. Most residents are gifts from the bevy of fawning world leaders who came to visit Tito in his island hideaway. A motley collection of confused animals, including giraffes, llamas and zebras, now idle away their days here.

Regular day tours leave from Fažana, Pula and Rovinj on the mainland, but the experience is a shepherded and rushed one, with the island sightseeing conducted aboard a tourist train with an obligatory stop at a souvenir shop. Those who really do want to explore the islands for themselves would do better to stay overnight.

North to Rovinj

A short drive northwest up the E751 highway from Pula is **Rovinj ❸**, Istria's most attractive coastal resort and an excellent base for exploring the region. An island until connected to the mainland in the 18th century, Rovinj has flourished as a fishing port for centuries and you will still find a flotilla of colourful fishing boats bobbing in

the harbour. Its main attraction is it Venetian-style architecture dating from the 14th to 18th centuries, when it wa controlled by the Divine Republic This Venetian connection was to cos Rovinj dearly as Venice's great rivals the Genoans, frequently harassed th town when they were causing mischie in the Adriatic.

Rovinj is home to Croatia's larges cigarette manufacturer, TDR – also th city's largest single employer. The tou ist industry is becoming increasingl important, both for mass tourism Istria's traditional market, and mor exclusive customers, for whom a luxur boutique hotel and niche shops cate Plans brew to build a luxury resort o the nearby island of Sveti Katarina, bu for now there are plenty of places t stay in and around Rovinj, as well a all the tourist trappings, such as boa tours, multilingual menus and souve nir shops. Yet somehow this ancien town manages to retain its character.

For many visitors the highligh of visiting Rovinj is just wanderin around the old town and explorin the narrow lanes. Old women sit i

Venetian Influences

The Venetian-style architecture that you see all over Istria is evidence of Istria's close ties with the Divine Republic from the Venetian conquest of the Adriatic coast in 1420 until its fall in 1797. Control of the coast was vital to securing the republic's all-important trade routes against the Genoans and the notorious pirates of Senj *(see page 188)*. Istrian and Dalmatian ports were fortified with enclosing walls and lookout towers, and also beautified as they developed their own prosperous merchant class. Istria's quarries were a handy source of fine white stone, which was also used to build many of the finest palaces in Venice.

Soon the Adriatic Sea was known as the "Gulf of Venice", and from here the republic quickly pushed on to conquer Greece, Cyprus and many territories in mainland Italy.

Venetian Gothic is the most visible style of architecture throughout Istria, most splendidly seen in the elegant piazzas of Rovinj and Poreč, but also in bell towers of quite small villages. Typical features include rose windows, ogival (pointed) arches, loggias and fine slender columns. Facades sometimes incorporate the traditional symbol of the Divine Republic, the winged Lion of St Mark holding a book inscribed with the word *Pax*.

Map on
page 148

flower-shrouded windows and tiny bars fill with grappa-drinking locals. Rovinj's reputation as an enclave of artists and painters was rediscovered after World War II, when the government lured local artists into the old town with cheap rents. Myriad small galleries and workshops line the winding streets – follow **Grisia** as it tumbles seaward from St Euphemia's Church, a street lined with small galleries, jewellers and other niche shops showcasing Rovinj's bountiful artistic talent and creative spirit.

The atmospheric old town rambles around a small limestone peninsula, culminating in the voluminous **Church of St Euphemia** (Crkva sv. Eufemije), named after Rovinj's patron saint. The present building only dates from the 18th century, but it dominates Rovinj's skyline and has Istria's tallest bell tower, said to be modelled on the campanile in Venice. Look out also for the statue of St Euphemia rotating at the top. Local fishermen, who pray here for a good catch, have complained that since a recent renovation, using a helicopter to bring the

statue down, she no longer gives such accurate weather forecasts. Today the church hosts classical concerts during the Rovinj Summer Festival in July and August when musicians from Germany, Russia, Slovenia and elsewhere join domestic talent.

Many legends and myths haunt the church, including the particularly intriguing story of St Euphemia herself. She is said to have been thrown to the lions for her Christian beliefs at the order of Emperor Diocletian and her body later vanished from Constantinople before appearing off the Istrian coast aboard a ghostly transport in the 9th century. Local legend has it that moving her 6th-century sarcophagus from the shore to the lofty church seemed an impossible task until a local boy herding cattle received a divine calling and spirited the sarcophagus up the hillside.

Look out for the small and very faded 14th-century marble relief of St Euphemia to the right of the church's side door, as well as the altar dedicated to her on the apse's right-hand side. The saint's heavily waxed remains

In August Istria's artists head to Rovinj for the annual arts festival. Grisia is transformed into an open-air gallery with some unusual works on sale for those prepared to delve beneath the touristy watercolours depicting Rovinj's skyline.

BELOW: the old town of Rovinj in the early morning.

The glut of souvenir stalls, multilingual menus and touts selling boat tours do not detract from Rovinj's charm. The tourist office can help you find reliable merchants.

RIGHT: one of the many fine sunsets viewed from Rovinj.

are visible through a panel in the sarcophagus. A poignant recent addition is the wooden altar donated by refugees from Vukovar to thank the local people for their help during and after Serbia's siege of the city in 1991.

Rovinj's **Heritage Museum** (Zavičajni muzej; high season Tue–Fri 9am–3pm and 7–10pm, Sat–Sun 9am–2pm and 7–10pm, low season Tue–Sat 9am–3pm; charge) is housed in a Baroque creation. The eclectic exhibits range from paintings from the 15th and 16th centuries, including Pietro Mera's *Christ Crowned with Thorns* and works by Venetian artists, right through to the works of Rovinj's own painters. There are a number of traditional folk costumes on display, as well as various artefacts unearthed on digs in the surrounding region. Also in the museum are a few moderately interesting Etruscan pieces and some fine examples of antique furniture.

Back east over the channel that originally rendered Rovinj's old town an island, before it was paved over, is the **Franciscan Monastery** (Franjevački samostan), built at the beginning of

the 18th century in Baroque style atop a hilly mound. The monastery contains an old library and a museum displaying18th- and 19th-century paintings as well as ecclesiastical robes and religious artworks.

On the waterfront to the north, just outside the old town, is the **aquarium** (*akvarij*; high season 9am–9pm, low season 10am–5pm; charge), part of the **Ruđer Bošković Centre for Maritime Research** (Institut Ruđer Bošković; www.irb.hr) and a good alternative for those unable to snorkel or dive in the clear waters around Rovinj. The aquarium dates from 1891 and houses a collage of colourful Istrian sea life, from sea bed dwellers through to brightly coloured and poisonous fish. It may not be particularly high tech, but it is a useful distraction for younger visitors bored with churches and art galleries.

Sensational sunsets

Rovinj's sunsets are justly famous, with the island of **Sveti Katarina** a particularly good place to watch the old town and the church of St Euphemia

The Italians of Croatia

While relations between Serbs and Croats have received endless attention, the no less complicated situation of its significant Italian minority has had less international attention. Anyone visiting Istria will find Italian influences aplenty, from the food to the bilingual signs, and the considerable ethnic Italian minority is particularly active in cultural life. However, the Italian population was once much higher. Some 90 percent of Italians in Croatia live on the coast. Many migrated to what is now Croatia when Istria and some other regions became part of Italy between 1918 and 1943, but others are descended from much earlier immigrants.

Under Mussolini the Fascist troops forced Croats to Italianise or leave. The 1936 census indicated some 194,000 Italian speakers in Croatia. From 1945 to 1953 around 200,000 Italians left Croatia and took up Italian citizenship, leaving only 36,000 in the whole of Yugoslavia, most of them in Croatia. Emigration continued under Communism, although mostly to the US, Australia, South America and Canada. Although most Italians live near the sea and do not work in agriculture, there is also a smaller inland community descended from farmers who migrated at the turn of the 20th century. Today there is a well-organised Italian Federation *(Unione Italiana)* representing the interests of Croatia's Italians, as well as several Italian-language newspapers and magazines.

illuminated by an explosion of red and orange hues. Regular boats to and from Sveti Katarina leave from the jetty next to the Delfin Travel Agency. Back in town the rocks at Valentino's Cocktail Bar are the best place from which to view the sunset – cushions are dispensed on arrival and mellow music accompanies the sun's slow descent into the Adriatic.

After sundown the action moves on to the many bars, cafés, trattorias, pizzerias and osterias that line the waterfront, with the scene taking on a distinctly Italian feel.

Best boat trip

A worthwhile day or half-day trip by boat from Rovinj is to **Crveni otok ➍**, or Red Island, which is actually two islands connected by a causeway. One islet has two tourist hotels, while the other is home to a popular naturist resort. Both are heavily wooded and provide peaceful walks. The islands are also much better for swimming than Rovinj, which is often crowded. Boats leave regularly from Rovinj's waterfront in high season.

From Rovinj to Poreč

Limski zaljev ➎, or Lim Fjord, is a 9km (5-mile) long flooded karst fjord that looks unlike anywhere else in Istria, with its massive rock walls, emerald-green waters and unusual vegetation. Adriatic pirates used to plan ambushes from the sanctuary of this hidden world, but today the only evidence of human activity are the seafood restaurants and the remains of two prehistoric caves. Those with their own transport, who are planning to head from Rovinj to Poreč, are well advised to avoid rejoining the fast inland road and instead curl around the old route passing the fjord. This diversion provides easy access to the seafood restaurants at the head of the fjord, which are ideal for a lazy lunch – specialities include the bountiful local oysters and mussels that are landed in the fjord. From the waterside the Poreč road climbs past a wooden viewing tower that opens up a cross-section of the forest-shrouded fjord as it snakes away seaward bound.

Just before the road reaches Poreč it comes to the small town of **Vrsar ➏**,

The Istrian village of Žejane is the centre of what is claimed to be the smallest ethnic and linguistic group in Europe, the Istro-Romanians, with an estimated population of around 1,000. Their language, which is closely related to Romanian, is, according to Unesco "seriously endangered", with only around a few hundred mostly elderly speakers.

BELOW:
the market on Trg Valdobora, Rovinj.

TIP

Boat tours of the Limska
zaljev leave daily from
Rovinj's waterfront from
May to September.
Lunch is usually
included.

which is quieter and less brash than
its larger neighbour. Vrsar's facilities
include a small marina and the usual
tourist hotels that line this stretch of
coastline, but it has a pleasant character, with a church and bell tower
presiding over its compact old town, a
jumble of old streets that lead down to
a wide waterfront.

Just south of Vrsar things are more
relaxed still at pleasantly traffic-free
Koversada, one of the world's largest and oldest naturist resorts – twice
voted Croatia's best beach – which
can handle the naked needs of more
than 10,000 naturists at a time.

Croatia's largest resort

For many people arriving in **Poreč** ❼
alarm bells start ringing when they
hear that this is the largest tourist
resort in Croatia, the epicentre of one
of the country's fastest expanding
industries. The approach from the east
takes one through the massive Zelena
laguna resort, almost a town in its own
right. Since the 1960s Poreč has been
geared towards taking in thousands
upon thousands of tourists from all

over Europe, catering for them for one
or two weeks, and then spitting them
back out – admittedly with a friendly
smile – at the end.

There may be only 10,000 residents
in the town, but Poreč manages to
accommodate more than 700,000
visitors annually with the two massive
companies of Riviera and Plava laguna
soaking up most of the business. This
all too obvious mass tourism can
put people off visiting Poreč, but to
avoid the town is to miss out on one
of Croatia's most alluring attractions,
the Basilica of Euphrasius, on Unesco's
World Heritage List since 1997.

St Euphrasius

In almost any other European city the
6th-century **Basilica of Euphrasius**
(Eufrazijeva bazilika; daily 7am–8pm;
free), housing some of the Adriatic's
finest Byzantine art, would draw long
queues and charge a hefty admission
fee, but in Poreč there are rarely queues
and entry is free. Its highlights are the
iridescent gold-laced frescoes, embellished with mother-of-pearl and precious and semi-precious stones, which

BELOW: fresh fish
being unloaded on
Limski zaljev.

dorn the main basilica's apse. The work of craftsmen from Constantinople and Ravenna, they include *Christ and the Apostles*, the *Virgin enthroned with Child*, and scenes of the Annunciation and Visitation. One interesting feature to look out for is Euphrasius himself, the bishop who commissioned the frescoes; he is depicted to the left of the largest fresco, holding a scale model of the church. In front of the apse, the 13th-century ciborum (canopy) is also decorated with mosaics. The wooden pews are a perfect place to sit and admire the intricate handiwork of the Byzantine artists and craftsmen.

The site's antiquity is further revealed in the mosaics on the floor on both sides of the entrance, originating from a previous church on the site, dating from the 4th century. The wooden pews in the basilica are 15th-century, as is the bell tower, which is accessible through the baptistry across the courtyard from the basilica. The steep and narrow climb up the bell tower is well rewarded with views out across Poreč and the Adriatic Sea; it is said that on a clear day you may even see Venice.

Roman Poreč

Just outside the basilica is **Eufrazijeva**, one of the two sturdy thoroughfares that, along with **Decumanus**, form the centre of Roman Poreč. When the Romans arrived this was little more than a sleepy Illyrian fishing village, but they transformed it beyond recognition. The town's ancient heritage is still very much alive, its old Roman thoroughfares lined with Venetian-style buildings very much in use as restaurants, cafés and shops.

Decumanus's southern fringe used to culminate in the Roman Forum, but little of the original buildings remain, bar the scattered ruins of two temples, the Temple of Neptune and another thought to pay homage to Mars. Little reliable information is available on either, despite what the creative local guides may tell you.

Towards the southern end of Decumanus is the **Romanesque House**, dating from the 13th century. The unusual wooden balcony on the upper level would make a delightful vantage point for overlooking this stretch of the Decumanus and the orange-tiled

TIP

The tourist office in Vrsar publishes a guide to cycling around the town. Cycle paths run beside the main road to Poreč and into the countryside.

BELOW: Madonna and Child in the Basilica of Euphrasius, Poreč.

BELOW LEFT: the
statue of Joakim
Rakovac, a
renowned partisan
who died in 1945,
is one of several
memorials marking
Poreč's liberation
from Fascist forces
at the end of World
War II. **RIGHT:** aerial
view of Novigrad's
old town and
marina.

roofs of Poreč, though at present this
is not open to the public. The ground
floor displays an ever-changing exhibition of the work of local artists and
sculptors, with many of the exhibits on
sale at reasonable prices.

In 2001 fresh Christian mosaics were
uncovered in a courtyard behind the
Istrian Assembly Hall (Istarska sabor-
nica) and research is underway to find
out more about them. The hall was
built originally as a Franciscan church
in the 13th century and its interior was
revamped in Baroque style in the 18th
century. In the 20th century an Istrian
assembly used to have its meetings
here and today the local government
still convenes in the hall. During summer classical concerts are held here,
along with art exhibitions.

Entertainment in Poreč

Poreč's Roman history warrants at
least a few days' exploration, but on
longer stays you may want to take a
break from mining Poreč's rich cultural seam. The many tourist-oriented
facilities, including a number for families, are at their peak in high summer.

The resort developments offer some
thing for everyone, from all the usua
water sports and the simple pleasure
of sunbathing to more adrenalin
pumping activities such as paintbal
paragliding and skydiving. The loca
tourist office also produces a series o
leaflets on the network of cycling path
in the Poreč area. More sedentar
thrills include scenic flights over Istria'
dramatic coastline and all the majo
west coast towns.

North of Poreč

While Poreč and Rovinj are the
best-known Istrian resorts there are
another couple of historic resor
towns on the coast curling north
west towards the border with Slov
enia. A short drive north of Poreč i
Novigrad ❽, a miniature Rovinj with
its old town clinging to the shore and
a bell tower rising above a smatter
ing of orange-tiled roofs. Some of it
former charm was sacrificed in the
Communist-era drive to attract low
margin mass tourism, resulting in an
untidy collection of hotel develop
ments, but it is worth at least a day

JOAKIM RAKOVAC
NARODNI HEROJ
RODEN 1914 - POGINUO 18.I.1945
U BORBI
PROTIV OKUPATORA

KOTARSKI ODBOR
SAVEZA BORACA NOB

rip with lunch or dinner in one of its well-regarded fish restaurants. There s also an 11th-century church with a arcophagus said to contain the little-known St Pelagius's remains.

Further north on the coastal road s **Umag 9**, a compact town of 6,000 nhabitants whose old centre is scenially located on a peninsula. Umag has Roman heritage and an old town vith a Venetian-style bell tower. Historical attractions that have survived its ransformation from a modest Istrian own into a tourist resort include ections of the old town walls, the Church of Mary's Assumption and the **Town Museum** (high season Tue–Sun am–10pm, low season Tue–Sat 10am– oon; charge).

The Istrian west coast comes to an nd at the small fishing village of **avudrija 10**, a good spot for a simple neal comprising the fresh catch of the ay. One tall village tale concerns its 6-metre (118ft) high lighthouse, the ldest on the Croatian coast. The story oes that Count Metternich fell head ver heels in love with a Croatian voman at a ball in Vienna. His shy-

ness prevented him from making a move and instead he decided to build a lighthouse in an attempt to win the heart of his love. Tragically the object of his desire is said to have died on the very night his illuminated messages of love began beaming over the rocky Adriatic coastline.

Istria's east coast

Istria's east coast is far less explored than the west and is not as saturated with tourists, though there is also no town that really has the appeal or facilities of Poreč, Pula or Rovinj. The landscape is dominated by wild, pine-covered mountains and a rambling, rugged coastline, though a number of power stations and industrial scars spoil the vistas across the Kvarner Gulf and towards the island of Cres. The coastal E751 road is a more inviting route to the Kvarner Gulf than that offered by the express toll road, which speeds through the interior, but expect delays because of roadworks.

The road northeast of Pula reaches the village of **Raša 11** after meandering through the Raška valley. This is

Since 1990 Umag has gained worldwide attention with its annual ATP Tour Croatia Open tennis tournament in July. This men-only event has attracted big names such as Thomas Muster, Carlos Moya and, of course, Croatian hero Goran Ivanišević to the 16 clay courts of the International Tennis Centre in the tourist development of Stella Maris.

BELOW: Savudrija's rocky shore.

When travelling around coastal Istria look out for the kažuni, the dry stone dwellings that were traditionally the homes of local shepherds. Scale replicas of the fat round buildings make unusual souvenirs.

the first of a number of villages offering clues to the region's main industry prior to tourism.

The east of Istria offers a rich seam of coal and this part of Croatia was first mined by the Italians in 1937. The neat rows of dwellings were built to house the coal workers during the Italian regime. Yugoslavia continued coal production after gaining control of Istria after World War II, but mining in the region finally ceased in 1989 and the village feels somewhat stranded in a time warp.

The most impressive building is **St Barbara's Church** (Crkva sv. Barbare) – look out for the bell tower sculpted to resemble a pithead.

Town on a hill

The largest and most interesting settlement on the east coast is **Labin** ⑫, consisting of an old town perched on a high hill and a newer settlement that has mushroomed over the last century. The town's original name, Albana, is said to be of Celtic origin, meaning simply "town on a hill", but this aspect of the area's history has been little

explored. Major subsidence problem caused by mining and careless planning put the old town in danger of collapse and at one point it looked as though it would have to be abandoned altogether. Thankfully the subsidence was shored up and the jumble of winding streets, tumble of church spire and sprinkling of craft shops make it a pleasant place to visit.

The most impressive of Labin's churches is the **Church of the Birth of the Blessed Mary** (Rodjenje Marijino), a fascinating place of worship built on 11th-century foundations although the present structure date from 1336. It incorporates both Renaissance and Gothic styles. Look out for the 17th-century Venetian lion above the Gothic rose window on the church's facade and the six sturdy marble altars inside.

Next door to the church the town's eclectic history is explored in the **Town Museum** (Gradski muzej; high season Mon–Sat 10am–1pm and 5–7pm, low season Mon–Sat 10am–1pm; charge). The display are housed in an 18th-century palace

BELOW:
view of Labin.

nd range from traditional costumes nd musical instruments, through to n exhibit on the town's coal min- g days. One of the most intriguing oal-related stories concerns a period 1 1921 when the local mine work- rs defied the Italian authorities and eclared the "Labin Republic" as they eld a strike in protest at poor condi- ons. The helpful English-speaking aff at the museum are usually only o keen to fill visitors in on Labin's 5 minutes of fame.

oastal Rabac

n sweltering Istrian summer days the oastal resort of **Rabac** ❸ is a good scape, reached after a 30-minute walk r a 3km (2-mile) drive from Labin. he first settlers in Rabac were fisher- en with a handful of boats operat- g out of the village.

The first hotel along the pretty ay was opened in 1889, but it did ot develop as a proper resort until he Italian authorities promoted the illage as the perfect getaway for the xhausted mine workers during their ccupation of Istria. Today's visitors

tend to be holiday-makers seeking a quieter alternative to the west coast resorts, or young Croatian ravers looking for a party. In summer Rabac hosts enormous dance parties with some of Europe's most celebrated DJs. The only other real attraction as such is a sculpture park.

Kvarner Gulf views

The last settlement of note on the E751 before the Kvarner Gulf is the village of **Plomin** ❹, set on a high forested ridge. You are unlikely to find any other tourists in this hill vil- lage, and very few locals for that mat- ter. The small settlement may have a sense of foreboding and decay, and the fishing bay nestling below has long since silted up, but its narrow streets and relaxed atmosphere war- rant a quick stop. The Church of St George has a fine early example of Glagolitic script.

Superb views from Plomin take in a wide sweep of the Kvarner Gulf and the beautiful Adriatic island of Cres and the village provides an atmos- pheric last stop in Istria. ❑

Istria's fish restaurants are among the best in Croatia.

BELOW:
Rabac harbour.

INLAND ISTRIA

Often overlooked by the tourists on Istria's coast, the attractions of inland Istria – rolling vine-clad hills and perched villages – are making it a successful centre for rural tourism

G iven the millions of tourists who descend on the Istrian coastline every year it is surprising that so few think about heading into the region's rural hinterland. Travel professionals have often described it as the new Tuscany or Umbria, and its rolling green hills, sweeping vineyards and idyllic hill towns certainly bring Italy to mind.

Getting into Istria's hinterland could not be easier. In high season plenty of day trips operate from Poreč, Rovinj and other resorts, and there is also a passable public transport system, with both rail and bus connections. However, if you really want to explore the region in some detail, rather than just dipping in for a taste, it is advisable to hire a car and spend a few nights in at least one of the hill towns. Just a short journey north of Poreč is Istria's rather unlikely regional capital, Pazin, which year-round makes a good base and starting point. Nearby is Motovun, one of the most delightful of all the hill towns and perhaps the most visited.

One of the real joys of exploring inland is driving aimlessly around stopping off whenever you feel like it. There are many pleasant surprises, such as the village of Vižinada, where you are almost guaranteed not to find any other tourists, and few inhabitants either, as like many of the hill towns it suffered serious depopulation during and after World War II, with about two-thirds of all ethnic Italians leaving.

One of the upsides of the population drift away from the hill towns has been the availability of homes for local artists. The enlightened local authorities have opened up many of the towns' deserted houses on low-rent or even rent-free schemes to attract colonies of artists, sculptors and craftspeople. The shining example of the success of this programme is Grožnjan, in itself a scenery-rich hill town, where dozens of artists work in the rambling old stone buildings. It is easy to spend a whole day in Grožnjan browsing through the

Main attractions
PAZIN
MOTOVUN
VIŽINADA
GROŽNJAN
BUJE
BUZET
HUM
ISTARSKE TOPLICE

PRECEDING PAGES: frescoes in St Mary's, Beram. **LEFT:** house in Pazin. **BELOW:** rustic items in the Ethnographic Museum of Istria.

Stone carving in the wall of Pazin's 9th-century castle.

BELOW: Istrian produce for sale.

galleries and studios and picking up some interesting art.

Since independence the Istria County Tourist Association has been very proactive in pushing the attractions of Inland Istria. It has set up a wine trail, published a guide to the region's gastronomic highlights and initiated the *Agroturizam* programme, which encourages local people to open up their farms and homes to fee-paying guests from abroad. Its emphasis is on meeting local people and sampling the fine wines and foods that the region has supplied in such abundance since Roman times.

Inland to Pazin, Motovun and Vižinada

A 35km (22-mile) drive north of Poreč is Istria's rather unlikely regional capital, **Pazin** ⑮. While Pula is the *de facto* capital of the peninsula on account of its being the largest settlement in Istria, after World War II the Communist authorities designated this modest inland town the official seat of the regional government as they attempted to wrest power away from

Pula and Poreč and thank Pazin for i role as a partisan stronghold during t fighting. First mentioned in historic records by Emperor Otto II, the tow today is largely unappealing, mode and industrial. The old town and i austere castle teeter on the brink of dramatic limestone gorge that dro over 100 metres (330ft) below ar was said to have been the inspiratic for Jules Verne when he hurled t eponymous protagonist of his nov *Matthias Sandorf* over the abyss. Som Pazin residents insist that the vertig inducing gorge was also the inspiratic for Dante's *Inferno*.

Pazin's castle, a utilitarian 9t century fortress that overlooks t Fjoba stream, is not particularly exc ing to look at, although it is Istria largest and best preserved. Fifteent century additions include the stur defensive walls. Cross the drawbrid into the castle itself to visit the **Ethn graphic Museum of Istria** (Etnogr skog muzej Istre; www.emi.hr; dai 10am–6pm; charge). It displays selection of historical costumes fro the surrounding region and an arr

Ecotourism

Istria has not been slow to realise the increasing popularity of "ecotourism", an environmentally friendly form of vacation offering holiday-makers the chance to spend time in a rustic setting very different from the kind of faceless tourist hotels often found in the built-up coastal resorts. They are usually much cheaper, too. The Istrian County Tourist Association's *Agroturizam* programme lists well over 100 cottages, farms, guesthouses and rural hotels dotted over the peninsula. It also has details of places where passing travellers can pop in for lunch if they book ahead.

All of the establishments listed in the programme offer the chance to sample the excellent food and drink of Istria. Specialities you can expect to savour include *pršut* (locally produced wind-dried ham), wild asparagus, black and white truffles, local blood sausages, honey and a range of local cheeses. There are also many excellent Istrian wines such as Malvazija, Terrano and Istrian Muscatel, as well as *biska*, a fiery but very enjoyable mistletoe brandy.

Further details and information on the *Agroturizam* programme in Istria can be found at www.istra.com/agroturizam, and are available from the Istria County Tourist Association, tel: 052 880 088, or from any local tourist office.

of jewellery, and documents the history of the fishing and agricultural industries in Istria. Look out also for the collection of bells, some dating back as far as the 14th century, and finds from local archaeological digs. The museum's atmospheric galleries also house a number of temporary exhibitions. If you are looking for an unusual activity, the museum runs weaving workshops on request. The town museum (high season Tue–Sun 10am–6pm, low season Tue–Thur 10am–3pm, Fri noon–5pm, Sat–Sun 11am–5pm; charge), at the same location, displays items from the castle's history. In the castle's courtyard is a water cistern that was installed to provide fresh water in the event of a siege, an ever-present danger in Pazin for centuries.

Pazin also has a couple of interesting churches. The **Church of St Nicholas** (Župna crkva sv. Nikole) on the town's southern perimeter was built in 1266 in austere Romanesque style, with the bell tower an 18th-century afterthought. The rather plain exterior gives way to a more elaborate interior

with three naves and a series of Gothic frescoes from the 15th century, depicting scenes from the bible and the life of St Nicholas. A Gothic sanctuary and vault were also added in the 15th century – look out for the coat of arms of Pazin, the oldest surviving in the town. Meanwhile the Franciscan monastery and attached church were built between 1463 and 1477 with a late Gothic presbytery from the same period. According to tradition, anyone who visits it on 2 August will be absolved of their sins.

Another good time to visit Pazin is the first Tuesday of the month, when it runs a traditional market. Honey is a particularly good buy.

Fine frescoes around Pazin

The main attraction in the area surrounding Pazin is the bucolic little village of **Beram** 5km (3 miles) to the northwest. It is renowned for its cemetery church of St Mary (Crkva sv. Marije na Škrilinah), containing a fine collection of 15th-century frescoes. Getting access to see the frescoes can be problematic as the church is not often left

Scene from the lives of Mary and the saints in the church of St Mary in Beram.

BELOW: view from the castle in Pazin.

TIP

Keen cyclists should click on the cycling link at www.istra.com, where there is information on cycling routes throughout the Istrian peninsula, with nine inland routes ranging from 20km (12 miles) to a 56km (35-mile) ride through the Istrian countryside. Another useful resource is the website www.istria-bike.com.

open – either ask locally for the key or plan ahead and make enquiries at the tourist office in Pazin, which may be able to point you in the right direction. It is well worth the effort.

Depicted on the medieval frescoes are scenes from the lives of Mary and the saints, with Adam and Eve also featuring on one. Look out for the signature of the man who crafted them, Vincent of Kastav. Perhaps the most dramatic of all the works is the vividly portrayed *Dance of Death* in which a procession of citizens headed by the Pope is attended by scythe-wielding skeletons. Unfortunately, some of the frescoes were damaged when new windows were added to the church and also when they were covered up by mortar, not to be rediscovered until just before the start of World War I. The church is a small, mainly Gothic structure, but in the 18th century the entrance was widened and a wooden roof built to shore up the building.

Perched town

Motovun  ⓰, 20km (12 miles) from Pazin, is perhaps the archetypal inland Istrian town and the best place to hea if you are short of time and want quick taste of what the region has t offer. Its chocolate-box beauty unfold atop a rocky 280-metre (920ft) hig outcrop, which rears seemingly fror nowhere amidst the rolling green field and vineyards of the Mirna River valle Getting up to Motovun is fun in itsel the winding road meanders up th green slopes, seemingly in search of way through the Venetian stone wall The forests surrounding the town ar renowned for the excellent truffles tha are unearthed here in autumn. The fo est once covered a massive area, but th Venetians cut down large parts, floatin the trees downstream to the Adriati where they used them for shipbuildin. A small section of the original forest now protected by conservation laws.

Venetian inspiration

Venice's influence is apparent as yo enter the town, in the trademark Ven tian lion casting a watchful eye ove all new arrivals, and palatial home dating from the 15th and 16th cer turies. Motovun has some of the be

BELOW: Motovun.

Motovun.

preserved defensive walls in the region with a single line encircling the historic core and two smaller semicircles aiding defence. The best way to get an understanding of the place is to climb on to the town's walls and walk around, taking in the views of Motovun and the Istrian countryside stretching away into the distance. Look out for the rich collage of architecture that Motovun embraces. Gothic, Venetian and Romanesque buildings are squeezed into a town that today has fewer than 600 inhabitants.

St Stephen's Church (Crkva sv. Stjepana; daily 10am–1pm and 4–8pm) is Motovun's only real must-see sight, a Renaissance parish church with a lofty campanile built in the 17th century by the Venetian architect Andrea Palladio, while the marble statues on the altar of St Laurence and St Stephen were sculpted by another Venetian artist. When the bell tower is open (times vary depending on staffing levels) head up the stairs of the campanile for an unforgettable view of the town and the Istrian landscape, which is even more impressive than that from the town walls. The Motovun forest is also the world's largest natural habitat for truffles.

For an unusual perspective of Motovun, attempt to climb the 1,052 steps that lead up to the old town from the valley floor, a feat that is practically impossible in the height of summer.

Apart from truffles, it would be rude to visit Motovun without sampling the renowned local Malvazija and Teran wine varieties. The second goes especially well with *pršut* (prosciutto).

Encapsulating the best of Istria

Southwest of Motovun the small village of **Vižinada** 🔟 is a real find and well worth a stop. There are only a few small agrotourism places in town to stay or eat at, but Vižinada has all of the best bits of inland Istria without many tourists: unspoilt countryside, panoramic views, impressive old churches and the historical relics of the various civilisations that have influenced the region through the centuries. Its tiny old town covers the hillside away from the main road. Crowded around the small central

Woodcarving – one of the crafts practised in Motovun.

BELOW: umbrellas up in Motovun.

BELOW: Venetian elegance in Buje.

square are a jumble of old churches, Roman remains and the foundations of a Venetian-era loggia, while all around are sweeping views of the peninsula's countryside. There is nothing much to do but congratulate yourself on finding this little hidden-away slice of inland Istria. In summer outdoor classical concerts brighten up the main square.

From Vižinada you can take a 27km (17-mile) long bike trail that brings you back to where you started via some impressive views, an old wine railway track and the village of Kaštelir. Details of the route are available from the small MTB information office on the main road through Vižinada.

Artists' town

Farther west towards the mountains that mark the border with Slovenia is the hill town of **Grožnjan** ⓲. Since Croatian independence the local authorities have breathed new life into it, with many public buildings revamped and the infrastructure restored from its dilapidated state. Wandering along the cobbles of its well-preserved medieval

centre is a joy. With Communism gone a number of young people have moved back and set up small businesses and the population has been boosted by fresh young blood. Grožnjan also has the distinction of being the only locality in Croatia with an Italian majority – 51 percent at last count.

Since World War II Grožnjan has also become an oasis for artists and writers as the enlightened local authorities offered them the empty homes that had been left by fleeing Italians and young people heading to find jobs in nearby cities. The result is an artistic colony that has become a tourist attraction. It offers the opportunity to buy a broad range of paintings, sculpture and ceramics, along with the chance to talk to the artists.

Strolling around the various studios and workshops, having a nose into any that look interesting – doors are left open for passing visitors – is the main pleasure in the town. A group of musicians have formed the International Centre for the Young Musicians of Croatia in previously uninhabited buildings, and the sound of their music

often wafts through the narrow stone streets, adding to the artistic ambience. In summer students from many other European countries come to work with the Croatian students, giving the town's cafés a cosmopolitan air.

Events and exhibitions

There are myriad cultural events with exhibitions, concerts and workshops taking place daily in rejuvenated venues such as the Fonticus Gallery and the Kastel Concert Hall. Grožnjan hosts a three-week jazz festival spanning late July and early August. In 2008 it won the Europa Jazz Award for best small festival

Apart from the main town gate, the Venetian walls have been pulled down, leaving uninterrupted views of the rolling countryside and over a dozen surrounding villages. When the visibility is especially good the naked eye can see as far as the Julian Alps in Slovenia and east to the rugged outline of Mt Učka, on the edge of the Kvarner Gulf. There are few historic sights apart from the 18th-century **Church of St Mary** (Crkva svete Mar-

ije). It is worth peeking inside to see the Baroque altars and the wooden choir stalls that were added in Renaissance style. The Venetians left a fine loggia in the centre of the old town. Built around four sturdy columns in the 16th century, it houses four Roman tombs, relics of the days when Grožnjan was garrisoned as a hill fort by the Roman rulers. The Italians returned in the 20th century and many locals are still bilingual; a large portion of everyday speech is in a local adaptation of a Venetian dialect.

Venetian-style Buje

Even farther east towards the Slovenian border is the hill town of **Buje ⓲**, still only 34km (21 miles) as the crow flies from Poreč, in the heart of Istria's leading wine-growing area. Buje's old town has a solid feel to it and it is less touristy than either Motovun or Grožnjan. It was fortified in the Middle Ages by a succession of Istrian counts, before the Venetians shipped in and took most of the fortifications down. A wealth of Venetian-style architecture survives, including the

Autumn produce at a roadside stall near Motovun.

BELOW LEFT: ornate entrance to the church of St Servulus, Buje.

The Wine Trail

All over inland Istria you will see vineyards and signs pointing to small local outlets where families sell their own wine from the cellars of their homes. Driving out to the vineyards to stock up on supplies is tremendously popular among Istrians themselves.

To help foreign visitors join in the fun, the Istria County Tourist Association has put together a *Guide to the Wine Roads of Istria*. It identifies three wine routes (Buje, Buzet and Poreč) and recommends specific vineyards and cellars where you can taste and buy. In addition, a Wine Day takes place on the first Sunday in May in Buje, Buzet and Vodnjan, when around 60 cellars open for wine tasting. The majority of the production is based in the western portion of inland Istria in the fertile land between Rovinj, Poreč and Buje, while to the east there is a much smaller district around Labin. You will also find local wines served by the jug in Istria's *konoba* (taverns), accompanied by hearty rustic fare.

Istrian wines vary greatly in price, ranging from just 20 kuna for a cheap litre bottle of the dry white Malvazija to around 80 or 90 kuna for a 75cl bottle of red Teran and more for a good vintage. In winter in Istria, look out for *supa*, made from red wine mulled with sugar, olive oil and pepper and scooped up with toasted bread.

town loggia, a classic of Venetian Gothic design with an elegant facade.

From the post-Venetian town walls the views from Buje are amongst the finest in the whole of Istria. The town spreads below, a picturesque collage of terracotta roofs, while in the background lush fields run into a patchwork of vineyards and rolling hills. Framing the scene is the crumple of peaks marking the backbone of the Slovenian border and the Adriatic Sea, with a sprinkling of the Istrian coastal resorts also visible on a clear day.

Buje's **Church of St Servulus** (Crkva sv. Servola) is worth entering. It has undergone many modifications since a Roman temple stood on the site, the current building owing much to an 18th-century facelift. Look out for the organ, which has survived on the site since it was installed in 1791. If the facade of the church looks a little ramshackle do not be too surprised as it was never actually finished. Nearby, the **Church of St Mary** (Crkva sv. Marije) dates from the 15th century, though the bell tower was added a century later.

The distinctive Lion of St Mark on the belfry once again emphasises the Venetian connection that crops up throughout Istria.

Best base

Heading back east across the northern portion of inland Istria, you come to the town of **Buzet** ⓴, a larger settlement than most and a good option if you would prefer to be based in the interior rather than in one of the coastal resorts. If you are planning on heading from coastal Istria to the Kvarner Gulf, with a few days exploring inland Istria in between, Buzet is also handy, as it is around 50km (30 miles) from both Poreč and Rijeka.

Buzet is a typical Istrian hill town, with green slopes rising to an old town core, overlooking a verdant valley with the ubiquitous River Mirna running through it. Settlement in Buzet dates back to before the arrival of the Romans, who knew it as Pinguentum. A number of major archaeological finds have been made in and around Buzet, some of which are on display in the **Buzet**

Region Museum (Zavičajni muzej; daily 11am–3pm; charge), inside a 17th-century palace. The museum's highlights include pagan carvings depicting sacrificial altars and grave-stones, as well as pagan gods. The Roman period is also well covered, as is World War II, which dwells on the heroic deeds of the local people. There is also a colourful collection of traditional Croatian folk costumes.

Buzet is not known as the "Truf-fle City" for nothing as it is at the centre of one of Istria's most bounti-ful truffle areas. The delectable fungi are harvested in the fields and woods surrounding the town in September and October, and are celebrated by an annual truffle festival in September, in which the locals prepare a truffle omelette in the town square. One of the highlights of visiting is eating in the local restaurants, which all feature truffles on their menus.

Glagolitic Alley

Blink and you will miss the tiny town of **Hum ㉑**, which is signposted just below the town of Roc. It lies at the head of a road known as **Glagolitic Alley** (Aleja glagoljaša), a kind of sculpture trail created in the 1970s to celebrate the Glagolitic script (*see page 193*), the precursor of Cyrillic. The 11 works include copies of important Glagolitic documents.

Hum claims to be the smallest town in the world, which may have some validity, as its 2001 population was just 17 inhabitants. It is certainly the smallest town in Istria, although it still manages somehow to pack in a couple of churches, a restaurant and a set of town walls.

Spa treatment

A good place to laze away an after-noon is at **Istarske toplice**, a health spa 10km (6 miles) outside Buzet on the road to Poreč. The spa has been famous since Roman times. It is renowned for its beneficial effects on aching backs, arthritis and skin con-ditions, especially acne, but as yet it offers no cure for an insatiable addic-tion to truffles. The sulphur-infused waters stay at around a constant 30–35°C (86–95°F) all year. ❑

Hum is a tiny town, which claims to be the smallest in the world.

BELOW LEFT: on the Glagolitic Alley, near Hum.

Across to Slovenia

Slovenia declared independence on the same day as Croatia in 1991, but since then their paths have gone in markedly different directions. While Croatia was dragged into the bitter conflict with Yugoslavia, Slovenia got on with modernising its economy and build-ing ties with its neighbours, Austria and Italy. Popping into Slovenia for a few days is well worthwhile. The "Slovenian Riviera" is not on the scale of Croatia's meandering coastline, but this patch of the Adriatic, tucked between Istria and the Italian city of Trieste, has plenty of attractions to offer.

Close to the border crossing is the resort of Portorož, but a better option is to continue on to Piran, a dreamy Venetian Gothic town set on a narrow peninsula, offering views west to Trieste and east to Istria, with the spires of Venice visible on the horizon on a clear day. Koper, 17km (10 miles) to the north of Piran, has a rambling old town that was built by the Venetians in the 15th and 16th centuries. Its main square has a Renaissance loggia and there are concrete beaches for those wanting to swim. Koper is connected by regular buses to Trieste and north to the Slovenian capital, Ljubljana, a small city with a blend of Austro-Hungarian and Italian architecture, that is enlivened by a large student population.

BIRDS

Of all the wildlife in Croatia,
birds are the most visible –
and the most rewarding

There are birds to see in every season in Croatia.
Spring brings migrating flocks from Africa,
and martins and swallows are busy in their
nests beneath the eves; in summer, towns
are filled with the shrill cries of swifts
careening around bell towers and
rooftops; and in early autumn
brilliant blue kingfishers flit through
rocky coves. Raptors soar over the
islands, woodpeckers tap away in the
forests that conceal owls and tits, and
warblers, buntings and wheatears flit
over more open ground. Croatia, with
its great variety of habitats, has a rich roll
call of birds, so it is not surprising that a
number of companies offer birdwatching
holidays. Many bird species will be unfamiliar. You
might not recognise the pale grey olive-tree warbler
or sombre tit, but a blue nuthatch, red-rumped
swallow, black-eared wheatear, bee-eater and rock
partridge are more easily identified.

July and August are not the best times, as birds are
on the whole inactive in summer. (Nature
compensates for this in Croatia by providing a
wide variety of butterflies.) But when on a boat
trip or wandering through meadowlands, there is
still usually something to see. Spring and autumn
bring the large migrations: more than 350 varieties
have been recorded in the country. In winter, water
birds collect in their thousands around Lake Vrana and
the Kopacevo marshes.

It can take a trained eye to know one songbird from
another, a gull from a tern, and to sort out
the difference between birds of
prey, and this is a good
place
to start
learning.

ABOVE: a white-backed woodpecker, which breeds in
Paklenica National Park.
ABOVE LEFT: the unmistakable bee-eater, which catches
insects only when they are in flight.

RIGHT: the
great white
pelican, one
of the world's largest
birds, is a visitor to the
coast.

ABOVE: a wood warbler, more colourful than the grey olive-tree
warbler, snacks on a ripening olive.

ALONG THE COAST

The coast presents three distinct types of habitat.
Mountains: choughs and larks and other mountain species
head for the Velebit mountains in Paklenica National Park,
which is also a breeding ground for capercaillie and white-
backed woodpeckers. Biokovo Nature Park is where the
ortolan bunting breeds, while the Dinari mountains
possess the only breeding population of shore larks. Eagles
and falcons can usually be seen in the high ground above
Trogir.
Rivers and lakes: the freshwater lakes and deltas are
breeding grounds for herons and coots, plovers, curlews
and terns. The largest delta belongs to the River Neretva,
scene of great spring and autumn migrations, and more
than 100 species nest here. Vransko Lake and the Krka and
Zrmanja rivers are important too.
The islands: terns, sheerwaters, shags and gulls all nest
among the islands. The endangered griffon vulture is
helped with a rehabilitation centre on the island of Cres,
and the only nesting area for
Eleanor's falcons is
on the Pelagic
islands where
Cory's
shearwaters
also breed.

ABOVE: don't forget to
pack your binoculars.
RIGHT: a griffon vulture,
which is being rehabilitated
at a special centre on Cres.
LEFT: swifts scream
around the streets and
squares of coastal towns
such as Split.

KVARNER GULF

This enormous bay has a long history of high-class tourism. The Opatija Riviera was popular in Austro-Hungarian times, while islands such as Krk and Rab are among Croatia's most beautiful

The vast, island-studded Kvarner Gulf (Kvarnerski zaljev) connects the Istrian peninsula in the north with the Dalmatian regions to the south. To the rear its coastal strip is backed by the hulking sweep of the Velebit Mountains, Croatia's largest range, cutting off coastal towns and villages from the interior and necessitating long trips along the Adriatic Highway (or *Magistrala*), which runs south all the way from Rijeka to Dalmatia. Tourism here began in the 19th century when rich citizens of Vienna and Budapest, many leaving for health reasons, fled their own harsh winters and sought refuge in the relatively balmy climes of the Opatija Riviera, running along the eastern flank of the Istrian peninsula. The area lies under the protective shadow of Mt Učka, which keeps away the worst of the wind and chill and offers good opportunities for hiking in summer, with spectacular views across the whole expanse of the Kvarner Gulf.

Tourism is once again flourishing, both in the Opatija Riviera resorts of Lovran, Volosko and Opatija and on the islands that litter the gulf, including Krk, the largest Croatian island, and Rab, home to Rab Town, one of the most attractive towns in Croatia. Unlike the barren islands of Northern Dalmatia those of the Kvarner Gulf are far more varied and include oases such as Cres and Lošinj that are dotted with interesting towns, beaches and lush landscapes, as well as Pag, where the eerie landscape, in which humans have struggled to survive for centuries, offers a taste of things to come further south in Dalmatia.

Back on the mainland, the only city in the Kvarner Gulf is Rijeka, Croatia's third largest city, which is interesting enough to detain the tourists passing through its port for a few nights. It receives nothing like the attention of Split or Pula, but it is worth exploring nonetheless. Elsewhere on the mainland there is little to stop off for on the route south, bar the Risnjak National Park, a mountain paradise, and the

Main attractions
OPATIJA
LOVRAN
MT UČKA
RIJEKA
PAKLENICA NATIONAL PARK
KRK
RAB
PAG
CRES
LOŠINJ

PRECEDING PAGES:
Opatija Riviera.
LEFT: a hilltop village overlooking the gulf. **BELOW:** 19th-century elegance at Opatija.

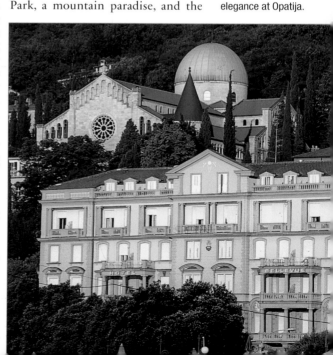

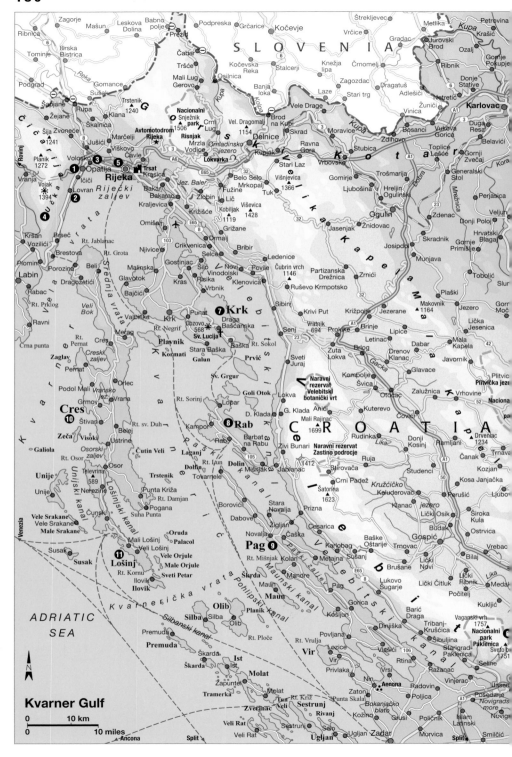

Kvarner Gulf

ADRIATIC
SEA

0   10 km

0   10 miles

town of Senj, famous for its 16th-century Uskok warriors.

A highlight in the extreme south is the Paklenica National Park with its many opportunities for walking and hiking and spectacular views of the Kvarner Gulf and its myriad islands.

Opatija Riviera

The **Opatija Riviera** (Opatijska rivijera) stretches for over 40km (25 miles) along the shores of the Kvarner Gulf, enjoying a unique microclimate that ensures year-round balmy temperatures and evergreen vegetation. It owes this to the hulking presence of Mt Učka and other lofty mountains, which stretch high above the coastal flatlands and protect them from the worst of the winds and rain. With such agreeable weather the riviera has been popular since the 19th century, when the wealthy classes of the Austro-Hungarian Empire, particularly those with respiratory problems, came to enjoy the climate – 2,200 hours of sunshine a year and an ever-present cooling breeze ensuring that summer temperatures average a very pleasant 22°C (72°F).

Opatija ❶ is still the main resort on this stretch of coastline. Up until the end of the 19th century it was little more than a few houses that clustered around the 15th-century abbey (*opatija* in Croatian). All that changed, largely thanks to one man and a railway. The man was Iginio Scarpa, a nature-loving patrician from nearby Rijeka, who built his Villa Angiolina – named after his late wife – in Opatija in 1844. He filled his garden with plants brought from South America, Australia, the Far East and other parts of the world, including the Japanese camellia, which later became the symbol of Opatija. Within a few decades distinguished visitors to the villa had been so impressed that many bought property there and Opatija's first hotel, the Quarnero, now the Kvarner Hotel, opened its doors in 1885. Several sanatoria opened soon afterwards. The rail line from Vienna to Trieste was also in the process of being built and when it reached the Adriatic at Rijeka in 1873 Opatija's tourist industry blossomed. By the 1910s Opatija was the most visited resort in

EAT

Opatija's has an air of faded grandeur. The terrace Caffe Wagner in the luxury Millennium Hotel on the waterfront sells *Sachertortes* brought in all the way from the Hotel Sacher in Vienna.

LEFT: Krk Town marina. **BELOW:** keeping a close watch.

BELOW: an autumn stroll in Opatika's Botanical Park.
RIGHT: fishing from the marina at Lovran.

the Austro-Hungarian Empire after Karlsbad (Karlovy Vary).

With the growth of tourism and the opening of yet more hotels and sanatoria Opatija began to expand and its waterfront was landscaped with a promenade, the *lungomare*, which today stretches for 12km (7½ miles), all the way from the town of Volosko in the north to Lovran to the south of Opatija. Ornately planned gardens also flourished, as Opatija became a sort of Vienna-on-Sea for Austrian holiday-makers. Famous people queued up to see and be seen in Opatija. They included such diverse luminaries as Mahler, Chehkov, Puccini and various European royal, aristocrats and politicians.

The best place to start a tour of Opatija is where it all started – at the Villa Angiolina. This stylish neoclassical creation is in the leafy Opatija Park, close to the Adriatic, which is full of exotic plants from all over the world brought by Scarpio's varied friends. As a landmark in the history of tourism, the villa is a fitting co-host for the **Museum of Croatian Tourism** (Hrvatski muzej turizma; Tue–Sun

10am–6pm; charge), opened in 2007 and housing the permanent collection, entitled "Opatija–Golden Beginnings of Croatian Tourism", which contains many historic travel guidebooks among other exhibits. The other venue, the Juraj Šporer arts pavilion, next to the church of St James (Crkva sv. Jakova), hosts temporary exhibitions.

From the garden the *lungomare* is just a short stroll away. This boulevard circles the resort's rocky outcrops and small coves, in an explosion of pavement cafés, concrete swimming pools and shady cypress, oak and palm trees. In summer it fills with bronzed bodies topping up their tans, and splashing children, giving some credence to Opatije's nickname, the "Nice of the Adriatic", while in winter it is the venue for bracing walks.

The **Church of St Mary** (Crkva sv Marije) was built on the site of the abbey at the start of the 20th century, designed by the German architect Gabriel Seidl. Neither its exterior nor interior arouse paroxysms of visual ecstasy, but for a glimpse into Opatija's history it warrants a quick look.

Lovran

Just 6km (4 miles) south of Opatija, easily reached by local bus or along the *lungomare*, the resort town of **Lovran** ❷, is a sort of mini-Opatija clustered on the peninsula. Like its more illustrious neighbour there was nothing much to Lovran until the 19th century when a road was opened through to Rijeka in 1885. Then a sprinkling of hotels arrived to cater for wintering Austro-Hungarians convalescing on the riviera with various ailments, mostly respiratory. Lovran's stretch of the *lungomare* is lined with parks of evergreen vegetation and chestnut trees.

To the rear of Lovran is **Gorica Hill** (Grešna gorica), which in turn is part of the Mt Učka range. With the major exception of tourism, Lovran's history is more gripping than Opatija's as it saw battles between Uskok (Fugitive) pirates (*see page 188*), who were based in the Kvarner Gulf town of Senj, and the mighty Venetian Republic, confrontations which ensured that little of Lovran's old architecture has survived. One remnant is the Church of St George (Crkva sv. Jurja), rebuilt in Gothic style in the 14th century with a vault that dates from 1470. Look out also for the ceiling frescoes that are not dissimilar to those found in Beram in Istria. Lovran's frescoes were the work of Croatian artists in the 15th century.

Instead of heading south from Opatija to Lovran it is also worth walking a few kilometres north to the old fishing village of **Volosko** ❸. The halcyon days of Volosko, when the small harbour used to be alive with the frantic hollering and bustle of tuna fishermen, are long gone, but the old stone buildings crowded around the harbour are alluring. Compared with increasingly slick Opatija there is not much to do in Volosko, but wandering around the narrow alleyways and reclining in the modest seafood restaurants is a pleasant way of spending a few hours.

Opportunities for hiking

Keen hikers may find spending time in the shadow of the **Mt Učka** ❹ range tempting. The rugged limestone hills are not as impenetrable as they may appear, even for less experienced walkers. The 20km (12-mile) long range is

TIP

Walking maps of the Učka range are available from the tourist offices in Opatija and Lovran.

LEFT AND BELOW: the old town and seafront at Lovran.

Risnjak National Park

Despite its proximity to Rijeka, and its rich flora and fauna, this haven for mountaineers, hikers and botanists remains largely unknown to travellers in the Kvarner Gulf.

Compared with the Plitvice Lakes and the Kornati Islands, Risnjak National Park, just 18km (11 miles) north of Rijeka, is far less visited. It became a national park in 1953 and commercial development has been strictly limited. It was extended in 1997 to encompass the Kupa area as well, bringing the total land mass to 64 sq km (25 sq miles), making it a paradise for walkers, mountaineers and botanists.

The park is made up of the Snježnik and Risnjak massifs, which are part of the larger sweep of the Dinaric range. This rugged limestone and sandstone landscape separates the heavily wooded Gorski Kotar inland region from the Kvarner Gulf coast and comprises tree-shrouded slopes and karstic features such as caves, precipitous drops, sinkholes and disappearing streams. Various species of flora and fauna inhabit the park at different heights, but only the hardiest survive on the upper slopes, where bitter winds and heavy snowfalls are common. At lower altitudes tree species include sycamore maple, wych elm, fir, birch and, on the upper stretches, mountain spruce and juniper. As the area has never been heavily logged, much of it is virginal forest. Many parts of the park are off-limits to visitors.

The fauna is also interesting. The lynx, which disappeared from Risnjak for over a century before its return from across the Slovenian border in 1974, is flourishing; indeed the park takes its name from *ris*, the Croatian for lynx. Wolves and wild boar are among the residents, alongside red and roe deer, brown bears, capercaillie, chamois, poisonous horned vipers, wild cats and pine and stone marten. The 51 native bird species include woodpecker, hedge sparrow, lesser whitethroat and black redstart, as well as eight species of birds of prey. During winter rangers have to leave food out to help the most desperate animals stay alive. Hunting and fishing are permitted but strictly licensed. Hunters can organise trips in search of chamois, deer, wild boar and capercaillie; anglers can fish for trout and grayling.

One of the best times to visit the park is in late June and early July when a multitude of wild flowers bloom. Highlights are the edelweiss, mountain milfoil, alpine clematis, violet, alpine snowbell, alpine rock rose and the orange lily. This is also a good time for hiking. (Hiking is inadvisable in winter or early spring, as there are more than 100 days of snow on average a year and layers of snow reach 4 metres/13ft deep.)

The highest peak is Veliki Risnjak (1,528 metres/5,952ft), which has a mountain lodge, but perhaps the most appealing peak is Snježnik (1,506 metres/4,940ft; also with a modest lodge). A good base for accessing both is Bijela Voda, close to the little highland village of Crni Lug, where there is a small hotel and restaurant. There is also a shelter in the village of Kupari. Another good base is Platak, a 26km (16-mile) bus ride from Rijeka, with special buses in summer laid on for hikers. In winter it is possible to access the Snježnik ski field.

Visitors to the park need to buy a ticket, with proceeds going to help with maintenance. There are various restrictions on visits. For further information about the park, visit its website www.risnjak.hr or tel: 051-836 133. ❑

LEFT: red deer are among the park's fauna.

easily accessible from towns and villages along the coast between the Poklon Pass in the north to Plomin Bay (Plominski zaljev) in the south. The main peaks are Plas (1,285 metres/4,216ft), Brgud (907 metres/2,975ft), Sisol (835 metres/2,739ft), Kremenjak (827 metres/2,713ft), Suhi vrh (1,333 metres/4,373ft) and the highest of them all, Vojak, which rises 1,394 metres (4,596ft) above the Kvarner Gulf. Sweeping views from the top of Vojak take in everything from the Bay of Trieste to the north through to the island of Dugi otok on the edge of the Kornati Islands to the south.

Facilities along the Mt Učka massif are not extensive, but you will find a few mountain lodges and stone cottages that can house hikers. There is also a *pension* and restaurant at Poklon and a viewpoint tower on the peak of Vojak. For those wanting to take Vojak head on the best bet is to climb through Lovran's old town and follow the steps that break off up the hillside to the village of Liganj and on to the small settlements of Dindici and Ivulici, where all traces of civilisation are

left behind as the ascent begins through the evergreen forests. Usually it is possible to manage the whole climb in less than four hours, but allow for time at the top and for the descent. Climbers should take plenty of water and provisions, as there are few places to procure anything en route. The Croatian National Tourist Board website (www.htz.hr) has details of Mt Učka walks.

Main port

Rijeka ❺ is by far the largest settlement in the Kvarner Gulf, with more than 140,000 inhabitants. It's a working port city that those heading to the gulf's celebrated islands often overlook but it has much to recommend it for those prepared to delve past the industrial scars and untidy port district, Croatia's busiest. Locals take great pride in their shipbuilding tradition; today Rijeka's shipyards specialise in ships for transporting cars, and continue to thrive despite the recession because the orders are made years in advance.

Rijeka came to prominence at the end of the 19th century when it benefited from the new rail links to both

Entrance to the fortress of Trsat, the best place to begin a tour of Rijeka.

BELOW: view of Rijeka from the fortress.

TIP

It is worth timing a visit to Rijeka to coincide with the Rijeka Carnival, which runs from mid-January through to mid-February. Events include balls, parades and various cultural events.

Vienna and Budapest, and from its increasingly busy port; the majority of its impressive architecture dates from this period. These days Croatia's third largest city has a spring in its step once again. Public works of art brighten up its old streets, cultural events are blossoming and there is a buzz about the waterfront, the Riva, in summer. It may not be as pretty as Split, but if you are catching a ferry or passing through it merits a night or two, especially if you have been on an outlying island without any of the mod-cons that Rijeka offers in abundance.

A tour of Rijeka

A good place to begin a tour of Rijeka is the fortress of **Trsat**, set spectacularly above the city and offering panoramic views of the gulf. For those who would have liked to enjoy the sweeping views from Mt Učka, but were unprepared to do the leg work, Trsat, accessible by public bus from Rijeka city centre, offers a good alternative. For Učka veterans the 561 steps connecting the city below to Trsat are still something of a test.

Trsat's fortifications date back to pre-Illyrian times, and the Romans are among those who have exploited the site's strategic importance over the centuries. Today's fortress owes its design to the 13th-century Frankopan kings, who came from the Kvarner Gulf island of Krk. Defences were strengthened over the next few centuries, but once the Ottoman threat had receded and military technology had moved on, the castle was less strategically vital and fell into disrepair. It is now being restored and in summer hosts outdoor concerts.

Just across from Trsat's castle is the **Church of Our Lady of Trsat** (Gospa Trsat), associated with several legends. Devout residents of Rijeka claim this was where the House of Mary and Joseph came to rest after fleeing Nazareth on its way to Italy. The house is said to have remained on this spot for three years before continuing on its unusual journey west. The church contains tributes and messages of thanks, in various languages, from those who believe their prayers have saved loved ones from a litany of disasters. Among

BELOW:
Art Nouveau
facade, Rijeka.

he petitions and messages are many
from local fishermen, recounting the
dangers they have faced. Donated in
the 14th century, the supposedly mir-
acle-working icon of the Virgin Mary
– whose cult in Croatia is massive – is
said to have been the work of St Luke.

The 16th-century steps lead down
from Trsat to the regal **Hotel Continental**, a good place to stop off for
a refreshing drink, a bite to eat or
to make use of its Internet café. Just
across from the hotel is the **Mrtvi
kanal**, which accompanies the sleepy
Rječina river on its final run towards
the Adriatic. Head south and you will
come to the new metal bridge across
the channel that takes you from the
suburb of Sušak into the city centre.
Under Italian occupation Sušak was
part of Yugoslavia, while the Italians
controlled Rijeka's western flank.
These days the local tourist office is
trying to promote the merits of Sušak,
but in reality there is little to see and
do and you are far better off spending the lion's share of your time in the
city centre.

Directly across the canal is the
**Croatian National Theatre (Hrvat-
ko narodno kazalište)**, an elegant
neoclassical concoction with a pale
yellow facade and decorative pillars
beneath its green-tinged dome. It was
designed by the Austrian architects
Fellner and Helmer at the end of the
19th century and a major renovation
in the 1980s brought it back to something approaching its former glory. The
interior is spectacular, with a fabulous
rococo ceiling. Acoustically it is one of
Croatia's most impressive venues and it
attracts international as well as domestic artistes. Its first performance was
Verdi's *Aida* back in 1885. Look out for
the statue of Croatian composer Ivan
Zajc outside the theatre.

Just across the square from the theatre is the **Main Market (Velika tržnica)**,
dating from 1880 and lined with cheap
and cheerful eateries and beer terraces.
The interior is an architectural free-for-
all that has evolved over the ages, but

the facade retains its Austro-Hungarian
elegance, with a grand arch welcoming customers. Construction of the
superstructure by the architect Izidor
Vauchning was a pioneering effort in
the use of metal and glass, reflecting
the period's changing architectural
ideas. The market is a good place to
get a snapshot of Rijeka life, with lashings of local colour, especially in the
Liberty-style fish market.

Rijeka's Korzo

From the theatre walk northwest to
the **Korzo**, an elegant boulevard running through the heart of Rijeka. It
is flanked by Austro-Hungarian era
buildings evoking more a provincial
Austrian city than an Adriatic port.
It encompasses the stretch of land
between the canal and the main railway station, but the most interesting
section is just behind the waterfront
north of the Riva. Its basic design and
many of its buildings owe much to
Trieste-based architect Anton Gnamb,
who arrived in Rijeka in 1773 and
worked in the city until his death in
1806. Even the fast-food outlets and

*Overlooking the
Korzo, Rijeka's
main boulevard.*

BELOW:
café on the Korzo.

The double-headed eagle, symbol of the Austro-Hungarian Empire, on a building in Rijeka.

RIGHT: the Church of St Vitus.

tacky shops cannot impair the air of elegance. Several stately cafés offer the chance to take in the ambience and watch local people flitting by or enjoying their evening promenades, and the quality of the shops is rapidly improving.

Roughly halfway along the Korzo on its north side is the **City Tower** (Gradski toranj) with four clocks, which was built on top of the old medieval gateway into Rijeka and was one of the few buildings to survive Rijeka's 1750 earthquake. The 18th-century Baroque design incorporates an ostentatious Austro-Hungarian eagle over the entrance to remind the citizens of just who was in control. Look out for the busts of the emperors Charles IV and Leopold I. The former first designated Rijeka a free port, leading to a rush of prosperity that funded the construction of much of the city centre and enriched the local merchants. In the 1980s the tower underwent extensive restoration work, which shored up its superstructure but left it a rather unsettling shade of lime green. Today the City Tower marks the fault line

between the order and harmony of the Austro-Hungarian section of the city and the more shambolic **Old Town** (Stari grad), beyond the arch. The rambling streets are still fairly shabby, but there have been a few attempts at restoration and the introduction of modern street sculptures.

The main square in the old town is **Trg Ivana Koblera**. One interesting feature is the Stari kolodrob fountain, the work of Croatian architect Igor Emilio. Two large concrete wheels sit atop the spouting water, forming an arresting sight that manages to divert attention from the square's ugliest post-World War II buildings. Close by a 4th-century **Roman Arch** (Stara vrata) is the oldest standing structure in the city.

Farther to the north is the **Cathedral of St Vitus** (Katedrala sv. Vida), one of Rijeka's most impressive churches, dedicated to the city's patron saint. The 17th-century cylindrical design is unusual. Its construction dragged on for over 100 years and was never really finished, as the two bell towers that were part of the original design were

Pirates of Senj

Today the sleepy Kvarner Gulf town of Senj is somewhere that most visitors glimpse fleetingly as they zoom past on the Adriatic Highway between Rijeka and Northern Dalmatia. The town's history, though, is steeped in the exotic tales of the 16th-century Uskoks, piratical warrior oarsmen.

Refugees kicked out of the hinterland by the advance of the Ottoman Empire, the belligerent Uskoks bore a grudge against the Turks that the Austro-Hungarian rulers of the Kvarner Gulf were only too happy to exploit. With the tacit support of Vienna they built their Nehaj Fortress overlooking the town and used the forested cove of Senjska Draga to launch surprise attacks on Ottoman vessels plying the lucrative trade routes to Venice.

Their attacks were so successful and savage that they triggered war between Venice and the Austro-Hungarians in 1615, culminating in the Treaty of Madrid two years later. The Uskoks were forced inland, and the Austro-Hungarian navy sank many of their ships.

Today the legacy of the Uskok pirates is resurrected during Senj's August carnival and is recorded in the Nehaj Fortress. From the hillside ramparts you can see the stretch of the Adriatic that the Uskoks brutally made their own.

itched. The most noteworthy part of the interior is the Gothic crucifix above the main altar. Local legend has it that a blasphemer once hurled a stone at the crucifix, whereupon it began to bleed and the ground beneath the assailant opened up and swallowed him.

Further north is the green expanse of the **Park Nikole Hosta**, containing the Rijeka City Museum and the Historical and Maritime Museum. In Communist times the modern building housing the **City Museum** (Muzej grada Rijeke; Mon–Fri 10am–1pm, 5–8pm, Sat 10am–1pm; charge) used to be the Museum of National Revolution and it has been a little slow to find its feet in its new role. Its highlights tend to be the temporary exhibitions that occasionally pass through.

The **Historical and Maritime Museum of the Croatian Littoral** (Pomorski i povijesni muzej Hrvatskog primorja; Tue–Sat 9am–1pm; charge) occupies a far grander building next door, which used to house Rijeka's governor. You can walk along the arcade from the City Museum, passing some outdoor sculptures on the way. Inside, the highlights of the maritime exhibits include replicas of Rijeka-built tankers, paintings of old sea dogs, stuffed sharks and replicas of the sailing ships that once used the city's port. Other displays include weapons, traditional folk costumes and assorted finds from local archaeological digs. Look out for two torpedo-firing cannons – torpedoes are said to have been invented by Croatian pioneer Ivan Lupis (Baron von Rammer) in Rijeka in 1878.

South to Paklenica National Park

If you head south along the *Magistrala* towards the Paklenica National Park there are few reasons to stop off, as the towns of Bakar, Kraljevica, Crikvenica, Karlobag and Jablanac have little to recommend them. Senj was the base of the piratical Uskoks *(see page 188)*, but there is little to see apart from a small castle once used by the pirates. As the 145km (90-mile) Velebit range reaches its final flourish, this sheer karst fortress concedes a brace of gorges that cut deep into

Making a great escape to the Paklenica National Park.

BELOW: rock climbing is popular near the entrance to the park.

TIP

There are numerous caves within the boundaries of Paklenica National Park. One of the most impressive is Manita peć, which is over 170 metres (560ft) long and contains a number of large underground chambers.

the massif, opening up a wild landscape where four types of eagle and both honey and mouse buzzards wheel overhead and bears roam. This spectacular corner of Croatia has been protected as the **Paklenica National Park** (Nacionalni park Paklenica) ❻ since 1949, with hunting and hotels banned within its confines and all visitors paying an admission charge to help cover conservation costs. The best base for exploring the national park is Starigrad, increasingly referred to as Starigrad Paklenica, more a gaggle of *pensions*, grill restaurants and campsites littered along the coastline rather than a real town. Be sure to secure a room with a view of the Velebit for unforgettable multi-hued mountain sunsets.

Paklenica National Park itself is divided into two main gorges: Mala Paklenica and Velika Paklenica, literally "small" and "big" Paklenica. The former has been preserved as much as possible in its original condition, with no amenities and loosely marked trails that deter day-trippers. Being well-prepared with good local advice and

accurate maps for exploring this part o the park is essential. Velika Paklenica more user-friendly, with drinking four tains and a well-marked main trail tha snakes up in a two-hour walk from th car park to a mountain hostel, wher more serious hikers and climber spend the night before starting earl ascents of the park's lofty peaks.

As you enter the park you will usuall see rock climbers tackling the faces of th sheer rock walls. Organised mountair eering excursions are possible, if booke seven days ahead: see www.paklenica.h for details. Look out for a small door o the left that leads into a secret bunke (opening hours change monthly) use by the Yugoslav Army until 1990. O the way up to the mountain hostel tw paths break away from the main arter to the peak of Anica kuk, a steep bu straightforward scramble that most rea sonably fit people can manage. To th left of the main path a trail leads to th Manita peć, a cave with a fine array o stalactites and stalagmites.

The main path has plenty of inter est, with voluminous rock skyscraper rising hundreds of metres above an

BELOW: it is essential to book ferries in summer.

section running alongside a gurgling stream surrounded by Alpine trees and vegetation. From the mountain hostel those with the necessary equipment can tackle various climbs and hikes depending on their level of expertise. Croatian climbers conquered the highest peaks in the 1940s, and today mountaineers from all over Europe come to pit themselves against peaks and ridges ranging from easy to extreme, with some routes having an X+ rating for free-climbing.

Do not underestimate the weather; even on a bright day in summer a violent thunderstorm can quickly whip up and crash over the Velebit. Whether you are just dipping in for an afternoon walk or embarking on a week-long assault of the most challenging peaks, the Paklenica is a highlight of the Kvarner Gulf.

nner Kvarner Gulf Islands

Krk ❼, the largest island in Croatia, is the most easily accessible of the Kvarner Gulf islands, as you can drive over the bridge from the Croatian littoral. The island also has its own inter-national airstrip, which functions as Rijeka's city airport. As it is so close to the major road arteries to Zagreb, Istria and Slovenia the island is maddeningly popular with tourists in summer and many of the island's 68 settlements struggle under the strain of thousands of Slovenes, Austrians, Germans and citizens of the former Soviet Bloc states. In fact, tourism on Krk dates back to at least 1866, when the island's first postcards were produced.

The most attractive and historically interesting settlement on Krk is **Krk Town** (Grad Krk) itself. Its rambling old town is complemented by an attractive modern section that reclines by the sea in a collage of villas and stone cottages. It is over an hour's drive from the mainland bridge to Krk Town, but in high season there is little appeal in stopping off in the congested resorts of Omišalj, Njivice and Malinska on the way south. In summer, it is essential to book accommodation in Krk Town.

The town's sturdy defensive walls date from Roman times, though the Venetians added parts in the 15th

TIP

The Krk Summer Festival is the pick of the Kvarner Gulf island festivals. Krk Town's old quarter is the main venue for classical concerts and folk music, but there are events all around the islands from late July until late August.

BELOW:
island-hopping
from Krk to Cres.

View over the small, attractive resort of Baška on the island of Krk.

BELOW: on the beach at Baška.

and 16th centuries. The highlight of the old town is the Romanesque **Cathedral of the Assumption** (Katedrala Uznesenja), constructed over the foundations of a 6th-century church. Particularly interesting are the nave and the 15th-century Frankopan chapel, as well as the graves of local bishops dating from the 16th century.

In an adjoining gallery there is a collection of works by Italian 16th- and 17th-century masters. One of the most interesting is an earlier work, a rare painting by the 14th-century Venetian artist Paolo Veneziano.

Other attractions in Krk Town include the **Canon's House** (Kanonička kuća), with its Croatian Glagolitic script, the Romanesque basilica of the Church of Our Lady of Health (Crkva Majke Božje od zdravlja) and the Decumanus Art Gallery (Galerija Decumanus), showcasing the work of some modern Croatian artists, particularly those from in and around Krk. The town's castle has also been reinvented and now stages a varied summer-long programme of cultural performances.

Best beach

The most dramatically located resor on Krk, and the one with the be beach, is **Baška**, on the island's soutl ern tip, with the lofty ridge of th Velebit mountains rising like a wa out of the Adriatic in the distanc Baška is no secret and is very popula in summer, but its 2km (1-mile) swee of beach (a European Blue Flag wi ner since 1999) is impressive, its re taurants fairly good and its old tow full of cosy *pensions* with a splash c personality unobtainable in the larg resorts that cover Krk. If you are lool ing for a few days of seaside relaxatio with all the facilities that you nee before heading south or north, the Baška is a recommended stop. Th town is also within easy reach of th village of Jurandvor, where St Lucy Church (Crkva sv. Lucija) houses replica of the 12th-century Baška Tal let (Baščanska ploča) that was foun here. The tablet is the oldest exis ent example of Glagolitic script an also includes the first mention of th Croatian kings who presided ove Croatia a millennium ago. The orig

al tablet is at the Academy of Arts nd Science in Zagreb.

If you have more than a couple of ays on Krk and have fallen in love with Croatian wine then head for the north oast town of **Vrbnik**. This scenic town, et atop rugged cliffs with views back o the sweeping mountains of the main- and, is renowned for its first-rate white vines, especially Vrbnička žlahtina. In Croatian *žlahtina* means "noble" and his straw-coloured wine impresses most isitors who savour it in the old town's vine cellars and restaurants. The main roducers to look out for are Katunar, oljanić and Juranić.

Rab's medieval bell towers

rom Baška regular ferries make the hort and enjoyable crossing over to the own of Lopar on the northern tip of **Rab Island** (Otok Rab) ❽. Rab's north oast is much less developed than Krk's, ut it is hard to find much reason to ang around in sleepy **Lopar** for more han a few hours when **Rab Town** (Grad Rab), one of the most beautiful towns n Croatia, is less than an hour's drive outh. Rab Town is quite simply daz-

zling, a medieval oasis stretched out in a riot of church spires and winding streets on a narrow peninsula surrounded by crystal-clear water. Whether you prefer exploring the churches or just swim- ming off the pine-shrouded beaches it is hard not to fall in love with the town. A feature of Rab, captured on many a post- card, is the lovely silhouette of bell tow- ers on the skyline. A good place to start a walking tour of the churches to which they belong is Trg svetog Kristofora, where you can climb the steps into the old quarter of Rab Town. Take a quick diversion up the short section of the medieval walls that are open to the pub- lic to gain a good overview of the town's layout. The Church of St John (Crkva sv. Ivan) is just a short walk along Gornja ulica. In the 19th century much of the 6th-century original was scavenged for building materials, but the crumbling remains retain plenty of charm.

A little further along Gornja ulica is St Justine's Church (Crkva sv. Justina), with its 16th-century bell tower, today home to the **Museum of Sacred Art** (Muzej sakralne umjetnosti; high sea- son 7.30–10pm; charge). Its collection

TIP

Rab Musical Evenings is a very popular festival that takes over Rab Town from June through to the end of August. One of the main venues is the Church of the Holy Cross. Also look out for the Rab Tournament in August, with jousting and other medieval sports and games.

LEFT: view of the old town of Rab.

Glagolitic Script

Until well into the Middle Ages the Croatian language was usually written down using a unique alphabet known as the Glagolitic script, introduced by the monks Cyril and Methodius in the 9th century, and a precursor of Cyrillic. But as Renaissance influences grew stronger in Croatia, the Roman alphabet overtook Glagolitic and grad- ually the languages of the Serbs and Croats began to merge. After World War I and the establishment of the Kingdom of Serbs, Croats and Slovenes, this similarity was officially recognised as Serbo-Croatian, which came to be the chief language of Tito's Yugoslavia. Opposition to this merger, and the consequent relegation of pure Croatian to a local dialect, became a rallying point for nationalist feelings following the break-up of Yugoslavia.

Today Croatians take enormous pride in surviving examples of Glagolitic text, and "Glagolitic Alley", as the road to Hum in Central Istria is called *(see page 173)*, celebrates this unique heritage with a series of sculptures based on Glagolitic characters. Look for examples of the real thing in some of the country's museums, usually inscribed in stone. The oldest and longest example is the 12th-century stone tablet known as the Baška Ploca, which records a gift to the church from King Zvonimir.

St Antony's, one of Rab's many interesting churches.

BELOW:
taking cover from the sun on Rab.

includes a painting by the 14th-century Venetian painter Paolo Veneziano and a 12th-century reliquary containing the skull of St Christopher, with scenes of his martyrdom worked into the design along the sides. The last of the churches on Gornja ulica is St Andrew's (Crkva sv. Andrija), a 12th-century construction topped by a Romanesque bell tower.

The most magnificent campanile in Rab Town belongs to the 11th-century **Cathedral of St Mary the Great** (Katedrala sv. Marija Velika), tucked towards the end of the peninsula. Actually it lost its cathedral status in the 19th century but everyone still calls it one. You can climb the 25-metre (82ft) high bell tower for a sweeping view of Rab Town and the surrounding area, but it is also worth taking time to savour the calm simplicity of the interior. In particular, look out on the left wall for the relief of Christ, originally belonging to a 7th-century church on this site. Also look out for the fine *Pietà* by Petar, an artist from the Dalmatian town of Trogir, which was positioned over the main altar in the 15th century.

Behind the cathedral, on the tip of the peninsula, is the Church of St Antony (Crkva sv. Antuna Malog), which has a wooden sculpture of the saint said to date from the 12th century.

St Marinus, who founded the world's oldest republic, San Marino, in AD 301, was born on Rab and the two places have a twinning agreement.

Holiday mood

Away from its churches Rab Town is perfect for aimless wandering, with a tight warren of medieval streets enlivened by small bars and boutiques opening out to café-strewn squares, with glimpses of the sparkling Adriatic waters around every corner. Even at the height of summer the old town is quiet during the day as its many tourists are either at the beaches dotted around the peninsula or on one of the myriad tour boats lined up along Rab Town's wide waterfront every morning, offering a huge selection of day tours. At night in high season things are a different proposition altogether, as thousands of visitors crowd the streets and a number of discos thump on into the small hours.

The rugged Frkanj Peninsula just west of Rab was one of Croatia's oldest naturist resorts. In August 1936 it was visited by Britain's Edward VIII and his American future wife Wallis Simpson, who obtained special permission from the town authorities to go skinny dipping there. However, there are records of naturism on Rab going back more than a century (see page 67).

From 1942 to 1943 Italy ran a concentration camp near the village of Kampor, 5km (3 miles) northeast of Rab Town by road. Most of the prisoners were Slovenian, with smaller numbers of Croats and Jews. After Italy signed the armistice in 1943, Italy allowed most of the surviving Jews to flee to the Italian mainland, although some who were too sick or elderly to travel remained in the camp and were deported to Auschwitz when the Germans took over the camp. After the war a memorial complex and cemetery were built on the site.

Pag

The last Kvarner Gulf island before the hump of Dalmatia is **Pag** ❾, a barren place with far fewer facilities than the other main gulf islands. It is celebrated for its eponymous hard and salty-tasting sheep's cheese (*Paški sir*), served with *pršut* (a Croatian version of prosciutto) in restaurants all over the country. Its other renowned product is the intricate lace (*Paška čipka*) that local women have been crafting for centuries.

Today tourism helps keep these two industries alive, but the captivating curl of Pag Town is rarely anywhere near as busy as Rab Town. The old town rises above the waterfront and is home to a small cathedral, a couple of churches, the Ducal Palace (Kneževa palača), an unfinished bishop's palace and a museum dedicated to lace production. Pag is developing a reputation as Croatia's party island, with the greatest concentration of bars and clubs around **Zrće beach**, near the island's second town, Novalja, on the south coast.

Outer Kvarner Gulf Islands

Within sight of the Opatija Riviera and the inshore islands is the long, thin stretch of **Cres** ❿, sometimes confused with the island of Lošinj as only a very narrow 11-metre (36ft) wide channel

Pag's famous sheep's cheese goes particularly well with pršut, *a tasty air-dried ham that is a speciality of Istria.*

BELOW: the marina on Lošinj.

TIP

A useful resource for anyone interested in buying property in Croatia is www.property-abroad.com. It is highly advisable to deal with solicitors and estate agents who know the Croatian property market well, and to allow plenty of time.

separates the two. This is a lush island, supposedly where Jason and the Argonauts came in search of the Golden Fleece. It is easy to reach the island by ferry from either mainland Istria or Valbiska on the island of Krk. If you are coming on foot your best bet is the catamaran from Rijeka.

Cres Town (Grad Cres) crowds around Cres Bay in the verdant northern half of the island, which offers a sharp contrast to the dry south. The town still owes much of its livelihood to fishing, and its restaurants are a treat, with a choice between the fresh seafood catch or the delicious lamb for which Cres is renowned. Cres Town's highlights include the **Church of St Mary of Snow** (Crvka sv. Marije Snježne), with its 15th-century relief of the Madonna and Child, a Venetian loggia, a Franciscan Monastery (Franjevački samostan) and a museum in the old town with many Roman artefacts – legacies of the time when Cres lay on one of the main Roman trade routes.

Farther north the town of **Beli** is known for its population of rare griffon vultures (*bjeloglavi supe*), which are

as fond of the local lamb as the tourist are. Today the vultures are a protected species and survive along the cliffs near the town. Beli also has the **Caput Insulae Ecology Centre** (Eko centar Caput Insulae; www.supovi.hr; Mar–Oct daily 9am–8pm; charge), set up as part of the conservation effort, but which is also open to curious tourists wanting to learn more about these massive birds. Sometimes it is possible to take a look at birds that have been rescued after being injured and are being nursed back to health. The centre also runs acclaimed activity holidays for paying volunteers.

Twin island

Across the channel **Lošinj** ⑪ first came to the attention of tourists in the 19th century when elderly Austrians came to spend the winter. Today tourism is the main industry and Mali Lošinj is a fully fledged resort town. In the summer stalls around the harbour sell all types of souvenirs, while bobbing boats also offer fresh fruit and vegetables in a colourful scene. There are plenty of pavement cafés dotted around the bay where you can relax and enjoy the action. Mali Lošinj's other attractions include a couple of art galleries, the 15th-century Church of St Martin (Crvka sv. Martin) and the Baroque Church of the Nativity of the Virgin (Crkva Rođenja Blažene Djevice Marije).

Veli Lošinj is much quieter than its bright sibling, and its fishing industry still manages to hold its own against the demands of tourism. The pedestrianised old town is an atmospheric place for aimless wandering, interrupted by visits to the many cosy cafés and inexpensive restaurants serving excellent seafood. The steep streets do not really house many tourist attractions as such, bar the 18th-century Church of St Anthony (Crkva sv. Antun) and a Venetian defensive tower built at the height of the Uskok threat, when the notorious marauders of Senj (*see box page 188*) were at their peak.

BELOW: ringing the church bell, Lošinj.

Buying Property

The recession notwithstanding, for a small but growing number of foreigners, living in Croatia is an affordable dream – or an exciting investment.

D rawn by its alluring way of life and impending EU entry, there has been an overall long-term rise since independence in the number of foreigners buying property in Croatia as a hot investment or main or second home. However, as in most European countries since 2008 the recession has dampened the market even as prices have fallen.

Yet foreign property ownership on any scale is a relatively recent phenomenon. In the past Croatia has had tight restrictions on foreigners buying property, partly because of vexed colonial memories. As the most recent example, during World War II, the Italian Army occupied the Yugoslav coast and Italy sponsored an Ustaše takeover of Croatia. In Istria Mussolini even banned the use of Croatian surnames, and using the Croatian language in public, while ethnic Italians and Germans – whose families had often been there for centuries – enjoyed privileged status. Unsurprisingly, after the war relations between Croats and the Italian minority were tense. Although not legally forced to leave, about two-thirds of ethnic Italians chose to do so for political, economic and religious reasons, while Italian citizens were banned from buying property.

The many ethnic Germans fared even worse, being stripped of citizenship and having their property confiscated without compensation. Many were even forced into slave labour. These issues are likely to resurface as Croatia moves towards EU entry, just as they did with Poland over compensation to ethnic Germans forced to leave the Sudetenland.

Since independence rules have slowly relaxed but the war and fears about Croatia's stability deterred many potential buyers and the market has been tepid, certainly compared with many other Mediterranean countries. The most typical foreign buyers have been those with business interests in Croatia, largely in major commercial and tourism centres. However, as Croatia is poised to join the EU, fears of instability are declining and there has even been a backlash from Croatians in places such as Dubrovnik, worried that they are being priced out of the market.

In the 1990s the government introduced so-called reciprocity laws allowing citizens of countries where Croatians were able to buy property to do the same in Croatia, albeit with many time-consuming bureaucratic hurdles. Many foreigners sidestepped the rules by setting up a Croatian company to buy property on its behalf. In February 2009 as part of its EU entry process the government liberalised the laws still further, allowing foreigners to buy property on the same basis as Croatians, although it is too soon to see what practical effect this will have.

Not wishing Croatia's coast to become another Costa Brava, the government enforces strict rules on development. This is good news for tourism but not always for property developers. Nonetheless there have been increasing numbers of residential developments in resorts aimed at holiday-let investors.

Croatia is attractive to those priced out of many other Mediterranean countries, although not especially cheap by former Yugoslav standards. Some of the most popular hotspots are resorts on the Istrian and Dalmatian coasts such as Rovinj, Pula and Poreč, as well as islands such as Hvar and Brač.

In January 2008 a mere 11,517 foreigners or foreign companies owned property in Croatia. So for investors, or those enamoured with the Croatian way of life, it is not too late to join the bandwagon. ❑

RIGHT: a typical seaside house on the Kvarner Gulf.

NORTHERN DALMATIA

This region has Venetian-style ports and Roman remains, but the highlights are its natural attractions – the lakes and waterfalls of Krka National Park and the Kornati archipelago

Crossing the Maslenica Bridge from the Kvarner Gulf transports travellers into the long, sinewy rump of Dalmatia, a slice of Croatia that stretches all the way around the belly of Bosnia to the Republic of Montenegro in the extreme south. Northern Dalmatia may not have the renowned cities and resorts of Central or Southern Dalmatia, however it does offer a wealth of history, superb coastal scenery and two of the most impressive natural parks in Europe.

During the 1990s' war the region was one of the worst affected parts of Croatia as rebel Serbs from nearby Knin and the Yugoslav army conspired to establish a sturdy front line and mount major attacks on the cities of Šibenik and, especially, Zadar, as well as terrorise and ethnically cleanse smaller towns and villages around the region. The Serbs blew up the Maslenica Bridge and it was not until the Croatian offensive of 1995 that the threat was lifted.

The effects of the war are still being felt economically with much of the heavy industry that used to power the economy still in the doldrums. Increasingly the regional authorities are looking towards tourism as a way of making ends meet, and new restaurants and hotels are starting to appear, though development outside mass tourist resorts like Solaris, just south of Šibenik, remains slow.

The highlights

While the cities of Northern Dalmatia are not as well known as those further south they have much to recommend them. The old centre of Zadar is dramatically situated along a peninsula and has a wealth of Roman architecture, while Šibenik is perhaps the most "Croatian" city on the whole coastline, largely devoid of Roman and Venetian embellishments. Smaller towns and resorts such as Vodice and Primošten are pleasant oases in which to spend a few days, enjoying the fresh

Main attractions
NIN
ZADAR
ŠIBENIK
KRKA NATIONAL PARK
PRIMOŠTEN
KORNATI ISLANDS
ZADAR ISLANDS

PRECEDING PAGES: monastery at Krka National Park. **LEFT:** St Donat's Byzantine church, Zadar. **BELOW:** a Dalmatian dog.

TIP

For those looking to get away from it all there is a string of idyllic sand bars a few kilometres north and east of Nin, though they have little in the way of tourist facilities.

local seafood and good Dalmatian wines. Nin is one of the most historically important towns in Croatia, but neglected by most foreign visitors who are more interested in reaching resorts farther south.

The non-urban highlights are the Krka National Park and the Kornati Islands. The former, in many ways every bit as impressive as Plitvice National Park in Central Croatia, is a breathtaking limestone landscape of plunging waterfalls, broad lakes and rugged ravines. The Kornati Islands are unique in the Mediterranean, an uninhabited and barren but beautiful playground for day-trippers and yachtsmen that is gaining a reputation as one of the most relaxing sailing destinations in Europe. To the north of the Kornati group is the large and rugged Dugi otok, where the main activity is taking it easy and enjoying the fact that there are no crowds or tour buses. It offers good food, plenty of low-key places to stay, and has a beautiful setting; in many ways it encapsulates the attractions of Northern Dalmatia.

Nin

The small town of **Nin** ❶ is something of a sleepy backwater, far from any major resort and relatively untouched by tourism. From the 7th to the 13th centuries it was a major hub for the Croatian bishops and kings – seven of whom were crowned here – though the Venetians practically levelled it in 1570 when they feared it would fall into Ottoman hands, and so little of its original grandeur remains.

The old town occupies an islet only 500 metres/yds in diameter, surrounded by a lagoon and linked to the mainland by a 16th-century stone bridge. The most significant building left standing is the **Holy Cross Cathedral** (Katedrala sv. Križ), whose claims to be the smallest cathedral in the world may indeed be valid. The stark stone structure was built in the shape of a domed cross in the 9th century with an inscription carved above its entrance that is thought to be the oldest inscription surviving from the age of the Croatian kings. In recent years there has been some debate over whether the irregular lines and angles of the superstructure

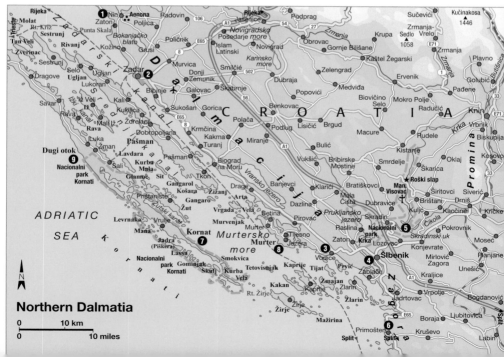

Northern Dalmatia

0   10 km

0   10 miles

were the result of shoddy design and workmanship, as some outside scholars have suggested, or a more calculated attempt to use the cathedral not only as a religious building, but also as a timepiece and calendar, an idea proposed by the Dubrovnik-born artist Mladen Pejaković.

A short distance southwest of town on the Prahulje hill, another important monument is the 12th-century **Church of St Nicholas** (Crkva sv. Nikole), a rare surviving example of the early Romanesque style, where the Croatian kings would vow to defend their nation.

On the coast on the outskirts of Nin are extensive mud plains. The mud is said to have curative properties and in the summer an out-patient programme allows visitors to sample one of the rejuvenating mud treatments. The set-up is not as slick as in most spa-type centres in other parts of Europe, but the treatments are not necessarily any worse for that.

Zadar

Take a 17km (10-mile) drive south of Nin and you will come to **Zadar ❷**,

Northern Dalmatia's most populous settlement, and once Dalmatia's largest town. Although Split may now have overtaken it in terms of size, it remains a lively city whose citizens overcame the trauma of devastating Allied bombing raids in World War II only to be subjected to a three-month Serbian siege in 1991. Then followed what the international community described as "low level warfare" (random artillery barrages and rocket attacks) up until 1995. Today Zadar is back on its feet and most of the damage has been repaired. The city is attempting to woo back the tourist business that its Roman heritage and dramatic old town so well deserve.

The centre of Zadar occupies a narrow peninsula overlooking the Zadarski Channel (Zadarski kanal), with the old Roman town hemmed in by sturdy walls and a wide seaside promenade circling the fortifications. The most dramatic entrance to the old quarter is the **Mainland Gate** (Kopnena vrata), accessible from the small harbour at Foša, the only surviving portion of Zadar's protective moat

Surrounded by a lagoon and with a strong north wind and long sandy beach, Sabunike, a short walk from Nin, is one of the best places in the Adriatic for windsurfing and kite surfing for all levels. Equipment and training are both available.

BELOW:
Zadar harbour.

Zadar Dreams (Zadar snova; www.zadar snova.hr) in August is an innovative arts festival showcasing new theatre and performance art at outdoor venues around the old town peninsula.

BELOW: ringside views in Zadar.

system. On the right as you approach the gate is a citadel that functioned as an active garrison from Venetian times until the 18th century; it lies over earlier, Roman fortifications.

Once inside the Mainland Gate turn right and three blocks in is Štroka ulica, an arrow-straight Roman road dissecting the old town, passing many of the main sights on its way west to the sea. Its old churches, squares and museums have been painstakingly restored, but they are interspersed with large areas of modern buildings, resulting in some odd juxtapositions.

On the way west the first church you come to is **St Simeon's** (Crkva sv. Šimuna), rebuilt in the 17th century in Baroque style, though there are elements of Renaissance and Gothic architecture, as well as evidence of a 5th-century church on the same site. The main attraction is St Simeon's gold sarcophagus, moved here from its original home in the Church of St Mary the Great when that was knocked down during the building of the city walls. The work of the Milanese goldsmith Francesco da Sesto, it is covered with reliefs depicting the life of the saint and the rescue of his relics from the Venetians by Louis I of Anjou. According to a local legend Queen Elizabeth of Hungary commissioned the church to atone for her attempt to chop off and keep the finger of St Simeon.

A short distance down the street is **Narodni trg**, one of the city's busiest squares. The 16th-century town watch tower presides over outdoor cafés, invariably packed with ice cream-licking locals, while the eastern side of the square is home to a Venetian-style **loggia** (loža; Mon–Fri 9am–noon, 6–9pm; Sat 9am–1pm; charge), which is now an art gallery housing temporary exhibitions. Its modern, glass-fronted design harmonises with the older building. Along with the modern exhibits, look out for a stone table dating from 1600.

Narodni trg was Zadar's main public space in the Middle Ages. The **Forum**, a short walk further west, was the city's original hub. Little remains of the Roman buildings apart from a few columns, but an information board gives some idea of the scale of the once mighty colonnades. A couple of cafés – Zadar is renowned for its vibrant café culture – spill out into the Forum, where you can sip a cappuccino or a cold beer on the very spot where the Romans once went about their business. Look out for the chains in one of the largest Roman pillars: these were used to shackle miscreants in Venetian times

Byzantine masterpiece

The most impressive building in the square is undoubtedly the 9th-century **St Donat's Church** (Crkva sv. Donata; high season only 10am–1pm and 5–8pm), for many years the symbol of Zadar but no longer functioning as a church. This Byzantine monolith was commissioned by the Irish saint and built using stones from the Forum. Look closely and you may be able to make out jumbled snatches of Latin script on the stone walls and columns. The church is reputed to bear a similarity to the court chapel in Aachen, and in

act Bishop Donat visited Aachen during his mission to Charlemagne before commissioning the church. The severe exterior encloses a stark interior, whose acoustics are perfect for the classical concerts performed here in summer.

Nearby is the **Archaeological Museum** (Arheoloski muzej; Mon–Sat 9am–1pm and 6–8.30pm; charge), the oldest museum of its kind in Croatia. It is best to start on the upper floors, which house neolithic and Liburnian artefacts that pre-date the Roman collection on the first floor. The Liburnian materials are some of the most interesting, with jewellery and weapons over 2,000 years old. The collection culminates with exhibits from the Middle Ages and the time of the first Croatian kings. Look out also for artefacts preserved from Zadar cathedral.

Just off the Forum is the **Cathedral of St Anastasia** (Katedrala sv. Stošije), a vast Romanesque structure that was substantially rebuilt after World War II bombing and Serbian shelling in the 1990s, not to mention an attempt to destroy it by 13th-century crusaders. The original was consecrated in 1177 by Pope Alexander III. Although it blends in well, the bell tower was added in the late 19th century by an English architect, who may have been inspired by the bell towers on the Adriatic island of Rab further north.

The cathedral's ornate facade has three portals leading into a vast interior with three apses. Look out for the frescoes of John the Baptist, Christ and St Anastasia dating from the 13th century. You should also seek out the marble sarcophagus of St Anastasia, located in the left aisle. A six-sided baptistry used to stand on the southern wall, but it was destroyed by bombing during World War II. Look, too, for a marble plaque commemorating Pope Alexander III's visit, which has remained intact since 1177 and has survived the various travails of the cathedral.

Zadar's Serbian community

The Orthodox heritage of local Serbians, something that few local people are interested in today, surfaces behind the cathedral in Zadar's Serbian **Church of St Elijah** (Crkva sv. Ilija). Built in 1563 and originally

View over Zadar with the Cathedral of St Anastasia in the foreground.

BELOW: a handicrafts stall in Zadar.

Alfred Hitchcock once enthused that "the sunset is more beautiful in Zadar than California". It is hard to disagree with the director as you watch the sun sink into the Adriatic, turning the sky from a melting orange to a fiery red.

consecrated by the Greek Orthodox Church, it passed into the hands of the local Serb community in the 18th century. It contains a small collection of Orthodox icons. Architecturally it is not the most fascinating church in Zadar, but coupled with the knot of streets around it that makes up the small Serbian community, it is a reminder that the two communities co-existed peacefully before the disintegration of Yugoslavia.

Boat trips and beaches

In the 19th-century Cosmacendi Palace, overlooking the Jazine harbour, the **Museum of Ancient Glass** (Muzej antičkog stakla; daily 9am–9pm; charge) has a superb collection from Roman times and one of the best souvenir shops in town, selling replicas from the exhibition.

Further west, at the end of the Zadar peninsula, regular ferries leave for Ancona in Italy. To the right, you will find a confusing array of local ferries and tourist boats, where a gaggle of operators tout day tours to the Kornati Islands. These are not bad value, but it is worth shopping around as busines is highly competitive and a subtle hag gle out of earshot of the other opera tors is often well rewarded.

A more interesting walk, particularl when sunset is approaching, is to hea left away from the boats and strol back around the tongue-twistingl named **Obala kralja Petra Krešimir IV** to Foša. The walk takes you alon a breezy boulevard with sweepin views south across the Zadarski Chan nel to the island of Ugljan; these view are particularly enchanting at sunse There is a sprinkling of cafés and res taurants where you can savour the view and the expansive seafront; like the res of this underrated city, they are neve too crowded with tourists.

Less than an hour's drive south o Zadar is the resort town of **Vodice ❸** Vodice may be the most popular beac resort on the Northern Dalmatia coastline, but many of its beaches ar made of concrete and there is little o historical interest. The town grew as bulwark against the Ottoman Empire i the 14th century and by the 16th it ha its own protective walls, but the onl

emnant of these today is the three-
torey **Ćorić Tower** (Ćorića kula).

Mass tourism came to Vodice with
vengeance in the 1960s, leaving a
umber of bland hotels and a sprin-
ling of tourist-related facilities. Those
eking a relaxing day at the seaside in
igh season would do far better to head
ut of Vodice on one of the ferries to
he nearby islands of **Cogorun**, **Tijat**
r **Prvic**, which has a naturist beach.

ibenik

ist another 11km (7 miles) south
own the E65 from Vodice is the city
f **Šibenik ❹**. Until 1991 Šibenik
vas the chrome- and aluminium-
roducing capital of Croatia, a wealthy
ity known for having one of the fin-
st cathedrals on the Adriatic coast.
he Serbian shelling that followed the
reak-up of Yugoslavia, though, dented
s prosperity and now it is one of the
ost economically depressed cities in
ne new nation. There is little sign of
ne heavy industry coming back and
ne local authorities are pinning their
opes on tourism. This is slowly grow-
ıg, as the war-damaged old town is

patched up and a string of restaurants
and cafés revive some of the city's
former lustre. It is also a good base for
visiting **Krka National Park**, one of
Croatia's most spectacular landscapes
(*see box on page 209*).

Unlike most of Croatia's coastal cities,
Šibenik has no Roman heritage, built as
it was 1,000 years ago during the reign
of the Croatian kings. This Croat ances-
try gives it a unique feel, with winding, narrow streets and small buildings
instead of wide Roman thoroughfares
and spacious houses. The best way into
the old core is through the public gardens on the east of the old town, with
their trickling fountains. The garden
benches are a good place to sit and read
up on the city before you delve in.

The **Franciscan Church and Monastery** (Franjevački samostan i crkva)
at the southern end of the gardens
was built in Gothic style in the 14th
century, but it is relatively plain and
simple. The ceiling was embellished
later in the 17th century with various
depictions of the life of St Francis. Hiding away in the treasury is the *Šibenska
molitva*, or "Šibenik Prayer", said to

*A market in
workaday Šibenik, a
good place on the
coast to get a feel for
the real Croatia.*

BELOW:
overview of Šibenik.

Carvings from Šibenik Cathedral, one of the finest cathedrals on the Adriatic.

BELOW: a waiter at work in Šibenik.

be the oldest manuscript using the Croatian language in Latin script.

Just a few metres away is the waterfront, offering fine views out towards the narrow channel leading from the city's protected harbour to the open sea. A string of cafés and restaurants hug the seafront as it meanders round to the **Town Museum** (Gradski muzej; main collection daily 7.30am–3.30pm, temporary exhibitions 10am–1pm, 6–8pm; free), a small venue for temporary exhibitions with Croatian themes. There is also a permanent collection recounting the history of the city from prehistoric times through to the present day.

Shortly after the museum, steps lead up to Trg Republike Hrvatske, the city's imposing main square. The 15th-century **St Jacob's Cathedral** (Katedrala sv. Jakova), a World Heritage Site, dominates the scene. The cathedral took over a century to build; the bulk of it is the work of Zadar-born Juraj Dalmatinac, who came over from Venice. The cathedral is a cocktail of architectural styles, as the original relatively modest Gothic plans were repeatedly revised, becoming ever more elaborate as ambitions grew.

The upper sections of the exterior were constructed in the Renaissance style the interior is a visually pleasing blend of Gothic and Renaissance forms.

The interior is dominated by the dome, inspired by Brunelleschi's dome in the Duomo in Florence, which is supported by four immense columns Crowded around the cupola are the statues of various saints, the work o Dalmatinac, though he never lived to see his masterpiece finished (his son wa among those who completed the work) Look out for the sarcophagus of St Jacob to whom the cathedral is dedicated.

Among the most striking feature of the exterior are the 74 stone head depicting local luminaries of the day – they hang like Christmas decora tions from the apse. The best place to appreciate the beauty and scale of th cathedral is from the excellent seafood restaurant Gradska vijećnica, which has outdoor tables huddled under the old loggia on the opposite side of th square. The square, with its old, pol ished stones, is an agreeable spot, where children play in the day and Šibenik citizens go for their evening strolls,

r cry from 1991 when Serbian shells
it the square, damaging the cathedral,
though it was soon repaired. Look
ut for patches of bright white stone
n the cathedral's walls, indicating
here they have been patched up.

Farther west still, the waterfront is
acked with café-bars, which get busy
a the evenings. The buzz lasts until
round midnight, after which the
rowds dissipate, the hardy heading
ff to Vodice or Primošten in search of
eir resort nightlife.

Inland, the old town's streets run
iggledy-piggledy in a confusing pat-
rn, but wherever you go you will prob-
bly end up climbing to **St Nicholas
ortress** (Tvrđava sv. Nikola), built dur-
g Venetian times to keep the Ottomans
t bay. Most of the original fortress has
allen into ruin, but its sturdy cliff-top
amparts offer panoramic views of the
ity and out towards the Šibenski Chan-
el and the Adriatic islands. There are
aree other fortresses inland, the medie-
al Fort of St Anne (Tvrđava sv. Ana), the
7th-century Šubićevac Fort (Tvrđava
ubićevac) and the 15th-century Fort of
t John (Tvrđava sv. Ivan).

The resort of Primošten

Southeast of Krka National Park and
30km (18 miles) south of Šibenik on
the E65 is the pleasant coastal resort
of **Primošten 6**. The best approach
is from the sea, from where you can
best appreciate its position on a jut-
ting peninsula. At first sight there are
echoes of Rovinj, further north on
the Istrian coast.

The dramatic setting and the sheer
brilliance of the local light, which
gives the waters deep-blue hues, help
hide the fact that much of Primošten
is a 20th-century construction, partly
due to devastating bombing during
World War II and partly because of
the tourist boom in the 1960s, when
concrete monoliths sprang up.

Many of Primošten's main tourist
hotels have little allure, but there are
plenty of good spots for swimming
and relaxing. Primošten works best as
a place in which to lie back and recover
from the nearby cities as there is little
actually to do apart from sunbathe and
enjoy eating in the many local restaurants. The local Babić dry red wine is
also likely to enhance a stay here. For

TIP

For those who do not
have their own transport,
regular tours to the Krka
National Park operate
from Zadar, Šibenik and
other coastal resorts in
the region.

Krka National Park

Some Dalmatians reckon the lakes, rivers, gorges and
waterfalls at Krka are even more impressive than those
in Plitvice Lakes National Park in Central Croatia.

Northern Dalmatia's most striking natural mainland
attraction is the **Krka National Park 5** (Nacionalni park
Krka; www.npkrka.cro.net; charge). The Krka river forges
its way through 72km (45 miles) of countryside from its
lofty source in the Dinara Mountains to its effluence at
Šibenik. Since 1985 the area south of Knin as far as Skradin has been protected as a national park.

To access the park you can take a car to Lozovac and
park at the entrance, where a free bus will pick you up (in
winter visitors can drive the extra 4km/2½ miles on their
own). There are also daily buses from Šibenik. But a more
popular way of accessing it is by boat from the pretty little
village of Skradin, from where boats leave regularly for
Skradinski but, the area's most impressive waterfall. The
basic cruise to the waterfall is included in the entrance
charge. Forming one huge mass of pumping water and
solid rock are a spectacular array of 17 waterfalls; wooden

walkways help visitors navigate the site. There is a third
entrance at Roški slap (see below).

Additional cruises from both Skradin and Roški slap
explore the wetlands further upstream. They stop off at the
Visovac, where a monastery is set in the midst of the
Visovačko lake. The monastery was built in 1445 by Franciscans fleeing the Ottomans, and inside is preserved a
beautifully illustrated copy of Aesop's Fables, said to be
one of only three of its kind in the world. Another sacred
building, in the middle of the Krka River canyon, is the
Serbian Orthodox Monastery of the Holy Archangel, dating
from the 15th century or earlier.

The cruises also cover the early Croatian fortresses of
Trošenj and Nečven and **Roški slap**, another impressive
cascade of water. It is also possible to visit the remains of
a Roman military camp, **Burnum** (daily 9am–5pm). However, it is best to check on the latest park opening times
and boat schedules before visiting. There is no accommodation in the park itself but nearby Skradin has a couple of small hotels.

those looking for a different kind of relaxation there are also popular naturist beaches on the nearby island of Smokvica – take your own facilities – and 3km (2 miles) south of Primošten at Marina Lucica. Smokvica is accessible by taxi boat.

Kornati Islands

There is perhaps nothing to say about the **Kornati Islands** (Kornatski otoci) that has not been said before. George Bernard Shaw summed up the ethereal charm of the archipelago best when he first sighted them: "On the last day of the Creation God desired to crown his work, and thus created the Kornati Islands out of tears, stars and breath." This lofty praise is well deserved as there is nowhere else in Europe quite like this string of stark white islands strung out like a necklace in calm, balmy waters. For centuries locals dismissed the Kornati Islands as an arid, infertile wasteland, but to today's tourists and yachtsmen they are as near to paradise on earth as many can imagine getting. Local legend has it that when God threw the white hulks of rock into

the sea, intending to sculpt them into fertile land, he was so taken by their perfect beauty that he chose to leave them as they were.

The Kornatis form the largest archipelago in the Adriatic, with a total of 147 islands, many of them completely uninhabited and others abandoned outside the summer. From the large island of **Dugi otok** (Long Island) in the north the archipelago stretches 35km (21 miles) south to the island of **Žirje**, both of which help form the natural barrier against the open sea that makes the region so perfect for untroubled yachting and boating. As there are no sources of fresh water anywhere on the islands, populating the area has always been difficult.

Roughly speaking, the islands fall into four strips running north–south toward Žirje, with the two closest to the coast known as Gornji Kornat. The two outer strings make up the **Kornati National Park** (Nacionalni park Kornati; www.kornati.hr), comprising over 100 islands in total, three-quarters of which are no more than 1 hectare (2½ acres) in size. The park's main island, **Kornat**  which is around 25km (15 miles) long and 2.5km (1½ miles) wide, is the largest uninhabited island in the Adriatic.

Attempts are being made to promote Kornati as an ecotourism destination where man has done little to change or damage the environment. This is somewhat ironic as man has already wrought havoc on the environment by burning down the indigenous oak trees for firewood, while sheep introduced by local farmers have destroyed much of the original vegetation. Only tough grass and wild herbs such as sage survive amidst the crumbling old stone dykes that used to pen in the sheep.

Thankfully the very barrenness of the area and the logistical difficulties of setting up large-scale tourism have stopped real development, and the establishment of the national park in 1980 has also helped keep the developers at bay. Although in summer there are plenty of yachts and

BELOW: ship-shape and ready to sail.

boat day trips, the sheer size of the archipelago means that things seldom feel too crowded. Facilities are low-key – almost nonexistent outside high season – and rustic, with many sailors just choosing to moor in one of the many tempting bays rather than looking for a proper harbour. The restaurants that exist on some of the islands are informal and small-scale, serving simply cooked seafood. Accommodation tends to be in characterful old stone cottages and small houses, rather than in hotels. Camping is permitted only at the Levrnaka and Ravni Zakan campsites.

The most convenient marina for accessing the islands is on **Murter** ➑, an island just off the Northern Dalmatian coast, connected to the mainland by a bridge some 25km (16 miles) south of Biograd. Murter has hotel accommodation, restaurants, shops, supermarkets, travel agencies and all of the necessary facilities for setting out on a sailing expedition. The experience of sailing around the archipelago is relaxing, but sailors must have proper navigation tools, as there are many dangerous shallows around the various islands. The best time for sailing is May or June, when a pleasant breeze is present; July and August can be a little too calm unless you use a motor. Novice sailors will be safer joining one of the organised day trips; regular boat tours of the Kornatis leave from Murter, Šibenik and Zadar.

The Zadar Islands

Dugi otok ➒ (Long Island), north of the Kornati Islands, stretches for over 50km (30 miles) and is the largest of the so-called Zadar archipelago, which comprises some 300 islands. It is home to around 2,500 inhabitants and characterised by the same haunting beauty that pervades the Kornatis, as, like its neighbours, it has no natural fresh water supply. The rocky land undulates through a series of rocky ridges, coves and bays, with the highest point the limestone crest of Vela

straža, which reaches a height of 338 metres (1,110ft).

The main settlement on Dugi otok is **Sali**, which is a thriving fishing port. It also has a reasonable supply of accommodation and a sprinkling of pavement cafés and restaurants. Boat tours leave from Sali in high season for **Telašćica**, frequently cited as one of the most beautiful bays in Croatia. The sweeping bay is usually littered with yachts in summer, but there are no cruise liners, ferries or hotels to clog up the view. As elsewhere on the Dalmatian islands, the main pleasure is relaxing and enjoying the clean seawater and the natural beauty. If you are visiting on a yacht it is well worth heading ashore to walk around to **Lake Mir**, a lagoon separated from the sea by a narrow band of rocks.

The other inhabited islands of the archipelago – Pašman, Ugljan, Premuda, Olib and Molat – are similar in character, with isolated churches, the occasional monastery, small farms and, on Ugljan and Pašman, which are greener than the others and linked by a bridge, second homes. Accommodation is available in a few small hotels and private homes. ❏

Northern Dalmatia has a long history of salt mining, going back at least to Roman times. Croatia's leading salt producer is on Pag Island and the superior taste of the island's lamb is attributed to the saline soil.

BELOW: view over the bay from the island of Dugi otok.

BEACHES AND BOAT TRIPS

With a dazzling coast and more than 1,000 islands, there is so much to explore

It has been estimated that, if you count the islands and reefs, there are 5,385km (3,625 miles) of coastline in Croatia. It's a country just made for blissing out on the beach. Most beaches are pebbly or rocky and not very wide, and though this might seem a hindrance, it does help to keep the waters of the coast wonderfully clear, as very little sand is churned up by the waves. A lack of tides, which never rise beyond a metre, also means that debris is not continually washed up. Around 100 beaches have earned a EU Blue Flag for cleanliness.

There are, however, some spectacular sandy beaches, both on the mainland and, more often, on the islands, some reached only by boat. Beaches are universally safe, with few currents or undertows, and the water is warm from May to October. Facilities vary, depending on how remote the beaches are, but the main resorts are fully kitted out for windsurfing, sea kayaking and other water-borne activities.

If you are swimming in rocky areas, forget your image and put on plastic shoes – there are often sea urchins with nasty spines. Apart from an influx of jelly fish, these are the only nasties to worry about. Speedboats and jet skis are the only real hazards, though the larger beaches have designated areas.

As to etiquette, topless is normal, and there are always nudist beaches nearby. In high summer try to keep out of the sun in the middle of the day. You will see local people descend on the beach in the late afternoon for a swim and a touch of sun – not a bad habit to follow.

ABOVE: the shore at Orebić, a family holiday resort in a town was once known for its sea captains.

BELOW: Paradise Beach in sandy Crnika Bay in the Lopar peninsula, Rab island, is very shallow and ideal for children.

BELOW: Baška beach on Krk island is a fine pebble shore away from commercial centres.

BOAT TRIPS

Croatia has some of the best sailing waters in the world, and you should not visit the coast without taking a boat trip, particularly in the Kvarnar Gulf and on the Dalmatian coast. To the people of this region, water transport is a way of life, but for visitors it is still something special. Small boats in towns and resorts everywhere will ferry you to island villages and beaches, to hidden coves and special sites, often offering a fish lunch on the way, with perhaps some local brandy.

Take a trip from Zadar or Šibenik to Murter and the Kornati archepelago, or make a round trip from Dubrovnik to Koločep, Lopud and Šipan, and as you sail among the islands, around headlands and through channels, you will get closer to feeling what it is like to be not just a Croatian fisherman, but to have been an adventurer in ancient times, a Greek explorer, a Roman soldier, a Venetian merchant – a timeless traveller in the ancient sea.

r: though
and, Pag is
ust off-
, reached
causeway
Zadar.
one of the
st shores,
hing 270
70 miles).
ed with
coves,
s and
nes, it
limitless
tunities for
activities
kinds.

TOP: a traditional sailing boat is just one of the many vessels to take you to the island idylls.

ABOVE RIGHT AND BELOW: many excursion boats have on-board fish meals included in the price of the ticket.

CENTRAL DALMATIA

With its rich culture, stunning coast and myriad islands, Central Dalmatia is hard to beat. Its main city is Split, whose inhabitants have a reputation for being cosmopolitan, hedonistic and chic

Central Dalmatia is becoming one of the most popular regions to visit in Croatia and it is not difficult to see why. It is easy to spend a month, never mind a week, here, exploring its intriguing historical towns and cities, and relaxing on its many rugged islands with their pristine beaches and warm breezes scented with wild lavender and rosemary.

The region largely escaped the 1990s' war, though the Serbian blockade further north served to emphasise the region's isolation on a narrow strip of land to the south of Bosnia. To this day the region has poor railway links with the rest of the country. While the Serbs failed to make a real breakthrough, previous invaders such as the Romans, Venetians and Austro-Hungarians were more successful and their legacy is evident in the rich collage of architectural styles in the main ports.

Mercifully Central Dalmatia was also largely spared the hotel building boom that changed the face of Istria in the 1970s and 1980s and as a result it has far fewer large, anonymous-looking hotels. Tourism is only now starting to emerge as the main industry and many tourist developments are pleasantly small-scale with family-run restaurants and *pensions* offering a cheap and atmospheric alternative to impersonal eating places and large hotels.

The region has also been discovered by the extremely wealthy international yachting community and you will see plenty of multimillion dollar yachts in the marinas. Indeed, sailing is a great way to explore the islands and coast; the marinas are well-equipped and there are far fewer boats than in the Greek Islands. Add the first-rate seafood, the relaxed pace of life, the openness of the local people and the quality of the scuba diving and Central Dalmatia is hard to beat as a summer holiday destination.

South of Šibenik

Less than an hour's drive south of Šibenik is the picturesque town of **Trogir ❶**, set on a narrow island that

Main attractions
TROGIR
SPLIT
SALONA
BIOKOVO MOUNTAINS
MAKARSKA
PLOČE
BRAČ
HVAR
VIS

PRECEDING PAGES: the old town and marina of Trogir. **LEFT:** Diocletian's Palace, Split. **BELOW:** Kamerlengo Fortress, Trogir.

Trogir's elegant Riva, a fine venue for the evening promenade.

is linked by bridge to the mainland on one side and by another bridge to the island of Čiovo across the Trogir Channel on the other. Trogir has been inhabited for around 4,000 years. Some 3,000 people live in the old town, which they like to refer to as the "town museum", in acknowledgement of the rich range of architectural influences – medieval fortifications, Renaissance palaces and Venetian Gothic mansions meet on narrow medieval lanes and wide waterside boulevards. Unesco placed the town on its World Heritage List in 1997.

A good place to get acquainted with the layout of the town is from the ramparts of the **Kamerlengo Fortress** (Tvrđava Kamerlengo; daily 9am–10pm; charge), originally built by the Venetians in 1420 to fend off Turkish attacks. The ramparts offer good views across the old town's spires and rooftops and out to sea, with the suburbs of Split visible in the distance. During summer film screenings and other open-air events take place in the courtyard.

From the fortress head east along the **Riva**, Trogir's main boulevard,

which in summer is lined by expensive yachts, tour boats and crowded pavement cafés. This emphasis on leisure and tourism has resulted in the loss of some of the old town's traditional features; during a fairly recent facelift of the area, for instance, the characterful fish market that used to occupy a 16th-century loggia at the boulevard's eastern end was evicted and relocated on the mainland. Rearing up behind the loggia is the best preserved stretch of old town walls, now home to the immensely popular Padre Café and Big Daddy Bar.

Head through the late 16th-century South or Sea Gate (Južna vrata) and you come on to **Gradska**, the old town's main artery. Many of the town's key attractions are on this narrow street, which runs the length of the island and culminates in the Land Gate (Sjeverna gradska vrata), where a sculpture of St John, Trogir's patron saint, overlooks proceedings.

At the southern end of Gradska, just inside the South Gate, the 11th-century Benedictine **Convent of St Nicholas** (Samostan sv. Nicole; opening times

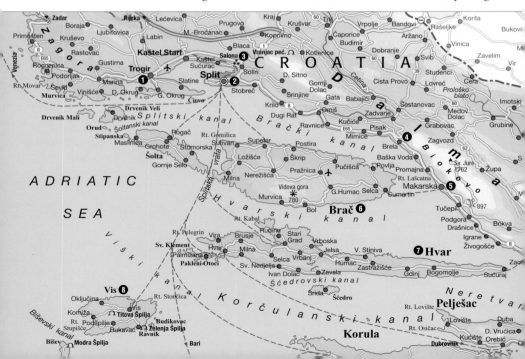

erratic and limited) is inhabited by just two priests and three nuns. The original building dates from the 11th century with the interior constructed in the Baroque style. Highlights include a 13th-century Romanesque painting of the Madonna and Child and Croatia's finest example of Greek art (the Greeks arrived in Trogir from Issa, now the Croatian island of Vis) – the 3rd-century reliefs of Kairos that were unearthed in the 1920s.

Further along Gradska the narrow street opens out upon **Trg Ivana Pavla II** (John Paul II Square, honouring the pontiff who made three episcopal visits to Croatia), which has a number of pavement cafés that are busy by day but fairly quiet by night. Looking across the square, the eye is drawn to the **Cathedral of St Lawrence** (Katedrala sv. Lovre; Mon–Fri 9am–7pm, Sat–Sun no fixed hours; charge), which appears to be in the final stages of a very long period of restoration.

The interior of the cathedral is breathtaking in its level of adornment. Enter from the side door of the three-nave building rather than the main portal and you will face the superb **St John's Chapel** (Kapela sv. Ivana). This ornate work by Nikola Firentinac just manages to stay on the right side of overblown, with more than 160 sculpted heads of angels, cherubim and saints surrounding the figure of God. Look out for the flower-embellished torches that are Firentinac's signature (also visible in a relief in the loggia across Trg Ivana Pavla II). St John's sarcophagus lies in the centre, a focus of devotion for many devout citizens of Trogir.

Leave the cathedral via the **West Portal** (Portal zapadnih), a 13th-century Romanesque masterpiece by the sculptor Radovan, with assistance from his many talented protégés. The upper section depicts scenes from the life of Christ and also scenes of local Dalmatian life, with hunting and fishing featuring strongly. The lower sections depict large figures of Adam and Eve hiding their modesty atop a couple of lions and, reflecting the politics of the time, exhausted Jewish and Ottoman figures bearing the weight of the door on their shoulders. The portal merits detailed viewing; make sure you come

Taking place in various indoor and open-air venues, the Trogir Summer Festival (Trogirskog ljeta) is a 10-week celebration of classical, choral and folk music in June, July and August. For more information visit www.trogir.hr.

BELOW: the altar in Trogir's cathedral.

Central Dalmatia

TIP

The Split Card gives holders free or reduced entrance to the city's museums, discounts at some hotels, on excursions and at the theatre. Valid for 72 hours, and costing just €5, and free if you are staying more than three nights, it is excellent value if you are planning on spending some time in the city. The card is available from the Tourist Information Centre in the Peristyle and other authorised outlets.

early in the day before the tour groups descend en masse.

Also on Trg Ivana Pavla II is Trogir's 15th-century **loggia** (loža), formerly the city court, which is topped by a clock tower. On the inside wall there is a slightly incongruous Meštrović relief of Petar Berislavić astride a rather strange-looking steed, while on the other wall is another Firentinac relief, which used to hang above the judge's chair when the loggia was used as a court. More interesting in some ways than what is still there is what is not: the sculpture of a Venetian lion that was destroyed by Croats opposed to Italian expansion in Dalmatia in the 1930s, something that the local guides claim to know nothing about. At the western end of the loggia there is a small shrine to the victims of the 1991–5 war and three Roman sarcophagi. At the other end of the loggia a door leads to the **Picture Gallery** (Pinakoteca; Mon–Sat 8am–8pm, Sun noon–4pm; charge), which houses a small but valuable collection of sacred art from the 13th to 16th centuries, including a 13th-

century polyptych of the Virgin and Child with Saints from the main altar of the cathedral. Another branch on the other side of the road (same hours; charge), next door to the tourist office, houses a small collection of medieval stone masonry.

From the square continue north along Gradska to Trogir's Town Museum (Gradski muzej), which is housed in an old Venetian palace. The family who built the villa kept a private library that was the largest in Trogir, with more than 5,000 books, many of which are still on display today. The main exhibition consists of stone artefacts, some Roman and others attributed to the Dalmatian sculptors Ivan Duknović and Nikola Firentinac. There is also an art gallery showcasing the work of local painter Cata Dujšin-Ribar (1897–1994).

Any sightseeing tour should finish up on the Riva, perhaps after a stroll west around the island, past the Kamerlengo Fortress. By evening the Riva is packed with tourists, and teenagers from Split, who scream aboard a fleet of mopeds as night falls. The

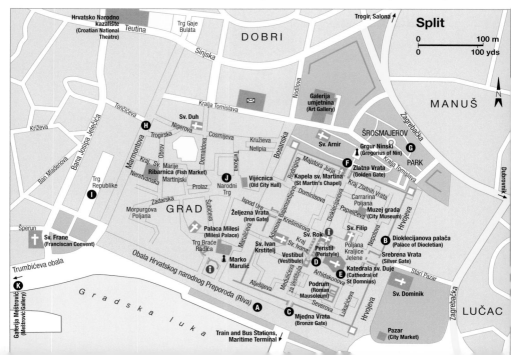

bars, cafés and waterfront restaurants stay open late; when they close hard-core revellers continue on to clubs in nearby Primošten and Split.

Second city first

Split ❷ is one of the Adriatic's liveli-est and most alluring cities and often manages to seduce visitors initially planning on passing through to stay for months or even years. Croatia's second city is a proud place; the local Splićani cultivate a fierce rivalry with Zagrebi-ans, a rivalry that reaches fever pitch on the football field when Hajduk Split lock horns with Dinamo Zagreb. The Splićani like to see themselves as infinitely more stylish and glamorous than their inland brethren, a view that the proliferation of fashionable shops and nightclubs and the local passion for people-watching support.

But Split has its problems, with high unemployment due to the decline of the city's traditional industries such as shipbuilding, high levels of crime in the housing developments that radiate from the centre, and suburbs blighted by the scars of heavy industry. But there is no denying the city's dramatic setting, with sheer karst mountains on one side and the Adriatic on the other. Arriving in Split on an early ferry and catching sight of its old town shim-mering in the morning light creates a wonderful first impression, and one that many people experience, given that the city is an important hub for island-hopping, with its ferry harbour conveniently located right next to the train and bus stations.

Diocletian's Palace

The centre of Split life still focuses upon Diocletian's Palace (Diokleci-janova palača), built on the waterfront by the Roman emperor Diocletian as a retirement home between AD 295 and 305 and later inhabited by the citizens of the neighbouring Roman city of Salona after invading Avars and Slavs destroyed their homes in the 7th cen-tury. Over the centuries Split's citizens chose to build into and around the palace structure rather than demolish it, offering today's visitors the unique chance to eat, sleep and drink in the footsteps of a Roman emperor. Unesco

You cannot miss Ivan Meštrović's gigantic statue of Grgur Ninski, outside the palace's Golden Gate. Touch the statue's toe for good luck.

BELOW: the cathedral of St Domnius, Split.

listed the complex in 1979. Two reasons for the remarkably well-preserved state of the ground floor are the high quality of limestone used – brought in from the island of Brač – and the fact that townspeople filled it with rubble from building works above.

The palm-fringed waterfront **Riva** is the most obvious place to begin a walking tour of the palace area. Its pavement cafés, cheap restaurants and waterside benches, all built around the grand facade of the palace, make it a natural focus. The waterside scene is all the more alluring now that the Riva has been pedestrianised.

From the waterfront you can delve straight into **Diocletian's Palace** Ⓑ through the **Bronze Gate** Ⓒ, which used to be right on the water's edge and only accessible by boat. The gate leads up through a tunnel to the Peristyle, where the Cardo joins the Decumanus, a simple layout that makes navigating the palace area very easy.

Diocletian was born in Dioclea, near Salona in AD 245, the son of former slaves, and rose to emperor through a distinguished career in the army. His retirement palace, which he began about half-way through his 21-year reign, was conceived on a grand scale and completed in AD 305 – the year he abdicated, the only Roman emperor to do so – and six years before his death. More than 200 buildings remain inside the original dimensions: his old chambers and garrisons have been converted over the centuries into shops, bars, cafés, hotels and homes, with more than 3,000 people still living where refugees from nearby Salona originally moved in. As you enter the Bronze Gate look out for the entrance to the subterranean museum, with artefacts from Roman times laid out in the emperor's old living quarters.

Once you are back above ground continue on through the tunnel, which is lined with souvenir stalls, and at its end some steep stairs bring you up into the **Peristyle** Ⓓ (Peristil). This remarkable Roman set piece features a sunken square, which houses a couple of cafés, while to the right are a line of Roman columns and the octagonal **Cathedral of St Domnius** Ⓔ (Katedrala sv. Duje; Mon–Sat 7am–noon, 4–7pm), whose

BELOW: café in the Peristyle.

lofty bell tower, one of the symbols of the city, was a later addition. Head past the Egyptian sphinx, once the guardian of Diocletian's tomb, and into the octagonal cathedral.

It is somewhat ironic that the last resting place of a man notorious for his persecution of Christians, and who was present at the beheading of St Domnius, the first bishop of Salona, should have been converted into a Christian cathedral – albeit one of the world's smallest – and that the nearby Roman temple has become a baptistry. Look out for the intricately carved reliefs of scenes from the life of Christ on the entrance doors.

Inside, the highlights include a portrait of Diocletian with his wife Prisca, which somehow survived the post-Roman makeover; the main altar, with paintings by Croatian artist Matija Pončun; and the north altar, sculpted in the 18th century by the Venetian Giovan Maria Morlaiter.

Other eye-catching things to look out for are the sacristy, dating from the beginning of the 17th century, and the ornately decorated 13th-century Romanesque choir stalls.

Golden Gate

From the Peristyle continue north past the tourist information office on Dioklecijanova towards the Golden Gate and the minuscule **St Martin's Chapel** (Kapela sv. Martina), occupying an old Roman guard house and probably built in the 5th or 6th century. Today it caters to a Dominican nunnery next door. Most of Diocletian's garrison was housed in the northern portion of the palace. It is worth seeing the memorial to St Domnius. The **Golden Gate ⑤** (Zlatna vrata), which led to the Roman town of Salona, used to sport a figure of Diocletian amongst other statues, but these have long gone.

Pass through the Golden Gate and you will be struck by the massive sculpture of **Grgur Ninski**, the 9th-century bishop who challenged Rome by advocating that the Croatian Church use the Slavic tongue and Glagolitic script rather than Latin. The toe much rubbed for luck, this is one of Ivan Meštrović's best-known works, though perhaps not among his best. The sculpture stood by the Peristyle inside the palace complex until the occupying

Olive leaves outside the Cathedral of St Domnius on Palm Sunday.

BELOW: intricate carving on the entrance to Split Cathedral.

TIP

The reputation of the Split Festival (mid-July–Aug) is growing year on year, both nationally and internationally. It includes opera, theatre, jazz and ballet – all staged in the city's sumptuous historic buildings.

BELOW: portrait of Ivan Meštrović.

Italian authorities moved it out, fearing its symbolic importance to Croatian national consciousness.

Near the statue at Lovretska 11, the **Art Gallery** (Galerija umjetnina; Tue–Sat 11am–7pm, Sun 10am–1pm) spans the 14th to 20th centuries. Some of the most valuable works are three pieces by Meštrović.

Built in the early 16th century and catering to a 100-strong community, Split's **synagogue** (sinagoga; Mon–Fri 10am–2pm; donations requested) on Židovski prolav (Jewish Passage) inside Diocletian's Palace is one of only a handful still functioning as such in Croatia. It is the third oldest in Europe in continuous use. Visitors are welcome. Under Nazi occupation this street formed part of the Jewish ghetto but most Jews were interned on Rab Island. In 1942 Italian Fascists took most of the synagogue's ritual objects and religious books and made a bonfire in the main square, but local people rescued some and returned them to the Jewish community. Jews have lived on the Dalmatian coast since Roman times. There is also an old Jewish cemetery on the eastern slope of Mt Marjan above Split. Although the Jewish community took over the site in 1573, plots were initially recycled and the oldest surviving tomb dates from 1717.

The rest of Split

From the palace area, walk west through **Šrosmajerov Park**  and follow the outline of the city walls that were added as Split outgrew the original confines of Diocletian's Palace. Eventually you will come to **Trg Gaje Bulata**, home to the grand Croatian National Theatre. Its impressive facade was restored after a devastating fire in the 1970s.

Stroll south back towards the sea and down **Marmontova** and you will see the shiny, modern face of Split. The locals descend on this polished and recently revamped promenade every evening to browse in the fancy designer shops and to see and be seen. The street shows how seriously the Splićani take their fashion, as prices are not much cheaper than in London or Paris in spite of the much lower local wages.

Ivan Meštroviç

An apprenticeship as a stone-cutter in Split at the age of 15 set Ivan Meštrović (1883–1962) on the path to becoming one of the most highly regarded sculptors of the 20th century. The classical remains in his home city are said to have inspired the unschooled artist and he soon attracted the attention of benefactors. With their help, he went on to study at the Academy of Art in Vienna during the heyday of Secessionism and then worked first in Paris, where he won the admiration of Rodin, and then Rome, where he achieved first prize for the Serbian pavilion at the International Exhibition of 1911 for a series of bronzes commemorating heroic Serbians warriors fighting the Ottomans at the Battle of Kosovo.

Meštrović was intensely nationalistic, and much of his work was inspired by his desire to shake off the shackles of first the Austro-Hungarians and later the Italians. His politics took up almost as much time as his art. Believing that the way forward was for Croatia to forge a union with Serbia, he was a founding member of the Yugoslav Committee. However, he was bitterly disillusioned by the first Yugoslavia created after World War I, in which Croatia was subordinate to Serbia, and refused to live in Tito's Yugoslavia after World War II. In 1954 he became a citizen of the United States. His later themes tended to be religious rather than political.

As Marmontova approaches the sea turn right on to **Trg Republike** ❶, a neglected square that most visitors do not notice. After the throngs of people and general vibrancy of Diocletian's Palace this sombre Austro-Hungarian imperial square is a marked contrast. As the crowds pass by on Marmontova a few metres away, this elongated square with its attractive colonnades and buildings and view towards the Adriatic lies forgotten, with only an unremarkable café and the neglected Bellevue Hotel providing any life. But increasingly the annual Split Summer Festival is bringing live music to the Trg Republike and there has long been talk of a refurbishment of the Bellevue; so it may not be too long before the square finds itself on the tourist map.

To find the most impressive Venetian portion of Split walk back along the Riva to **Narodni Trg** ❶ (People's Square). This graceful space looks as if it has been transported from the Divine Republic, a little corner of Venice on the edge of Diocletian's Palace. In the 15th century, as the city expanded beyond the confines of the palace, this square took on the mantle of the most important in the city. A legacy of those glory days is the town hall, dominating the square on the northern flank, and several palaces, the most impressive of which is the Renaissance Karapić Palace. Pop around the corner to Trg Preporoda, home to another Meštrović work, this time a striking sculpture of the 15th-century writer Marko Marulić, one of Split's greatest literary sons and the author of the play *Judita*, one of the first secular works of Croatian literature.

If the Meštrović sculptures around town have sparked an interest in the controversial Croatian sculptor then consider venturing to the **Meštrović Gallery** ❾ (Galerija Meštrović; high season Tue–Sun 9am–7pm, low season Tue–Sat 9am–4pm, Sun 10am–3pm; charge) at 39 Šetalište Ivan Meštrovica. Housed in what he intended to be his retirement home, before his decision to emigrate to the United States, this is the largest collection of his work – in bronze, wood, stone and marble. Standout sculptures include *Distant Accords*, *Vestal*, *The Madonna and Child*

The aptly named Goli otok (Barren Island), an uninhabited dot midway between Rab and the mainland, was from 1949 the site of a little-known gulag where political prisoners had to carry out hard labour in a stone quarry. The subject of many books, it closed in 1988 and is now falling into ruin.

BELOW: floral delivery in Split.

Enjoying a drink in a quiet candlelit passageway in Split.

BELOW: at the barbers in Split.

and his bronze of Job. The entrance fee includes admission to Kaštelet (same hours), at No. 39 in the same street, devoted to his series of wood carvings portraying the life of Christ.

Summer nights

One of the most alluring aspects of Split is its vibrant nightlife. As the sun comes down over the Adriatic people gather in the cafés along the Riva. As the night progresses the wealthier, trendier participants move on to Diocletian's Palace, where several chic bars hide away on the upper level (take the stairs by the Hotel Slavija). Suitably attired and discreet visitors are welcome, but anyone bearing a camera or guidebook may not even get served at these trendy haunts. They offer the unusual experience of sipping a cocktail by candlelight right in the heart of the 2,000-year-old Roman palace. Nights in Split, especially in summer, are long and sultry; activity later moves on to the seafront south of the centre, where a string of bars and clubs cater for various different crowds.

Roman Salona

Outside Split itself the old Roman city of **Salona ❸** (Solin in Croatian) is well worth discovering. The No. bus stops near its main entrance. Salona's ruins are extensive, and it is best to arrange a guide through the local tourist office. The story of its destruction in the 7th century and the panic that accompanied the citizens' flight to Split is gripping.

The Romans first established Salona in the 1st century BC, under the Emperor Augustus's rule. It quickly prospered on the local salt industry (*sal* in Latin) and Diocletian liked it so much – he was born near Salona – he chose to build his retirement home on the waterfront to the south-east in modern-day Split. Salona later fell under the control of the Eastern Roman Empire, but in the 7th century Avars and Slavs descended to rout and sack the city. Those lucky enough to escape with their lives fled to Split and never looked back.

You can easily cover the 156 hectare (385-acre) site on foot. There is a modest museum at the main entrance

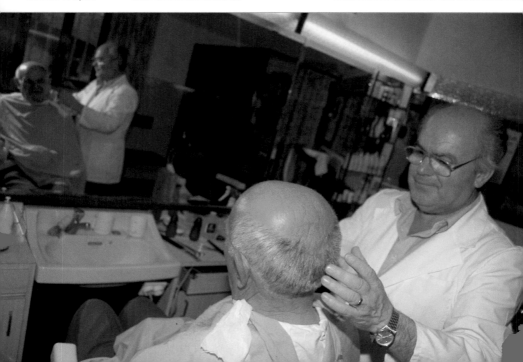

nd a café for those needing a drink
o counter the baking heat of a sum-
ner's day. You can still make out
ome of the old city walls, as well as
he ruins of a 5th-century cathedral,
2nd-century amphitheatre able to
ccommodate 18,000 spectators, and
medieval fortress. Look out too for
he remains of the aqueduct by the
outh wall, which used to supply
vater to Diocletian's Palace.

outh to the Makarska Riviera

outh of Split the *Magistrala* runs
hrough some of Europe's loveliest
oastal scenery. The **Biokovo Moun-
ains** sweep precipitously up one flank
1 a massif of karst hulks and forested
avines, while on the other the coast-
ne is punctuated by bays and coves,
vith the islands of Brač and Hvar glit-
ering just offshore. Expect to spend
he first 30 minutes of the drive out
f Split trying to shake off its suburbs
nd the mushrooming complexes of
oliday homes on the way to the heav-
y developed Makarska Riviera, the
quivalent of the Spanish costas for

Croatians, Bosnians and citizens of the
former Soviet Bloc. Despite the sometimes down-market resorts and eye-
sores that pass for hotel developments
the glorious mountains and sea are
ever present, as are long, clean shingle
beaches backed by pine trees.

The first substantial resort is **Brela** ❹,
probably the most tasteful and understated, though it gets very busy in high
season and finding a room can be a
problem. To the north and south are
sweeping beaches with a line of pine
trees set just back from the shingle to
provide shade during the hottest hours
of the day. Brela sprawls across a large
area, but the old town is surprisingly
compact with twisting narrow streets
leading seawards.

Just 12km (7½ miles) further south
is **Makarska** ❺, a long-established
resort that is big, brash and bolshy,
with a dramatic backdrop provided
by the Biokovo Mountains. It mainly
consists of a tangle of cafés, cheap
restaurants and *pensions*, though the
waterfront Riva is a pleasant place
to while away a few hours by day or
survey the smorgåsbord of humanity

*Central Dalmatia
enjoys the sunniest
weather in Croatia,
with more than 200
days of sunshine a
year. However,
beware the Bura,
a chilly and fierce
wind that rips along
the coast in the colder
months, playing
havoc with the ferry
services.*

BELOW: the popular
resort of Makarska
sits below the
magnificent
Biokovo Mountains.

TIP

On busy summer weekends Brač and Hvar can be saturated with tourists. If you are looking for a relaxing day trip, consider the island of Šolta instead. It is only a short ferry trip from Split and is popular with locals for its pine-shaded walks.

BELOW:
Zlatni rat (Golden Cape), Brač.

cruising past by night. Most remnants of the town's Ottoman and Venetian heritage are long gone, but the central Trg Kačićev does contain the Baroque **St Mark's Church** (Crkva sv. Marka), which has a fine 18th-century Venetian altar. Just outside the church look out for a work by the sculptor Ivan Rendić – a statue of the 18th-century Franciscan friar and poet Andrija Kačić Miošić. The **Town Museum** (Gradski muzej; hours vary) documenting Makarska's maritime past, only merits a visit if you are spending a few days in town.

The area has plenty of shingle beaches on which to laze away the days. More adventurous types may want to set off and conquer some of the peaks and ridges of the Biokovo Mountains, which are easily accessible from the town and rise from the sea to afford a magnificent panorama of the Makarska Riviera and Zabiokovlje. Do not underestimate this steep range: seek local advice before setting out and take plenty of water and warm clothing. The highest peak is **Mt Sveti Jure** (1,762 metres/5,781ft),

accessible from the villages of Maka and Veliko Brdo.

Other resorts on the Riviera include the tourist-saturated **Baška Voda** and the slightly better **Tučepi**, **Podgora**, **Drvenik**, **Zaostrog** and **Gradac**. Accommodation tends to be geared to mass tourism and one-week minimum stays are common.

Securing a room for just one or two nights in high season can be tough. I you are travelling independently, a better option is to look for hotels and restaurants off the *Magistrala*, which are used to catering to the passing trade. Many of these are much more tranquil than the resort hotels and usually near quieter beaches.

A dip into Bosnia?

South of Gradac the *Magistrala* bypasses the shabby port of **Ploče**, which could make a strong claim to be the least appealing settlement on the entire Croatian coastline. Rail enthusiasts and any travellers interested in visiting Bosnia can take the reopened rail line from Ploče to the Bosnian city of Mostar and on to its capital, Sarajevo.

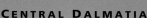

From Ploče the *Magistrala* curls round the Neretva Delta, a sweeping plain reclaimed from the once broad river. Myriad waterways and small settlements dot the fertile valley floor, while in the background a curtain of chunky limestone hills disappear over the horizon towards Bosnia. Tourism is still very low-key in this part of Croatia, but it is possible to rent a boat and explore. There are eight lakes and 12 river branches in a delta that spreads over an area of around 90 sq km (500 sq miles).

The island of Brač

For centuries **Brač** ❻, Croatia's third largest island, has made a living from the limestone laboriously hacked out of its rugged hills. Among the many illustrious buildings constructed from this stone are Diocletian's Palace in Split, the Hungarian Parliament in Budapest and even the White House in Washington, DC. These days tourism has become equally as important as quarrying, with most visitors arriving in the island's main town of **Supetar**. The ferry from Split arrives just east of the centre, which consists of a curving bay

lined with palm trees and orange-roofed buildings dating from Venetian times. A string of pebble beaches lies within easy striking distance to the west.

The first pre-Roman settlement on Brač was unearthed on a peninsula near Supetar's beaches. The peninsula today is occupied by a cemetery with some impressively ornate tombs, many the work of Ivan Rendić, a contemporary of Meštrović. The most dramatic, the **Petrinović Mausoleum** (Mauzolej obitelji Mate Petrinović), was created in 1924 by another Croatian sculptor, Toma Rosandić, adding Byzantine influences to the range of Dalmatian styles seen elsewhere in the cemetery.

Windsurfing off Bol

From Supetar, the most popular route is eastwards towards **Zlatni rat**, the Golden Cape, near the town of Bol across the mountains on Brač's southeast coast. This stark white peninsula with its backdrop of pines is a dramatic sight. Arguably Croatia's best beach, it attracts huge crowds at the height of summer, but many are only daytrippers from Split and Hvar. So it is

TIP

The Brač Summer Cultural Festival runs from June to September. Traditional folk music and classical concerts are held in Brač's main towns – most of them free.

BELOW LEFT: Supetar town and marina.

Extreme Sports in Bol

Croatia has in recent years become something of a centre for "extreme sports" and on the Dalmatian island of Brač there is a summer festival dedicated to them.

Brač's Vanka regule Festival, based in the town of Sutivan, is no Olympic Games, more of an ad hoc gathering of like-minded individuals looking to have fun, but for the increasing number of fans of this branch of sports it is well worth a visit. The festival covers six days in June or July every year and is becoming more and more organised and popular as it develops.

One of the main events is a summer "ice" climbing contest in which competitors use pickaxes and spiked boots to climb an artificial rock covered in Styrofoam. Events vary from year to year but have included free diving, similar to scuba diving but without the luxury of an oxygen tank; mountain biking across Brač's rugged landscape; and free-climbing – climbing without most of the usual equipment. A series of lectures and talks supports the events, providing a platform for debate amongst participants. The festival has its own Croatian and English language website through a link at www.sutivan.hr.

For those dedicated to raising their adrenalin levels, there are also emerging extreme-sports festivals in Zadar and in Istria.

It's hard to get away from the scent of lavender on Hvar. Lavender bags, water, oil and balm are sold all over the island.

RIGHT: one of the many olive groves on the island of Hvar.

best to stay overnight and visit outside peak season. **Bol** merits visiting in its own right. This small town of tightly packed houses has a trio of large hotels and a Dominican monastery. Skulking in the background, Vidova gora (780 metres/2,560ft), is the highest peak in the Adriatic islands. The summit is accessible from Bol, on foot or by car. Other activities include diving and windsurfing – Bol being one of the best places in Croatia for the latter.

Plans are afoot for a smooth road along Brač's southern coast, but for now the drive west is an arduous journey, not for nervous drivers, with terrifyingly tight bends and hairpins. The wild southern coastline is dotted with remote and sheltered coves.

The pretty town of **Milna** is one of several places that have so far escaped development. All the classic Dalmatian components are there: a higgledy-piggledy old town, a crumbling old church, a wide waterfront and some excellent seafood restaurants, but there are few tourists, which is probably why you will see some very smart yachts in the harbour.

Hvar

With its lush forests, sweeping Sve Nikola mountain range, the omnipresent aroma of lavender, and a sprinkl of historic towns, **Hvar** ❼ is one o the most enticing of Croatia's Adriati islands. On the downside it is the mo visited Croatian island and tends to b more expensive than other places. Th Greeks occupied it in the 4th centur but it was the Venetians in the 15th an 16th centuries who left their stamp o the architecture, much appreciated b the many Italians who visit on Adriati ferries in summer.

Hvar Town enjoys an idyllic settin in a protected island-studded bay, wit the old town unfolding on a pine covered slope that reaches to the water edge, with clumps of wild lavender an herbs growing among the Venetian pa aces. In high season the town and i harbour are packed with shiny yach and tour boats and the pavemen cafés and trendy bars are bursting . the seams. All available rooms usuall go by mid-morning; those looking t appreciate the island's special beaut and atmosphere would do best t

Lavender Island

The Romans are said to have believed "As the rose is the scent of the heart, so is lavender the scent of the soul". Whether or not the Romans first cultivated the aromatic plant on Hvar, the lavender industry – now one of the island's chief sources of income – took off in the 1930s, when the plant was brought in en masse and quickly spread across the rocky hillsides.

Conditions are perfect on an island that is the sunniest in Croatia. Today for much of spring and summer (the harvest is in late June/ early July) the scent of lavender wafts across the whole island, giving it the aroma of a luxury spa.

Most of the production centres on small, family-owned plots of land, and so you are unlikely to see the great swathes of lavendar fields that you find, say, in the south of France.

Nonetheless, Hvar lavender, *Lavandula Croatica*, is among the finest in Europe. It comes ready packaged in a bewildering array of oils, creams, bath foams and balms, which are said to aid everything from mosquito bites and sore muscles, through to migraine headaches and depression. For a wonderfully aromatic experience in high summer, visit the fragrant lavender stalls that line the streets of Hvar Town, Stari Grad, Jelsa and Vrboska.

visit outside the main summer season.

The best place to begin a walking tour is in front of the Palace Hotel at the **municipal flagpole** (štandarac), where government decisions used to be announced to a largely illiterate population. Directly east is **Trg sveti Stjepana**, known locally as the pjaca (piazza), but more of a wide boulevard than a square. The main focal point of the town – and the largest square in Dalmatia – it is the setting for the nightly promenade in summer.

At the western end of the square is the 16th-century **arsenal** (oružana; high season 9am–1pm and 5–11pm, low season by appointment), once capable of housing and repairing entire Venetian warships. Unusually the upper level was transformed into one of Europe's first public theatres, a function it performs to this day, although it is temporarily closed for restoration. Far from symbolising a united and enlightened community, the theatre's genesis seems to have been a crude attempt by the town's nobles, who lived in hillside palaces, to placate the disenfranchised masses living in the maze of streets south of Trg Sveti Stjepana. The arsenal also houses a modest collection of paintings by Dalmatian artists.

Strolling to the other end of Trg Sveti Stjepana, you come to **St Stephen's Cathedral** (Katedrala sv. Stjepana), visible from all over Hvar Town. In 1571 the Ottomans razed the original Benedictine monastery on the site, just before their landmark defeat at the Battle of Lepanto. Today's incarnation was built in Venetian Renaissance style in the 16th and 17th centuries. The striking bell tower attached features a biforium, triforium and quatroforium. You can usually enter the cathedral shortly before Mass. If you examine the nave closely, you will notice segments of the earlier cathedral. Also worthy of attention is the understated 13th-century Madonna and Child on the altar.

Up the hillside from Trg Sveti Stjepana, on Matije Ivanića, are many of Hvar Town's old family palaces, symbols of the prosperity of this Venetian trading town when it was a stopping point for northbound ships en route to the metropolis. Look out for the coats of arms lining the street above

Hvar has more sunshine than anywhere else in the country, with more than 2,700 hours a year. Some local hoteliers even offer discounts if the temperature dips below a certain level.

BELOW: a popular café-bar in Hvar Town.

TIP

The Hvar Festival runs from late June to late September in Hvar Town, with theatre performances from domestic and international groups in the historic buildings, as well as open-air jazz concerts.

the many restaurants that have moved into the buildings. Particularly striking is a roofless palace with Gothic windows, which was never finished because of lack of funds.

The steep hike from sea level up through the hillside park to the **Spanish Fortress** (Fortezza Spanjola; high season 9am–7pm) is well worth it for the panoramic views that the ramparts offer. The town walls join each flank and Hvar Town spreads around the harbour below, while Hvar's offshore islands and the island of Vis are visible further afield. The fortifications were commissioned by the Habsburg monarch Charles V in 1551; today the fort is used as a café during the day and a nightclub in the evening. It also has a collection of rare weapons.

The beaches around Hvar Town are nothing special and tend to be overcrowded in summer. A better bet are the unfortunately named Pakleni Islands (Pakleni otoci – Islands of Hell). Numerous boat operators run day trips and also offer taxi services out to the islands, with a one-way fare priced between 20 and 30 kuna.

The three most popular islands are **Sveti Island**, the largest, **Marinkovac**, which has a couple of good beaches, and **Jerolim**, where clothes are very much optional.

Exploring the Rest of Hvar

Stari Grad (Old Town) on Hvar's north coast earned its name on account of being the island's first major centre before the Venetians developed Hvar Town. These days Stari Grad is going through something of a renaissance, fuelled to a large extent by a new purpose-built ferry terminal just outside the town, which serves most of the car ferries from Split as well as services run by the Jadrolinija ferry company from as far afield as Rijeka and Dubrovnik. In contrast to its southern sister, Stari Grad grew to prominence as a Greek town in the 4th century BC when it was known as Faros; although no buildings from that time remain, the structure of the town is unchanged. Since 2008 the Stari Grad plain has been a Unesco World Heritage Site.

Stari Grad was the home of the 16th-century Croatian poet and visionary

BELOW: Hvar's main town square and cathedral.

Petar Hektorović, who possessed a social conscience rare amongst his fellow nobles of the time. Hektorović's best work was the epic *Ribanje i ribarsko prigovaranje (Fishing and Fishermen's Conversations)*, though islanders perhaps best remember him for his attempt to build a sanctuary in which citizens could seek refuge when the town came under attack.

Work on the **Tvrdalj** (July–Aug Mon–Sat 10am–noon and 7–9pm, Sun 7–9pm, May, June, Sept Mon–Sat 10am–1pm; charge) began in 1520, though it was damaged by the Turkish attack of 1571. Unfortunately the building was never completed and in the 19th century it underwent a facelift that smoothed over the delicate Renaissance facade. The Tvrdalj now doubles as an ethnographic museum as well as a memorial to the poet – look out for his etchings in Croatian, Latin and Italian, which are carved into the walls and around the fish pond in the garden.

Next door, housed in the former palace of the Biankini family, is the nautically themed Stari Grad Museum

(Muzej Staroga Grada; same hours as the Tvrdalj; charge), which displays items retrieved from a 4th-century Roman shipwreck.

Just a short stroll away is Stari Grad's other main attraction, the **Dominican Monastery** (Dominikanski samostan; daily 10am–noon and 6–8pm; charge), which houses a museum with a number of Hektorović's belongings, including a 16th-century collection of Petrarch's sonnets and portraits of the poet. The original building dates from the 15th century, though it has been modified over the years, with a church added in the 19th century. The church may be unspectacular in itself, but look out for Tintoretto's *Disposition* inside.

West of Stari Grad are the towns of Jelsa and Vrboska. **Jelsa** offers a far more relaxed resort experience than the maelstrom of Hvar Town, despite the two large hotels that share the wooded slopes with the old fishing village. The main pleasure is

The small village of Jelsa makes a pleasant island base.

BELOW: Stari Grad's Dominican Monastery and marina.

BELOW: a quiet day in Vis Town.

strolling along the waterfront, but there are a couple of interesting churches. As in all the churches in Jelsa and Vrboska opening times are erratic, but popping in just before a service gets underway is often the best bet. In the **Church of SS Fabian and Sebastian** (Crkva sv. Fabijana i Sebastijana) look out for a wooden statue of the Virgin Mary said to have been brought to Jelsa by Christians fleeing the Dalmatian hinterland in the wake of Turkish attacks. The Chapel of St John (Crkva sv. Ivana) dates from the 16th century.

Vrboska is even more relaxed, though the atmosphere was considerably less sleepy when the crews of Venetian vessels used to stop by to enjoy the seafood caught by local fishermen. Again, idling away the day on the waterfront is the chief attraction, but there are a couple of churches worth seeing.

The Church of St Lawrence features a Madonna of the Rosary attributed to Leandro Bassano, while St Mary's Church was built in the wake of devastating Turkish attacks, hence its sturdy construction. There are good views over Vrboska and the Adriatic from the roof of St Mary's.

Magical Vis

The island of **Vis** ❽ holds a special place in the hearts of many Croatians as well as with many regular visitors who have discovered the last inhabited Croatian island before the Italian coastline. It is one of the least densely populated areas of Croatia, in part thanks to its being an off-limits military base until 1989. On the approach to Vis its rugged, mountainous beauty is reminiscent of a Scottish Hebridean isle with lofty peaks and sheer rock walls looming large.

The first inhabitants were the Greeks in the 4th century BC – it was their biggest colony in Croatia – but its strategic position at the heart of the Adriatic with views towards both the Croatian and Italian coastlines, has made it a prized possession historically and ownership has changed hands numerous times. Since the demise of the Venetian Republic in 1797 the Austrians, British, French and Germans have all battled

over Vis, with the British leaving the most indelible imprint in the fortifications ringing Vis Town.

Aesthetically Vis Town is not as immediately striking as some of the other Dalmatian settlements such as Hvar Town or Rab Town. Its hotchpotch of architectural styles is an indication of its turbulent history. There are two parts to the town: the area where the ferry docks, with its cafés, souvenir stalls and bus station, and the old aristocratic enclave of Kut, to the east around the bay.

From the ferry dock, turn right and a 10-minute walk will bring you to the 16th-century **Franciscan Monastery** (Franjevački samostan). Though of no special interest in itself, and usually closed, its cemetery is worth seeing, not least for the fine views of Vis Town and the harbour, with verdant slopes rising to meet the sea on all sides. Some of the headstones are spectacular, such as a fine sculpture of a maiden watering flowers on the grave of one Toma Bradanović by the Croatian sculptor Ivan Rendić. Look out also for the mass tomb built to

house a group of Austrian sailors killed during a fierce naval engagement with the French off Vis in 1866.

Heading east back past the ferry dock, you will come to a small palm-fringed park that gives way to a promenade lined with yachts on one side and cafés on the other. Keep walking away from the crowds and you will come to the 16th-century **Church of our Lady of the Cave** (Župna crkva Gospe od Spilica). The three-nave interior is quite striking, but in a sad state of repair. Even a solid-looking altar on the left has developed a serious crack through its centre. One fine surviving artwork is the *Madonna with the Saints* by Girolamo da Santacroce.

Just past the church is a small jetty with a pebble beach that is a good spot for a refreshing swim. Next to this a path leads south past two hefty cannons to the old bastion that used to house a military museum. A celebration of Communist-era military might and Tito's victories did not sit well with the new independent Croatia and the bastion now functions as an **Archaeological Museum** (Arheoloski muzej;

Though sparsely populated by humans, Vis has plenty of goats.

BELOW: entrance to the cave where Tito and his Partisans sheltered for several months during 1944.

Islands of the Adriatic just off the Vis shore.

BELOW: well-tended vineyards on Vis produce the excellent Plavac wine.

high season Mon–Sat 10am–1pm and 6–9pm, Sun 10am–1pm; charge). On the lower level of the main building is an interesting collection of Greek and Roman artefacts, including many from Issa. Upstairs (where there are English language signs) look out for the replica of a bronze bust of Aphrodite (the original is in storage on Vis) that is captioned "the most celebrated Greek sculpture in Croatia". Also interesting are vases and amphorae taken from wrecks around Vis.

Across the courtyard another exhibition space displays amphorae recovered from a Greek wreck in 1971. Thought to date from the 4th century BC, these shed new light on when the Greeks first came to Vis, or Issa as they called it.

During 1944 Tito set up his headquarters in a cave on Vis following the collapse of Italy. Bolstered by the Allies, who were determined to stop the Nazis from recovering the Italian losses, Tito had fled to Vis from Bosnia, transported there by the British navy. The network of underground tunnels and caves made it an ideal location and Tito coordinated many a significant military operation from his cave in Mt Hum above Komiža, and even Winston Churchill visited the island to meet him.

A national shrine in Yugoslav days, it now functions as a not terribly exciting World War II museum, with carved lyrics celebrating Tito and his troops, exploring a period when the island helped form the destiny of Yugoslavia and, in many ways, the post-war map of the Balkans.

Wine tasting

Further towards Kut there are a number of family-run wine cellars (look for signs saying "Domaće vino pradajem", where you can sit with different generations of local families and taste and buy some of their produce. Vis is renowned for the quality of its wines, with 20 percent of its surface area given over to viticulture. Both the ruby red Plavac and honey-hued Vugava are very drinkable and available for next to nothing. Most families also concoct their own Prošek dessert wines; these vary tremendously but the best of them are an excellent way to round off a meal.

Kut, the old aristocratic quarter, was built by the wealthy Venetian nobles of Hvar as a retreat. The elegant Gothic **St Cyprian's Church** (Crkva sv. Ciprijana) and its bell tower preside over a hillside covered with beautiful Venetian-style homes and family palaces. Look out for the family coats of arms adorning many buildings and the decorative balconies where old women still stoop out to hang up their washing. Over the last half decade a number of first-rate restaurants have opened their doors in refurbished houses in Kut, offering lovely outdoor settings and lashings of atmosphere.

Komiža, Biševo and the Blue Cave

The island's main road straddles the mountains on a 10km (6-mile) route

across to Komiža, the only other town on Vis, whose livelihood is based on sardines. It is even sleepier than Vis Town, except during the daily rush to get the boats out to the nearby island of **Biševo**, the location of the celebrated Blue Cave (Modra špilja). This is a grotto where the waters are illuminated with a brilliant blue light, a natural phenomenon, often compared with a similar grotto on the Italian island of Capri. The only way to get to the cave is on an organised boat tour or a scuba-diving trip (details available from the tourist office on the Riva in Komiža), with the latter providing the best view of the spectacle. Be aware that the phenomenon only happens in summer – best around 11am – and that all trips are cancelled during rough weather. After visiting the cave most boat trips stop off for a few hours swimming at Porat Bay (Porat uvala) on the west side of Biševo; it is one of the few sandy beaches on the east side of the Adriatic.

Divine diving

Thanks to its long period as a military base, the waters around Vis have never been commercially fished and have a particularly lush sea life as well as six diveable wrecks. Unsurprisingly Vis offers some of the best scuba diving in Croatia with something to suit everyone, from inexperienced PADI (Professional Association of Diving Instructors) beginners, right through to seasoned divers in search of challenging deep dives. In addition there are around a dozen submerged wrecks within easy reach of Vis, with everything from a World War II bomber through to a Venetian galleon. There are two dive operators in Vis Town.

Komiža itself is an unassuming little place with enough distractions for a leisurely few days. The town's single most impressive attraction is the **Church of St Michael** (Crkvica sv. Mihajla), picturesquely set on a vine-covered bluff overlooking the town and the sea. The church served as a refuge for

local people during pirate attacks. The original church on the site dated from the early 12th century, and a monastery has also existed here for centuries, with the present structure owing much to a refurbishment in the 17th century. Look on the church floor for the gravestones of local noble families.

Also worth visiting next door is a sprawling cemetery that enjoys fine views over Komiža, out across the Adriatic and back to Mt Hum (the highest peak on Vis); it also has a number of grand headstones and tombs. On the road up to the church a track, signposted Plaža (beach) leads down to a series of rocky coves and secluded beaches.

Back in town in the 16th-century Venetian tower on the promenade (Riva), the **Fishing Museum** (Ribarski muzej; hours vary by season; charge) offers an insight into an industry that is still important to Vis. You can walk around the outer wall of the harbour and you will come across a plaque to British sailors killed off the island during World War II, when Vis was of major strategic importance. ❑

A glimpse of Komiža's harbour.

BELOW: a pleasant waterfront restaurant, Komiža.

SOUTHERN DALMATIA

The walled city of Dubrovnik is the most beautiful city on the Adriatic, and offshore lie some of Croatia's most enchanting islands, including Mljet with forest walks, twin lakes and a monastery

he long sliver of Southern Dalmatia is the domain of one of the most beautiful cities in Europe. Dubrovnik, frequently hailed as the "Pearl of the Adriatic", was one of the few medieval city states to fend off all aggressors, ruling over the surrounding towns and maintaining its incredible walls intact.

The city's star status attracts many visitors including daily fleets of cruise ships, none of whose passengers ever have the opportunity of visiting the parts of the city beyond the walls, or the whole of the rest of Southern Dalmatia, a region rich in beauty and culture. In the north, Korčula is a smaller version of Dubrovnik, while the nearby Pelješac peninsula is one of the country's most bountiful larders. A short drive south are the gardens at Trsteno and quiet resorts such as Slano and Zaton. Some 17km (10 miles) south of Dubrovnik, Cavtat has a spectacular setting between the mountains and the sea. Offshore, the islands are far less developed than those off central and northern Dalmatia. Scheduled ferry services are geared more to the needs of local people, but a plethora of excursion boats provide a service for visitors. The most beautiful island is undoubtedly Mljet, about a third of which is a verdant, forested national park.

Dissecting the narrow strip of land, just south of the Neretva Delta, is a 10km (6-mile) corridor of land belonging to Bosnia Herzegovina. This once

belonged to Dubrovnik but, fearful of being overrun by the Venetians who bit by bit were taking over the coast, it was ceded to the Ottomans in 1699, in the hope that they would act as a buffer against La Serenissima's advance. Today it provides Bosnia with its only outlet to the sea, and the coast around the main town of **Neum** is overdeveloped. The road inland is poor, and visitors planning on trips to **Mostar**, with its famous bridge over the Neretva, need to go back up the *Magistrala* and pick up the E73 at Opuzen. Plans by Croatia

Main attractions
KORCULA TOWN
STON RESTAURANTS
TRSTENO BOTANICAL GARDENS
DUBROVNIK
ELAPHITE ISLANDS
MLJET NATIONAL PARK
CAVTAT

PRECEDING PAGES:
an overview of
Dubrovnik.
LEFT AND BELOW:
Dubrovnik's Church
of St Blaise
and the old town.

Bougainvillaea thrives on the island of Korčula.

to build a bridge to skirt around this corridor by hopping across the Neretva Channel (Neretranski kanal) to the Pelješac peninsula have been debated for some time.

The Pelješac peninsula

The *Magistrala* is soon back in Croatia where it funnels down towards the Pelješac peninsula, whose mountains rear up on the horizon across the Neretva Channel. Pelješac is renowned for its fine food and wine: the first-rate red wines Dingač and Postup both originate from the peninsula, and the seafood is legendary, with huge mussels, lobster, oysters and many kinds of fish.

The twin villages of **Ston ❶** and **Mali Ston** (Little Ston), either side of a narrow isthmus connecting the peninsula to the mainland, are two unspoilt little backwaters, though you can see at once from the 5km (3 miles) of fortified walls that link the two settlements across a hill, that these have had glory days. The walls of the great fortress **Veliki Kastio** are the longest in Europe, and date from 1333, when the rapidly expanding city of Ragusa

(modern-day Dubrovnik) bought the town and wanted to protect it – as well as the surrounding salt pans – from attack. Sections of the walls were taken down in the 19th century, but the remaining parts withstood Serbian shelling in 1991 and an earthquake in 1997, both of which wrecked parts of the town below. While the historical merits are intriguing, most Croatians come here to eat and drink. Just off shore from the tiny fortified port of Mali Ston, fishermen can be seen working the fertile waters of the Neretva Channel in small wooden boats, and a crop of poles indicate the mass of oyster beds. Fresh from the boats, oysters, mussels and a lot of other fish and seafood besides are served in a handful of restaurants that hug the waterfront.

Ston, the larger of the two villages, lies a kilometre to the southwest, and it is from here that you can clamber up the wall to the Pozvizd Fortress, with views down both sides. The village is an attractive little place, with an ornate Rector's Palace and a tree-shaded central square.

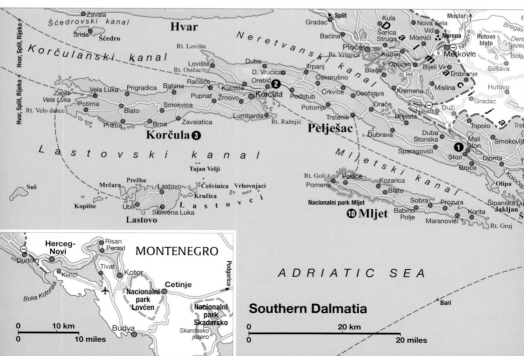

Southern Dalmatia

The road out of Ston into the peninsula passes the great salt beds, still in use, and heads into the winelands, where produce can often be bought direct from the vineyard. There are beaches and a handful of small resorts on the peninsula. On the south side ferries go to the island of Miljet (see page 254), while ferries cross the Nervetna Channel on the north side from Trpanj to Ploče.

The largest town on the peninsula is **Orebić ❷**, with wonderful sweeps of sandy beaches, ideal for a family holiday. Windsurfers take off from here, too. Its reputation otherwise rests on its native sea captains who were famous in the days of sail, and its seafaring past is laid out in a small Maritime Museum. The 15th-century Franciscan monastery high on the hill overlooking the town and the coast has some interesting works of art, and there are some good walks to be had in these hills.

Korčula

From the port of Orebić, car- and passenger-ferries cross to the nearby island of **Korčula ❸** (the island also has ferry links to Dubrovnik, Hvar and Split), though many visitors leave their cars at the port and take a passenger ferry. Korčula town is the main attraction, a walled, chocolate-box ensemble of terracotta-hued roofs and spires, set on its own peninsula. The medieval town plan is straightforward and makes walking around easy: the main thoroughfare runs right through the heart of the old centre and a waterside boulevard circles the peninsula.

The town's most impressive building is **St Mark's Cathedral**, constructed, like most of Korčula's buildings, from the mellow limestone that made the island, and its stonemasters, famous. The tower and cupola, dating from around 1480, are the work of Marko Andrjić, whose sons, Petar and Josip, worked on numerous prestigious buildings in Dubrovnik, including the Sponza Palace and the Rector's Palace. The triple-naved interior of the basilica is impressive, with a blend of architectural styles, in which Gothic and Renaissance predominate.

Inside St Mark's Cathedral is the richly coloured Tintoretto altarpiece (1550) depicting St Mark with St Bartholomew and St Jerome.

Marco Polo

A number of families today in Korčula bear the name of de Polo, and it is entirely likely that Marco Polo was born here in 1254. The town has documents going back to its original communal statute of 1214, which gave the town some degree of independence from the Venetians on whom they relied for business. At the time of Marco Polo's birth, the island had come under the domain of the Venetian duke of Dubrovnik. There are documents mentioning the Polo family being from Dalmatia, and archives on the island have a document from 1430 of a Mateo Polo applying for land for shipbuilding "as his forefathers had been making small ships here for centuries". The Polos had shipbuilding yards on the shores on both sides of the town and there were also smiths, stonemasons, tradesmen, priests, and notaries in the family. After he had returned from his legendary travels to China, Marco Polo went to live in Venice. It is thought that it was while he was on a ship in the Venetian fleet that engaged the Genoan fleet at the battle of Korčula in the Peljesac Channel in 1298 that he was captured and imprisoned in Genoa, where he dictated his book of travels to a fellow prisoner, the writer Rustichello da Pisa. He was released the following year and his book (pre-printing press) became a bestseller. The adventurer settled in Venice as a famous and increasingly wealthy merchant, where he died at the age of 70. Korčula celebrates his birthday every May.

The Adriatic Highway

Keep your eyes straight ahead – if you can – as you head down Croatia's beautiful but challenging coastal road.

The Adriatic Highway (*Jadranska Magistrala*) is one of the world's great corniches, heading south from its starting point in Rijeka and dramatically following the coast as far as – and over into – Montenegro. It is a stretch on the European route E65, a chain of major roads that starts in Malmö in Sweden and ends 3,800km (2,400 miles) away in Chaniá, Greece. The *Magistrala* is undoubtedly the most picturesque part of it, and also the most potentially hazardous. Much of it is a single-lane road wedged between karst mountains and the sea, chasing the curves and contours of the edge of the land, with lanes tipping over the side to reach hidden villages and communities out of sight way below.

Bit by bit new motorways are extending down the coast, though in some parts of this narrow strip of coast, there simply isn't room for another road. This is taking much of the traffic, including lorries, away from the *Magistrala*, but it can still be a pretty slow road, especially in high summer. Hindered by lorries

and hairpin bends, drivers can become impatient and take risks. There is also a danger that a tourist, finding so much to see, forgets to concentrate on the road, though skid marks and holes in the crash barriers will provide sharp reminders.

The E65 from Zagreb reaches the Adriatic at Rijeka, meeting the coast road that has swept round from Istria and the Opatija Riviera. Keeping hard by the sea, the Adriatic Highway plunges down towards Split, passing village after village and offering broad views across the Kvarner Gulf. Just south of Rijeka, a turning leads off to the island of Krk, reached by a bridge that bad weather – notably the *bura* wind, which is capable of blowing cars off course – can keep closed for days.

At Senj the road inland to Karlovac is called the Josephina, named after the wife of Emperor Josef II, who had it built – or rather rebuilt, as it had been a Roman road. The *Magistrala* scurries past to Karlobag, beneath the Velebit mountains, Croatia's only biosphere reserve. Ducking under the A1 main road coming down from Zagreb it then crosses into Dalmatia over the Maslenika Bridge, which had to be rebuilt at the end of the Homeland War. This bridge may also be closed in high winds, in which case you may go back to the A1, rejoining the highway shortly afterwards to continue into Zadar.

From Zadar the road continues along the edge of the sea and through Krka Nacional Park and crosses the River Krka shortly before arriving in Šibenik. A stop here would allow a visit to the beautiful cathedral of St James. It continues down past the fine beaches and vineyards around Primošten to Trogir and Split, which definitely need checking out. At the small port of Ploče the road skips over the islands of the Nerveta delta, returning to the coast at Kremena before sneaking through the brief seaward incursion of Bosnia Herzogovina, where you must be prepared to show your passport at customs posts a few kilometres apart.

On then beneath the karst cliffs of southern Dalmatia, round the little bays of Slano and Zaton – with no sign of the famous Trsteno botanical gardens hidden down below, between the highway and the sea. Then it's over the Dr Franjo Tudjman suspension bridge to reach the walls of Dubrovnik, scraping by the Minčeta Tower in its northern corner. Then on to the last lap, which passes by Cavtat and Dubrovnik airport, before heading off into Montenegro where a bridge is planned to cross the Verige strait to shorten the highway around the Kotor Fjord. ❏

LEFT: the Maslenika Bridge.

There is a Tintoretto altarpiece (1550) depicting saints Mark, Bartholomew and Jerome, who were credited with helping stave off the Ottomans when they besieged the town on their way north to the Battle of Lepanto in the 16th century. The cathedral also contains a School of Tintoretto *Annunciation*.

Next door to the cathedral is the **Treasury Museum** (Opatska riznica; summer 9am–2pm, 5–8pm, winter 9am–1pm; charge), which crams a surprising number of works by an eclectic array of artists into its small confines. The building was restored in the 17th century with the addition of an attractive hanging garden. Spread across seven small halls the museum contains works by Bassano, Carpaccio and various Croatian luminaries, as well as gold, silver and porcelain artefacts, medieval pottery and, in a stone-flagged kitchen, a huge number of Roman pots and jars, recovered from the sea in the 1960s.

The **Town Museum** (Gradski muzej; summer Mon–Sat 9am–1pm, 5–7pm, winter 9am–1pm; charge) is housed in an impressive 16th-century palace opposite. The story of Korčula is told here, from the arrival of the Greeks through to modern times. The stories of Korčula's famous stonemasons and shipbuilders are covered in some detail; there is furniture, costumes, and photos of Tito's Partisans, and signs in English help illuminate the collection.

Not far from the cathedral square, in Ul. Depolo, you can visit the **Marco Polo Tower** (9am–8pm; charge), adjoining the building where the explorer was said to have been born in 1254 *(see page 243)*. There are stunning views from the top of the tower, and the attached building – a graceful, ruined palace – was purchased by the town council in 2004 and is to be renovated and opened to the public. The nearby church of **St Peter** (summer daily 10am–7pm; charge), a simple little chapel with a facade featuring reliefs by the Milanese artist Bonino, has an extremely kitsch exhibition portraying the life of Marco Polo.

All Saints' Church (Svih svetih), to the southeast of town, was founded at the start of the 14th century and has

Korčula is known locally as the "Island of Wine". Among the best wines are the Pošip, Rukatac, Grk and Plavac varieties.

BELOW: view of Marco Polo Tower.

TIP

There are three places
to swim under the
Dubrovnik city walls:
on the Popporela
breakwater by the old
port, through a doorway
in Ispod Mira Street by
St Stephen's Tower and
in od Margarite Street
beneath the Buza Café.

BELOW:
a classic view of
Dubrovnik's old
town and beach.

one of the most impressive Baroque altarpieces anywhere in the country, a *Pietà* by the Austrian sculptor George Raphael Donner. There is also a beautiful 15th-century polyptych by Dalmatian artist Blaž Trogiranin. The ceiling was a later addition, designed by Tripo Kokolja, an artist from present-day Montenegro, who died in Korčula Town in 1713. Next door is the **Icon Museum** (Zhirka ikona; 10am–2pm, 5–7pm; charge), housed in the Hall of the Brotherhood of All Saints.

Outside the city walls, the **Church and Monastery of St Nicholas**, on the harbour-side, were founded in the 15th century and later embellished in Baroque style. Look out for the medallions in the monastery, attributed to Tripo Kokolja.

After you have covered Korčula's sights, relax on the **beaches** around the town. Luka Korculanska Bay, a safe sandy beach with shallow water, is just 15 minutes' walk away. There is also a string of good beaches near the town of **Lumbarda** to the south of the island, and at **Blato**, a pleasant village to the west. There are excellent local wines on sale all over the island, although you will really need your own vehicle if you want to explore deeper into the smaller villages and the vineyards. If you came as a foot passenger, scooters and cars can be hired in Korčula Town, and there are taxis and taxi boats to take you to the beaches.

Back on the Highway

South from Ston, the highway curls into a deep bay at **Slano** ❹, a well-protected yaching resort. It's a small village, with just over 500 inhabitants, but it has several beaches and is in striking distance of Dubrovnik (27km/17 miles away), making it an option as a place to stay. Illyrian burial mounds and the walls of an old Roman fortress attest to Slano's historical importance, and after coming under the control of Ragusa in 1399, villas and palaces were built here for the nobility. The Franciscan church has a triptych by the 15th-century artist Lovro Dobričević.

Another worthwhile stop on the route south to Dubrovnik is **Trsteno** ❺, where there is an early 16th-century **Arboretum** (summer daily 8am–7pm, winter 8am–5pm; charge). Croatia's oldest botanical gardens were created by the aristocratic Gučetić family in 1502, although local legend claims that they originated from a single oak planted by a member of a Dalmatian noble family as he set out for the Crusades. The central fountain, with statues of Neptune and nymphs, and the accompanying aqueduct, were added in 1736. Serb shelling destroyed a quarter of the gardens in 1991 and a substantial fire in 2000 further hampered their renaissance. However, painstaking reconstruction work, and the rejuvenating microclimate of Trsteno, have combined to bring the gardens back to life. Parking can be difficult, but you can get round the problem by parking in the private car park of the café at the garden's entrance and enjoying a drink among the lime trees.

The 18km (11-mile) drive from Trsteno to Dubrovnik runs along a beautiful

stretch of coast with good views across a number of islands, including Mljet in the distance (see page 254) and the Elaphite Islands (see page 254), easily accessed from Dubrovnik. Some 8km (5 miles) from Trsteno you reach the seaside resort of **Zaton** (divided in two – Veliki and Mali), in a deep bay that causes the highway to scuttle inland around farmland. This was another choice spot for Ragusa's nobility to build summer villas.

Dubrovnik

The most attractive settlement on the whole of the Croatian seaboard, **Dubrovnik ⑥** has prospered within its walls for centuries. The city – Ragusa – was settled in the 7th century by the citizens of nearby Epidauram (Cavtat), who fled here when it was a small island, to escape invasion. Over the centuries, Slavs settled on the hillside on the mainland opposite and gradually links between the two settlements grew stronger. In the 11th century the channel separating the island from the mainland – today's Stradun – was filled in and the two towns became one.

Backed by sweeping limestone cliffs and flanked on three sides by the sparkling Adriatic Sea, Dubrovnik's setting is breathtaking. The water reflects the perfectly preserved fortifications, which, unlike those of most medieval European towns and cities, were not removed to accommodate an expanding population or rendered unnecessary when military technology moved on. The result is a living history book that feels very far from 21st-century Europe. The fact that no motorised vehicles are allowed inside the walls adds to this impression.

The best place to start a tour of Dubrovnik is **Pile Gate ⓐ** (Vrata Pile), its most dramatic entrance, on the western side of the city. It crosses the old moat, now a leafy garden, and a stone bridge. As you enter the old town, look up to see the statue of the city's patron saint, Sveti Vlaho (St Blaise), the handiwork of the ubiquitous Croatian sculptor Ivan Meštrović.

Instead of heading down the steps, take the ramp, which leads to a map detailing the attack by rebel Serbs, volunteers from Montenegro and the

Pile Gate provides the most dramatic entrance to the old town. During the days of the republic the city gates were locked at 6pm sharp and opened at 6am.

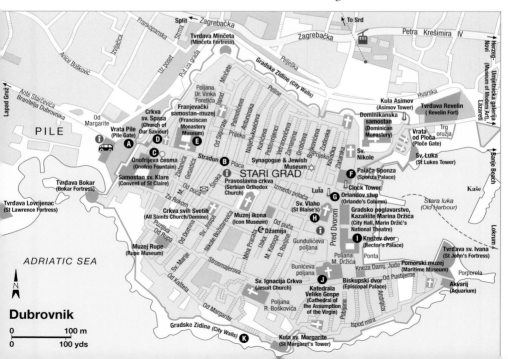

Dubrovnik

0   100 m
0   100 yds

TIP

High on Mount Srđ
above Dubrovnik a
new Museum of the
Homeland War has
been established in
the remains of a
Napoleonic fort. Plans
to extend the bus
service and rebuild the
cable car (destroyed in
the war) are underway.
Views from the top are
stunning.

BELOW: art for sale
below the city
walls. **RIGHT:** the
Small Fountain of
Onofrio.

Yugoslav Army in 1991–2. This map details the cascade of shells that battered the old town during the fighting. The Siege of Dubrovnik made headline news around the world as the World Heritage-listed city, which had no strategic value nor any real Serb claim of ownership, was attacked from the surrounding hills. In May 1992, Serb forces withdrew, partly as a result of international pressure and partly because by then priorities had changed. Some residents of other Croatian cities, such as Vukovar and Osijek, which suffered greater damage and loss of life, feel that Dubrovnik was helped on account of its appearance and reputation. The fact that Dubrovnik is a World Heritage Site has certainly helped with reconstruction. However, there is no doubt that the residents, who lived for months without electricity and running water, suffered greatly. More than 40 of them, mainly young men, gave their lives in defence of their city and many more were traumatised.

The main artery through the old town is **Stradun** Ⓑ (Placa), a wide boulevard of marble that has been polished by the feet of thousands of visitors. To take the pulse of the city and soak up some of its ambience, sit for a while on the terrace of one of its cafés (the Festival Café is a good place to start), watch the crowds and admire the architectural details that help the thoroughfare retain its beauty: mellow-stoned buildings with uniform arched doorways and window shutters in the same shade of dark green, and lamp-posts all of the same design.

At the western extremity of Stradun is the **Large Fountain of Onofrio** Ⓒ (Onofríjera česma), the culmination of a system that has brought fresh water to the city since 1444. The circular domed well, with its 16 water-spouting stone heads, is named after its designer Onofrio della Cava, an Italian who worked in the Dubrovnik region for a number of years. During the siege it was seriously damaged, but has now been fully restored. Some tourists consider it lucky to drink at the well, but it was originally intended merely for washing on entering the city. A second fountain, known as the **Small**

Fountain of Onofrio, lies at the far end of Stradun, next to the Clock Tower.

Just across Stradun from the well is the **Church of Our Saviour** (Crkava sv. Spasa), built in Renaissance style, and one of the few buildings to survive the great earthquake of 1667. It is usually closed during the day, but is the venue for chamber recitals several evenings a week in summer.

Next door is the **Franciscan Monastery and Museum** (Franjevački samostan; daily 9am–6pm; charge). If possible plan an early or late visit, to avoid the crowds. On the left as you enter is a delightful little pharmacy, which has been here for centuries and is still functioning today. The lovely Romanesque-Gothic cloisters, which survived the 1667 earthquake, are the work of master stonemason Mihoje Vrajkov of Bar. There are double pillars with ornamental capitals, a garden, once used to grow herbs for the pharmacy, and a 15th-century well.

Among the most intriguing exhibits in the **museum** are 14th- and 15th-century objects from the pharmacy, but there are also some fine paintings, among which a 15th-century polyptych featuring St Blaise, by Lovro Dobričević, stands out. The **church** (6.30am–noon, 4–7.30pm; free if entered from the street), has Baroque altars, replacements for those destroyed in the earthquake, and a plaque commemorating the revered Dubrovnik poet Ivan Gundulić (1589–1638) who is buried here.

Luža Square

Continue on down the Stradun, saving until later the little lanes that break away to the north and south, and you will come to the 16th-century **Sponza Palace** (Palača Sponza; daily 9am–6pm; free) on the far side of lively **Luža Square**. The palace, a mixture of Venetian Gothic and Renaissance, has had many roles. The word *Dogana* on the metal studded door indicates that it was once the customs house. The courtyard houses temporary art exhibitions, and is one of the most atmospheric venues for musical performances during the Dubrovnik Festival. Look out for an inscription that served as a warning to shady traders:

You will find figures of Sv. Vlaho (St Blaise), Dubrovnik's patron saint, all over the city, often in little niches, offering succour and protection to the good citizens.

BELOW:
the Franciscan Monastery church.

The colonnaded facade of the Rector's Palace. The rector was a civil leader chosen from the city's nobility.

BELOW RIGHT:
Orlando's Column.

"We are forbidden to cheat and use false measurers. When I weigh goods, God weighs me."

To the left of the entrance is the **Memorial Room of the Defenders of Dubrovnik** (daily 10am–4pm; free), with photos of those who died in defence of the city during the 1991–2 siege, some of them little more than boys. Above them are pictures of burning boats and buildings, while a video plays scenes of devastation.

In the centre of Luža Square is **Orlando's Column ⑥** (Orlandov stup), also known as Roland's Column. The carved figure of a knight represents Roland, who is said to have helped Dubrovnik vanquish Saracen pirates in the 9th century. Although this is highly unlikely, the statue is a symbol of freedom, and very dear to the city. It was once used for public proclamations, when citizens of Ragusa came to hear news and decrees, and criminals were exhibited at its foot. Directly in front of the column (if you are facing east, towards the harbour) is the **Clock Tower**, whose bell is chimed by the hammers of little green men.

Behind the column is the 18th-century **Church of St Blaise ⑪** (Crkva sv. Vlaho; opening times vary; free), named after the patron saint of Dubrovnik. Above the high altar stands a silver figure of Sv. Vlaho that is paraded through the streets on 3 February each year. The saint is portrayed holding a scale model of the city, providing one of the few records of how Dubrovnik looked before its destruction in the 1667 earthquake. The attractive stained-glass windows, depicting saints Peter and Paul, Cyril and Methodius, are by Ivo Dulčić (1916–75), Dubrovnik's most renowned modern artist.

The Rector's Palace

To the left of the church are the imposing buildings of the **Gradska vijećnica** (Town Hall), the **Marin Držić Theatre** and the recently revamped **gradskakavana** town café, within the arches of the old arsenal. Next door is the **Rector's Palace ⑪** (Knežev dvov; closed in 2009 for renovations, but usually open daily 9am–6pm; charge). The first palace on the site was erected in 1200, but it was destroyed and rebuilt several times

The Heyday of Ragusa

The republic of Ragusa was established in 1358 when Hungary granted the city freedom in exchange for an annual payment. The hinterland was rich in silver and lead, and Ragusa soon became the main port for exporting these materials as well as an entrepôt for the growing east–west trade. By the 16th century the city had a highly respected merchant navy, with 4,000 sailors and more than 180 large vessels, which sailed across many a distant sea. When the Ottomans dominated the wider region, many Bosnian and Croatian Catholics fled to Ragusa; generally highly educated, these newcomers contributed to an intellectual flowering in the city-state.

In spite of Ragusa's strength, its rulers constantly worried about being attacked. Nobles were not allowed to flaunt their wealth by constructing ornate palaces, and the decoration of buildings was restricted to a family coat of arms above the main door. Even the wearing of jewellery was curtailed.

Ragusa managed to rise from the ashes of the devastating earthquake of 1667, as the wealth of Baroque buildings prove, and by the end of the 18th century it had 673 ships, and consulates in 80 cities (diplomacy being a key facet of its success). However, its demise was not far off. In 1808, Napoleon invaded and dissolved the city-state.

over the centuries. The current palace, incorporated into the remains of an earlier one by Florentine Michelozzo Michelozzi (1396–1492) has a stunning loggia with intricately carved capitals – both Gothic and Renaissance – atop pillars of Korčula marble. Dubrovnik's well-developed democracy limited the rector's term of office to a month, forbade his family to move in with him and banned him from leaving the confines of his palace for anything other than official business. Just in case he should forget his responsibilities an inscription in the palace also reads: "Forget personal worries, worry about public matters." The beautiful atrium is the venue for summer concerts by the Dubrovnik Symphony Orchestra, and the acoustics are excellent. The staterooms display period furniture and paintings – among them a lovely *Baptism of Christ* (1509) by Mihajlo Hamzić – as well as an unusual collection of clocks.

Outside the palace you will see, to our left, the Baroque **Cathedral** **J** (Katedrala Velike Gospe; usually open 8am–8pm; free). Legend has it that the original 12th-century cathedral (all but destroyed in the 1667 earthquake) was commissioned by a grateful Richard the Lionheart, said to have been saved from a shipwreck on the island of Lokrum by the citizens of Ragusa during a journey back from the Crusades.

There are three naves with solid Baroque altars, and a severe, modern, main altar (the earlier one was destroyed in another earthquake in 1979), above which is a School of Titian polyptych. The **Treasury** (small charge) to the left of the altar, is packed with revered objects. Chief among them are an enamelled gold reliquary of St Blaise's head, and reliquaries in delicate gold and silver filigree of his arms and one leg, which are carried in procession around Dubrovnik on the saint's day, 3 February.

Behind the Cathedral, Gundulićeva poljana (Gundulić Square) is the site of a lively fresh **produce market** every

morning except Sunday. A flight of steps leads from the south side of the square to the imposing bulk of the **Jesuit Church** (Crvka Sveti Ignacija; daily 8am–6pm; free), which was completed in 1725, its interior modelled on the Gesù Church in Rome.

Dubrovnik's walls

The best way to get an idea of the layout of the old town is to walk around the **City Walls** **K** (summer 8am–7pm, winter 10am–3pm; charge). There are entrances by the Pile and Ploče gates and another by St Ivan's Fort in the harbour. The 2km (1-mile) walk can be arduous in the heat of a summer's day and is not recommended for anyone who suffers from vertigo. Early evening is the best time for ambling around the old fortifications as the fading light softens the hard lines of the stone and casts peachy hues across the terracotta-tiled roofs. There is surprisingly little evidence of war damage, but look closer and you will see the different shades of the roof tiles. The older tiles were sourced from a local quarry that has long since closed down, so restorers

Well-groomed customers in a stylish Dubrovnik café.

BELOW: altar in the Baroque cathedral.

had to import as close a match as they could get from Slovenia and France.

North from the Pile Gate is the highest point on the walls, the **Minčeta Fortress** (Tvrdava Minčeta), designed by the Florentine artist Michelozzo Michelozzi, though local luminary Juraj Dalmatinac executed his plans. From atop the fort there are great views of the old town rooftops, gardens, domes and spires. Head along the northern wall, peering down into the narrow lanes below, and you eventually come to the **Ploče Gate** (Vrata od Ploča) from where you can see the busy harbour and most southerly bulwark, **St Ivan's Fortress**, which houses the **Maritime Museum** (Pomorski musej; Tue–Sun 9am–6pm; charge). Laid out over two spacious floors the cool, air-conditioned museum gives an interesting glimpse into the history of this maritime city.

As you circle the southern walls, the Adriatic lies on one side while Dubrovnik spreads towards the limestone hills on the other; eventually you come to the **Bokar Fortress** (Tvrdava Bokar), another creation of Michelozzi and Dalmatinac, from

where you can descend to street leve back where you began near the Pil Gate. (If you keep your ticket you ca leave the walls and return to them a any of the three entrance points.)

Off the beaten track

Other sights worth visiting includ the **Dominican Church and Monas tery** (Dominikanska crkva i samostan 9am–6pm; charge), just inside the Ploč Gate. You enter through a peacefu cloister, where late-Gothic arcades ar embellished with Renaissance motif. In the centre is a huge well that was las used to supply water for the besieged city in 1991–2. There are some excellen paintings by artists of the 16th-centur Dubrovnik School in the museum while the church has a number o modern art works, including a bronz *Virgin and Child* by Ivan Meštrović, on of the foremost 20th-century Croatia sculptors. The small **Synagogue an Museum** (Sinagoga musej; Sun–Fr 10am–8pm; charge) in Zudioska – on of the narrow streets leading north between Stradun and the restauran lined Prijeko – is also interesting.

Venture outside the Ploče Gate to visit the **Museum of Modern Art** (Umjetnička galerija; Tue–Sun 10am–8pm; charge), a few hundred metres/yds along Frana Supila, which runs beside the sea. It is housed in a beautiful building that looks pure Renaissance but was actually built in 1935 for a wealthy shipowner. The gallery's collection, housed over four floors, with sculpture in the airy courtyard, is rotated, but includes works by Ivo Dulčić and by Vlaho Bukovac (1855–1922), who was born in Cavtat (*see page 255*).

When your sightseeing is done, join local people and visitors in the pavement cafés on Stradun, where people-watching is the main activity, especially in the early evening when people dress up to stroll up and down and children play on the shiny paving stones. Later, move on to enjoy a seafood dinner in the port or in one of the many restaurants in the narrow side streets of the old town.

Beyond the walls

Most people staying in Dubrovnik will be in one of the large hotels around **Lapad**, centred on a bay on the northwest of the city, an easy bus journey away. On the same side of the city is **Gruž**, the city's main harbour, where ferries go to the islands and to Italy. A few Renaissance villas remain behind high walls, and there is a a daily produce market and local shops. Beyond Gruz is **Rijeka dubrovačka,** the estuary of the River Ombla which the suspension bridge crosses. The city's main yachting marina is here.

On the opposite, south side of the city is **Banji Beach** Dubrovnik's recreational shore, just outside Ploče Gate and beneath the **Lazereti**, the former quarantine station aimed at keeping disease from the city. The half a dozen buildings are today used as workshops and cultural centres, and it is here that the local Lindo folk group regularly performs songs and dances.

Just offshore and a 10-minute boat ride from the old port is the island of **Lokrum**, which makes a pleasant excursion: take your swimming things for a dip. You pay a small charge to step ashore. The former Benedictine monastery was turned into a summer

BELOW: Cavtat town and marina.

Cool down with a colourful cocktail in an island café-bar.

residence by Archduke Maximilian who purchased the island in 1859. There is a café, and peacocks roam everywhere.

The Elaphite Islands

A huge range of boat trips operate out of Dubrovnik, from Gruž Harbour and Lapad, and from the Old Port. The **Elaphites** (Deer Islands) lie just north of the city. Today any deer that once lived here are long gone, and the human population is much reduced. All three of the inhabited islands, Koločep, Lopud and Šipan, are easy to visit on a day trip from Dubrovnik, but there is accommodation if you want to stay overnight.

Nearest to Dubrovnik is **Koločep** ❼, which has two small settlements, Donje Čelo and Gornje Čelo, with just 150 inhabitants between them. The main attractions are wandering through the pine forests and olive groves and relaxing on the sands at Donje Čelo. Slightly further west is **Lopud** ❽, which has the most to offer. In the 15th century it had its own fleet of some 80 vessels and a shipyard; nobles from Ragusa often built summer houses on the

BELOW: St Mary's Island, Mljet National Park.

island. The town, built around a sandy bay, has several grand old palaces, a testament to its golden age. A Franciscan monastery (currently under restoration) has a lovely cloister, and the adjoining church of St Mary of Spilica (beside the elegant Hotel Villa Vilena) can be visited. From the harbour front lined with restaurants, a path marked Plaža Sunj leads for about half an hour through pine-scented woods with conveniently situated benches to the lovely, sandy beach at **Sunj Bay**.

Šipan ❾, the largest of the Elaphites, a 90-minute trip from Dubrovnik, is the most agricultural of the islands, with small vineyards and olive groves. Excursion boats stop at Sudurad and ferries also go to the little settlement of Šipanska Luka.

Mljet National Park

The largest of the Southern Dalmatia islands after Korčula is **Mljet** ❿, a third of which is protected as a national park. It is unspoilt, wild and beautiful and, according to myth, it was here that Ulysses was kept captive for seven years. A fast catamaran

and slower ferries go to Polače, from where a minibus will take you to the **National Park** if you buy a park entrance ticket in the kiosk near the jetty. Main attractions are the saltwater lakes of Malo jerezo (Small Lake) and Veliko jerezo (Big Lake), which have cycling and walking paths leading around them and off through the pine forests to the village of Pomena, where there is a hotel and a number of restaurants. There is also a boat to **St Mary's Island**, where an abandoned Benedictine monastery, now being restored, houses a restaurant with tables set out on an attractive terrace.

South of Dubrovnik

The highway continues down the coast, heading around to **Župa dubrovačka**, a community made up of a string of small resorts around the attractive Župa Bay, where the water is beautifully clear and the white pebbly beaches a delight. A handful of small communities, hardly resorts, include Mlini, which takes it name from its water mills, and Srebreno (Silver), the administrative centre. A fragment of 10th-century Glagolithic script, inscribed in stone, has recently been found here.

The relaxed town of **Cavtat** ⓫ (pronounced "tsavtat") is just beyond the bay. Close to the airport, this is another good springboard for Dubrovnik but it is also a destination in its own right. There are regular boats from Dubrovnik harbour. Its picturesque houses crowd around a couple of bays, which form good natural harbours. The waterfront is lined with palm trees, restaurants and cafés, and a 7km (5-mile) promenade circles both bays. At one end is the Renaissance Rector's Palace, containing a museum and gallery (currently closed), and the Baroque parish church of St Nicholas. At the other end is the **Franciscan Monastery Church** (Franjevački samostan crkva; usually open; free) with an eye-catching polyptych of St Michael (1510) to the left of the door, the work of Vicko Dobrečević.

The monastery itself is now a hotel. The street behind the church leads up to a cemetery containing one of sculptor Ivan Meštrović's most important works, the **Račić Family Mausoleum**, built for a wealthy shipping family in 1922. Constructed of white Brač stone it is adorned with angels, rams and eagles. From behind the cemetery there is an attractive walk all the way round the peninsula.

Half way along Cavtat's harbour front, in a steep narrow street, is the **Galerija Vlaho Bukovac** (Tue–Sat 9am–1pm, 4–8pm, Sun 4–8pm; charge), dedicated to the work of Bukovac, the highly esteemed and prolific artist who was born here.

The region south of here, down to Montenegro, is **Konavle**, an agricultural district where the silk moth is cultivated and the silk used in local costumes worn at the Sunday folk gatherings in **Čilipi**. Hillside hamlets make up **Pridvorje**, a town eulogised by Dubrovnik's Renaissance poets. Now a series of hamlets, the community includes a Franciscan monastery and a former palace of the rector of Konavle. ❑

Ivan Meštrović's fine mausoleum for the wealthy Račić family in Cavtat.

BELOW: day at the beach on the Elaphite Island of Koločep.

MONTENEGRO EXCURSION

A small, wild, mountainous nation – neighbouring Montenegro has scenic splendour from peaks to shore and can be visited on a day excursion from Dubrovnik

Main attractions
BAY OF KOTOR
BUDVA RIVIERA
LAKE SKARDASKO
DURMITOR NATIONAL PARK
CETINJE
LOUVĆEN NATIONAL PARK

BELOW: the old section of Kotor in the late evening sunlight.

Visitors to Dubrovnik have the opportunity of a day excursion to the Bay of Kotor (Boka Kotor-ska), which lies just over the border in Montenegro 40km (25 miles) to the south. Behind the bay is the old royal city of Cetinje, and further forays into the sunny mountainous country a quarter of the size of Croatia will reward the more intrepid traveller.

Kotor Fjord

A World Heritage Site, the huge **Kotor Fjord** is a sunken river canyon, 28km (16 miles) long and 30 metres (100ft) deep, with four distinct bays. It is the nearest that the Mediterranean has to a real fjord and is a breathtaking sight especially for anyone arriving by boat. The bay has a number of beaches, resorts and small islands, and much of the ancient architecture in the fishing and boat-building villages is from the Venetian period.

The road runs around the bay from the resort of **Herceg-Novi** to reach **Risan**, the oldest settlement, adjoining a smaller, inner bay. Here are remains of a Graeco-Illyrian acropolis and some impressive Roman mosaics, particularly one representing Hypnos, the god of sleep. Beyond Risan is **Perast**, the last city in the Venetian Republic to surrender to the French. Its elegant Venetian buildings make it one of the most attractive towns in the bay, and there are even a few remaining people who speak a Venetian dialect called Perasto. Offshore are two small islands with pretty churches.

The road soon reaches **Kotor**, set spectacularly beside the bay. Kotor's delightful old town is encircled by sturdy walls and it is a pleasure to wander its music-filled streets. The most important among its impressive palaces and churches is the Romanesque cathedral of St Tryphone, which has 14th-century frescoes and a rich treasury. The excellent seafood restaurant Galion, with a view of the bay, is alone worth the trip.

The airport for the region is 4km (2½ miles) outside **Tivat**, a largely 19th-century town in the southernmost bay. The naval base built by the Austrians is now in private hands and in 2009 it opened as Porto Montenegro, with 800 berths proposed for mega-yachts and the depressing ambition of becoming the Monaco of the Adriatic.

Budva Riviera and the national parks

Beaches and resorts continue down the coast to the **Budva Riviera** (Budvanska rivijera), a boundless playground with 11km (7 miles) of fine sandy beaches. This is Montenegro's millionaires' paradise, and as money has poured in over the past few years, locals selling their land to Russian and other foreign developers have suddenly found themselves wealthy. There is a buzzy night-life, and star performers at Jaz beach have included the Rolling Stones and Madonna. Budva's attractive walled old town was almost entirely rebuilt after an earthquake in 1978.

Shortly after Buvda, at Petrovac, the main road leaves the coast and heads inland to the capital, Podgorica, crossing the northern end of **Lake Skardasko**. This is the largest lake in the Balkans, shared between Montenegro and Albania. Now a national park (Nacionalni park Skadarsko jezero), it has abundant birdlife and has adopted the scruffy looking curly pelican as its emblem.

Montenegro has several other national parks. **Biogradska Gora**, based at Kolašin, has glacial lakes, streams, virgin forest, and mountains topping 2,000 metres (6,500ft). At Eko Katun Vranjak above Kolasin, you can stay in mountain huts and enjoy rural life. But the main focus of mountain tourism – climbing in summer and skiing in winter – is the **Durmitor National Park**, around the Durmitor massif, cut through with magnificent canyons such as the 80km (50-mile) Tara River Canyon, which descends 1,300 metres (4,250ft).

Capital cities

Montenegro's capital, **Podgorica**, is a modern city of around 140,000. Much of it was destroyed in World War II, but there is still an old Turkish quarter and some interesting restored churches. The city has an active cultural life, and socialising takes place out of doors in the main square, Trg Republike.

Montenegro's old royal capital is **Cetinje**, on the inland road between Podgorica and Kotor, and it remains the country's cultural and educational centre. Its fine museums and galleries provide an idea of Montenegro and its past. These include an art museum with the most valuable murals in Montenegro. Icons can also be seen in the Museum of Cetinje Monastery. The National Museum is housed in the palace of Nikola I Petrović-Njegoš, Montenegro's only king, who reigned 1910–18.

The Petrović ruling family came from Njeguši, in the nearby **Lovćen National Park**, which extends over twisting mountain roads behind Kotor. Traditional farm buildings are scattered around the park, and there are fine views over the coast that are hard to forget. ❑

TIP

One of the best – and certainly the cheapest – ways to stay in Montenegro is to rent a room. Montenegrins keep their doors open and are universally hospitable. Ask in any café where you can find lodgings.

BELOW: sailing into the Budva Riviera.

※ INSIGHT GUIDE — TRAVEL TIPS
CROATIA

T RANSPORT

GETTING THERE AND GETTING AROUND

GETTING THERE

By Air

Flights from Europe

Zagreb's small but functional airport, situated 17km (12 miles) south of the city, is Croatia's main international airport. The country has another six international airports at Split, Dubrovnik, Pula, Rijeka, Osijek and Zadar. Croatia's national airline Croatia Airlines (www.croatiaairlines.hr) and its partners connect the country to more than 30 European destinations including London, Paris, Brussels, Rome, Vienna, Zurich, Frankfurt, Munich and Dusseldorf. British Airways (www.ba.com) flies from London Gatwick to Dubrovnik. The only low-cost carrier linking the UK with Zagreb is Wizz Air (www.wizzair.com), with three flights weekly from London Luton. Other no-frills airlines with direct flights from the UK and Ireland include easyJet (www.easyjet.com), which flies from Bristol and London Gatwick to Split and from London Gatwick and Liverpool to Dubrovnik; Jet2.com (www.jet2.com), with flights from Belfast and Leeds Bradford to Dubrovnik and Newcastle to Split; Flybe (www.flybe.com) connecting Dubrovnik with Belfast, Birmingham, Exeter, Glasgow, Jersey and Southampton; and Ryanair (www.ryanair.com), linking Dublin,

Timetables

A useful resource for domestic and international bus timetables as well as domestic ferry routes is www.autobusni-kolodvor.com.

Edinburgh and London Stansted with Zadar and Stansted with Pula.

Other cheap options include indirect flights to Dubrovnik or Split via various airports in Germany with TUIfly (www.tuifly.com) or Germanwings (www.germanwings.com), or flying to Pescara, Bari or Ancona in Italy and taking a catamaran to Dalmatia.

Two useful price-comparison websites for airfares are www.skyscanner.net and www.kayak.com.

Airport information

Zagreb
Tel: 01 626 5222
www.zagreb-airport.hr
Split
Tel: 021 203555
www.split-airport.hr
Dubrovnik
Tel: 020 773333
www.airport-dubrovnik.hr
Pula
Valtursko Polje bb
Tel: 052 530105
www.airport-pula.hr
Rijeka
Tel: 051 842132
www.rijeka-airport.hr
Zadar
Tel: 023 205800
www.zadar-airport.hr
Osijek
Tel: 031 514400
www.osijek-airport.hr

Travel to and from the airport

Bus services from Zagreb airport to the city's bus station, run by Pleso prijevoz (tel: 01 633 1982; www.plesoprijevoz.hr) operate almost every half hour daily from 7am to 8pm, with additional services after later flights have landed. In the return direction services run from

5am to 8pm but also leave 90 minutes before aircraft departure on domestic flights and 120 minutes on international flights. At the bus station, look for the Croatia Airlines terminal sign. It takes around 45 minutes and costs 30 kuna.

Taxis collect passengers from outside the international arrival hall. Fares to the city are usually between 150 and 250 kuna, depending on distance and hour. It is best to order a cab on tel: 970.

Croatia's other international airports also have bus connections to the city centre. Distances and journey times are as follows:

Split 24km (14 miles), 35 minutes; Dubrovnik 18km (11 miles), 20 minutes; Osijek 3km (1½ miles), 10 minutes; Zadar 15km (9 miles), 15 minutes; Rijeka 27km (17 miles), 35 minutes; Pula 7km (4 miles), 10 minutes. Check airport websites for the most up-to-date information.

Airlines

Zagreb
Croatia Airlines
Zrinjevac 17
Tel: 01 481 9633
www.croatiaairlines.hr
Aeroflot
Trg Nikole Šubića Zrinskog 6
Tel: 01 487 2055
www.aeroflot.ru
Adria Airways
Praška 9
Tel: 01 481 0011
www.adria.si
Air France
1st Floor
Hotel Westin
Kršnjavoga 1
Tel: 01 489 0800
www.airfrance.com

Austrian Airlines
Pleso bb
Tel: 01 626 5900
www.aua.com

Czech Airlines (ČSA)
Trg N. Š. Zrinskog 17
Tel: 01 487 3301
www.csa.cz

Hungarian Airlines (MALEV)
Hotel Westin
Kršnjavoga 1
Tel: 01 483 6935
www.malev.hu

Lufthansa
Bantel Travel Lufthansa City Centre
Ilica 191
Tel: 01 390 7284
www.lufthansa.com

Polish Airlines (LOT)
Trg Bana Josip Jelašića 2
Tel: 01 483 7505
www.lot.com

Turkish Airlines
Zabreb Airport
Tel: 01 456 2008
www.turkishairlines.com

SWISS
Zrinjevac 1/III
Tel: 01 481414
www.swiss.com

Split
Croatia Airlines
Hrvatskog Narodnog preporoda 9
Tel: 021 362997
www.croatiaairlines.hr

Zadar
Croatia Airlines
Poljana Natka Nodila 7
Tel: 023 250101

Rijeka
Croatia Airlines
Jelačićev trg 5
Tel: 051 330207

Pula
Croatia Airlines
Carrarina 8
Tel: 052 218909

Dubrovnik
Croatia Airlines
Terminal A
Dubrovnik Airport
Tel: 020 773232

Flights from Australia, New Zealand, Canada and US

There are no direct flights from the USA, Canada, Australia or New Zealand to Croatia. However Croatia Airlines has representatives in all these countries except Canada and connections are possible through various European cities. Two useful websites for planning flights and

ABOVE: towing a boat just off Vis Town shore in Central Dalmatia.

comparing prices are www.skyscanner.net and www.kayak.com.

Sky Air Services (GSA)
7/24 Albert Road
Sth Melbourne
Victoria 3205
Australia
Tel: +61 (3) 9699 9355
Email: lidia@skyair.biz

Croatia Times Travel Ltd (GSA)
131 Lincoln Road
Henderson
Auckland
New Zealand
Tel: +64 (9) 838 7700

Sea/Ferry

International car ferries connect Italy to Croatia. Jadrolinija operates the majority of these services. The main routes are from Ancona to Zadar, Ancona to Split and Stari Grad (Hvar) and Bari to Rijeka via Dubrovnik, Korčula and Split. Jadrolinija offices are usually close to the ferry dock.

Jadrolinija Offices at Main Ports:
Rijeka, tel: 051 211444
Zadar, tel: 023 250555
Split, tel: 021 338333
Dubrovnik, tel: 385 51 666 111
Pula (Jadroagent), tel: 052 210431
Other offices are listed on Jadrolinija's website: www.jadrolinija.hr.

From mid-June to early September **SNAV** operate international car and passenger ferry services between Ancona and Split. **SNAV** also operates a service from late July to the end of August from Pescara to Split via Stari Grad. From early April to the end of October BlueLine Ferries sails from Ancona to Split, with some services also stopping in Stari Grad or Vis. From July to September Azzurro Line

operates a ferry from Bari to Dubrovnik. From mid-April to mid-October Venezia Lines runs ferries from Venice to Rovinj via Poreč, and from mid-July to the end of August from Venice to Pula and Mali Lošinj and from early June to late September from Venice to Rabac. From the end of May to mid-September it also runs ferries from Venice to Rovinj via Piran (Slovenia). A useful ferry-booking website is www.traghettiweb.it.

SNAV (Società Navigazione Alta Velocità)
Ancona
Ancona Maritime Station
Tel: +39 (0) 71 207 6116
Pescara
Pescara Maritime Station
Tel: +39 (0) 85 454 9089
www.snav.it

Tickets are also available from Jadroagent in Split.
Tel: 021 460999
www.jadroagent.hr

Azzurra Line (sales agents)
Agestea, Bari Maritime Station
Tel: +39 (0) 80 592 8400
Email: booking@azzurraline.com
Elite Shipping Agency, Dubrovnik Maritime Station
Tel: +385 020 313178
Email: port.office@elite.hr, shipping@elite.hr
www.azzurraline.com

BlueLine Ferries (sales agents)
Split Tours, Gat sv. Duje, Split
Tel: +385 021 352533
Agenzia Mauro, Ancona Maritime Station
Tel: +39 (0) 71 204041
www.blueline-ferries.com

Venezia Lines
Isola di Tronchetto 21, Venice
Tel: +39 (0) 41 242 4000

Call centre for Italy and overseas:
Tel: +39 (0) 41 272 2646
Call centre for Croatia: 052 422 896
www.venezialines.com

By Train

There are direct international rail connections to Zagreb and Rijeka from Italy, Austria, the Czech Republic, Slovakia, Germany and all neighbouring countries except Montenegro. EuroCity services to Zagreb run from Munich via Salzburg and Ljubljana, from Villach and from Belgrade. InterCity services link Vienna to Zagreb via Maribor, Budapest to Rijeka and Zagreb and Budapest to Osijek, while EuroNight sleeper services connect Venice and Ljubljana with Zagreb and Budapest with Split. From mid-July to early September there is also a daily train from Prague to Split via Brno, Bratislava, Szombathely and Split, with sleepers and couchettes available. A less obvious international rail option is the 13¾-hour train from Zagreb to Ploče, the nearest station to Dubrovnik, travelling via Mostar, Sarajevo and Banja Luka in Bosnia Herzegovina.

From London to Zagreb the most convenient route involves changing in Paris and Munich and takes about 24 hours. Comfortable sleeper accommodation with showers is available on the overnight *Cassiopeia* train between Paris and Zagreb.

Croatian Railways provides timetable and station information in Croatian and English on its website, www.hznet.hr and by telephone, tel: 060 333444. Two useful websites for planning European railway travel are www.seat61.com and www.sbb.ch.

Various InterRail and Eurail passes – for European and non-European residents respectively – are available that cover Croatia. However train fares in Croatia are low and it is generally better value to buy point-to-point tickets. See www.eurail.com and www.raileurope.co.uk for details.

Bus/Coach

International coach services connect Croatia to its neighbouring countries as well as Macedonia, Austria, Hungary, the Czech Republic, Slovakia, Italy, Germany, France and Switzerland.

Eurolines, with its extensive network, is the biggest international service provider. Its local partner in Croatia is Eurotrans (www.autotrans.hr), although there are also other

companies running international services. Links to individual country websites are available through the main site www.eurolines.com.

International Bus Terminals

Zagreb
Avenija Marina Držića 4
Tel: 060 313333 (+385 (0) 1 611 2789 from outside Croatia)
www.akz.hr
Rijeka
Žabica 1
Tel: 060 302010, 051 660360
Dubrovnik
Put Republike 19
Tel: 060 305070, 020 357020
www.libertasdubrovnik.hr
Pula
Istarske divizije 43
Tel: 052 500012
Split
Obala Kneza Domagoja 12
Tel: 060 327777; (+385 (0) 21 329199 from outside Croatia)
www.ak-split.hr
Osijek
Trg Lavoslava Ružičke 2
Tel: 060 334466
Šibenik
Draga 14
Tel: 060 368368
Zadar
Ante Starčevića 1
Tel: 023 211555

GETTING AROUND

Choosing Transport

Travelling around Croatia can be a frustrating experience. The old Yugoslav government built few highways and there were few stretches of dual carriageway – even along the main coastal road between Rijeka and Dubrovnik, the Jadranska *magistrala* (Adriatic Highway). This is gradually being redressed and new highways are under construction in preparation for EU entry.

However, at present, single-lane roads often lead to traffic jams triggered by slow vehicles and accidents caused by reckless overtaking. Driving can therefore be a white-knuckle experience.

Often the only viable alternative is to catch a bus. Villages, towns and cities are well connected by extensive national and local bus services, but these stop frequently for rest breaks, a joy for smokers, drivers and the incontinent but a pain for many others. The standard of vehicle also varies from luxury air-

Taxis

Taxis can be caught at ranks, hailed on the street or booked by telephone. Reputable taxis have meters. As a general guide, the starting fare is 30 kuna and each additional kilometre costs 10 kuna. Fares for long journeys should be agreed in advance. Hotels, restaurants, tourist offices and travel agencies all carry flyers for local taxi firms. Compared with other living costs in Croatia taxis are expensive.

conditioned coaches to run-down buses with poor ventilation.

Domestic train travel is not really an option if you want to get around Croatia quickly, as the Austro-Hungarian rulers were more interested in connecting Croatian cities to Austria and Hungary than to each other. Little changed under Yugoslav rule and many lines became damaged or fell out of use during the war. Split, Pula and Rijeka all have a direct rail link by diesel train to Zagreb, but services are slow and those requiring connections are subject to backtracking and long waits. Many lines remain non-electrified and single track, there is no direct rail link between Istria and the rest of Croatia, and Dubrovnik has no railway station. Unsurprisingly most locals scarcely use the railway, though for rail buffs the run-down system can be fun to ride. There is a night train between Split and Zagreb, taking eight hours and with comfortable if not very spacious sleeper accommodation in one-, two- or three-berth compartments.

Travelling by ferry can also be exasperating. Jadrolinija has a near monopoly over ferry travel in Croatia, with infrequent and oversubscribed services to destinations along the coast and on the islands, especially in summer. Foot passengers can buy tickets for immediate or future travel on any service; however, those driving cars often experience lengthy waits. So book in advance, if possible. The timetables and regulations are confusing. It's best to get local advice.

By Air

Domestic flights with Croatia Airlines connect Zagreb to Bol (Brač), Dubrovnik, Osijek, Pula, Split and Zadar. Taxi flights from destinations in Croatia, Germany, Austria, Slovenia, Italy, Bosnia Herzegovina and other countries in the region also land in the small airport at Mali Lošinj. Airport information for international airports are included in the Getting There section *(see page 260).*

Brač Airport
Tel: 021 559711
www.airport-brac.hr

Lošinj Airport
Privlaka 19
Mali Lošinj
Tel: + 385 51 235148
www.airportmalilosinj.hr

By Bus/Coach

It is possible to travel almost anywhere in Croatia by bus or coach. Autotrans (tel: 051 660360, fax: 051 211988; www.autotrans.hr) is the main company operating domestic services. Buy tickets at the local bus station or – if you are not boarding at a station – from the conductor. Fares are not especially cheap, with 3–4 hour journeys costing around 100 kuna, with an extra charge on most journeys of 7 kuna per item for baggage stowed under the bus.

By Train

Most Croatians rarely travel by train. The network is small with few connections between major towns and cities. Where connections do exist, services are often much slower than the bus. Tickets are cheap and available from railway stations. There is rarely any need to book ahead.

The main routes are between Zagreb and Split and Split and Rijeka. Croatia's dreamiest railway journey is from Zagreb to Split, cutting through the heart of the country and culminating in the harsh karst mountains of the Dinaric range. A new express service began to operate on this route in June 2004, cutting the journey time down from seven and a half to five hours. This high-tech train offers passenger radios and power points for laptops. There is also a slower night train, all second-class, bearing reasonably priced sleeper carriages with one, two or three berths as well as seats. For arrival and departure information, visit the Croatian Railways (Hrvatske željeznice) website at www.hznet.hr or tel: 060 333 444.

Zagreb Railway Station
Tomislavov trg 12
Split Railway Station
Obala Kneza Domagoja 10

Rijeka Railway Station
Trg kralja Tomislava 1
Pula Railway Station
Kolodvorska 5
Šibenik Railway Station
Fra Jerolima Milete 24
Zadar Railway Station
Ante Starčevića 3

Island-hopping

There are two ways to island hop in Croatia. The first is to use the regular passenger- and car-ferry services that connect towns and cities along the coast and many of Croatia's islands. The second is to charter a yacht.

The main car and passenger service provider is Jadrolinija (www.jadrolinija.hr), whose main offices are listed in the Getting There section *(see page 261).* Local offices are near the ferry dock. Jadrolinija provides more than 30 direct connections, with the main tourist routes being: Krk–Cres, Krk–Rab, Mali Lošinj–Ilovik, Prizna–Pag, Zadar–Mali Lošinj, Zadar–Dugi Otok, Split–Trogir, Split–Brač, Split–Hvar, Split–Vela Luka, Split–Vis, Hvar–Vis, Dubrovnik–Mljet and Rijeka–Dubrovnik via Split and Korčula.

The following is a list of routes, some of which are seasonal:

Jadrolinija Services
Biograd na moru–Tkon
Brestova–Porozina
Dominče–Orebić
Drvenik–Sućuraj
Drvenik Mali–Trogir
Dubrovnik–Sobra
Dubrovnik–Suđurađ
Makarska–Sumartin
Split–Drvenik Mali
Split–Hvar
Split–Jelsa
Split–Rogač
Split–Stari Grad
Split–Supetar
Split–Ubli
Split–Vela Luka
Split–Vis
Sućuraj–Drvenik
Sumartin–Makarska
Šepurine–Šibenik
Šibenik–Šepurine
Šibenik–Vodice
Šibenik–Zlarin
Šibenik–Žirje
Tkon–Biograd na moru
Trogir–Drvenik Mali
Zadar–Brbinj
Zadar–Bršanj
Zadar–Ist
Zadar–Mala Rava
Zadar–Mali Lošinj
Zadar–Molat
Zadar–Preko (Ugljan)

Zadar–Premuda
Zadar–Rava
Zadar–Sali
Zadar–Zaglav
Zaglav–Zadar
Zlarin–Šibenik
Žigljen–Prizna
Žirje–Šibenik

Tickets for cars and their passengers can – and in summer should – be purchased in advance, because traffic queues to board the ferry are lengthy, with waits of up to four hours frequently reported.

Foot passengers do not face the same problems and can purchase tickets immediately before departure. Tickets cannot be purchased on board and those requiring seats or cabins on the journey between Rijeka and Dubrovnik are also advised to book well ahead.

SEM Maritime
Tel: 021 338219
Fax: 021 338267
www.sem-marina.hr
Operates catamaran and ferry routes. Catamaran services from Šolta to Split, and from Vis to Split, run year round. Summer ferry and catamaran routes include Pelješac to Mljet and Milna to Split. Return fares start at 40 kuna and rise, depending on the distance travelled.

Bura Line & Off Shore
Put Porta 19, Slatine
Tel: 091 727 1244
www.slatine.com/bura line.html
Operates between Trogir and Split via Slatine.

G&V Line
Vukovarska 34, Dubrovnik
Tel: 020 313119
Mateja Bošnjaka (Zadranina), Zadar
Tel: 023 250733
www.gv-line.hr
This Dubrovnik-based company operates the following routes: Zverinac–Božava–Sestrunj–Rivanj–Zadar; Zadar–Mali Iž–Veli Iž–Mala Rava–Rava; and Dubrovnik–Luka Šipanska–Sobra (Mljet)–Polače (Mljet)–Korčula–Ubli (Lastovo).

Ivante
Obala boraca 8, Zlarin
Operates services between Šibenik and Žirje via Kaprije.

Mediteranska Plovidba
Trg kralja Tomislava 2, Korčula
Tel: 020 711156
www.medplov.hr
Runs services from Orebić to Korčula.

Miatrade
Sv. Vinka Paulskog 23, Zadar
Tel: 023 254300
www.miatours.hr
Runs services from Zadar to Olib via
Premuda and Silba.

Rapska Plovidba
Hrvatskih branitelja domovinskog rata
1/2, Rab
Tel: 051 724122
www.rapska-plovidba.hr
Runs services from Jablanac to
Mišnjak (Rab).

Split Tours
Boktuljin put, Split
Tel: 021 338310
www.splittours.hr
Runs services from Split to Milna; Split
to Rogač; Split to Stomorsko; Pula to
Zadar via Unije and Mali Lošinj; and
Lopar to Valbiska.

UTO Kapetan Luka
Poljička cesta-Krilo 4, Jesenice
Tel: +385 21 872877
www.krilo.hr
Runs services from Korčula to Split via
Hvar.

Vrgada
Biograd na moru
Runs services from Biograd na moru to
Vrgada and Pakoštane to Vrgada.

Chartering a Yacht

Numerous companies offer yacht
charters in Croatia. Contacts for some
of the bigger companies are listed
below. To charter a yacht you need a
qualified skipper who must hold a
navigation permit (people who have
held a captain's certificate for at least
three years can take an examination to
gain their permit). For those without
formal qualifications it is usually
possible to hire a skipper through the
various yacht charter companies.

ACI (Adriatic Croatia
International Club)
Charters boats throughout Croatia.
M. Tita 15, 51410 Opatija
Tel: 051 271288
Fax: 051 271824
www.aci-club.hr

Adriatic Yacht Charter
ACI Marina Pomer, Rizanska 16,
52100 Pula
Tel: 098 366735
Fax: 052 573848
www.ayc.hr

ACI Marina Dubrovnik
20000 Dubrovnik
Tel: 098 335554
Fax: 020 456502
www.ayc.hr

Asta Yachting Ltd
Put Murata 1a , 23000 Zadar
Tel: 023 316902
Fax: 023 316765
www.croatia-yachting.com

Club Adriatic
Tel: 01 466 8220
Email: info@clubadriatic.com
www.clubadriatic.com

Driving

Main Routes

Croatia's limited motorway network
connects Zagreb to Karlovac, Krapina
and Slavonski Brod, Varaždin to
Cakovec and Rijeka to Kupjak. All
motorways are toll roads. Croatia's
other main route is the Jadranska
Magistrala (Adriatic Highway)
connecting Rijeka and Dubrovnik,
subject to roadworks. For the latest
traffic news, check out www.hak.hr.

Car Hire

It is fairly expensive to hire a car in
Croatia – around €280 (£255 or $425)
per week for a small car in high season.
This will include unlimited mileage,
third party insurance, collision damage
waiver and theft waiver, and local
taxes. For the international car hire
firms, it generally works out cheaper to
hire in advance of arriving in Croatia,
but you may manage to get a good
deal on the spot from a local company.

Drivers must be at least 21 years
old and have held a full driving licence
for two years; they also need a valid
passport or national identity card.
When hiring your car, check the
insurance carefully to be clear about
any excess charges that may be
applied in case of accident.

Major hire companies such as
Budget, National and Avis have offices
throughout Croatia, with many at
major transport terminals. It is best to
book through a central reservations
number or online.

Budget
Tel: 01 480 5688
Fax: 01 480 5690
www.budget.hr

Avis
Tel: 01 483 6006
Fax: 01 483 6296
www.avis.hr

National
Tel: 021 399043
Fax: 021 399044
www.nationalcar.hr

Insurance

When hiring a car it is advisable to
purchase collision damage waiver
(CDW) and theft protection (TP) for the

duration of the hire. Personal accident
insurance (PAI) is optional. Damage to
a vehicle must be reported to the
police immediately (Tel: 92). Otherwise
the insurance becomes invalid, leaving
the hirer liable for the repair bill.

Rules of the Road

To enter Croatia by car drivers need a
valid licence, an automobile
registration card and evidence of
insurance cover. Official speed limits
are 50kmph (30mph in built up areas,
80kmph (50mph) outside residential
areas, 100kmph (62mph) on major
roads and 130kmph (80mph) on
motorways. However, many Croatians
drive faster. Buses and vehicles with a
trailer have a maximum speed of
80kmph (50mph).

The wearing of seat belts is
compulsory and using mobile
telephones that are not hands-free is
banned. It is a legal requirement to
inform the police about traffic
accidents (tel: 92) and to use a hazard
warning triangle. A variety of violations,
including speeding, not wearing a seat
belt and not observing the right of way,
incur an on-the-spot fine. Fines range
from 100 kuna to 500 kuna depending
on the severity of the incident. Drivers
under the influence of alcohol will have
their licence revoked.

Many of Croatia's old towns are
officially closed to traffic except for
those accessing residential property.
Although there is lax enforcement of
this rule, old town streets are very
narrow, hard to navigate and can
become unexpectedly blocked.

In case of a breakdown, tel: 987.
The Croatian Auto Club (Hrvatski
Autoklub – HAK) can provide more
information about toll roads, driving in
Croatia and traffic updates, tel: 01
464 8800, www.hak.hr.

Parking

Car parks in Croatia are well signposted with a white "P" inside a blue
square. The main car parks in many of
Croatia's historic towns are just
outside the pedestrian zones and cost
4–6 kuna an hour. Parking is usually
available for 24 hours.

Distances from Zagreb		
Karlovac	56km	35 miles
Varaždin	98km	61 miles
Rijeka	182km	113 miles
Slavonski		
Brod	190km	118 miles
Osijek	280km	173 miles
Pula	292km	181 miles
Dubrovnik	572km	355 miles

ACCOMMODATION

HOTELS, YOUTH HOSTELS, BED AND BREAKFAST

Price categories are for the cheapest available double room in high season, including breakfast (unless indicated otherwise). On the coast there is often a supplement for sea views.

Choosing a Hotel

Croatia has hotels to suit all tastes and budgets from vast concrete resorts to small luxury hotels and even renovated lighthouses. The country is also in the process of developing high-quality small-scale accommodation. Prices and facilities vary greatly, but most hotels offer spacious, clean rooms. It is highly advisable to book in advance in high season. For those travelling on a tighter budget, Croatia has a wealth of private accommodation and camping grounds with excellent facilities (see pages 259–262). Except in Zagreb and some five-star hotels, hotel prices are seasonal, being highest in July and August and up to 40 percent less off-season. In Zagreb prices rise during trade fairs. You can find a list at www. zv.hr. A useful website for booking hotel accommodation in Croatia is www. adriatica.net. Hotel prices are often better if booked online. There is often a supplement for sea views.

Private Accommodation

Private accommodation is popular in Croatia and many resorts, villages and towns throughout the country have more beds in private accommodation than in hotels. The standard of private accommodation varies considerably, ranging from simple rooms in private houses (called sobe) to self-contained studios or apartments, ideal for longer visits. Although it is common for people to approach travellers at

transport terminals offering rooms, it is best to go through an agency.

The cheap rates for a room **$** and **$–$$** for an apartment can be hiked by supplements for short stays (30–100 percent depending on the location) taxes, registration fees and single occupancy. Generalturist, Atlas and Kompas are among the biggest agents and have offices throughout Croatia. A useful resource is www. hostelworld.com.

Lighthouses

For a truly unique holiday experience you can stay in one of 13 renovated lighthouses in Croatia. Located on beautiful islands and promontories they offer a real getaway. Most lighthouses have their own keeper and a stay of seven days, from Saturday to Saturday, is required (three days out of season). More information is available on tel: 021 390609, www.plovput.hr.

Camping

Croatia has 520 campsites with accommodation in tents or mobile homes, categorised on a star system from one to four. Some cater to naturists. Facilities are generally good and include hot water, showers and loos as a minimum. Camping is seasonal and the campsites listed are open from April through to October. All of them fall in in the $ price code. The **Croatian Camping Union** can provide information. Pionirska 1, Poreč, tel: 052 451324, www.camping.hr.

Youth Hostels

Hostels affiliated with Hostelling International are prefixed YH and can

be booked at www.hfhs.hr. You will need a membership card. There is a 50 percent discount for those aged 12 to 29 and under-12s go free.

YH Zagreb
Petrinjska 77
Tel: 01 484 1261 www.hfhs.hr
After a major overhaul Zagreb's oldest hostel has mainly ensuite doubles, triples and quads, an internet bar and its own art gallery. Prices for national youth hostel association or Hostelling International cardholders range from €16.70 in a six-bed dorm to €51.15 in a private room. The location is convenient for stations and the centre.

Hostel Lika, Zagreb
Pašmanska 17
Tel: 01 618 5375
The Lika has air con, a beer garden and bar, barbecue nights, free WiFi and friendly owners. A bed in a six-bed dorm is €12.50.

Ravince Youth Hostel, Zagreb
I. Ravince 38d
Tel: 01 233 2325
www.ravnice-youth-hostel.hr
Excellent family-run hostel, a 20-minute journey from the centre (trams 12 and 11 or buses 4 and 7). Accommodation is in two-, four-, six- and 10-bed dorms, with prices starting at €15, including one hour's internet access. Wooden furniture and garden views give the rooms a light airy feel.

YH Pula
Zalijev Vasaline 4
Tel: 052 391133
www.hfhs.hr
This hostel has a tranquil location in a pine forest just out of town (bus No 7). Bar and restaurant. Prices range from €12 to €19 (plus €10 one-off registration fee). Camping is also possible and you can even hire a tent.

ACCOMMODATION LISTINGS

ZAGREB

Arcotel Allegra Zagreb
Branimirova 29
Tel: 01 469 6000
www.arcotel.cc
This Austrian-owned design hotel is centrally located, offers spacious rooms and a Mediterranean styled restaurant. If you can get one of the lower online rates the hotel is great value. **$$–$$$$$**

Best Western Premier Hotel Astoria
Petrinjska 71
Tel: 01 480 8900
www.bestwestern.com
Built in 1932 and recently refurbished, this hotel has a great location on a quiet street midway between the train station and the town centre. **$$$**

Central
Branimirova 3
Tel: 01 484 1122
www.hotel-central.hr
A recently renovated hotel 100 metres/yds from the train station with reasonably priced rooms. **$$$$**

Dubrovnik
Gajeva 1
Tel: 01 486 3555
www.hotel-dubrovnik.hr
Built in 1929, the Dubrovnik is at the heart of Zagreb's busy shopping centre and surrounded by buzzing cafés. Refurbished rooms and bathrooms make this hotel a good option. Its café is a popular meeting place for politicians, journalists and businessmen. **$$$$**

Four Points by Sheraton Panorama Zagreb
Trg Sportova 9
Tel: 01 365 8333
www.starwoodhotels.com
At the heart of Zagreb's business district the former Hotel Panorama became a member of the Sheraton group in 2004. This modern hotel has high-tech rooms, its own restaurant and meeting facilities. Book a mountain-view room. **$$$$–$$$$$**

Palace Hotel
Trg Strossmayera 10
Tel: 01 489 9600
www.palace.hr
Zagreb's oldest hotel (built in 1891) is also one of its most impressive, overlooking a leafy square near the Art Pavilion. It has a pleasant Viennese-style café. **$$$$$**

Regent Esplanade
Mihanovićeva 1
Tel: 01 456 6666
www.regenthotels.com
Croatia's grandest hotel since 1925, when it opened to service the needs of passengers from the *Orient Express* alighting at the train station next door, has recently emerged from a major refurbishment. Now part of the Regent Hotel group it offers 209 luxurious rooms and suites that combine traditional decor with the

latest technology. **$$$$$**

Tomislavov dom
Sljeme
Tel: 01 456 0400
www.hotel-tomislavovdom.com
Surrounded by forest and near Medvednica's peak, this comfortable hotel makes a good location for active holidays and has an excellent wellness centre. **$$$**

Villa Tina
Bukovačka cesta 213
Tel: 01 244 5204
www.vilatina.com.hr
This new hotel, opposite the Maksimir Park, has 16 individually styled rooms and a good restaurant. **$$$$**

CENTRAL CROATIA

Karlovac

Hotel Carlstadt
Vraniczanyeva 2
Tel/Fax: 047 611111
www.carlstadt.hr
A modest hotel situated in the heart of town, featuring its own casino and a nightclub. **$$$**

Plitvice Lakes

Hotel Jezero
Tel: 053 751400
www.np-plitvicka-jezera.hr
Many of the rooms at the park's top hotel have fantastic views and balconies. Ask for one specifically. Don't come expecting much luxury; the location is the main reason to stay here. The lack of air conditioning can be a problem in the height of summer.
$$$–$$$$

Hotel Plitvice
Tel: 053 751100
www.np-plitvicka-jezera.hr
If you cannot get a room at the Jezero, which is often full with groups, stay here.
$$$–$$$$

Hotel Bellevue
Tel: 053 751700
www.np-plitvice.com
A modestly priced hotel with a dreary facade and equally uninspiring rooms.
$$–$$$

Hotel Grabovac
Tel: 053 751999
Email: grabovac@np-plitvicka-jezera.hr
Plitvice's most affordable hotel offers comatosely tired motel-style accommodation a short distance from the main entrance. **$$–$$$**

Villa Mukinja
Tel: 053 774061
www.plitvice-lakes.com
Plitvice hotels tend to have a Communist

time warp feel to them. For a more personal and homely if not particularly cheap experience, try this friendly, family-run guesthouse. The homemade food is a high point and the room rate includes breakfast and dinner. **$$$$**

Samobor

Hotel Livadic
Kralja Tomislava 5
Tel: 01 336 5850
www.hotel-livadic.hr
This small hotel has luxurious rooms and attentive service. **$$$**

Varaždin

Hotel Turist
Aleja kralja Zvonimira 1
Tel: 042 395395
www.hotel-turist.hr

This centrally located hotel is only five minutes' walk from the bus and railway stations. Facilities include restaurant, terrace bar, hairdresser's, fitness centre and disco. Ask to see the room first. **$$$**

PRICE CATEGORIES

Prices categories are for a double room including breakfast:
$ = under 250 kuna
$$ = 250–400 kuna
$$$ = 400–600 kuna
$$$$ = 600–1,000 kuna
$$$$$ = over 1,000 kuna

EASTERN CROATIA

Osijek

Hotel Osijek
Šamačka 4
Tel: 031 230333
www.hotelosijek.hr
After a thorough renovation this is now the most comfortable hotel in the region with large and funky rooms, some of them specially adapted for athletes and people taller than 2 metres (6ft 6in). It is on the bank of the Drava River. Ask for a room with a water view. **$$$–$$$$**

Hotel Central
Trg Ante Starčevića 6
Tel: 031 283399
Email: hotel-central@os.htnet.hr
Faded 19th-century hotel in the town centre. Reasonably comfortable, with large rooms, a sweeping staircase and a library. The Viennese-style café is lovely. **$$$**

Hotel Mursa
Bartola Kašića 2a
Tel: 031 224900
www.zug.hr
A characterless tower block, five minutes' walk from the bus station, redeemed by its comfortable if small rooms and reasonable prices. **$$**

Vukovar

Hotel Dunav
Trg Republike Hrvatske 1
Tel: 032 441285
Completely rebuilt after the Homeland War, Vukovar's only centrally located hotel enjoys a riverside setting and has reasonable rooms. **$$$**

Hotel Lav
Strossmayera 17
Tel: 032 445100
In central Vukovar on the banks of the Danube, this stylish hotel has a convenient location. Ask for a room at the back with river views. **$$$$**

ISTRIAN COAST

Brijuni Islands

Hotel Karmen
Veliki Brijun
Tel: 052 525400
www.brijuni.hr
Well-located hotel next to the sea. Most rooms have balconies and minibars. Prices are considerably lower outside high season and there is a supplement for rooms with a sea view. **$$–$$$$$**

Hotel Neptun-Istra
Veliki Brijun
Tel: 052 525861
www.np-brijuni.hr
Hotel Karmen's larger sister hotel is also on the waterfront and has good-sized rooms. There is also a supplement for rooms with a sea view and prices are much lower outside high season. **$$$–$$$$$**

Poreč

The **Valamar** and **Plava laguna** hotel groups have a duopoly on resort-style hotels geared towards mass tourism. They are large, with pools and a wide range of facilities. Book online for the best deals. **$$–$$$$**

Valamar Hotels and Resorts
Tel: 052 465000
www.riviera.hr

Plava Laguna
Rade Končara 12
Tel: 052 410101
www.plavalaguna.hr

Hotel Diamant
Tel: 052 465000
www.valamar.com
One km (½ mile) from the centre of town it has modern and comfortable rooms, an outdoor pool, gym and wellness centre. Sea-view rooms with balconies are the best. **$$$$–$$$$$**

Pula

Hotel Histria
Verudela
Tel: 052 529444
www.hotel-histria-pula.h-rez.com
With panoramic sea views and an excellent restaurant, this hotel in the Verudela marina resort is a good choice for families not needing to be too close to the historic centre, 4km (2½ miles) away. Book online for the best deals. **$$$**

Hotel Valsabbion
Pješčana Uvala IX/26
Tel: 052 218033
www.valsabbion.com
This is a stylish hotel, with an award-winning restaurant overlooking the marina. The rooms are elegant with air conditioning and a minibar. **$$–$$$**

Rovinj

Jadran-Turist Rovinj manages the majority of Rovinj's hotel accommodation.

Jadran-Turist Rovinj
Vladimira Nazora 6
Tel: 052 813055
www.istra.com/jadranturist

Adriatic
Pino Budicin
Tel: 052 803510
www.maistra.com
This is a small town house hotel on Rovinj's main square with comfortable air-conditioned rooms, minibars and sea views. **$$$–$$$$**

Angelo D'Oro
Via Svalba 38–42
Tel: 052 840502
www.rovinj.at
In the heart of the old town, this 17th-century bishop's palace has been turned into an exclusive boutique hotel. It has an attractive garden bar, a restaurant and a sauna and jacuzzi. **$$$$–$$$$$**

Hotel Rovinj
Svetog Križa 59
Tel: 052 811288
hotel-rovinj@pu.t-com.hr
An independent hotel attractively situated beneath the town's famous church. Clean and functional rooms, many with balconies and sea views. **$$–$$$$**

Umag

Istraturist
Istraturist manages the majority of Umag's hotels.
Jadranska 66
Tel: 052 700700
www.istraturist.com
$$$–$$$$

INLAND ISTRIA

Buje

Hotel Mulino
Škrile 75a
Tel: 052 725300
www.mulino.hr
Bling has well and truly come to Buje. Decked out like a cruise liner, this luxury casino hotel has enormous rooms decorated with Swarovski crystal, an impressive indoor and outdoor swimming pool and three

types of sauna, not to mention 20 roulette tables and 260 slot machines. **$$$$$**

Motovun

Hotel Kaštel
Trg Andrea Antićo
Tel: 052 681607
www.hotel-kastel-motovun.hr
With clean and reasonably priced rooms, this spa hotel occupies a former 18th-century palace atop a hill

and with excellent views. It has various wellness deals including the exciting option of chocotherapy. **$$–$$$$**

Vižinada

Agroturizam Ritossa
Vižinada 46
Tel: 052 446211
www.agroturizam-ritossa.com
Right in the centre of town, this lovingly restored 19th-

century traditional stone house belonging to the Ritossa family is agrotourism at its finest, with picturesque views. **$**

KVARNER GULF

Cres

Hotel Kimen
Melin 1/16
Tel: 051 573305
www.hotel-kimen.com
This large concrete hotel shrouded with trees offers a choice of park or – for a small supplement – sea views. **$$$$**

Krk

Hoteli Baška
Emila Geistlicha 39
Tel: 051 656111
www.hotelibaska.hr
This group has the monopoly on Baška's accommodation. Rooms fill up fast in summer.
Dražica
Ružmarinska 6
Tel: 051 655766
www.hotelikrk.hr
The Dražica dominates the hotel scene in Krk Town, with the adjoining Hotel Marina (the least expen-

sive) and Hotel Tamaris. **$$–$$$$**

Mali Lošinj

Jadranka
Drazica 1
Tel: 051 661122
www.jadranka.hr
Jadranka has the monopoly on hotel and private accommodation, as well as camping.
Hotel Alhambra
Čikat
Tel: 051 232022
www.jadranka.hr
The Alhambra is smallest and most appealing of the Jadranka hotels. **$$–$$$**
Villa Diana
Čikat
Tel: 051 232055
www.jadranka.hr
The jewel in the crown of the Jadranka hotel chain offers tranquil accommodation in a small villa with renovated en suite rooms. **$$$$–$$$$$**

Opatija

Milenij
Maršala Tita 109
Tel: 051 278007
www.milenijhoteli.hr
The resort's premier accommodation with luxurious rooms, a gym, heated outdoor pool and seafront café.
$$$$–$$$$
Milenij Grand
Maršala Tita 85
Tel: 051 202000
www.milenijhoteli.hr
This former Austrian villa in the midst of Opatija's verdant gardens has 26 de luxe rooms with wooden floors and classic furnishings. Some rooms have terraces.
$$$$$
Hotel Mozart
Maršala Tita 138
Tel: 051 718260
www.hotel-mozart.hr
This attractive family-run boutique hotel has 27 rooms, two apartments and one suite. The public areas are impressive and the classic rooms uncluttered. The Wellness Oasis has saunas, baths and a whirlpool.
$$$$–$$$$$
Hotel Opatija
Trg V. Gortana 2/1
Tel: 051 271388
www.hotel-opatija.hr
This mid-range hotel exudes an air of faded grandeur. It has clean, basic rooms, many with sea views, and an indoor seawater swimming pool. **$$–$$$**

Pag

Hotel Restaurant Biser
Pero Jeliniae
Tel: 023 611333
www.hotel-biser.com
Wonderful small hotel with 20 balconied rooms.
$$–$$$$

Paklenica National Park (Starigrad)

Bluesun Hotel Alan
Jadranska 14
Starigrad Paklenica
Tel: 023 209050
www.bluesunhotels.com
This refurbished high-rise hotel offers flexible accommodation in single, double, triple and family rooms and apartments. It also has a beachside restaurant, pool and sports facilities and private parking. Rooms come with half board. Those travelling on a budget can stay in the hotel's campsite.
$$–$$$$
Hotel Rajna
Dr. F. Tudmana
Starigrad Paklenica
Tel: 023 369130
Email: ranja-paklenica@inet.hr
Not as well located as the Alan, but with more inspiring

BELOW: the Opatija Riviera.

ABOVE: Pazin Castle and Abyss.

rooms. **$$$$**

Hotel Vicko
Joze Dokoze 20
Tel: 023 369304
www.hotel-vicko.hr
A pleasant family-run hotel.
Some rooms have sea
views. **$$–$$$$**.

Rab

Imperial
J Barakovićka
Tel: 051 724522
www.imperial.hr
The group dominates hotel

accommodation in Rab Town
and Kampor. **$$$–$$$$**

Hotel Imperial
Palit
Tel: 051 724522
The Imperial group's signa-
ture hotel has large modern
rooms, some with balco-
nies. Rooms come with half
board. **$$$–$$$$**

Hotel Istra
M. de Dominisa
Tel: 051 724134
www.hotel-istra.hr
Run by the Renić family
this is the only independent

hotel in town. Good loca-
tion, friendly staff and clean,
minimalist bedrooms make
this a good choice. **$$–$$$**

Rab
Obala P. Krešimira 4
Tel: 051 602000
The hotel has an excellent
harbour-side location in the
thick of it all and adequate
rooms but is short on frills.
$$$

Rijeka

Grand Hotel Bonavia

Dolac 4
Tel: 051 357100
www.bonavia.hr
This elegant hotel has
comfortable rooms and vies
with the Milenij in Opatija to
be the best hotel in the Gulf.
$$$$$

Hotel Continental
Šetalište Andrije Kačića-Miošića 1
Tel: 051 372008
www.jadran-hoteli.hr
An Art Nouveau hotel with
clean if basic en suite
rooms and a fantastic
internet café. **$$$**

NORTHERN DALMATIA

Šibenik

Hotel Jadran
Obala dr. Franje Tuđmana
Tel: 022 242000
www.rivijera.hr
A charmless hotel with a

BELOW: a pavement café
in Zadar.

prime city centre location.
$$$$

Hotel Panorama
Šibenski most
Tel: 022 213398
www.hotel-panorama.hr
Modern, medium-sized
hotel located outside the
city, with spectacular sea
views. **$$$**

Solaris Holiday Resort
Hotelsko naselje Solaris
Tel: 022 361048
www.solaris.hr
An overhaul in 2004 has
made this large holiday
resort, located 6km (4 miles)
out of town, far more appealing. It offers five hotels (Hotel
Ivan is the best), apartments,
a campsite and its own
marina. Its attractive setting,
enormous wellness centre
and large number of indoor
and outdoor pools com-
pensate for the impersonal
feel of the resort. There is a
regular shuttle service to the
town centre. **$$$**

Zadar

Hotel Kolovare
Bože Peričića 14
Tel: 023 203200
www.hotel-kolovare-zadar.htnet.hr
This is a business-
oriented hotel, but it is
good for leisure travellers
too (it has swimming
pool), quietly located in a
park a 10-minute walk
outside of the old town.
$$$–$$$$

Hotel Mediteran
Matije Gupca 19
Tel: 023 331188
www.hotelmediteran-zd.hr
Run by the Ćoza family and
located near the beach in
Borik, 3km (2 miles) from
the old town, this small
hotel is a great escape
from the concrete resort
complexes that tend to
dominate the hotel scene in
Dalmatia. **$$$**

Hotel President
Vladana Desnice 16

Zagreb

Tel: 023 333696
www.hotel-president.hr
Hotel President is a small,
elegant hotel with 15
rooms and 12 junior suites.
It provides a welcome
taste of luxury close to
Zadar's old heart.
$$$$$

PRICE CATEGORIES

Prices categories are for a
double room including
breakfast:
$ = under 250 kuna
$$ = 250–400 kuna
$$$ = 400–600 kuna
$$$$ = 600–1,000 kuna
$$$$$ = over 1,000 kuna

TRANSPORT
ACCOMMODATION
EATING OUT
ACTIVITIES
A – Z
LANGUAGE

CENTRAL DALMATIA

Brač

Bluesun Grand Hotel Elaphusa
Zlatni rat
Tel: 021 635288
www.zlatni-bol.com
This is the best hotel on Bol's celebrated beach. **$$$$**

Hotel Restaurant Villa Britanida
Hrvatskih velikana 26
Tel: 021 631038
www.supetar.hr
This is a 30-bed hotel in the heart of town with clean and functional rooms, some with sea views. **$$$–$$$$**

Waterman Resorts
Put Vele Luke
Tel: 021 631133
Waterman Resorts operates a central reservations number for the Kaktus Hotel, its annexes and apartments and the Hotel Palma, all located in a sprawling holiday resort just west of Supetar town centre. **$–$$/$$–$$$$**

Hvar

Sunčani Hvar (www.suncani hvar.hr) has a monopoly over hotel accommodation in Hvar Town, with many of its rather anonymous resort hotels hogging the prime harbour-side locations. **$$$–$$$$$**

Hotel Croatia
Majerovića bb
Tel: 021 742400

Fax: 021 741707
Email: croatia-hvar@st.tel.hr
This hotel contains 36 pleasant rooms, some with balconies. Its only drawback is the 20-minute walk into town. **$$$$**

Hotel Podstine
Zagrebačka 13
Tel: 021 740400
www.podstine.com
This small family-run hotel enjoys a peaceful location and also has a four-bed-room apartment for rent. **$$$–$$$$**

Hotel Riva
Riva
Tel: 021 750100
www.suncanihvar.hr
Croatia's only member of Small Luxury Hotels of the World, this waterfront hotel offers fine rooms with a few rough edges. **$$$$**

Makarska

Biokovo
Kralja Tomislava bb
Tel: 021 615224
Fax: 021 615081
www.hotelbiokovo.hr
A well-located but charac-terless hotel. Many rooms have sea views. **$$$$**

Hotel Makarska
Potok 17
Tel: 021 616360
www.makarska-hotel.com
More like a pension than a hotel, with some very small rooms, the Makarska doesn't offer good value for

money. Parking and good views over the Biokovo Mountains are among its more redeeming features. **$$$**

Split

Hotel Bellevue
Bana Josip Jelačića 2
Tel: 021 345644
Fax: 021 362383
Superbly located on one of Split's most underrated squares and overlooking the water. Its grandeur may be faded, but it retains much of its charm. **$$$**

Hotel Marjan
Kneza Branimira 8
Tel: 021 399211
Fax: 021 399210
www.hotel-marjan.com
Waterfront hotel just five minutes' walk from Split's old town, with recently renovated rooms. **$$$**

Hotel Park
Hatzeov Perivoj 3
Tel: 021 406400
Fax: 021 406401
www.hotelpark-split.hr
Split's most luxurious hotel by far and recently refurbished. Located a short walk from the Riva. **$$$$**

Slavija
Buvinova 2
Tel: 021 347053
Fax: 021 591558
This basic hostel-like hotel has double, twin, triple and quad rooms. Its situation in the heart of Diocletian's

Palace makes this the place to stay in Split. **$$**

Trogir

Hotel Concordia
Bana Berislavića 22
Tel: 021 885400
Fax: 021 885401
www.concordia-hotel.htnet.hr
Less luxurious guest rooms than the Fontana, but still a very pleasant place to stay. **$$$**

Hotel Fontana
Obrov 1
Tel: 021 885744
Fax: 021 885755
www.fontana-commerce.htnet.hr
This small hotel has good modern rooms, some equipped with jacuzzis. The hotel's apartment is the best room in town and great value for money. There is a 10 percent discount if you pay with cash. **$$$–$$$$**

Vis

Hotel Biševo
Ribarska 72
Tel: 021 713095
Fax: 021 713098
Large hotel that is well-placed for the beach and reasonably priced. **$$**

Hotel San Giorgio
Petra Hektorovića 2
Tel: 021 711362
Fax: 021 711362
www.hotelpaula.com
This is good value accom-modation in a small family-run hotel hidden away in the old town streets of Kut. Seafarers can even moor their boats outside. **$$$**

Hotel Tamaris
Sv. Jurja 30
Tel: 021 711350
Fax: 021 711450
Superior to the nearby Issa and situated right in the heart of Vis Town. **$$$–$$$$**

BELOW: preparing to fish off the Split coast.

SOUTHERN DALMATIA

Cavtat

Hotel Supetar
Obala S. Radiča bb
Tel: 020 479833
Fax: 020 479858
www.hoteli-croatia.hr/supetar
In a traditional stone building right by the bay with 28 rooms, a restaurant and bar. Friendly staff. **$$$**

Hotel Villa Kvaternik
Kvaternikova 3
Tel: 020 479 800
Fax: 020 479 808
www.hotelvillakvaternik.com
Five rooms and a suite in a 15th-century building with a courtyard tucked behind the Franciscan Monastery, just off the bay. Personal friendly service from the the owners, who came here from Australia in 2002. As of 2005 there are also eight simple rooms available in the former monastery. **$$**

Dubrovnik

Accommodation in Dubrovnik is expensive, with hotels in Ploče the most costly. More affordable accommodation can be found in Gruž or Lapad, 3km (2 miles) west of town. Prices are higher during the Summer Festival in July–August. *Also see Private Accommodation, page 273.*

Dubrovnik Palace
Masarykov put 20
Tel: 020 430000/430100
Fax: 020 437285
www.dubrovnikpalace.hr
This ultra-smart 307-room hotel on the Lapad headland reopened in 2004 and offers sea views, 3 pools, cafés, several restaurants and a conference centre. **$$$$$**

The Excelsior
Frana Supila 12
Tel: 020 353353
Fax: 020 353295
www.alh.hr
Dating from 1913, but renovated in the late 1990s, it has stunning views back to the old town from many rooms and suites.

Fresh Sheets
Smokvina 15
Tel: 020 322040
www.igotfresh.com
The only hostal in Dubrovnik's old town, run by Croatian Canadians. Clean, comfy, friendly, sleeping 2–4 per en suite dorm. Free breakfast smoothie. **$**

Grand Villa Argentina
Frana Supila 14
Tel: 020 440555
Fax: 020 432524
www.gva.hr
A luxurious hotel in Ploče, set in lush gardens with sea views and two pools. **$$$$$**

Hotel Komodor
Masarykov put 5
Tel: 020 433500
Fax: 020 433510
www.hotelimaestral.com
The oldest and most traditional of the hotels in the Maestral chain (which has five on Lapad Bay); recently refurbished. Restaurant and pool. **$$$**

Hotel Lero
Iva Vojnovića 14
Tel: 020 341333
Fax: 020 332123
www.hotel-lero.hr
Modern, functional and handy for the bus station. **$$$–$$$$**

Hotel Petka
Stjepana Radića 38
Tel: 020 410500
Fax: 020 410127
Email: hotel-petka@du.hinet.hr
Large, impersonal hotel, renovated in 2008, with good standard rooms, close to ferry port in Gruž. **$$$–$$$$**

Hotel Uvala
Masarykov put 10
Tel: 020 433890
Fax: 020 433591
www.hotelimaestral.com
The newest in the Maestral group offers spa, massage and fitness services. Minimalist decor, indoor and outdoor pools. **$$$$**

Pucić Palace
Od Puča 1
Tel: 020 326222
Fax: 020 326223
www.thepucicpalace.com
Opened in August 2002, this luxurious 19-room hotel is one of only two hotels in Dubrovnik's Old Town. Push the boat out and stay in a suite overlooking the bustling Gundulić Square. **$$$$$**

Stari Grad
Od Sigurate 4
Tel: 020 322244
Fax: 020 321256
www.hotelstarigrad.com
This small three-star hotel (only eight rooms) occupies an aristocratic family house, a tall narrow building just off Stradun. Furnished with antiques, it has a café-bar on the ground floor and a rooftop terrace for breakfast in summer. No lift. **$$$$**

Villa Dubrovnik
Vlaha Bukovka 6
Tel: 020 422933
Fax: 020 423465
www.villa-dubrovnik.hr
The lovely old hotel has been demolished and a smart new one, with all mod cons, is due to open for the 2010 season. The setting is incomparable. **$$$**

Villa Orsula
Frana Supila 14
Tel: 020 440555
Fax: 020 432524
www.gva.hr
Offers luxurious accommodation in 15 rooms, most of which have views of the sea and Dubrovnik's old town. **$$$$$**

Villa Wolff
Nika i Meda Pučića 1
Tel: 020 438710
Fax: 020 356432
www.villa-wolff.hr
An elegant boutique hotel with stunning views across the bay and a pleasant palm tree-shaded terrace on which to have breakfast. Internet access in all rooms. The Casa-Bar by the water's edge is part of the hotel. No pool, but safe swimming from the rocks immediately below. **$$$**

Hotel Zagreb
Šetalište Kralje Zvonimira 27
Tel: 020 436146
Fax: 020 436006
A comfortable, traditional hotel with a palm-shaded garden. Under five minutes' walk to Lapad beach. **$$$**

Korčula

Hotel Korčula
Šetalište F. Kršinća 102

Tel: 020 726336
Fax: 020 711746
Elegant hotel right by the harbour. Well-furnished rooms. **$$$**

Lešić Dimitri Palace
Don Pavla Poše 1–6
Korčula 20260
Tel: 020 715560
Fax: 020 715561
www.lesic-dimitri.com
Elite boutique hotel in 18th-century bishop's palace and five medieval cottages, opened in 2009. **$$$$**

Mali Ston

Vila Koruna
Tel: 020 754999
www.vilakoruna.cjb.net
Comfortable accommodation and an excellent seafood restaurant. **$$**

Mljet National Park

Hotel Odisej
Tel: 020 475 777
Fax: 020 475 973
www.hotelodisej.hr
Overlooking Pomena bay in the Mljet National Park. **$$$–$$$$**

Orebić

Grand Hotel Orebić
Kraj Petra Kresimira IV 107
Tel: 020 798 800
www.grandhotelorebic.com
A big modern hotel by a sandy beach with lots of facilities. Ideal for a family stay. **$$$–$$$$**

PRICE CATEGORIES

Prices categories are for a double room including breakfast:
$ = under 250 kuna
$$ = 250–400 kuna
$$$ = 400–600 kuna
$$$$ = 600–1,000 kuna
$$$$$ = over 1,000 kuna

TRANSPORT

ACCOMMODATION

EATING OUT

ACTIVITIES

A – Z

LANGUAGE

CAMPING

Coastal Istria

Novigrad

Baia Bianca
Tel: 052 758616
Email: autokamp.baiabianca@inet.hr
A small one-star rated campsite with no recreational facilities.

Mareda
Tel: 052 735291
Email: camping@laguna-novigrad.hr
A 2,400 capacity beachside site surrounded by oak trees.

Poreč

Bijela Uvala
Tel: 052 410102
www.plavalaguna.hr
Poreč's largest campsite with a capacity for 6,000 visitors.

Campling Laterna
Tel: 052 465010
Email: lanternacamp@riviera.hr
A 9,000-capacity waterside camping ground with a wide range of sport and recreation facilities.

Zelena Laguna
Tel: 052 410700
www.camping-adriatic.com
A sprawling campsite that overlooks the bay and has sports facilities.

Pula

Camping Stoja
Tel: 052 387144
www.arenaturist.hr
This campsite is 3km (2 miles) outside of Pula on the attractive Stoja peninsula.

Puntižela
Tel: 052 517433
Email: puntizela@pu.tel.hr
A basic campsite on a peaceful stretch of coastline.

Rovinj

Polari
Polari bb
Tel: 052 801501
www.maistra.com
This huge campsite is 2.5km (1½ miles) outside town, with excellent facilities and sea views.

Valdaliso
Monsena bb
Tel: 052 815822
This relatively small campsite has good general facilities.

Veštar
Veštar bb
Tel: 052 829150
www.maistra.com
This large modern campsite 5km (3 miles) out of town and has good facilities.

Umag

Stella Maris
Savudrijska Cesta bb
Tel: 052 710900
www.istracamping.com
This site is just 2.5km (1½ miles) outside Umag. Guests can use the facilities of the adjacent holiday village.

Kvarner Gulf

Cres

Kovačine
Melin I br. 20
Tel: 051 573150
www.jadranka.hr
On a small peninsula near Cres, this eco-friendly campsite caters mainly to families and has a naturist section.

Krk

Bor
Tel: 051 221581
www.camp-bor.hr
This small campsite is handy for Krk Town.

Zablaće
Tel: 051 856909
This sprawling beach-front caravan site has average facilities.

Mali Lošinj

Čikat
Tel: 051 231125
www.camps-cres-losinj.com
This campsite is 2km (1 mile) outside Mali Lošinj.

Kredo
Tel: 051 233595
www.kre-do.hr
This small campsite is next to a low-key hotel and restaurant.

Lopari
Tel: 051 237127
www.losinjplov.hr
Large, well-equipped beach-front site.

Polijana
Tel: 051 231726
Fax: 051 231728
www.losinjplov.hr
Large site 3km (2 miles) from Mali Lošinj.

Rapoča
Tel: 051 237145
www.losinjplov.hr
A small site in picturesque Nerazine.

Rab

AC Padova III
Tel: 051 724355
www.imperial.hr
The closest site to Rab's historic old town, just 2km (1 mile) away.

San Marino
Tel: 051 775133
www.imperial.hr
Located in Lopar on a 1.5km (1-mile) long beach.

Dalmatia

Dubrovnik

Agava
Tel: 020 485 229
www.autocamp-agava.com
Small site with basic facilities, on the coast at Srebreno 7km (4 miles) southeast of Dubrovnik.

Camp Solitudo
Tel: 020 488 249
www.cmping-adriatic.com
Dubrovnik's only campsite is in Babin Kuk, a 20 minutes bus ride from the town. Swimming pool and tennis.

Korčula

Camping Kalac
Tel: 020 711182
Located 2km (1½ miles) from Korčula Town and only 50 metres/yds from the sea.

Hvar

Jurjevac
Stari Grad
Tel: 021 765843
email:helios-faros@st.t-com.hr
This is a cut above the Mina in Jelsa.

Mina
Jelsa
Tel: 021 761227
email: komunalno-jelsa@st.t-com.hr
Basic but adequate site.

Šbenik

Solaris Camping Resort
Hotelsko Naselje Solaris bb
Tel: 022 364000
www.solaris.hr
Located within the Solaris holiday resort, this shares access to all its facilities, including pools. Seaside location.

Trogir

Vranjica Belvedere
Tel: 021 798222
www.vranjica-belvedere.hr
Campsite and apartments 5km (3 miles) from Trogir; also the closest site to Split 8km (5 miles) away.

Zadar

Borik
Tel: 023 332074
Located within the nearby Borik holiday complex.

BELOW: a secluded home away from home in the open air.

PRIVATE ACCOMMODATION

Apart from the travel agencies listed below, tourist offices usually have lists of people renting out private accommodation. A useful resource is www.camping.hr.

Coastal Istria

Poreč

Adriatic
Trg Slobode 2a
Tel: 052 452663
www.adriatic-istra.com
This agency has more than 1,000 beds in Poreč and Vrsar on its books.
DI tours
Prvomajska 2
Tel: 052 432100
www.di-tours.hr
This company books family apartments in detached houses. Breakfast prepared by the owners is an optional extra.
Generalturist
Aldo Negri 3
Tel: 052 451839
www.generalturist.com
One of Croatia's largest travel agencies, founded in 1923, they can arrange private rooms throughout the country.
Olea Europaea
Istarska 10
Tel: 052 443664
www.istra.com/olea
Olea Europaea arranges private accommodation throughout Istria.

Rovinj

Eurostar Travel
P. Budicin 1
Tel: 052 813144
Email: eurostar-travel@pu.tel.hr
This general travel agency can also arrange private accommodation in Rovinj.
Marco Polo
Istarska 2
Tel: 052 816616
www.marcopolo.hr
This agency offers a small range of private rooms in Rovinj.

Kvarner Gulf

Krk

Aurea
Vršanska bb

Tel: 051 221777
www.aurea-krk.com
Aurea can book private rooms in both urban and rural locations throughout Krk.
Primaturist
Zvonimirova 98
Tel: 051 856132
www.primaturist.hr
This is one of the main accommodation booking agencies in Baška.
Polo line
Emila Geistlicha 12
Tel: 051 864039
www.polo.hr
This agency is also in Baška.
Splendido
Zvonimara 148
Tel: 051 856116
Fax: 051 856616
www.splendido.hr
This agency, which is also in Baška, offers a range of family houses, apartments and villas.

Mali Lošinj

Cappelli Tourist Agency
Kadin bb
Tel: 051 231582
www.cappelli-tourist.hr
This agency has a small range of apartments in Mali Lošinj.
Palma
Vladimira Nasora 22
Tel: 051 236179
www.losinj.com
Palma has a wide range of apartments in both Mali Lošinj and Veli Lošinj accommodating up to nine people.
Val
Vladimira Nazora 29
Tel: 051 236352
www.losinj-val.com
Val can book local private apartments and villas.

Opatija

Atlas
Maršala Tita 116/2
Tel: 051 271032
www.atlas-croatia.com
Atlas books private rooms and hotels throughout the Adriatic.
Da Riva
Maršala Tita 162
Tel: 051 272990

www.da-riva.hr
Da Riva's private apartments are a good deal for groups of up to six.
Katarina line
Maršala Tita 75/1
Tel: 051 603400
www.katarina-line.com
This company books hostel and hotel rooms throughout much of Croatia.

Rab

Katurbo
M. de Dominisa 5
Tel: 051 724495
www.kristofor.hr
Katurbo can arrange anything from a private apartment to a whole house.
Kristofor
Poslovoni Centar
Mali Palit
Tel: 051 725543
www.kristofor.hr
Kristofor is near the bus station in Palit on the edge of the old town.

Dalmatia

Brač

Maestral
1. G. Kovačića 3
Tel: 021 757233
www.travel.maestral.hr
Maestral can book rooms along the Adriatic coast.

Dubrovnik

Atlas
Head office: Cira Carica 3
Tel: 020 442222
www.atlas-croatia.com
Headquartered in Dubrovnik, Atlas holds comprehensive local listings.
Dubrovnikturist
Put Republike 7
Tel: 020 356959
www.dubrovnikturist.hr
Dubrovnik Travel
Metohijska 2
Tel: 020 313555
Fax: 020 313550
www.dubrovniktravel.com
Generalturist
Obala Stjepana Radica 24
Tel: 020 432937
www.generalturist.com
Generalturist can help with a wide range of Dubrovnik rooms including hotels apartments and more.

Gulliver
Obala Stjepana Radica 25
Tel: 020 410888
www.gulliver.hr
Gulliver can arrange private accommodation throughout Dalmatia.

Hvar

Pelegrini Tours
Riva bb
Tel: 021 742250
Pelegrini handles a good range of island listings.

Makarska

Delfintours
Kačićev trg 16
Tel: 021 612248
www.delfin-tours.hr
Private and hotel room bookings.
Turist Biro
Kralja Tomislava 2
Tel: 021 611688
www.turistbiro-makarska.com
Conveniently located near the waterfront.

Split

Adriatic Travel
Jadranska 6
Tel: 021 490129
www.adriatic-travel.hr
Atlas
Nepotova 4
Tel: 021 343055
Email: atl.split@atlas.tel.hr
Generalturist
Lazareta 3
Tel: 021 345183
www.generalturist.com

Vis

Darlić & Darlić
Riva Sv. Mikule 13
Tel/Fax: 021 713760
www.darlic-travel.hr
This family-run agency can help with private accommodation, hotel and apartment bookings on Vis.

Zadar

Miatours
Vrata sv. Krševana
Tel: 023 254300
Fax: 023 254300
www.miatours.hr
Miatours books private and other types of rooms. The agency is also able to help with hydrofoil and catamaran bookings, car hire and excursions.

TRANSPORT
ACCOMMODATION
EATING OUT
ACTIVITIES
A – Z
LANGUAGE

E ATING OUT

RECOMMENDED RESTAURANTS, CAFES AND BARS

Where to Eat

Although not always especially cheap, eating out is one of the high points of visiting Croatia and you won't have to look far to find somewhere specialising in fresh tasty local delicacies. There are also many places serving international cuisine, especially Italian.

Wine Cellars

There are two main wine regions in Croatia: the continental region – covering Plešivica, Zagorje, Prigorje, Moslavania, Pokupulje, Slavonia and Podunavlje – and the coastal region of Istria and Dalmatia. Istria currently has the best infrastructure for wine tourism and there are numerous wine cellars open to the public in the region. The Istria County Tourist Association, tel: 052 452797; www.istra.hr, can provide a road map showing locations and giving contact details for each cellar.

The island of Vis is another great place for wine lovers. Alongside bigger producers such as Roki's and Rukatac, the island has lots of small wine cellars, where people go to enjoy a glass of their favourite tipple with the producer. Many vinoteke bear the sign Prodajem domaće vino (domestic wine). Opening times are usually 9am– noon and 6.30–11pm.

What to Eat

Croatian cuisine varies regionally. In coastal areas fresh fish features heavily on the menu, whilst staples inland include mlinci (a type of pasta), roast lamb, roast suckling pig and boiled or baked štrukli (pasta with ham and cheese). Each region also has its own local dishes. Pršut (prosciutto), brudet (fish stew with polenta), pašticada (beef goulash and gnocchi) are Dalmatian specialities. Istrian specialities include pršut, manestres (dried meat and vegetable broth), ombolo (pork fillets) and truffles. In the Kvarner Gulf look out for Pag cheese (hard and salty sheep's cheese). Inland specialities include kulen (paprika flavoured salami) and češnjovka (garlic sausages from Zagorje). A useful source of information about eating and dining in rural Croatia is at www.ruraltour.org.

Vegetarian Food

Vegetarian restaurants are a rarity in Croatia although many restaurants offer a very small number of vegetarian dishes and Zagreb has an excellent vegan eatery. Most restaurants specialise in fish and traditional meat dishes, and even many of the pasta staples served as starters have meat sauces. Vegetarian options are commonly available in pizzerias and in fast-food outlets that sell sandwiches.

Cafés

Croatians have an average annual consumption of 4.8kg (10lb) of coffee per capita and Croatia has one of the most vibrant café societies of any country in the world. Croatian even has a word – špica – to describe the traditional caffeine-laced post-shopping Saturday-morning get-together between friends. While at home Croatians drink Turkish coffee (turska kafa), in a café (kavana or, if it is small, kafić) they ape the Italians and are likely to order a cappuccino (kapućino), espresso (espresso), macchiato (macchiato) or simply a black coffee (crna kava) or milky white coffee (kava s mlijekom). It is rare to find bad coffee in Croatia. Fruit, herbal and black teas are also popular. But you can order just about any drink you can think of – soft or alcoholic – and almost every café also serves pastries and ice cream. A slastičarnica is a pastry shop or ice cream parlour that also sells soft drinks. Since May 2009 there has been a smoking ban in all enclosed public spaces including bars, restaurants and cafés, but since there is such a culture of outdoor dining and drinking on terraces the ban has had little effect on business, simply making finding a table inside easier.

Taverns

In Croatian a konoba is a tavern where fishermen would eat some of their catch. While this practice is not quite as common as it used to be, the term konoba usually indicates a historic venue serving traditional local delicacies at reasonable prices, usually doubling as a bar in the evening, although a few places have gone up-market. If you're looking for generous helpings of authentic Croatian food lashed down with carafes of home-made wine in a homely environment, head for your nearest konoba. If you're looking for a cheap meal, try a gablec, a workers' restaurant usually offering inexpensive set menus at lunchtime.

Ordering Fish

It is normal for restaurants to charge for fish and seafood by weight, although there are usually a few set-price dishes too. A typical helping is about 250g (9oz) but to avoid confusion and unpleasant surprises on the bill it is best to specify the amount wanted when ordering.

RESTAURANT LISTINGS

ZAGREB

Dubravkin put
Dubravkin put 2
Tel: 01 483 4975
www.dubravkin-put.com
Award-winning restaurant with outstanding service and delicious fish specialities. A great place for a romantic meal. **$$$**

Le Bistro
Hotel Regent Esplanade
Mihanovićeva 1
Tel: 01 456 6611
www.theregentzagreb.com
This conservatory restaurant recalls the ambience of a Parisian bistro and is your best bet in town for French cuisine. It also offers local dishes including its very own Esplanade struckli. **$$$$**

Nova
Ilica 72/I
Tel: 01 484 7119
Part of Zagreb's macrobiotic centre, this great first-floor

vegan restaurant serves food good enough to tempt meat-eaters. The centre also organises cooking and healthy-living classes. There is also a good food shop attached to the restaurant. **$**

Opium
Branimir Shopping Centre
Branimirova 29
Tel: 01 461 5679
www.opium.hr
Part of the city's newish shopping and entertainment complex and one of Zagreb's trendiest restaurants, with a chic interior and tasty Thai food prepared by a Thai chef. Also a café and cocktail bar open till 1am daily. **$$**

Paviljon
Trg Kralja Tomislava 22
Tel: 01 481 3066
www.restaurant-paviljon.com
Dine in style whilst

overlooking one of Zagreb's most picturesque parks. The tagliatelle with white truffles and the grilled swordfish are delicious. It is closed on Sunday. **$$$$**

Placa
Radićeva 42
Tel: 01 481 3390
www.placa.hr
One of the city's finest dining experiences with excellent service and good Italian food in intimate surroundings. **$$$$**

Stara Vura
Opatička 20
Tel: 01 485 1368
www.stara-vura.hr
The city museum restaurant, well situated in historic Gradec, with rich game and seafood specialities. **$$$$**

Takenoko Sushi Bar
Centar Kaptol

Nova Ves 17
Tel: 01 486 0530
www.takenoko.hr
Another fashionable restaurant, with a stylish dining space, an extensive sushi menu and excellent cooked dishes like chicken teriyaki. **$$$$**

Zinfandel's
Hotel Regent Esplanade
Mihanovićeva 1
Tel: 01 456 6666
Recall the glory days of the *Orient Express* at Zagreb's swankiest restaurant in the hotel built to serve its passengers. It combines superb views over the Fountain Park, a choice of perfectly executed Croatian and Mediterranean dishes and a cosmopolitan atmosphere. Its sumptuous buffet breakfast is well worth an early rise. **$$$$**

CENTRAL CROATIA

Plitvice Lakes National Park

Lička kuća
Tel: 053 751024
licka.kuca@np-plitvica-jereza.hr
This cosy restaurant has roasted meat and sausage specialities. **$$**

Poljana
Tel: 053 751092

poljana@np-plitvicka-jezera.hr
The Hotel Bellevue's signature restaurant. Try the central Croatian specialities of delicious suckling pig or spit-roasted lamb. **$$$**

Karlovac

Dobra
Hotel Korana-Srakovčić

Perivoj Josipa Vrbanića 8
Tel: 047 609090
www.hotelkorana.hr
With a summer terrace in an ancient park on the bank of the Korana river, this elegant see-and-be-seen restaurant features imaginative new Croatian dishes and top-notch service. **$$**

Kristal
Bakin Business Center
Matka Laginje 1
Tel: 047 645320
www.restoran-kristal.com
A popular venue for functions, Kristal also has an à la carte restaurant specialising in fish, meat and high-class home-made cakes and pastries. **$**

Pivnica Raj
Ivana Gundulićeva 11
Tel: 042 213146
A fantastic beer hall with an extensive menu and fixed-price buffet lunch. Open until 1am on Saturday. **$**

BELOW: relaxing over drinks in a stylish urban bar.

PRICE CATEGORIES

Prices are for a three-course meal for two people, including a litre of house wine but excluding tip:
$ = under 220 kuna
$$ = 220–330 kuna
$$$ = 330–440 kuna
$$$$ = over 440 kuna

TRANSPORT · ACCOMMODATION · EATING OUT · ACTIVITIES · A–Z · LANGUAGE

EASTERN CROATIA

Osijek

El Paso
Tel: 031 203500
www.kubo.hr
A stylish pizzeria on board a boat. Be sure to try the house speciality – *pizzaiola* with a cheese-stuffed crust, ham, cheese, tomato, egg, *pršut* and sour cream. $

Slavonska kuća
Kamila Firingera 26
Tel: 031 208277
A cosy Slavonian restaurant in the heart of the old town renowned for its *fiš paprikaš*, a spicy fish stew made from carp, catfish, pike, tomatoes, chilli peppers, and paprika. $$

ISTRIAN COAST

Pula

Restaurant Valsabbion
Pješčana uvala IX/26
Tel: 052 218033
www.valsabbion.com
The award-winning Valsabbion serves delicious dishes that fuse Istrian and international cuisine. Home-made desserts served on a mirror add an unusual finishing touch. $$$$

Vela Nera
Tel: 052 219209
www.velanera.hr
A modern and light restaurant by the marina. Try the *pljukanci* (home-made macaroni) or shrimps served with artichokes. $$$

Scaletta
Flavijevska 26
Tel: 052 541599
www.hotel-scaletta.com

Fine-dining restaurant in the Scaletta Hotel close to the amphitheatre, with fish and meat specialities. Try the scampi soup, gnocchi with gorgonzola and excellent fish platter. It also serves lobster for special occasions. $$$$

Tomaso
Zagrebačka 13
Tel: 052 216027
One of Pula's centrally located pizzerias, serving good Italian staples like spaghetti bolognese and filling pizzas. $

Poreč

Peškera
Nikole Tesle
Tel: 052 432890
An unpretentious self-service restaurant selling substantial

pasta dishes and salads at reasonable prices. $

Pizzeria Barilla
Eufrazijeva 26
Tel: 052 452742
This traditional Italian-style pizzeria serves tasty staples on a lively terrace in one of Poreč's most beautiful squares. $$$

Pizzeria Dali
Istarskog razvoda 11
Tel: 052 452666
A small and traditional pizzeria serving up good wood-oven pizzas and pasta dishes in the heart of Poreč. Closes for the first half of January. $

Sofora
Maršala Tita 13
Tel: 052 432053
This restaurant has a pleasant seafront location and offers a good-value

tourist menu featuring Croatian staples such as fried calamari (squid) and *grah salata* (bean and onion soup). $

Rovinj

Al Gastaldo
Iza Kasarne 14
Tel: 052 814109
This cosy *konoba* serves up Italian and Istrian staples and specialities. The beefsteak with truffles is sensational. $$

Giannino
Ferrija Augusta 38
Tel: 052 813402
A first-rate Italian *osteria* serving fresh fish and located away from the main tourist throng. You cannot go wrong with a platter of the grilled mixed seafood. $$$$

INLAND ISTRIAN

The Istrian tourist office publishes a useful annual *Istria Gourmet* guide to the region's gastronomy and where to sample it, available from Istrian tourist offices or for download on www.istria-gourmet.com.

Buje

Bioagro Dvi None
Lozari
Tel: 052 776197
Gabriellea Damiani serves up delicious local specialities including roast beef with a choice of white or black truffles. Off the beaten track,

the restaurant is a great example of the current trend in farmhouse dining. It closes from January to March and on Monday. $$

Grožnjan

Agroturizam Deskovic
Kostanjica
In 2009 the Istrian tourist office voted this the best inn in the region.

Pintur
Mate Gorjana 9
Grožnjan-Grisignana
Tel: 052 776397, 098 586188
This *konoba* offers some standard international fare

served on a peaceful tree-shaded terrace. $

Momjan

Konoba Rino
Dolinja vas 23
Tel: 052 779170
This elegant cellar restaurant with rustic stone walls is a great place to sample the local truffles. $$$$

Vižinada

Fatorić
Ferenci 36a
Tel: 052 446146
Tourism in Vižinada means

agrotourism and this restaurant comes up with the goods in a cosy stone house with a balcony. Home-made *fuži* (Istrian pasta) and *pršut* (dry-cured ham) are house specialties. In 2009 the Istrian tourist office voted this the second best inn in the region. $$

Jadruhi
Jadruhi 11
Tel: 052 446194
www.jadruhi.com
Dario and Beba Šimonovič run a traditional kitchen restaurant offering the usual Croatian staples in pleasant surroundings. $$

KVARNER GULF

Krk (Baška)

Bistro Funtana
Hotel Corinthia Baška
Tel: 051 656838
The Corinthia's signature restaurant offers an excellent-value set menu, which changes daily. Among the regular specials are mushroom risotto and fillet of fish cooked in local wine. **$$**

Franica
Ribarska 39
Tel: 051 860023
Try the delicious local speciality *surlice i gulas* (home-made pasta with beef goulash) washed down with the best locally produced white wine, Vrbnička zlahtina. Open from June to November. **$$**

Opatija

Konoba Elita
Maršala Tita 156
Tel: 051 271014

This small grill serves simple fish dishes and basic pizzas. Worth visiting for the bird's-eye view of the pulsating main street and Kvarner Gulf. **$$**

Restaurant Amfora
Črnikovica 4
Tel: 051 701222
On the road to Volosko, this restaurant's elegant terrace is a great place to head for a romantic dinner. **$$$**

Sveti Jakov
Hotel Milenij II
Maršala Tita 105
Tel: 051 202066
This elegant restaurant in the middle of an attractive park serves delicious local fish dishes in one of Opatija's most luxurious villas. **$$$$**

Vongola
Tel: 051 711854
Has a great location on the waterfront in the heart of Opatija. The meat and fish dishes are only average in quality, but it is worth

coming for the views and ambience. **$$$$**

Rab

Labirint
Srednja ulica 9
Tel: 051 771145
This is a fine place to escape from the tourist hordes on the Riva. Courteous staff serve local specialities such as Pag cheese. We recommend the St Christopher seafood platter for two. **$$**

Paradiso
S. Radića 2
Tel: 051 771109
Enjoy Italian pizza and pasta whilst listening to classical music on an ornate terrace, or simply relax with a coffee or glass of wine beneath the pillars of an old Roman atrium. **$$$**

Santa Maria
Dinka Dokule 6
Tel: 051 725695
Dine on the fabulous terrace of this long-established

restaurant known for its tasty meat and fish dishes. Cash only. **$$**

Rijeka

Brasserie AS
Trg Republike Hrvatske 2
Tel: 051 212148
An ever-popular pizzeria-cum-café, despite the excruciatingly slow service, in the heart of Rijeka's shopping district. **$$**

Rijeka
Municipium
Trg riječke rezolucije 5
Tel: 051 213000
www.municipium.hr
In the former town hall and widely considered Rijeka's top restaurant, Municipium delights well-heeled diners with a light modern twist on Croatian classics. **$$$$**

Svid Rock Café Pizzeria
Riva 12
Tel: 051 338105
This Hard Rock Café-styled late-night eatery serves tasty pizzas. **$$**

NORTHERN DALMATIA

Šibenik

Gradska Vijećnica
Trg Republike Hrvatske 1
Tel: 022 213605
If you only eat out once in Šibenik make sure it is here. The former town hall is now an elegant restaurant that offers dining with an unbeatable view over the Unesco World Heritage-listed cathedral. **$$$$**

Stari grad
Osbođenja 12
Tel: 022 219330
A good seafood restaurant in the port area. **$$**

Zadar

Foša
Tel: 023 314421
Kealja Dimitra Zvonimira 2
www.fosa.hr
Enjoy tasty grilled calamari

in this excellent fish restaurant just outside the old town walls in what used to be the city's customs house. **$$**

Marival
Don Ive Prodana 3

Tel: 023 213239
This rustic taverna enjoys local renown for its fresh fish and friendly staff. Bookings are advisable. **$$$**

BELOW: open-air refreshment at a city centre café.

PRICE CATEGORIES

Prices are for a three-course meal for two people, including a litre of house wine but excluding tip:
$ = under 220 kuna
$$ = 220–330 kuna
$$$ = 330–440 kuna
$$$$ = over 440 kuna

TRANSPORT

ACCOMMODATION

EATING OUT

ACTIVITIES

A – Z

LANGUAGE

CENTRAL DALMATIA

Brač

Centar Marijan
Tel: 021 717991
www.centar-marijan.hr
100 metres/yds from the beach at Bol, the centre has a variety of dining options including self-service, à la carte, bistro and fast food. $–$$$

Konoba Vinotoka
Jobova 6
Tel: 021 630969
A rustic Supetar restaurant serving tasty grilled fish and shellfish dishes. $$

Jastog
Bana Josip Jelačića 7
Tel: 021 631486
Another Supetar restaurant dishing up first-rate seafood dishes. The beefsteak is also excellent. $$$

Pizzeria Roso
Put Vele luke
Tel: 021 630326
The best pizza in Supetar if not the whole of Brač. $

Hvar

Bounty
Riva
Tel: 021 742565
www.hvar.hr/bounty
Ideal for watching the throng of beautiful people heading to the beach. Tasty grilled fish, too. $$

Lucullus
Petra Hektorovića
Tel: 021 742498
www.villanora.eu
Hvar's classiest pizzeria, housed in a former Venetian palace with an ornate stone courtyard. $$$$

Macondo
Groda
Tel: 021 742850
One of Hvar's finest fish restaurants located in a narrow alley behind the main square. Book in advance to secure a reservation in high season or take your place in the queue of eager tourists outside. $$$$

Palača Paladini
Petra Hektorovića 4
Tel: 021 745010
http://paladinihvar.com

Housed in a Renaissance palace, and renowned for its seafood and beautiful garden terrace. $$$$.

Pizza Kogo
Trg sveti Stjepana
Tel: 021 742136
Participate in a spot of people-watching whilst enjoying reasonably priced pizza in Hvar's central square. $

Makarska

Adrion
Obala kralja Tomislava
Tel: 021 615244
The Hotel Biokovo's fine-dining option promises an atmospheric waterfront terrace and delicious if expensive fish main courses. $$$$

Lungo mare
Obala kralja Tomislava
Tel: 021 615244
The Italian-style pizzas served at the Hotel Biokovo's pizzeria are among the best in Central Dalmatia. Beware the "pepperoni" – they are very hot pickled peppers. $

Split

Galija
Tončićeva 12
Tel: 021 347932
More like a local pub that just happens to serve the best pizza in town than a pizzeria. Choose from 27 pizzas and a seemingly endless list of extras. A particular plus in this popular place just outside Diocletian's Palace is the draught Union beer from Slovenia. $$

Ponoćno Sunce
Teutina 15
Tel: 021 361011
This small and pleasant vegetarian-friendly restaurant near the Golden Gate serves a variety of Dalmatian meat dishes and pasta. The gnocchi with salmon is excellent, as is the vegetarian salad bar. $

Sarajevo
Domaldova 6
Tel: 021 347454

A traditional restaurant in the centre of the old town serving delicious pašticada (beef goulash). $$$

Šumica
Put Firula 6
Tel: 021 389897
Excellent fish restaurant near Bačvice with a large outdoor terrace and top-notch wine list. $$$$

Trogir

Alka
Augustina Kažotića 15
Tel: 021 881856
This popular fish restaurant serves good-quality seafood on its pleasant terrace. It's also a great place to sample the local speciality Trogirska pašticada (beef stew with gnocchi). The pettiness of charging for each slice of bread may grate a little, but you can always refuse it if you like. $$

Fontana
Obrov 1
Tel: 021 884811
www.fontana-commerce.htnet.hr
Delicious seafood served on the waterfront. You cannot go wrong with the mussels and grilled calamari. $$

Monika
Budislavićeva 12
Tel: 021 884808
Arguably Trogir's best fish restaurant. Fine dining in an ornate courtyard with courteous service. $$$

Pizzeria-Spaghetteria Kristian
Bl. Augustina Kažotića
Tel: 021 885172
A small and pleasant pizzeria on a lively square, with an authentic wood stove. Try the home-made pasta with salmon sauce or gnocchi with seafood. Closed from November to mid-April. $$

Vis

Bako
Ribarska
Komiža
Tel: 021 713008
Stylish konoba serving

simple, tasty food, pasta starters and fish main courses. Outdoor terrace on waterfront. $$$

Fast Food Žuvić
29 Riva
Komiža
No tel.
Fast-food outlet with superb marina and fort views. $

Manta Diving Centre
Vl. Lorenz Marović
Tel: 098 534714
Try this for its great view of Komiža. Waves lash the terrace when the sea is rough. $

Pizzeria Dionis
Matije Gubca 1
Tel: 021 711963
www.dionis.hr
Average pizza served in a great location. Take a table on the stone steps and enjoy views over a lively square, the harbour and the monastery. $$

Pojoda
Don Cvjetka Marasovića 8
Tel: 021 711575
A busy yet relaxing fish restaurant with a pleasant courtyard shaded by orange and lemon trees. It sells delicious fish by weight, but service can be a touch slow. The chef-owner, Zoran Brajčić, is a well-known Croatian gourmand. $$$$

Restaurant Paula
Hectorovica 2
Tel: 021 711362
Fine fish dishes, both local and European, served in an ornate courtyard beneath a white sail. Unbeatable service. $$$

Villa Kaliopa
V. Nazora 32
Tel: 021 711755
Dine on tasty grilled fish beneath towering pines in the sculpture garden of the 16th-century Garibaldi Palace as candles flicker and jazz drifts on the breeze in Vis's most romantic restaurant. There is no menu and no price list; customers discuss what's available with the waiter. It is popular with the yachting set and open for dinner only. $$$$

Cavtat

Dalmacija
Trumbiev put 9
Tel: 020 478018
Set in a busy little triangle at the southern end of the harbour promenade, the popular Dalmacija has been in business since 1979. As you would expect from the name, it offers Dalmatian cooking, and is usually bustling at lunchtime. **$$**

Konoba Ivan
Uvala Tiha 5
Tel: 020 478160/478485
On the other side of the peninsula, Konoba Ivan is a small, cheerful place by the water's edge, where fresh fish and grilled meat, accompanied by house wine, make a good lunch. **$**

Leut
Trumbiev put 11
Tel: 020 478477
Run by the same family, since 1971, it enjoys its reputation as Cavtat's premier restaurant. Food and location are great. **$$$**

Taverna Galija
Vuliceviceva 5
Tel: 020 478566
A friendly seafront restaurant, with tables beneath shady pines, near the Franciscan monastery. Try prawns with honey, or the Orgasm – a platter of oysters, mussels, sea urchin eggs and olive sauce. **$$**

Dubrovnik

Atlas Club Nautika
Brsalje 3
Tel: 020 442526
Romantic views of Fort Lovrijenac and city walls combined with excellent food and service. **$$$$**

Defne
Pucić Palace Hotel
Od Puča 1
Tel: 020 326200/222
A roof-terrrace restaurant, smart without being stuffy. Some dishes have a Middle Eastern flavour, and there is also plenty of fish, including lobster with black risotto. **$$$**

Kamenica
Gundulićeva Poljana 8
Tel: 020 421499/323682
Long-established restaurant that serves food at tables outside in this busy square. Mostly fish – the grilled squid is particularly good – and they also specialise in oysters, after which the restaurant is named. **$–$$**

Levanat
Nika i Meda Pucića 15
Tel: 020 435352
A delightful place by the sea in Lapad. Prawns in honey with sage are among the more unusual dishes. **$$$**

Lokanda Peskarija
Na Ponti (Old Port)
Tel: 020 324750
This friendly, efficient little place by the harbour features fresh fish and seafood. **$**

Mea Culpa
Za Rokom 3
Tel: 020 435352
The biggest and best pizzas in town in a street parallel with Stradun. No reservations. **$**

Orhan
Od Tabakarije 1
(just outside Pile Gate)
Tel: 020 414183/891267
Hidden away by the water's edge, beneath Fort Lovrijenac, Orhan serves excellent fish and seafood indoors or outside on a small, vine-draped terrace. Best to book in high season. **$$–$$$**

Orsan Yacht Club
Ivana Zajca 2, Lapad
Tel: 020 435933
In a breezy corner of Gruz harbour with lots to watch, the yacht club provides good salads and snacks. **$**

Poklisar
Ribarnica 1 (Old Port)
Tel: 020 322176
Pizzas and fish dishes right beside the harbour. The atmosphere is cheerful, there's live music some evenings, and it often keeps going until midnight. **$$**

Posat
Uz Posat 1 (just outside Pile Gate)
Tel: 020 421194
The upper terrace view is over Fort Lovrijenac. The

home-cooked food is good, especially some innovative lobster dishes. **$**

Proto
Široka 1
Tel: 020 323234
In the heart of the old town, with a popular upstairs terrace. The fillet of turkey with truffle and crab sauce is delicious. **$$$$**

Ribar
Damjane Jude
Tel: 091 5372418
A friendly place, close to the Aquarium, the Ribar has been run by the Kovacic family for years. They specialise in fish dishes. **$–$$**

Rozarij
Marija Sjekavika 4 (corner of Prijeko)
Tel: 020 423791
Close to the Dominican Monastery. Fine Dalmatian food; cosy dining room and a few outside tables. **$$**

Sesame
Dante Alighieria bb
Tel: 020 412910
Family-run taverna near Pile Gate; good-value. Try the chicken wrapped in Dalmatian ham. **$$**

Taverna Rustica
Frana Suplia 12
Tel: 020 353353
www.hotel-excelsior.hr
Serves Dalmatian specialities in an elegant setting. The views of the old town are breathtaking. **$$$$**

Korčula

Adio Mare
Sveti Roka 2
Tel: 098 243845
Korčula's most atmospheric restaurant in the middle of the old town. Delicious grilled fish, long tables – you might have to queue. **$$$**

Fresh
Sveti Roka 2
Tel: 098 243845
A popular spot selling wraps, juices and a mix of Mexican, Asian and Mediterranean food. **$**

Kanavelić
Sv. Barabare 15
Tel: 020 711800

Set in the old walled town, and named after 17th-century poet Petar Kanavelić, who was born here, the restaurant is known for its well-prepared fish dishes. **$$**

Konavle

Konoba Konavle
Šiljeski, Vojski do
Tel: 098 674363
Stone farmhouse in the hills behind Cavtat with home-made food and meat cooked in a traditional iron bell embedded in embers. **$$**

Lopud

Konoba Peggy
Narikla 22
Tel: 020 759036
Right by the harbour, this is a popular spot with a leafy terrace and large helpings of fish and seafood. **$**

Obala
Obala I. Kuljevana 18
Tel: 020 759170
There are tables so close to the water you could almost dip your toes in as you eat. Fish couldn't be fresher and the salads are great too, especially when washed down with local wine. **$$**

Mali Ston

Bota Šare
Tel: 020 754482
A rustic-style restaurant with friendly service and excellent food. **$$**

Vila Koruna
Tel: 020 754999
Fish fresh from the tank or individually priced oysters. Ask for a table in the conservatory and enjoy the fine sea views. **$$**

PRICE CATEGORIES

Prices are for a three-course meal for two people, including a litre of house wine but excluding tip:
$ = under 220 kuna
$$ = 220–330 kuna
$$$ = 330–440 kuna
$$$$ = over 440 kuna

TRANSPORT

ACCOMMODATION

EATING OUT

ACTIVITIES

A – Z

LANGUAGE

BARS AND CAFÉS

Bars and cafés are often interchangeable in Croatia and relaxed licensing laws mean that most open between 6 or 7am and 11pm or midnight. A few café-bars have extended opening hours and do not close until 2am or later.

Zagreb

Bulldog XL
Bogovićeva 6
Tel: 01 400 2070
www.bulldog-zagreb.com
A buzzing bar, popular with expats. It is in the heart of town. There is occasional live music.
Tkalčićeva
This long, vibrant street brims with café-bars, and during the warmer months when the seating spills onto the pavements it is the place to see and be seen.

Central Croatia

Varadin
Caffe Bar Patačić
Trg Kralja Tomislava
Tel: 042 320914
www.hotel-turist.hr
A cappuccino in Varaždin's most ornate palace is highly recommended. The café also serves pizza.
Kavana Korzo
Trg kralja Tomislava
This wonderful coffee house with mirrors and pictures of old Varaždin spills out onto the Trg Tomislav.

Coastal Istria

Poreč
Comitium Bar
Trg Marafor 15
Sip cocktails in an ornate courtyard amidst Poreč's impressive Roman buildings.

Rovinj
Bethlehem
Vodnjanska 1
Enjoy a draught beer (*točeno*) with a mixed but friendly group of locals.
Caffe Bar Monte Carlo
Sv. Križa 21
Tel: 052 830610
Funky music pumps out

whilst a 20- and 30-something crowd relax on one of two small sea-view terraces on the rocks of the old city.
Valentino Café
Sv. Križa 28
Tel: 052 830683
Watch the sunset from the rocks (cushion provided), sipping cocktails. The cocktails may be over-priced as 35–40 kuna, but the ambience and sea-level lighting are worth the expense.
Zanzibar
Obala Pina Budicina
This is Rovinj's in place with cool seating, an extraordinary range of cocktails and great dance tunes until 2am.

Inland Istria

Gronjan
Caffe Bar Arta
Trg Cornera
Tel: 052 776405
A popular student bar that has commanding views over the surrounding hills. It is open until 2am most nights.

Kvarner Gulf

Krk (Baka)
Caffe Bar Forza
Zvonimirova 98
Tel: 051 856004
www.pdm-guliver.hr
On the main shopping street in Bašk, this is a good place for breakfast or a light lunch, or to use the internet kiosk.
Krok
Zvonimirova 115
A first-floor terrace with great sea views distinguishes Krok from the numerous other bars along Baška's seafront.

Opatija
Grand Café
Milenij Grand Hotel
Viktora Cara Emina 6
Tel: 051 278497
A relaxed and informal café with a raised terrace that is great for people-watching.

Rijeka
Café Bar Striga
Titiv Trg bb
Tel: 051 372311

A modern café in a pleasant square beneath the castle.
Hemingway
Zert 2a
Tel: 051 712333
Enjoy a hot chocolate in one of Croatia's most luxurious cafés. Make sure you pop in to the first floor, a concert hall and art gallery, to marvel at the opulent ceiling.

Dalmatia

Dubrovnik
Buza Cafe
Od Margarite
A hole in the wall leads to this precipitous café with rocks plunging into the sea.
Festival Café
Placa (Stradun)
Tel: 020 420888
Enjoy a Festival Cappuccino (chilled espresso, cream and Baileys) or drink a decent single malt whisky and watch the world go by.
Gradskakavana
Pred Dvorom 1
The town café in the old shipyards is where many locals take their coffee – join them to watch the activities in the old port.
Hemingway Bar
Pred Dvorom
Opposite the Rector's Palace, the Hemingway has little to do with its famous namesake, but it does have comfy padded armchairs and innovative cocktails.
Vinaria Arsenal
Pred Dvorom
Tel: 020 321414
A winery, cocktail bar, and restaurant, this classy spot by the harbour feels far from the tourist throng,

Hvar
Carp Diem
Riva bb
Tel: 021 384745
Carpe Diem has achieved almost legendary status. The cocktails are pricey but the DJs are Croatia's finest.
Konoba de Lupis
Nikole Karkovica 12
Take a break from the café-bars around the harbour in this friendly wine cellar.
Konoba de Teraca

Nikole Karkovica 16
A tourist-oriented wine cellar where the owner dresses in traditional costume.

Makarska
Art Café
Don M Pavlinovića 1
Tel: 021 616838
The best drinking venue in Makarska with a beach bar-style terrace, live DJs and theme nights.
Central
Kralja Tomislava 9
Tel: 021 612388
A great central location and comfortable chairs make this the perfect venue in which to relax over a beer.

Šibenik
Simply head for one of the popular bars that battle for musical airspace down on the waterfront.

Split
Dioklecijan
Dosud 9
Tel: 021 346683
Join the fashionable crowd for a drink in this buzzing beer hall on the second level of Diocletian's Palace.
Ghetto Club
Dosud 10
Tel: 021 346879
This favourite hang-out of the local 20-something crowd has great dance music and an atmospheric candlelit terrace.

Vis
Caffe Bar Bejbi
Šeet Stare Isse 8
A popular beach-style bar with funky music that attracts a young crowd.
Peronospora Blues
Biskupa Mime Pušiča 17
Enjoy a glass of local island wine beneath a vine-covered roof in this attractive wine bar-cum-art gallery.

Zadar
Caffe Bar Forum
Široka Ulica bb
Tel: 023 205505
The candlelit outdoor terrace offers an unbeatable location within the remains of the Roman Forum.

A CTIVITIES

THE ARTS, EVENTS, NIGHTLIFE, SPORTS AND SHOPPING

THE ARTS

Dance and Opera

Both Croatia's National Ballet and its National Opera are based at the Croatian National Theatre in Zagreb (Hrvatsko narodno kazalište u Zagrebu; www.hnk.hr), Trg maršala Tita 15, tel: 01 488 8418. Traditional folk dances are also popular in Croatia. The local tourist office will advise visitors about planned performances.

Concerts

Croatia has a strong tradition of classical and jazz music and these come to the fore in the country's musical events and festivals. Some of the highlights include the 22-day Zagreb Summer Evenings (Zagrebačke ljetne večeri), featuring classical music concerts, the Zagreb Music Biennale (www.biennale-zagreb.hr), the Čakovec Days of Croatian Music festival, Dubrovnik Summer Festival, and Musical Evenings in St Donatus in Zadar.

For pop music, the Croatian alternative-rock band Hladno pivo (meaning "cold beer"), formed in Zagreb in 1988, is the current market leader and frequently performs live. Its website is www.hladnopivo.hr. Listings and further information are available from local tourist offices.

Folk Music

Each region in Croatia has its own distinctive folk-music traditions ranging from male choirs specialising in a cappella (klappa), to the three-stringed lirica of Dalmatia to the oboe-like sopila of Istria. However, Slavonian folk music is the dominant sound, with its distinctive tamburica. The **Zagreb International Folklore Festival** (www.msf.hr) and the **Zlatne žice Slavonije** (Golden Strings of Slavonia), held in Požega, are two of the biggest folk events in Croatia. In more recent years the tamburica has extended its influence into the world of pop with groups like Najbolji hrvatski tamburaši **(Best Croatian Tambora Players)** and **Gazde** infusing it into rock music.

Theatre

The Croatian National Theatre based in Zagreb and listed under Dance and Opera also has three other locations:

Rijeka
Verdijeva 5a
Tel: 051 355917
www.hnk-zajc.hr
Split
Trg Gaja Bulata 1
Tel: 021 344999
www.hnk-split.hr
Osijek
Županijska 9

Tel: 031 220700
www.hnk-osijek.hr

Puppet Theatres

Children's theatre and puppet theatre are also popular in Croatia. Since 1968 Zagreb has hosted the PIF International Puppet Theatre Festival. **Zagreb Puppet Theatre (Zagrebačko kazalište lutaka)**
Trg kralja Tomislava 19
Tel: 01 487 8444
www.zkl.hr
Split City Puppet Theatre
Matošićeva 3
Tel: 021 395958
www.gkl-split.hr
Osijek Children's Theatre
Trg bana Josip Jelačića 19
Tel: 031 501485
www.djecje-kazaliste.hr

Cinema

Foreign films shown in Croatian cinemas are nearly always shown in their original language with subtitles, unless they are aimed at children. Tickets generally cost less than 40 kuna.

Some of the cinemas in Croatia's main cities are listed below.

Information and Tickets

Sources of information

Local tourist offices, tourist agencies and hotels are the best sources for information about cultural events in Croatia. Listings are also often posted on billboards. The free In Your Pocket guides, widely available locally and online (www.inyourpocket. com), to Zagreb, Dubrovnik, Opatije, Osijek, Rijeka, Split and Zadar provide detailed information about cultural events.

Buying tickets

There is no central ticket agency in Croatia and so tickets usually need to be purchased directly from the box office, but they can sometimes be bought online or from a local tourist agency.

Zagreb

Kinematografi Zagreb
Tel: 01 483 4900
www.kinematografi.hr
Provides film information and takes
bookings for many city cinemas.
Blitz CineStar
Branimirova 29
Tel: 060 323233
www.blitz-cinestar.hr
Thirteen-screen cinema opened in
2004, as part of new shopping centre,
with seats arranged in amphitheatre
style. It also has a branch at the
Avenue shopping mall.

Rijeka

Art-kino Croatia
Krešimirova 2
Tel: 051 323261
www.art-kino.org
Teatro fenice
Dolac 13
Tel: 051 335225
www.rijekakino.hr
Opened as a theatre in 1914, this
glorious building now doubles as
a wonderful cinema.

Split

Kino Central
Trg Gaja Bulata
Tel: 021 343813
www.ekran.hr
Kinoteka Zlatna vrata
Dioklecijanova 7
Tel: 021 361335
www.pouciliste-split.hr
Long-running arthouse cinema inside
Diocletian's Palace.

Dubrovnik

Kino Kivana Slavica
Put od Republike, Lapad
Outdoor cinema; foreign films, original
version/Croatian subtitles, in July and
August at dusk.

DIARY OF EVENTS

Winter Carnival (Zimski karneval),
Pag, January–February (from first
Saturday after Epiphany to Ash
Wednesday)
On every Saturday people attend
masked parties in various locations. It
is claimed to be the oldest carnival in
the Adriatic. www.pag-tourism.hr
Rijeka Carnival (Riječki karneval),
January–February
Month-long series of events including
a carnival queen pageant, a
children's carnival parade and
various concerts. For further
information, tel: 051 315710, www.
ri-karneval.com.hr

Mea Opatija festival, 13–15 June
To mark the Town of Opatija Day,
people dress up in period costume to
recall the town's heyday. For further
information, www.opatija.net.
**International Children's Festival
(Međunarodni dječji festival),
Šibenik,** late June–early July.
A festival featuring puppet shows,
ballet, art and performances by
children's theatre groups. For further
information, contact: tel: 022
213123, www.mdf-si.org.
Cultural Summer, Istria
During the summer season outdoor
venues throughout Poreč, Umag,
Rovinj, Pula and Grožnjan come alive
with concerts. For further
information, tel: 052 452797, www.
istra.hr.
Libertas Film Festival, Dubrovnik,
last week in June
See www.libertasfilmfestival.com for
details.
Summer Carnival (Ljetni karneval),
Pag, usually 27 June
This festival is another excuse to
dress up in colourful costumes and
party. For further information, www.pag-
tourism.hr.
Zlatna sopela, Poreč, late June/early
July
Seven-day festival incorporating an
opening parade and folk concerts with
performers from various countries.
For further information, tel: 052
431156, www.musicistra.org.
Musical Evenings In St Donat's
(Glazbene večeri u sv. Donatu), Zadar,
early July–mid August
A chance to hear musicians playing
classical music in this historical
church. For information, contact
Concert Office Zadar, Trg Petra
Zoranića 1, tel: 023 300430, www.
donat-festival.com.
Summer Events, Krk, early July to
late August
Stages throughout Krk are illuminated
with opera, plays and concerts. For
further information, tel: 051 221359,
www.krk.hr.
**Zagreb Summer Evenings
(Zagrebačke ljetne večeri)** July
This festival brings traditional
folklore, music, theatre and concerts
to stages across the capital. For
further information, tel: 01 450
1200, www.kdz.hr.
**Dubrovnik Summer Festival
(Dubrovački ljetni festival)** mid-
July–late August
One of Europe's great festivals, this
annual feast of folklore, music, opera
and drama takes place in numerous
outdoor venues. Contact Dubrovnik
Summer Festival, tel: 020 326100,
www.dubrovnik-festival.hr

The Summer of Split (Splitsko ljeto)
Mid-July–mid-August.
An outdoor festival of drama, opera,
ballet, concerts. For further
information, contact Croatian National
Theatre Split, www.splitsko-ljeto.hr
Days of Opatije, 17–26 July
Programme of musical, sporting and
art events celebrating the Feast Day
of St Jacob, the city's patron saint, on
25 July. For further information, visit
www.opatija.net.
Pula Film Festival, late July
An annual event held inside the city's
Roman amphitheatre. For further
information, tel: 052 210760,
www.pulafilmfestival.hr
Feast Day of St Theodore, Korčula,
27 July
A tradition probably brought to
Korčula by traders from Spain,
the moreška is a sword dance
commemorating the triumph of
Christians over the Ottomans.
This one celebrates the Feast Day
of St Theodore (sveti Todor), the
island's protector.
**International Folklore Festival,
Zagreb (Međunarodna smotra
folklora)**, Wednesday–Sunday in the
third week of July.
Most events are free. Various
venues. For further information
contact Zagreb tourist office or tel:
01 450 1194, www.msf.hr.
**Vinkovci Autumn Festival
(Vinkovačke jeseni)** Two days,
late September.
A national review of authentic
Croatian folklore. For further
information, tel: 032 332854, www.
vk-jeseni.com.
**Varaždin Baroque Evenings
(Varaždinske barokne večeri)**,
late September–early October
Opera and Baroque ensembles
feature amongst the daily
performances. www.vbv.hr.

Sightseeing Tours

For a fee, tourist offices throughout
Croatia can arrange guided walking
tours for groups and individuals.
The guides are generally excellent.
However, tourist offices will require
advance notice in order to book an
appropriate local guide.
Travel agents throughout
Croatia will organise city tours on
foot or by coach, and excursions by
boat or bus. Contact details for
some of these are given on pages
292 and 293. Companies offering
boat tours moor at marinas.
Booking in advance is not normally
required.

NIGHTLIFE

Nightclubs/Discos

Outside Zagreb and Split the nightlife scene is not as developed as it is in most Western European countries and much of it centres around bars and cafés – which stay open till midnight or sometimes later – rather than nightclubs. The majority of the large resort hotels have discos, but these are not recommended to anyone who takes clubbing seriously. But in recent years, as tastes have become more sophisticated, there have been signs of a move away from the ubiquitous sound of techno to more diverse dance music forms. On the islands and coastal resorts in summer nightlife tends to centre around the beaches.

The *In Your Pocket* guides to *Zagreb, Dubrovnik, Opatije, Osijek, Rijeka, Split* and *Zadar* provide up-to-date listings of nightclubs in those cities, as does *Time Out Zagreb*, which comes out in English.

Zagreb

An excellent place to kick off the evening is Tkalciceva street in Gornji Grad, which has so many bars and cafés that you would be hard pressed to visit more than a few in one evening. Most close around midnight and at busy times it can be difficult to get a table. There are also quite a few cafés around the main square. Especially in summer, many people head after dark to Lake Jarun (tram No. 5 or 17 will take you almost there), which offers a large choice of nightclubs, cocktail lounges and bars. There are however an increasing number of places to choose from in the city itself. Many clubs operate a dress code and there is usually an entry charge.

Aquarius
Aleja Matije Ljubeka, Jarun
Tel: 01 364 0231
www.aquarius.hr
Considered by many to be Zagreb's best mainstream club, Aquarius has a terrace overlooking the eastern edge of Lake Jarun and caters to a wide range of Croatian and international musical tastes, especially house and commercial, over two floors.

Bacchus Jazz Bar
Trg kralja Tomislava 16
Tel: 01 492 2218
Quirkily decorated with antiques, this little bar less than 100 metres/yds from the train station has a cosy garden

and live jazz a few nights a week.
BP Club
Teslina 7
Tel: 01 481 4444
www.bpclub.hr
A popular jazz club in the heart of Zagreb, with live music every night.
Gjuro 2
Medveščak 2
Tel: 01 468 3367
One of Zagreb's oldest and most popular nightclubs, attracting night owls with a different musical theme each day of the week except Mon. On Fri and Sun it is an unofficial gay club.
Močvara
Trnjanski nasip
Tel: 01 615 9668
www.mochvara.hr
Occupying a disused factory on the bank of the River Sava, Močvara, meaning "The Swamp", proudly touts itself as a popular sub-culture club. One of the few places in Zagreb where you are expected to dress down.
Piranha
Jarunsko jezero
Tel: 091 426 9234
www.piranha.hr
Another popular Jarun hangout, Piranha likes to keep its beats commercial. If it's in the charts you'll probably hear it here.
Saloon
Opened in 1970 this is the oldest dedicated nightclub in town. At weekends it hosts Zagreb's only after-party, starting at 4.30am. There is no dress code.
Škola
Second Floor, Bogovićeva 7
Tel: 01 482 8197
Retro-themed and achingly hip lounge bar. Ideally you want to be young, rich and beautiful to fit in here. The cocktail menu is one of the most extensive in town. It also has a restaurant above.

Kvarner Gulf

Opatija

Nightlife in Opatije tends to centre on the Lungomare and Maršala Tita.

Hemingway Bar
Zert 2a
Tel: 051 712333
www.hemingway.hr
To kick off the evening, this popular pub on the promenade is good to watch the world sashaying by and has occasional live music.
Disco Seven
Maršala Tita 125
www.discoseven.hr
Touting itself as the Temple of Good Vibrations, this popular summer beach disco next to the Hemingway dispenses

Information

Find Croatia, www.findcroatia.com, *the free In Your Pocket guides to Zagreb, Dubrovnik, Opatije, Osijek, Rijeka, Split and Zadar* – also online at www.inyourpocket.com – and billboard posters are all good sources of nightlife information.

mostly house till the wee hours.
Filter Bar
Zvonimirova 14
For less commercial sounds such as reggae and drum and bass, this swish venue is just the ticket.
Palach
Kružna 8
Opatije's main outpost of grunge attracts a bohemian crowd.

Pag

Aquarius
Zrće
Tel: 053 662038
Island outpost of the popular Zagreb club near the town of Navalja, doubling in the daytime as a beach bar. It throws afternoon after-beach foam parties.

Dalmatia

Brač

Faces Club
www.mastersfaces.com
Incredibly popular open-air summer disco in Bol. Its dancefloor can accommodate 2,000.

Biograd

Lavender Bar
Hotel Adriatic
Tel: 023 383165
www.ilirijabiograd.com
The first designer hotel on the Croatian coast has Croatia's first and probably only bed bar, with ambient music, clumps of lavender and soothing cocktails to help you chill out.

Dubrovnik

Carpe Diem
Kneza Damjana Jude 4
A restaurant by day but its minimalist interior becomes a cocktail bar in the evening and stays open late.
Eastwest Beach Club
Frana Supila bb
Tel: 020 412220
Join the smart set on the sofas and dance floor of this posh nightclub on Banje beach.
Exodus
Iva Dulcica 39, Babin Kuk
Part of the hotel complex at Babin Kuk (Lapad), west of the Old Town, this large club offers techno music for a

TRANSPORT · ACCOMMODATION · EATING OUT · ACTIVITIES · A – Z · LANGUAGE

young crowd.
Jazz Caffé Troubadur
Bunićeva poljana 2
Tel: 020 323476
A lively and trendy bar in the old town with regular live jazz performances.

Split

Hemingway Bar
I VIII Mediteranskih igara 5
Tel: 099 211 9993
www.hemingway.hr
This opulently furnished waterfront venue with a terrace overlooking the harbour has top-notch cocktails and some of the hippest customers in town. There is occasional live music.
St-Riva
Riva 18
There is no such thing as a bad table at this classy joint on the Riva set into the walls of Diocletian's Palace.

Zadar

Gotham Club
Marka Oreškovića 1a
Tel: 023 200289
www.gotham.zadar.net
Zadar's most fashionable club is in Voštarnica on the east side of the harbour. It offers great sounds of various genres and a relaxed terrace.
The Garden
Liburnska obala 6
Tel: 023 364739
www.thegardenzadar.com
A garden atop the city walls, this British-run terrace set up by two former members of UB40 has put Zadar firmly on the nightclub circuit.
Arsenal
Trg tri bunara 1
www.arsenalzadar.com
An art gallery, concert venue, bar and restaurant all rolled into one.

Gay and Lesbian Venues

Although the legal situation is broadly in line with that of most member states of the EU, attitudes towards homosexuals are hardly enlightened in Croatia, resulting in a largely under-ground gay and lesbian scene. There are, however, a few official or unofficial gay bars and clubs in Zagreb, some listed below, and the Zagreb Pride festival is a good time to plan a visit. Much of Croatia's summer gay and lesbian scene centres on the naturist beaches, such as Duilovo near Split, the Island of Youth (Otok mladosti) in Lake Jarun near Zagreb and Punta Kriza near Rovinj. Three useful resources for gay and lesbian visitors are www.croatia-gay.com, www.friendlycroatia.com and, for Zagreb, www.zagrebgayguide.blog.hr.

Denis
Mrazovićeva 9
Tel: 098 931 3836
Cruising club for men only.
G Bar
Mesnička 36
Tel: 091 234 2103
www.g-bar.hr
Filling two floors, this gay bar near the centre has a funky contemporary décor and gets packed at weekends with both men and women. Open till 1am.
Gjuro 2
Medveščak 2
Tel: 01 468 3367
See listing in Nightclubs and Discos, page 283.
Rush
Amruševa 10
Zagreb's newest gay club, opened in May 2009 right in the centre, popular with both genders. It is open Fri and Sat only, until 5am.
Studio Mobilus
Ignjata Đorđića 10
Tel: 01 481 1052
Near the centre this is another place rather oddly doubling as an internet café and cruising place for men.

Casinos

Most of Croatia's casinos are simple affairs with a roulette wheel, poker games and slot machines. Casinos generally open from 8am until 2am.

Buje

Casino Hotel Mulino
Škrile 75a Buje
Tel: 052 725300
www.mulino.hr

Opatija

Casino Opatija
Grand Hotel Adriatic
Maršala Tita 200
Tel: 051 719000
www.hotel-adriatic.hr

Poreč

Hotel Parentium
Zelena laguna
Tel: 052 411500
www.plavalaguna.hr

Split

Le Méridien Lav
Grljevacka 2a
Podstrana
Tel: 021 500500
www.lemeridienlavsplit.com

Zagreb

The Regent Esplanade
Mihanovićeva 1
Tel: 01 456 6666
www.theregentzagreb.com

SPORTS

Spectator Sports

Football is the biggest spectator sport in Croatia with basketball and tennis coming in joint second. Every major town and city in Croatia has a football team but the biggest are Dinamo Zagreb and Hadjuk Split. Croatia's greatest football victory to date was in the 1998 World Cup when they came an impressive third. Croatia's track record since then has been remarkably changeable.

Water polo also has a big following in Croatia, as both a spectator and participant sport.

Participant Sports

You can find more traditional sporting facilities such as sports centres and tennis courts in Croatia's main cities, towns, resorts and business hotels. If your chosen accommodation does not have its own facilities then seek advice from the staff or local tourist office.

OUTDOOR ACTIVITIES

Adventure Sports

Almost every adventure sport you can think of, from bungee jumping, skydiving and parachuting through to free climbing and paragliding, is available in Croatia. Many of these activities are most easily available in resorts in Istria and Dalmatia. It is best to seek the services of a tour operator specialising in adventure sports. If you are travelling in Dalmatia check out Adventure Dalmatia's catalogue of extreme sports (www.crochallenge.com).

Generalturist and Shuttle are two Split-based travel agencies offering rafting on the Cetina River.

Active Holidays, based in Omiš, offers windsurfing, free climbing, canoeing and kayaking.

Generalturist
Obala Lazareta 3
Tel: 021 345183
www.generalturist.com
Shuttle
R. Boskovica 15, Kaleta 1
Tel: 098 234913
www.shuttle.hr
Active Holidays Croatia
Knezova kačića
Tel: 021 861829
www.activeholidays-croatia.com

Birdwatching

Croatia's lush nature parks provide bird enthusiasts with some of the best birdwatching opportunities in Europe. More than 250 different species make their nests at Kopački rit in eastern Slavonia, including heron, storks, kingfishers and white-tailed eagles, whilst Lonjsko polje is home to some rare European birds including the white-tailed eagle and short-toed eagle. Park regulations are strict, with visitors only allowed access to certain areas in the company of a guide. There are a number of specialist bird-watching tours and holidays on offer.

Park prirode Kopački rit
Petefi 35, Bilje
Tel: 031 285370
www.kopacki-rit.com
Park prirode Lonjsko polje
Trg Kralja P. Svačića, Jasenovac
Tel: 044 672080
www.pp-lonjsko-polje.hr

Climbing

The Velebit, Učka, Papuk and Biokovo mountains afford many opportunities for climbing. Local tourist offices can advise visitors about travel agencies and companies that organise climbing.
Croatian Mountaineering Association
Kozarčeva 22, Zagreb
Tel: 01 482 4142
www.plsavez.hr

Cycling

Bicycles are relatively cheap and easy to rent in Croatia and cycling can be a wonderful way to explore the country's islands and more rural areas. Istria is particularly geared up for cycling tourism and the tourist association has produced **Istria Bike** – a map of cycling routes including distances, time, altitude and difficulty. You can pick this up from any local tourist office. More localised maps and routes are also available from many tourist offices throughout the country. Cycling along Croatia's frenetic coastal roads, especially the Jadranska magistrala, can be hair-raising at best. Only experienced cyclists should attempt it.

Meridien Ten
Zajceva 7, Split
Tel: 021 388951
www.bikerentalcroatia.com
Organises cycling tours, with or without a guide and with or without your own bicycle, throughout Croatia. It caters for individuals and groups.

Diving

The popularity of diving in Croatia has exploded, with the waters of the Adriatic offering seemingly limitless opportunities for discovery dives, wreck dives, night dives and certified diving courses. The tranquil waters around the Dalmatian island of Vis are particularly rich in shipwrecks.

For anyone wishing to dive, membership of the Croatian Diving Association (Hrvatski ronilački savez – HRS) is compulsory and only suitably qualified divers can get a permit. For more information on obtaining the permit contact:
Croatian Diving Association (Hrvatski ronilački savez)
Dalmatinska 12, Zagreb
Tel: 01 484 8765
www.diving-hrs.hr
The huge increase in diving tourism in Croatia has resulted in a correspondingly high number of dive operators. The majority of these advertise their services through local tourist offices, flyers and roadside hoardings. Never dive with an operator whose credentials you are unsure of. Most diving companies rent equipment, fill gas bottles and operate dive schools. A useful online guide to scuba-diving sites is www.diving.hr.

Coastal Istria
Poreč
Ronilački centar Plava Laguna
Plava Laguna
Tel: 098 367619
www.plava-laguna-diving.hr

Mali Lošinj
Diver Sport Centre
Uvala Čikat 13
Tel: 051 233900
www.diver.hr

Kvarner Gulf
A list of dive sites, diving centres and diving clubs on the Kvarner Gulf mainland and the Adriatic islands is available from the Kvarner County Tourism Office in Opatija. The brochure is entitled *The Joys of Diving*.

Kvarner County Tourism Office
Nikole Tesle 2
Tel: 051 272988
www.kvarner.hr

Northern Dalmatia
Primošten
Manta Diving
Auto camp Adriatic
Tel: 098 265923
www.crodive.info

Southern Dalmatia
Dubrovnik
Dubrovnik Diving Club (Ronilački Klub Dubrovnik)
Villa Solitudo, Ivana Zajca 35
Tel: 020 435737
www.diver.vdu.hr

Korcula
Gorgona Diving Croatia
Ulica 1, Vela Luca
Tel: 099 255 8001
www.kotcula-diving.com.hr
Diving on Korcula and Lastovo islands.

Hvar
Dive Centre Hvar
Near Hotel Amfora
Tel: 021 741603
www.divecentre-hvar.com

Vis
An Ma Diving Centre
Kamenita 12
Tel: 091 521 3944
www.anma.hr
Dodoro Diving
Trg Klapavica 1
Tel: 021 711913
www.dodoro-diving.com
ISSA Diving Centre
Ribarska 91
Komiža
Tel: 021 713651
www.scubadiving.hr
Manta Diving Centre
Komiža
Tel: 098 534714
www.crodive.info

Fishing

The seas off Croatia are rich in sea bream, grouper, mullet, bass, cuttlefish, squid and sea eels, making Croatia a popular destination for anglers. A permit is necessary to fish the waters of the Adriatic and anglers may keep no more than 5kg (11lb) of fish. Harpooning and diving for shellfish are forbidden. Local tourist offices and travel agencies will be able to advise visitors about where to obtain fishing permits or provide information about fishing excursions. Alternatively, look out for signs on the waterfronts.

Hiking

Hiking is very popular in Croatia. The country's various national parks make ideal starting points. Trail maps are available from the park information centres and many tourist offices.
Biokovo Active Holidays
Kralja Petra Kresimira IV 7b, Makarska
Tel: 021 679655
www.biokovo.net

Hunting

Anyone wishing to hunt must seek advice and organise his or her activities through an official organisation. In some areas of Croatia it remains unsafe to hunt because of land mines left over from the war. Traditionally Slavonia is a rich hunting area. Prospective hunters should contact the tourist offices in Osijek or Slavonski Brod for advice, as they will have up-to-date information about operators and the location of uncleared land mines.

Reputable companies that coordinate hunting trips in Istria and the Kvarner Gulf area include:

Adriatic
Trg slobode 2a, Poreč
Tel: 052 452663
www.adriatic-istra.com
Marina Tours
Obala 81, Punat, Krk
Tel: 051 854375
www.marina-tours.hr

Skiing

Croatia has yet to make its mark as an international skiing destination, but resorts do exist. Within easy reach of Zagreb is Medvednica, where the highest mountain peak stands at 1,035 metres (about 3,400ft). Facilities include a chair-lift and two T-bar lifts, equipment-hire shops, several mountain huts and a hotel. Bjelolasica in the Gorski Kotar region is also a winter skiing destination. Prospective skiers should contact a travel agent or the Croatian National Tourist Board, www.croatia.hr, for further information.

Water Sports

The wide array of water sports available includes kayaking, canoeing, rafting, windsurfing, sailing and water-skiing.

Active Holidays Croatia
Knezova kačića
Omiš
Tel: 021 861829
www.activeholidays-croatia.com
Diving, rafting, windsurfing, paragliding and free climbing specialists.
Atlas Dubrovnik
Vukovarska 19
Dubrovnik
Tel: 020 442222
www.atlas-croatia.com
This company offers a variety of activity holidays including canoeing, kayaking and rafting.

SHOPPING

What to Buy

Traditional Croatian souvenirs include handmade silk neck ties (kravate, singular kravata), Pag cheese, hand-made lace, fragrant herbal remedies, stoneware and glassware. Traditional morčić jewellery from Rijeka, natural cosmetics, high-quality silver jewellery made with red Adriatic coral are also popular. Local foods, wines and spirits such as fiery Croatian grappa (rakija), or šljivovica (plum brandy), truffles, honey and olive oil also make good gifts. In a nation obsessed with fashion, clothes and shoes are also a good buy. In Zagreb Nataša Mihaljčišin and Martina Vrdoljak-Ranilović are two voguish designers running the I-Gle Fashion Studio, which distributes its lines through the world's top stores.

Shopping Areas

The main shopping areas in Croatia's smaller towns and resorts are easy to locate because of the throngs of people. In most destinations it is possible to purchase high-quality jewellery, souvenirs, original artwork, candles, perfume, lace and clothing from small boutiques. Some unmissable shopping areas include Poreč's Ulica Decumanus, where the remains of Venetian villas brim with souvenir shops, and Rovinj's Ulica Grisia in the old town, where high-quality artwork and gifts abound. In Hvar, Trgovački Orbit is worth a visit with its boutiques and antique shops. In Split, the best place for shopping is around Diocletian's Palace and Marmontova, where designer stores abound. Zagreb is also a good place for fashion, centred in Ilica. The tourist office has a good selection of reproduction antiques and other gifts.

Markets

Most resorts, towns and cities in Croatia have both a green market – selling fresh fruit, veg, fish and meat – and a general market. Most markets in Croatia are open daily, except Sunday, between 8am and 2pm. Markets in major tourist destinations tend to have extended opening hours.

Books

Books are incredibly expensive in Croatia. Outside the main cities it can be difficult to buy English or foreign-language books. Algoritam (www. algoritam.hr), which has branches in Zagreb, Split, Dubrovnik, Pula, Osijek, Šibenik, Varaždin and Zadar, many inside shopping malls, stocks a good selection of English-language books, including Insight Guides, and magazines. In Zagreb, Brala and especially Profil Megastore also have plenty of imported reading material.

Zagreb
Algoritam, Gajeva 1
Tel: 01 488 1555
Brala, Mihanovićeva 32
Tel: 01 485 6687

Split
Algoritam, Bajamontijeva 2
Tel: 021 348030

Dubrovnik
Algoritam, Placa (Stradun) 8
Tel: 020 322044

Arts and Crafts

You can buy contemporary Croatian art from a wealth of small galleries that breathe a hard-to-resist energy into many of Croatia's smaller resorts and towns. Arguably the best places to buy original art in Croatia is in the hill town of Grožnjan, or Rovinj's Ulica Grisia.

Two more unusual places to buy original arts and crafts are the **Kristal Tuk** (Crystal Shop), Langova 63, Samobor, tel: 01 336 7101, www.crystal-shop.com, which sells handmade cut glass of exquisite quality, and the **Benedictine convent** (Samostan benediktinki), Nikole Karkovica 13, Hvar, tel: 021 741052, which sells unique lace handmade by nuns.

In Rijeka, Mala galerija, Užarska 25, tel: 051 335403, www.mala-galerija.hr, is a family workshop selling handmade table lamps, pottery and jewellery.

Food and Drink

Good purchases include the hard and salty Pag cheese, Croatian olive oil, artisan honey, grappa, truffles and an incredible variety of Croatian wines, spirits and liqueurs.

One of the best places to purchase such gifts is at Zigante Tartufi, www. zigantetartufi.com. The retail group that stakes claim to having found the world's biggest truffle – weighing 1.31kg (2lb 8oz) and unearthed near Buje in 1999 – sells its world-famous white truffles, black truffles and truffled sheep's cheese in branches throughout Istria. It also has a good range of high-quality Croatian wines and other alcoholic drinks.

Parklife

National Parks

Nacionalni park Brijuni
Brijunska 10
Fazana
Tel: 052 525888
www.np-brijuni.hr

Nacionalni park Kornati
Butina 2
Murter
Tel: 022 435740
www.kornati.hr

Nacionalni park Krka
Trg Ivana Pavla II br. 5
Šibenik
Tel: 022 201777
www.npkrka.hr

Nacionalni park Mljet
Pristanište 2
Goveđari
Tel: 020 744041
www.np-mljet.hr
Lovely wooded island with central monastery on a lake

Nacionalni park Paklenica
Dr. Franje Tuđmana 14a
Paklenica
Tel: 023 369155
www.paklenica.hr

Nacionalni park Plitvice
Plitvička jezera
Tel: 053 751132
www.np-plitvicka-jezera.hr

Nacionalni park Risnjak
Bijela Vodica 48
Crni Lug
Tel: 051 836133
www.risnjak.hr

Nacionalni park Sjeverni Velebit
Krasno 96
Krasno
Tel: 053 665380
www.np-sjeverni-velebit.hr

Nature Parks

Most Croatian nature parks have some restrictions on visitors, and facilities vary widely. Some allow camping, a few have hotels and others are best suited to day trips. It is advisable to get in touch with a tourist office or the park itself.

Park prirode Biokovo
Marineta – mala obala 16
Makarska
Tel: 021 616924
www.biokovo.com
Near Makarska and covering 196 sq km (75 sq miles), this park ranges in elevation from 200–1,762 meters (656–5,781ft), has more than 40 endemic plant species and has some unusual geomorphological phenomena including pits and depressions. It also has superb views. Many travel agencies in Makarska can arrange guided tours either hiking or by car. The park is open to the public from April to mid-November and visitors need to pay an entry charge. The main entrance is 6km (4 miles) from Makarska on the Vrgorac road.

Park prirode Kopački rit
Petefi 35
Bilje
Tel: 031 285370
www.kopacki-rit.com
A mixture of forests and swamps, this park in eastern Slavonia offers some of the best birdwatching opportunities in Europe. More than 250 species nest here including herons, white storks, kingfishers and white-tailed eagles. There is also an abundant variety of other aquatic life. The park is open all year. Visitors need an entry ticket and fishing permits and guided tours are available at an extra charge.

Park prirode Lonjsko polje
Krapje 30
Krapje
Tel: 044 672080
www.pp-lonjsko-polje.hr
Another dream destination for twitchers, this marshy park near Jasenovac in eastern Croatia is home to some rare European birds including the white-tailed eagle and short-toed eagle. It also includes Krapje, an "architectural-heritage village", and two ethnographic exhibitions. The park is open year-round and tickets are necessary. Guided tours are available at an extra charge if booked in advance.

Park prirode Medvednica
Bliznec
Zagreb
Tel: 01 458 6317
www.pp-medvednica.hr

Park prirode Papuk
Stjepana Radića 46
Velika
Tel: 034 313030
www.pp-papuk.hr
This park in central Slavonia features relatively low mountains from 200–953 meters (656–3,127ft) high covered in forest and is suitable for hikers, mountaineers and mountain bikers of all abilities. It also has thermal springs and Iron Age burial mounds and is Croatia's first designated "geopark". It is open all year and there is no entry charge.

Park prirode Telašćica
Danijela Grbin
Sali
Tel: 023 377096
www.telascica.hr
One of the largest and best protected natural harbours on the eastern Adriatic coast, Telašćica is a dramatic landscape of bays, capes and islands with extremely rich marine flora and fauna, numerous sea caves and living coral reefs. Naturally it attracts divers as well as hikers, anglers, sailors and cyclists. It is open all year and entry is free.

Park prirode Učka
Liganj 42, Lovran
Tel: 051 293753
www.pp-ucka.hr
One of the northernmost points of the Mediterranean and overlooking Istria's Kvarner Gulf, the Učka mountain range offers trails that are easily accessible from the Opatije Riviera resorts, culminating at Vojak peak (altitude 1,401 metres/4,626ft) and interspersed with pretty villages. There are few facilities but the far-reaching view from the summit is its own reward. The park is also a good place for spotting the Učka bellflower (Campanula tomassiniana), which grows nowhere else, as well as griffon vultures and golden eagles. It is open all year and entry is free.

Park prirode Velebit
Kaniža Gospićka 4b, Gospić
www.velebit.hr
Tel: 053 560450
The only Unesco biosphere in Croatia, this thickly forested park combines karst peaks, ridges and sinkholes, and is one of the best places in the country to spot brown bears, lynx and wolves.

Vransko Lake Nature Park (Parka prirode Vransko jezero)
Kralja P. Svačića 2, Biograd
Tel: 023 383181
www.vransko-jezero.hr
In northern Dalmatia, between Zadar and Šibenik, this lake is a haven for birds and their spotters. So far 241 bird species have been recorded here, of which 102 nest in the park area.

Žumberak
Slani Dol 1, Samobor
Tel: 01 332 7660
www.pp-zumberak-samoborsko-gorje.hr
This park covers 350 sq km (135 sq miles) of hilly and sparsely populated territory southwest of Zagreb.

A – Z

A HANDY SUMMARY OF PRACTICAL INFORMATION, ARRANGED ALPHABETICALLY

A dmission Charges

Most Croatian museums charge an entry fee between 10 and 30 kuna, with half-price entry for children, students and senior citizens, although a few have occasional free-entry days. For one day around the end of January, many institutions in Croatia participate in Museum Night, which offers free entry to museums and galleries from 6 pm to 1 am. Many museums have restrictions on still or video photography. In Zagreb the Zagreb Card (www.zagrebcard. fivestars.hr) offers discounts at nearly all the city's museums and many other venues as well as free public transport and is available for either 24 or 72 hours.

B udgeting for Your Trip

Here are some average costs. Note that costs in Zagreb and Dubrovnik are generally higher than elsewhere and many prices increase in high season (July and August).
Croatian beer (half a litre) or a glass of house wine (125ml) in a bar or café: around 12 kuna

Main course at a cheap restaurant: 40 kuna
Main course at a moderate restaurant: 75 kuna
Main course at an expensive restaurant: 110 kuna
Double room with breakfast at a cheap hotel in high season: 350 kuna
Double room with breakfast at a moderate hotel in high season: 700 kuna
Double room with breakfast at a deluxe hotel in high season: 2,500 kuna
A taxi journey from Zagreb airport to the city centre: 175 kuna
A single bus ticket: 10–35 kuna

City Transport

Tickets for local bus services are available from tobacco kiosks or from the driver at a slightly higher price. In larger towns and cities bus services start as early as 4am and run until around 11pm, with fares ranging from 10 to 35 kuna depending on the distance travelled. Local and national bus services can be caught at bus stations or hailed at designated stops. The main bus stations are listed in the Getting There section (see page 262).

Zagreb and Osijek both have a city tram service. Trams operate a similar timetable to the buses and tickets should be purchased from a newspaper kiosk. Passengers must first validate tickets using the on-board machines.

C hildren

Most hotels, restaurants and cafés are very accommodating to families. In many establishments under-3s can stay free, and discounts are frequently available for accommodation, travel and food for under-12s and even under-18s. The beaches and resorts, especially Istria and its islands, offer plenty of water-based activities for children as well as dry sporting facilities for older children. One thing that Croatia is very short on, however, is sand, and most of the beaches are shingle, rock, or man-made from concrete or gravel.

Climate

Croatia has four seasons and two distinct climatic zones. Inland Croatia enjoys temperate weather whereas

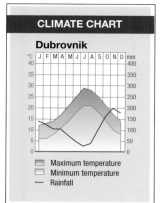

CLIMATE CHART

Dubrovnik

| | J F M A M J J A S O N D | |
|°C | | mm |

Maximum temperature
Minimum temperature
— Rainfall

the Adriatic coastline has a more Mediterranean climate with hot, sunny summer days and mild, wet winters. The Dinaric Alps, backing onto the Dalmatian coast, have hot summers and cold winters with lots of snow. Inland temperatures drop as low as −1°C (30°F) in January and reach highs of 26°C (79°F) in August. Coastal temperatures are around 5–10°C (40–50°F) in January and regularly reach 30°C (86°F) in August. The sea is warm all year round with a low of 12°C (53°F) in winter and a high of 26°C (79°F) in summer.

The tourist season is April–October. Spring and summer are the best times for hiking and biking. August is the time for nightlife, but at this hot, busy time of year car drivers have to queue for hours to board ferries for the islands, and many hotels and private rooms are booked up.

What to Wear/Bring

Croatia is a well-developed, modern country and visitors will be able to buy most of the things they need. The type of clothing required depends on the season and intended activities. At the height of the tourist season in July and August temperatures in the sun can reach 30°C (86°F), although they usually hover around 24°C (76°F), so it is essential to wear light, loose non-synthetic clothing, sunglasses and a sunhat. Night-time temperatures are mild, making it possible to wear shorts, T-shirts and sundresses through to bedtime. Mild, humid evenings attract mosquitoes and so a supply of insect repellent with 30–50 percent DEET is a good investment.

In spring, early summer and early autumn, when average temperatures are lower, a sweater or light jacket is also advisable. November through to March are cold months and a good

winter coat is necessary. Although parts of Dalmatia are renowned for long dry periods, be prepared for the possibility of rain whatever the season. It is also advisable to bring sturdy walking shoes or trainers for easy walks. More serious hiking will require hiking boots.

Useful Numbers

Weather forecast and road conditions: tel: 060 520520

Crime and Safety

Crime rates in Croatia are lower than in most European countries and crime against tourists is rare, violent crime extremely rare. Simple precautions such as not leaving valuables in vehicles, carrying personal belongings securely and avoiding walking alone in dark areas at night minimise the risk. Do not leave items unattended at beaches. It is advisable to photocopy the identification pages of your passport so that if it is lost or stolen the consulate will be able to issue a replacement quickly. The emergency number in Croatia is 112. Visitors to Croatia need to carry a passport or, where applicable, national ID card, at all times.

Land Mines

The Croatian government was quick to remove land mines at the end of the war and most areas are completely safe. However some more remote areas around Krajina and Eastern Croatia are still being de-mined, including areas close to main roads. Look out for warning signs with the skull and crossbones on a red triangle with black lettering saying *Ne prilazite* (Do not enter), and do not stray from roads and paved areas without a local guide. Particularly avoid overgrown areas and abandoned war-damaged buildings. A useful resource is the Croatian Mine Action Centre (Hrvatski centar za razminiranje; tel. 044 554151; www.hcr.hr).

Customs Regulations

Visitors can bring personal possessions, two litres of table wine, two litres of liqueur or dessert wine, 1 litre of spirits, 50 grams of scent, 250ml of toilet water, one package of homeopathic products and 200 cigarettes or 100 cigarillos or 50 cigars or 250g of tobacco into Croatia duty free. If you carrying more than a total of 10,000 euros in cash or cheques you must declare it at customs. The transportation of

domestic currency is restricted to 15,000 kuna. To prevent difficulties when trying to take them back out of the country, report expensive goods such as cameras and laptop computers to customs officials upon arrival. It is possible to bring cats and dogs into Croatia if they have a certificate confirming vaccination against rabies, issued within the previous six months and at least 15 days before the date of entry.

Electricity

220V, 50Hz, two-pin round pronged plugs.

D isabled Travellers

Many of Croatia's most interesting sights lie within the country's historic old towns, where streets are generally cobbled and buildings are old with narrow staircases, hallways and no lifts, making disabled access problematic. Access to beaches can also be difficult, requiring descents over steep steps or crossing rocky outcrops, although the town of Omiš, near Split, has a wheelchair-accessible beach with special ramps to lower disabled people into the sea, and the nearby town of Ivašnjak is also wheelchair-accessible. Travellers with disabilities should plan their visits in advance and check with local tourist boards that their needs can be catered for. In general, newly built hotels are more likely to have facilities for disabled travellers.

E mbassies and Consulates

Zagreb

Austrian Embassy
Radnička cesta 80
Tel: 01 483 4459
Email: agram-ob@bmeia.gv.at
Australian Embassy
3rd Floor, Kaptol centar, Nova ves 11
Tel: 01 489 1200
www.auembassy.hr
Canadian Embassy
Prilaz Đure Deželića 4
Tel: 01 488 1200
www.canadainternational.gc.ca

Emergency Numbers

All emergencies: 112
Police: 92
Fire Brigade: 93
Ambulance: 94
Emergency road service: 987
Coast guard: 985

TRANSPORT
ACCOMMODATION
EATING OUT
ACTIVITIES
A – Z
LANGUAGE

Hungarian Embassy
Pantovčak 225–257
Tel: 01 489 0906
www.mfa.gov.hu/emb/zagreb
Italian Embassy
Medulićeva 22
Tel: 01 484 6386
www.ambzagabria.esteri.it
British Embassy
Ivana Lučića 4
Tel: 01 600 9100
www.ukincroatia.fco.gov.uk
United States
Thomasa Jeffersona 2
Tel: 01 661 2300
http://zagreb.usembassy.gov

Etiquette

Croatians tend to be quite reserved with strangers, epecially away from the main tourist areas. A few words of Croatian go a long way. When addressing strangers it is polite to use the honorific *gospodine* (for a man), *gospodo* (for a married woman) or *gospođice* (for a young unmarried woman), followed by the family name. Beachwear is not acceptable in churches and visitors should cover their shoulders and knees. As a visit to any café will quickly confirm, Croatians take their fashion seriously and do not appreciate scruffy dress. If invited to a Croatian house for a meal, it is appropriate to give the hostess an odd number of flowers, from three upwards (but not chrysanthemums, which symbolise death) and the host a bottle of good wine or a box of chocolates. Do not start eating before the host. Croatians hold the fork in the left hand and the knife in the right. It is polite to wait for the host to insist before accepting a second helping. It is advisable to exercise tact when discussing politics or history.

G ay and Lesbian Travellers

Croatia is a religious country with a Roman Catholic majority. As a result, homosexuality is tolerated, but not embraced. As such there are not many official gay venues and public displays of affection are not welcome, though there are gay scenes in larger cities. Every year since 2002 a Zagreb Pride march has taken place in June with the support of the city authorities, but despite a strong police presence often with a backdrop of violence from protestors. There is also a Queer Zagreb festival every spring. There are several gay rights groups in Croatia including Iskorak (www.iskorak.org) and Kontra (www.kontra.hr), a group for lesbians and bisexual women. A useful online guide to gay Croatia, listing many clubs, bars and other meeting places, is www.croatia-gay.com.

H ealth and Medical Care

Health

A visit to Croatia does not carry any specific health risks and no vaccinations are needed. However, it is advisable to take precautions against sunstroke, sunburn and dehydration in the summer by bringing sunscreen, a sunhat, and drinking plenty of water. It is safe to drink the tap water throughout Croatia although mineral water is also widely available.

Visitors needing specific medication should take adequate supplies with them, including the packaging listing ingredients, which will help pharmacists supply replacements if necessary.

Those planning to travel for long periods in Croatia's mountains should think about vaccinating

against tick-borne encephalitis, a serious disease causing the brain to swell and sometimes leading to death. Another potential hazard is sea urchins, black spiky balls about the size of a child's fist that lurk around rocky beaches. If you tread on one, the spines can become implanted in the skin, causing great pain and potentially leading to infection if not removed.

Medical Treatment

Medical care in Croatia is of a high standard, with facilities on a par with those in Western Europe. Larger towns and cities have their own hospitals and most small towns have a medical centre with a doctor on call 24 hours every day. Most bigger towns and cities also have a 24-hour pharmacy. Local tourist offices and hotels can provide details of these. Also see Insurance (below) for information on payment for health services.

Insurance

Citizens of Britain, Ireland and most European countries are entitled to free medical care thanks to a mutual health-care agreement. If no such agreement exists patients pay according to a standard price list.

Credit cards often offer limited insurance when used to book a flight or holiday, and some household insurance covers personal possessions away from home including cover abroad. You should always check terms and conditions thoroughly prior to departure.

It would be unwise to rely on any of these forms of insurance alone. Without taking out adequate travel insurance you could face large medical bills, repatriation costs or expensive lawsuits.

The cover provided by travel-insurance policies varies greatly and so it is essential to read the small print and ensure that you have comprehensive cover that includes claims by a third party. Extra premiums may apply for covering adventure sports and expensive articles such as cameras, mobile telephones and laptop computers.

Maps

Good national maps are available from Croatian National Tourist Offices abroad, good local bookstores and also local tourist offices.

BELOW: pack a good road map when cycling.

Internet

Online Access

Croatia has embraced the World Wide Web with fervour and many organisations provide good dual-language websites. Internet cafés are also becoming an increasingly prominent feature of Croatian life. Most internet cafés open from 8am to 11pm or midnight.

Most Croatian cities and towns have internet cafés. A growing number of hotels also offer public internet access, commonly through coin-operated terminals. The local tourist office will tell you where to find the closest internet café.

Media

Television

Hrvatska radiotelevizija (HRT) (www.hrt. hr) operates Croatia's three state-controlled domestic television stations: HRT1, HRT2 and HRT Plus as well as an international station aimed mainly at the Croatian diaspora. All three domestic stations broadcast programmes in Croatian, English, German and other European languages. Funding for state TV comes partly from a licence fee and partly from advertising. Foreign-language broadcasts carry Croatian subtitles. The general quality of programmes is poor and repeats are very common.

Radio

Croatia's three main radio stations are Hrvatska radio 1, 2 and 3 (HR1, HR2 and HR3). HR1 and HR2 broadcast news, weather reports, travel news music, documentaries and sporting programmes. HR3 touts itself as an intellectual and spiritual channel and also broadcasts classical music. During the main tourist season Hrvatska radio regularly broadcasts news, reports on road and sailing conditions in English, German and Italian. www.hrt.hr.

Print

Croatia's four main daily newspapers are *Hina News Line* (www.hina.hr), *Vecernjilist* (www.vecernji-list.hr), *Vjesnik* (www.vjesnik.hr) and *Slobodna Dalmacija* (www.slobodnadalmacija.hr). The *Hina News Line* website is in Croatian and English. You can also access the *Novi list* (www.novilist.hr) and the business newspaper *Dnevnik* (www. dnevnik.hr) online, in Croatian only. The *Guardian Europe* and the *International Herald Tribune* are readily available in Croatia in summer as is a selection of other foreign language newspapers, though they are often not available on the day of publication. In the winter you may need to look for an international bookshop in a city.

Useful Number

News: tel: 060 440440.

Money

Cash

Croatia's official currency is the kuna: 100 lipa make 1 kuna, although prices are frequently quoted in both kuna and euros. It is not advisable to carry large sums of money, but it is useful to keep a small emergency fund if you are planning to visit remote areas of the country (you can change euros, US dollars, pounds sterling and other major currencies at banks and exchange offices throughout Croatia) and discounts from 10–20 percent are often offered for cash payment. Beware of changing money unofficially as you risk picking up counterfeit notes, especially for 200 and 500 kuna.

Approximate Exchange Rates:
1 euro = 7.3 kuna
1 pound = 8.5 kuna
1 US dollar = 5.2 kuna

Traveller's Cheques

Traveller's cheques offer the most secure way of carrying money. Euro or US dollar traveller's cheques can be exchanged at many banks and exchange offices for a commission of up to 2 percent when accompanied by a valid passport. American Express traveller's cheques can also be exchanged through Atlas travel agencies.

ATMs and Credit Cards

The easiest way to get cash in Croatia is to debit money from your bank account via one of the many ATMs, although try to avoid waiting until you reach one of the smaller islands. Debit cards carrying the Maestro, MasterCard, Visa and Cirrus symbols are widely accepted. When debiting money directly from a bank account the exchange rate is more predictable than when using a credit card, but commission charges vary greatly, with some banks charging as much as 4 percent. Credit card cash advances can also be made from ATMs.

Credit cards are a good way to settle bills, with American Express and MasterCard being more widely accepted than Visa. Do not assume that credit cards will be accepted, even in the most expensive restaurants. It is advisable not to depend on one card only and to inform your bank of your travel plans to prevent cards being blocked.

Most credit card companies will replace a lost or stolen credit card within 24 hours and arrange an emergency cash advance on the same day. Western Union money transfer services are also available at more than 1,000 post offices throughout Croatia.

Tax

Value Added Tax (PDV) is applied to nearly all purchases in Croatia and charged at 22 percent. Bread, milk, medicine and technical and educational books are exempt and there is a 10 percent rate for accommodation services, magazines and newspapers. Visitors can claim this tax back on purchases over 5,000 kuna from shops that display a Tax Free Shopping logo. Some local authorities also charge a 3 percent tax on certain transactions.

Tipping

Hotel and restaurant bills usually include tax and service. However it is common practice to round the bill up to the nearest 10 kunas or leave an additional tip of 10 to 15 percent if service has been good, especially in more expensive restaurants. In cheaper places it is normal to leave any coins from the change. Unless the service has been exceptional, do not feel obliged to tip taxi drivers as they often overcharge tourists or round up the fare.

Opening Hours

Office hours are generally 8am–4pm or 8.30am–4.30pm Mon–Fri. In the tourist resorts opening hours are often 8am–1pm and 5–11pm. Many large towns have a 24-hour pharmacy and some have 24-hour grocery stores. Banks are generally open 7am–3pm Mon–Fri and 8am–2pm Sat. Opening hours for museums vary but they generally close on Monday and public holidays. Try to avoid travelling without your own wheels on national holidays, when public transport grinds to a trickle. Most public transport also has a restricted Sunday timetable. Most shops and department stores open from 8am–8pm on weekdays, sometimes with a siesta from noon to 4pm, and until 2 or 3pm on Saturday. Some open till 10pm, especially in tourist areas in

Public Holidays

New Year's Day 1 January
Three Kings Day/Epiphany 6 January
Good Friday and Easter Monday March/April
Labour Day 1 May
Corpus Christi May/June (60 days after Easter)
Anti-Fascist Struggle Day 22 June
Croatian National Day 25 June
Victory Day/National Thanksgiving 5 August
Feast of the Assumption 15 August
Independence Day 8 October
All Saints' Day 1 November
Christmas 25 and 26 December
Names may vary slightly according to the translation from Croatian to English.

high season, and from 8am–2pm on Sunday. There are a few 24-hour shops in major cities, often in or near major transport terminals.

P hotography

Camera film and inexpensive shoot-and-snap cameras are widely available in Croatia and most tourist sites permit visitors to take photographs. Slide film, more expensive cameras, lenses and other professional equipment are not readily available outside Zagreb, and even there the range is very limited. There are correspondingly few camera shops to be found and getting cameras fixed outside Zagreb can be extremely difficult.

Postal Services

Croatia has an efficient postal service operated by Hrvatska pošta (www.posta. hr). It sell stamps and telephone cards, sends telegrams, faxes and packages, and gives credit card cash advances and changes foreign currency and traveller's cheques. Some towns have separate post offices for sending larger packages. Post offices are generally open from 7am–7pm Monday–Friday and until 1pm on Saturday. In smaller towns the post office may close at 4pm whilst those in tourist resorts operate a split shift, opening from 7am–1pm and 7–9pm.

R eligious Services

Around 85 percent of Croatians are Roman Catholic and Mass is held in Catholic churches and cathedrals throughout the county. According to the 2001 census, minority groups include Orthodox 4.4 percent, other Christian 0.4 percent, Muslim 1.3 percent, other and unspecified 0.9 percent and none 5.2 percent. The local tourist office will be able to advise visitors of service times or direct them to the office of the parish priest. Zagreb's Anglican chaplaincy hosts English-language services for Christians of any denomination at 10am each Sunday Sept–June at St Joseph's Chapel on the third floor of the Jesuit Centre, Jordanovac 110. According to the Constitution Croatia is a secular republic in which all religious groups are separate from the State. However, Roman Catholicism has long played a strong part in the national identity – before it collapsed, about half the population of Yugoslavia was Orthodox, 30 percent Catholic and 10 percent Muslim–and these faiths have made a resurgence since independence.

T elephones

You can make domestic and international direct-dial calls from any telephone in Croatia. Cellular (mobile) telephone numbers begin with 09 and have a third number and all the digits must be dialled.

To call Croatia from outside the country, first dial your international access code followed by the code for Croatia, 385. When calling from abroad omit the initial 0 in the regional access code. For example dial 1 instead of 01 for Zagreb. A cheap way to make international calls is to pick up a discount telephone card from a post office.

Useful Numbers

Directory enquiries: 988
International operator: 901
International directory assistance: 902
Fire, police, ambulance and other emergencies: 112

Tourist Information

Tourist Offices Abroad

The Croatia National Tourist Office (Hrvatska turistička zajednica) provides brochures, maps and leaflets about the country's many attractions, accommodation and facilities.

Time Zone

GMT plus 1 hour, with daylight saving time in summer.

Detailed information is also available on its website, www.htz.hr.

UK
2 The Lanchesters, 162–4 Fulham Palace Road, London W6 9ER
Tel: + 44 (0) 20 8563 7979
Email: info@croatia-london.co.uk

Tourist Offices in Croatia

Zagreb
Trg bana Josip Jelačića 11
Tel: 01 481 4051
www.zagreb-touristinfo.hr

Istrian Coast
Poreč
Zagrebačka 9
Tel: 052 451293
www.istra.com/porec
Pula
Forum 3
Tel: 052 212987
www.pulainfo.hr
Rovinj
Pina Budičina 12
Tel: 052 811566
www.tzgrovinj.hr

Inland Istria
Motovun
Trg Josefa Ressela 1
Tel: 052 617480
www.istria-motovun.com

Kvarner Gulf
Krk Town
Vela placa 1/1
Tel: 051 221414
www.tz-krk.hr
Opatija
Vladimira Nazora 3
Tel: 051 271710
www.opatija-tourism.hr
Rab
Trg Municipium Arba 8
Tel: 051 771111
www.tzg-rab.hr
Rijeka
Korzo 33a
Tel: 051 335882
www.tz-rijeka.hr

Central Croatia
Karlovac
Tel: 047 615115
www.karlovac-touristinfo.hr
Varaždin
Ivana Padovca 3
Tel: 042 210987
www.tourism-varazdin.com

Dalmatia
Dubrovnik
Od sv. Dominika 7
Tel: 020 323887
www.tzdubrovnik.hr
Hvar
Trg sv. Stjepana

Tel: 021 741059
www.tzhvar.hr
Šibenik
Obala dr. Franje Tuđmana 5
Tel: 022 214448
www.sibenik-tourism.hr
Split
Peristil
Tel: 021 345606
www.visitsplit.com
Trogir
Trg Ivana Pavla II. br. 1
Tel: 021 881412
www.dalmacija.net/trogir.htm
Zadar
Ilije Smiljanića 5
Tel: 023 212412
www.zadar.hr

Eastern Croatia
Osijek
Županijska 2
Tel: 031 203755
www.tzosijek.hr
Vukovar
J.J. Strossmayera 15
Tel: 032 442889

ABOVE: taking a break in Jelačić Square, Zagreb.

Tour Operators

UK companies offering charter flights and package holidays to Croatia include:
Holiday Options
49 The Martlets, Burgess Hill, West Sussex RH15 9NJ
Tel: +44 (0)8444 770451
www.holidayoptions.co.uk
Bond Tours
2 Upper High Street, Epsom, KT17 4QJ
Tel: +44 (0)1372 745300
www.bondtours.com
Balkan Holidays
Sofia House, 19 Conduit Street, London W1S 2BH
Tel: +44 (0)20 7543 5555
www.balkanholidays.co.uk
TUI Travel
Tel: +44 (0)2476 282828
www.thomson.co.uk

Specialist Holidays

Peng Travel Ltd
Broomfield Works, London Road, Swanley, Kent BR8 8TH
Tel: +44 (0)1708 471832
www.pengtravel.co.uk
Specialist providers of naturist holidays in Croatia.
Exodus Holidays
Tel: +44 (0)20 8772 3936
www.exodus.co.uk
Arranges sightseeing tours that take in Zagreb, Plitvice Lakes, Split, Bol and Dubrovnik.
Adriatic Holidays
1 Victor Street,

Oxford OX2 6BT
Tel: +44 (0)1865 516577
www.adriaticholidaysonline.com
Specialises in sailing holidays along the Dalmatian coast. Offers organised trips and charters.
Cottages to Castles
Tuscany House, 10 Tonbridge Road Maidstone ME16 8RP
Tel: +44 (0) 1622 775236
www.cottagestocastles.com
Offers agrotourism breaks in coastal and inland Istria, with accommodation ranging from bed and breakfast to castles and villas.

Croatian Tour Companies

Travel Agents in Croatia offer a variety of specialist tours, activities or holidays including cruising, climbing, sailing, water sports, hunting, fishing, diving, adventure holidays, horse riding, mountain biking, coach tours and wine tours. The two biggest travel agents are Atlas and Generalturist; they both have branches across the country:
Atlas
Vukovarska 19
Dubrovnik
Tel: 020 442222
www.atlas-croatia.com
Generalturist
Pile 1
Zagreb
Tel: 01 480 5652
www.generalturist.com
More specialist operators are listed in the Outdoor Activities section (see pages 284–5).

V isas and Passports

All foreign nationals entering Croatia must hold a valid passport, although those from EEA countries and European microstates can enter with a national ID card. For stays of less than 90 days many Europeans

(including all EU and EEA citizens) and those from the USA, Canada, Australia and New Zealand and many South American countries do not need a visa to enter Croatia. For longer stays the easiest way around the visa requirements is to leave the country temporarily by crossing the Croatian border with Slovenia, although a limit of 90 in 180 days applies. South Africans require a 90-day visa to enter Croatia and should seek advice from any Croatian Embassy.

Visitors to Croatia must register with the police even when visiting friends. Hotels, campsites and agencies offering private accommodation automatically take care of the paperwork. Those who do not register may experience difficulties if they need to report anything to the police. It is essential to travel with a passport at all times. Visas are not required for most nationals (EU, US and Australian) entering Montenegro.

Advice and a full list of countries whose citizens require a visa to enter Croatia can be obtained from:
Consular Department of the Croatian Foreign Ministry
Tel: 01 456 9964
www.mvpei.hr.

W omen Travellers

Many Croatian women work in low-status jobs and hold traditional roles within the home. Women travellers are usually treated courteously and unwanted attention can generally be discouraged by a firm response. As is the case anywhere, lone female travellers should use their common sense.

Weights and Measures

Metric.

TRANSPORT
ACCOMMODATION
EATING OUT
ACTIVITIES
A – Z
LANGUAGE

L ANGUAGE

UNDERSTANDING THE LANGUAGE

Pronunciation Tips

Croatians use a customised version of the Roman alphabet, with the pronunciation of many letters being the same in Croatian and English. Every single letter is pronounced and their sounds do not change from word to word.

c like the 'ts' in 'hats'
ć like the 'tu' in 'nature'
č like the 'ch' in 'chip'
d like the 'du' in 'endure' (sometimes written dj if the correct character is unavailable)
dž like the 'j' in 'juice'
j like the 'y' in 'yacht'
lj like the 'lli' in 'billion'
nj like the 'ny' in 'banyan'
š like the 'sh' in 'lush'
ž like the 's' in 'treasure'

BELOW: signs outside Visovac monastery.

Useful Phrases

Hello Bok
Good morning. Dobro jutro.
Good afternoon. Dobar dan.
Good evening. Dobra večer.
Good night. Laku noć.
Goodbye. Do viđenja.
Welcome. Dobro došli.
My name is ... Moje ime je ...
How are you? Kako ste?
yes da
no ne
Where? When? How? Gdje? Kada? Kako?
How much? Koliko?
Thank you very much. Hvala lijepo.
please molim
Excuse me, please. Oprostite, molim.
Do you speak (English, German, Italian, Croatian)? Govorite li (engleski, njemački, talijanski, hrvatski)?
I (don't) speak (ne) govorim
I (don't) understand (ne) razumijem
cheers živjeli

At the Hotel

Do you have ...? Imate li... ?
a room sobu
a single room jednokrevetnu sobu
a double room dvokrevetnu sobu
with a shower/bath sa tušem/banjom
one night/week jednu noć/tjedan
bed and breakfast noćenje i doručak
full board/half board pansion/polupansion
How much is it ...? Koliko košta za ...?
per night jednu noć
per person po osobi
balcony balkon
terrace terasa

Shopping

Do you have ...? Imate li ...?
How much is it ...? Kolika košta ...?
bakery pekara
bookshop knjižara
butchers mesnica
delicatessen trgovina delikatesen
department store robna kuća
fishmonger ribarnica
grocer dućan
laundry praonica rublja
market tržnica
pastry shop slastičarnica
souvenir shop suveniri
supermarket samoposluživanje
price cijena
cheap jeftino
expensive skupo

Travelling

Where is the ...? Gdje je ...?
railway station? željeznička postaja?
bus stop? autobusna postaja?
tram stop? tramvajska postaja?
What time does the ... leave? U koliko sati polazi ...?
train/bus/ferry? vlak/autobus/trajekt?
one way/return ticket jednosmjerna/povratna karta
1st/2nd class prva/druga klasa
booking rezervacija
airport zračna luka
timetable raspored
How much is the ticket to ...? Koliko košta karta za ...?

Sightseeing

Where is the ...? Gdje se nalazi
museum muzej
church crkva
monument spomenik
monastery samostan

cathedral *katedrala*
old town *stari grad*
exhibition *izložba*
main square *glavni trg*
palace *palača*
castle *dvorac*
How much is the ticket? *Koliko košta ulaznica?*
sightseeing *razgledanje grada*

Eating Out

restaurant *restoran*
breakfast *doručak*
lunch *ručak*
coffee house *kavana*
drink *piće*
one portion *jednu porciju*
Have you got a table for ...? *Imate li stol za ... osobe?*
May I have the menu (wine list)? *Molim vas jelovnik (vinsku kartu)?*
Have you got any food for vegetarians? *Imate li nešto za vegetarijance?*
Please could you bring ...? *Molim vas donesite ...?*
Thank you, it was delicious *bilo je jako dobro*
The bill please *račun molim*

Menu Decoder

beer *pivo*
black coffee *crna kava*
brandy *rakija*
fruit juice *voćni sok*
mineral water *mineralna voda*
plum brandy *šljivovica*
table wine *stolno vino*
tea (with milk/lemon, rum) *čaj (s mlijekom/s limunom/s rumom)*
wine (white, red, rosé) *vino (bijelo, crno, roze)*
bread *kruh*
egg *jaje*
ham omelette *omlet sa šunkom*
honey *med*
jam *marmelada*
cheese *sir*
cold meat *hladno pečenje*
ham (raw, cooked, smoked) *šunka (sirova, kuhana, dimljena)*
olives *masline*
sausage *kobasica*
soup *juha*
cod *bakalar*
lobster *jastog*
mussels *dagnje*
shellfish *školjke*
octopus *hobotnica*
oyster *kamenica*
scampi *škamp*
squid *lignje*
beefsteak *biftek*
beef goulash *goveđi gulaš*
chicken *pile*
roast suckling pig (cooked on the

spit) *pečeni odojak (na ražnju)*
pork chops *svinjski kotleti*
lamb on the spit *janje na ražnju*
turkey *tuka*
veal cutlet *teleći odrezak*
apple *jabuka*
banana *banana*
orange *Naranča*
strawberry *jagoda*
beans *grah*
cucumber *krastavac*
green pepper *paprika*
mushrooms *gljive*
onion *crveni luk*
potato *krumpir*
salad *salata*
cake *kolač*
fruit salad *voćna salata*
ice-cream *sladoled*
pancakes *palačinka*
whipped cream *šlag*
rice *riža*

Health

I am ill *Ja sam bolestan/bolesna sam (m/f)*
Where is the nearest ...? *Gdje je najbliža ...?*
chemist *ljekarna*
doctors *liječnik*
dentist *zubar*
hospital *bolnica*
I have a sore throat *boli me grlo*
I have a headache *boli me glava*
I have a stomach-ache *bolove u želucu*
I have ... *Imam ...*
nausea *mučninu*

Numbers

0	*nula*
1	*jedan*
2	*dva*
3	*tri*
4	*četiri*
5	*pet*
6	*šest*
7	*sedam*
8	*osam*
9	*devet*
10	*deset*
11	*jedanaest*
12	*dvanaest*
20	*dvadeset*
30	*trideset*
40	*četrdeset*
50	*pedeset*
60	*šezdeset*
70	*sedamdeset*
80	*osamdeset*
90	*devedeset*
100	*sto*
1,000	*tisuću*

diarrhoea *proljev*
toothache *zubobolju*
medicine *lijek*
I'm ... *Ja sam ...*
asthmatic *asmatičar*
diabetic *diabetičar*
epileptic *epileptičar*

On the Road

Is this the road to ...? *Je li ovo cesta za ...?*
Go straight ahead *Vozite ravno*
Turn right (left) *Skrenite desno (lijevo)*
I want ... litres of ... petrol *Molim vas ... litara ... benzina*
spare tyre *rezervna guma*
My car has broken down *Moje auto je pokvareno*
I have had a car crash *Imao sam sudar*
Could you please call ...? *Molim vas pozovite ...?*
the police *policiju*
the ambulance *hitnu pomoć*
the tow truck *vučnu službu*
driving licence *vozačka dozvola*

Emergencies

My ... has been stolen *Ukraden mi je ...*
money *novac*
suitcase *kofer*
car *auto*
watch *sat*
camera *foto-aparat*
passport *putovnica*
Could you please call ...? *Molim vas pozovite ...?*
the police *policiju*
the ambulance *hitnu pomoć*

Days of the Week

Monday *ponedjeljak*
Tuesday *utorak*
Wednesday *srijeda*
Thursday *četvrtak*
Friday *petak*
Saturday *subota*
Sunday *nedjelja*

Months of the Year

January *siječanj*
February *veljača*
March *ožujak*
April *travanj*
May *svibanj*
June *lipanj*
July *srpanj*
August *kolovoz*
September *rujan*
October *listopad*
November *studeni*
December *prosinac*

TRANSPORT

ACCOMMODATION

EATING OUT

ACTIVITIES

A – Z

LANGUAGE

FURTHER READING

History

The National Question in Yugoslavia by Ivo Banac, Cornell University Press (1998). An examination of the tension between Serbian nationalism, Croatian nationalism and Yugoslavianism in the Balkans from the mid-19th century to the 1921 Vidovan Constitution.

Yugoslavia's Bloody Collapse by Christopher Bennet, Hurst & Co. (1995). An examination of Milošević's role in the rise of Serbian nationalism and the collapse of Yugoslavia.

The Balkans 1804–1999: Nationalism, War and the Great Powers by Misha Glenny, Granta (2001). An ambitious attempt to explain the history of the Balkans and how the rest of the world meddled in its affairs. This informative but dry read features on many A-Level History reading lists.

The Fall of Yugoslavia by Misha Glenny, Penguin (1996). An eyewitness account of Croatia and Slovenia's struggles for independence and the ensuing five-year war. Glenny also considers the future in an unstable region and places the Yugoslavian war within a useful historical framework.

Croatia: A History by Ivo Goldstein, C. Hurst & Co (1999). Goldstein takes readers on a fascinating journey through Croatia's history right up to the present day.

The Impossible Country: A Journey Through the Last Days of Yugoslavia by Brian Hall, Minerva (1996). An engrossing account of the author's journey during the last days of Yuogoslavia in 1991. Reveals how everyday citizens can be persuaded to think the worst of their neighbours just because they happen to come from a different ethnic background.

The Death of Yuogoslavia by Laura Sibler and Alan Little, Penguin (1996). A riveting account of the events that contributed to the 1991 war and running on to the Dayton Accord, presented from a historical perspective.

Croatia: A Nation Forged in War by Marcus Tanner, Yale University Press (2001). Written by the author of the history chapters in this guidebook, this is a compelling account of Croatian history that ranges from the Greeks and Romans to the present day.

Forging War: the Media in Serbia, Croatia and Bosnia Herzegovina by Mark Thompson, University of Luton Press (1999). Examines the role of the Yuogoslav press in fanning the fires of ethnic hatred.

The Demise of Yugoslavia: A Political Memoir by Stipe Mesić, Central European University Press (2004). Unique and insightful account of the collapse of the former Yugoslavia, by the federation's last president, and the first democratically elected president of the independent Croatian state.

The Yugoslav Auschwitz and the Vatican: The Croatian Massacre of the Serbs During World War II by Vladimir Dedijer, Prometheus Books (1992). Written by a former Yugoslav ambassador to the UN, this detailed and impeccably researched book covers a secret episode of the 20th century and one that many Croatians – and Roman Catholics – would prefer had remained secret. It is probably a bit too harrowing for holiday reading.

Croatia Through History by Branka Magas, Saqi Books (2008). Despite being Croatian, historian and journalist Branka Magas bravely attempts to cover objectively the history of Croatia from the Middle Ages to the present and does it remarkably well.

Goli Otok–Hell in the Adriatic by Josip Zoretic, Virtualbookworm.com Publishing (2007). The former Yugoslavia's answer to Solzhenitsyn's *One Day in the Life of Ivan Denisovich*, this vividly written memoir is a harrowing account of life in the gulag on the Croatian island of Goli otok, where the author was a prisoner from 1962 to 1969. It is essential reading for anyone believing in the widespread popular image of Tito's regime as Communism with a human face.

Culture

A Taste of Croatia: Savoring the Food, People and Traditions of Croatia's Adriatic Coast by Karen Evenden, New Oak Press (2007). Not so much a cookbook as a well-written and lengthy love letter celebrating its subject.

My Favourite Croatian Recipes by Sandra Lougher, Pen Press Publishers (2005). One of very few books about Croatian food in English, this includes more than 60 recipes from all over the country.

The Best of Croatian Cooking – Expanded Edition by Liliana Pavicic

BELOW: a selection of Croatian newspapers.

and Gordana Pirker-Mosher, Hippocrene Books (2003). As well as 200 recipes, the book has an introduction covering Croatia's culinary tradition and local specialities and a useful wine guide.

Travel

Croatia: Travels in Undiscovered Country by Tony Fabijancic, University of Alberta Press (2003). Written by a Canadian-born son of Croatian immigrants who decided to explore the back roads of his ancestral homeland, this engaging travelogue deals insightfully and affectionately with the challenges facing rural Croatians rapidly adapting to life in a modern European state.

Fiction

How We Survived Communism and Even Laughed by Slavenka Drakulić, Vintage (2001). A collection of essays that examine different aspects of life under Communism, including censorship and consumerism.

As If I Am Not There: A Novel of the Balkans by Slavenka Drakulić, Abacus (1999). Set in Bosnia, not Croatia, this book takes the reader on a journey into the heart of the Balkan conflict through one woman's experiences. A harrowing and enlightening read.

Café Europa by Slavenka Drakulić, Abacus (1996). A collection of essays written between 1992 and 1996 that take a look at post-Communist life in Zagreb, Warsaw, Tirana and Budapest.

Balkan Express by Slavenka Drakulić, Hutchinson (1993). A compelling insight, given through a series of essays, into the effects of the Homeland War on the lives of ordinary people.

The Culture of Lies by Dubravka Ugrešić, Weidenfeld and Nicolson (1998). A collection of essays attacking the politics and culture of the Croatia that rose from the ashes of the Yugoslavian war, and of the war in Croatia and Bosnia. Also an insightful attempt to understand the nationalist aggression that triumphed at this time.

Have a Nice Day: From the Balkan War to the American Dream by Dubravka Ugrešić, Jonathan Cape (1994). A fictional diary of a life in exile in the USA through the eyes of a Croatian woman whose country is being destroyed by war.

The Museum of Unconditional Surrender by Dubravka Ugrešić Phoenix (1991). A well-written novel that weaves an intriguing mix of humour and bitterness. This prize-winning novelist hones in on the life of a 45-year-old Croatian woman living in exile.

Croatian Nights ed. Borivoj Radakoviç, Matt Thorne and Tony White, Serpent's Tail (2005). An eclectic but brilliant collection of short stories by Croatian and British writers, which grew out of a movement called FAK – Festival of Alternative Literature. It gives an insight into how young writers look at the country.

Other Insight Guides

Berlitz Croatian Phrase Book & Dictionary by Berlitz Publishing Pocket-sized but comprehensive companion that should see you through almost anything in Croatia.

Send Us Your Thoughts

We do our best to ensure the information in our books is as accurate and up-to-date as possible. The books are updated on a regular basis using local contacts, who painstakingly add, amend and correct as required. However, some details (such as telephone numbers and opening times) are liable to change, and we are ultimately reliant on our readers to put us in the picture.

We welcome your feedback, especially your experience of using the book "on the road". Maybe we recommended a hotel that you liked (or another that you didn't), or you came across a great bar or new attraction we missed.

We will acknowledge all contributions, and we'll offer an Insight Guide to the best letters received.

Please write to us at:
Insight Guides
PO Box 7910
London SE1 1WE
Or email us at:
insight@apaguide.co.uk

The classic **Insight Guides** series fulfils three distinct needs of a good travel guide: to inspire and motivate, to give accurate on-the-ground advice, and to arouse great memories of your trip long after you have come home. Other European titles include Austria, Italy, Venice and Western Europe.

Insight Smart Guides are packed with information arranged in a handy A–Z format that helps you find what you want quickly and simply. Titles include Prague, Salzburg and Venice.

Insight Step by Step Guides provide precise itineraries and recommendations from local expert writers. Titles include Croatia, Slovakia and Venice.

Insight Fleximaps make useful companions to the guidebooks. They combine clear, detailed cartography with essential travel information. The laminated finish make the maps durable, waterproof and easy to fold.

ART AND PHOTO CREDITS

AFP Getty 52, 53, 54, 84, 159
AKG London 26T, 29, 30, 34, 35, 36, 37/39, 41, 44L, 50, 72
Biblioteque Nationale 32
Corbis 51, 67
G. Dall'Orto 26B
Getty 158R
Hrvatski Povijesni Muzej, Zagreb 27T, 28, 43, 46, 48, 49
iStockphoto 6L, 79, 81, 85, 98, 127, 132, 133, 197, 211, 233T, 256, 257
Damil Kalogjera 70
Robin McKelvie 186, 195T
APA Mark Read 31, 32, 58, 62, 63, 64, 66, 75, 102T, 104T, 105T, 108, 109, 126, 166T, 170, 201, 208/T, 210, 219, 221T, 222, 223T, 225, 226, 235T
Mary Evans Picture Library 24/25, 44R, 47
NHPA 184
Topfoto 45, 224
Bruce Tuten 71
APA Corrie Wingate 2/3, 4B, 5B, 6M, 6B, 7BL/BR/ML/MR/TL, 8 all, 9 all, 10/11, 17B/M/T, 18, 19, 20, 21L/R, 22, 23, 56/57, 59, 65, 73, 74, 76, 77, 88/89, 92/93, 100,

101, 103, 105, 106T, 107, 110/111, 120/T, 123/T, 125/T, 149, 150, 153, 154, 157, 160, 165, 166, 168, 171T, 198/199, 221, 226T, 227, 230, 231, 232, 234, 235, 236/T, 237/T, 242, 243, 245, 254T, 258, 260, 261, 265, 267, 269T, 270, 274, 275, 277/T, 281, 288, 290, 293, 294/T, 296
APA Gregory Wrona 3B, 4T, 5T, 7TR, 12/13, 14/15, 16, 33, 40, 60, 61, 80, 82, 83, 90/91, 94, 95B/M/T, 104, 106, 112, 113, 115, 116, 117/T, 118/T, 119/T, 121, 110/T, 124T, 128/129, 130, 131, 135, 136/T, 139, 141/T, 141, 144/145, 146, 147, 148T, 151/T, 152, 154T, 155, 156, 158L, 160, 161T, 162/163, 164, 167, 169/T, 171, 172, 173, 176/177, 178, 179, 181, 182L/R, 183L/R, 185/T, 187/T, 188/T, 189/T, 190, 191, 192, 193, 194, 195, 196, 200, 203, 204, 205, 206, 207, 214/215, 216, 217, 218T, 222T, 223, 228, 229, 233, 238/239, 240, 241, 246, 247, 248L/R, 249, 250/T, 251/T, 252, 253/T, 254, 255, 269B

INDEX